Studies in Emotion and Social Interaction

Paul Ekman
University of California, San Francisco

Klaus R. Scherer
Justus-Liebig-Universität Giessen

General Editors

Interaction Structure and Strategy

Studies in Emotion and Social Interaction

This series is jointly published by the Cambridge University Press and the Editions de la Maison des Sciences de l'Homme, as part of the joint publishing agreement established in 1977 between the Fondation de la Maison des Sciences de l'Homme and the Syndics of the Cambridge University Press.

Cette collection est publiée en co-édition par Cambridge University Press et les Editions de la Maison des Sciences de l'Homme. Elle s'intègre dans le programme de co-édition etabli en 1977 par la Fondation de la Maison des Sciences de l'Homme et les Syndics de Cambridge University Press.

Interaction structure and strategy

Starkey Duncan, Jr., and Donald W. Fiske

with
Rita Denny, Barbara G. Kanki, and Hartmut B. Mokros
Department of Behavioral Sciences
The University of Chicago

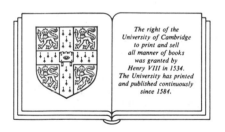

The right of the
University of Cambridge
to print and sell
all manner of books
was granted by
Henry VIII in 1534.
The University has printed
and published continuously
since 1584.

CAMBRIDGE UNIVERSITY PRESS

Cambridge
London   New York   New Rochelle
Melbourne   Sydney

EDITIONS DE LA MAISON DES SCIENCES DE L'HOMME

Paris

Published by the Press Syndicate of the University of Cambridge
The Pitt Building, Trumpington Street, Cambridge CB2 1RP
32 East 57th Street, New York, NY 10022, USA
10 Stamford Road, Oakleigh, Melbourne 3166, Australia
and
Editions de la Maison des Sciences de l'Homme
54 Boulevard Raspail, 75270 Paris Cedex 06

First published in 1985

Printed in the United States of America

Library of Congress Cataloging in Publication Data
Main entry under title:
Interaction structure and strategy.
(Studies in emotion and social interaction)
Includes bibliographical references.
1. Interpersonal communication.   2. Social interac-
tion.   3. Interpersonal relations.   I. Duncan, Starkey.
II. Series
BF637.C45I56   1985   302.3'4   84-22945
ISBN 0 521 30154 8
ISBN 2 7351 0131 2 (France only)

Contents

Introduction

Since about 1967, a program of research on face-to-face interaction has been pursued in our laboratory. Most generally, this work has been guided by McQuown's goal, as stated in *The Natural History of an Interview* (1971, but mainly completed in 1959). In his foreword, McQuown wrote that the purpose of the work leading to that monograph was to initiate first steps in a process aimed at developing "the foundation of a general theory of the structure of human communicative behavior" (p. 5). That is, interaction, like language, is seen as being guided or structured in part by rules for appropriate conduct. Interaction is a rule-governed activity. Rules provide a major source of regularity in the actions of participants in interaction. From this perspective, research is aimed at discovering and documenting rules and related phenomena. Although this view does not seem particularly unreasonable or even original, it will be seen that most of the research on face-to-face interaction to date has not been primarily concerned with interaction structure.

From the beginning of the work in this laboratory, a major concern has been the methods for studying interaction structure. The initial question was, what would a study of interaction structure look like? At the time that work started here, considerable conceptual treatment of the notion of structure and extensive systems for transcribing speech and body motion were available. However, there was rather less to be found in the way of methodological guidelines or approaches to data analyses for studies of this sort. Therefore, it was necessary to pay careful attention both to the process of generating and analyzing data, and to the manner of providing evidence in support of hypotheses. This methodological aspect of the research has been considered at least as important as the more substantive results that have emerged. Although most of the studies have been concerned with two-person conversations between adults, the goal has been to develop an approach to structural research that would apply to any interaction of interest.

Our first monograph

The first comprehensive report on our research (Duncan & Fiske, 1977) presented results from two large-scale studies. One was a structural study of the exchange of speaking turns and related phenomena in conversations. Based on intensive study of eight conversations, a *turn system* was hypothesized, which included signals, rules, and a number of other elements. The methods used in that study were described in great detail. We shall return to further consideration of that work presently.

The second study was aimed at exploring individual differences in conversational actions. This research was designed as an "external-variable" study (Duncan, 1969) in which data were generated primarily by counting or timing some action (such as gaze) over an interaction or some stretc ι of interaction. The raw counts or timings were then typically converted into rates by dividing them by some larger count or timing, such as total time with the speaking turn. Thus, one might calculate the rate or average duration of gazing while speaking for a participant in a given interaction. We shall call variables of this sort *simple-rate* variables. Studies based on simple-rate variables will be termed *external-variable* studies.

The defining characteristic of simple-rate variables is that they contain no information on sequences of action within the interaction. Thus, one might know a participant's overall rate of gazing at the partner but have no information on where the gazes occurred in the stream of interaction.

In the process of pursuing our own external-variable study, Fiske and I concluded that the lack of sequential information in simple-rate variables made them fundamentally flawed for research on interaction process. It is impossible to interpret such variables in interactional terms. For example, a positive correlation between rate of participants smiling and rate of partner's smiling could not be interpreted as reflecting a tendency toward mutual smiling because the data contained no information on who smiled when. From these data, one cannot be sure that the two participants ever smiled at the same time.

It became apparent that, in research on interaction process, it is necessary to know not only that an action occurs, but also where it occurs in the stream of interaction. The "where" is described in terms of interaction sequences. Accordingly, Fiske and I recommended (Duncan & Fiske, 1977, p. 315) that studies of interaction process abandon simple-rate variables altogether and replace them with studies using variables containing information on interaction sequences. These issues and others will be considered in detail in Chapter 1.

The discussion of external-variable research and simple-rate variables is not a review of that literature. The literature by this time has grown so large that it requires book-length reviews. We do consider methodological issues in that research and describe why we have elected to take an alternative approach. And we describe approaches to constructing variables that contain sequential information. This discussion is important because the research reported in Chapters 6–10 is based on these sequence variables.

Chapter 1 provides key elements of the rationale for the research described in subsequent chapters. It is also a critique of the standard approach to doing research in the field of "nonverbal communication."

Structure, strategy, and situation

At the same time, issues were arising regarding the structural research. It was becoming increasingly apparent that a full description of an interaction would extend well beyond its structure. Making the same observation from a researcher's point of view, one might say that structure is only one potential source of strong observable regularities in interaction. Two other major facets of interaction would be situation (or context), and interaction strategy. All of these issues will be considered in Chapter 2. This chapter presents the rationale for our studies of structure and strategy, setting the framework for all subsequent discussion. The notions of structure, strategy, and situation, together with their interrelations, are explored in some detail. (Evidence for yet another source of regularity – cognitive processing constraints – is also presented in Chapter 9.)

At the most general and intuitive level, the relation of interaction strategy to structure is simple and straightforward. If structure has to do with the "rules of the game" for interaction, then strategy represents the manner in which a participant or group of participants actually plays the game. It will be apparent that structure and strategy are inextricably related; one cannot participate in rule-governed conduct without simultaneously effecting some strategy within those rules.

From this perspective, it seemed inappropriate to go on to further applications of our structural work without first exploring interaction strategy as a research area. As with the structural research, the initial question was, what would a study of strategy look like? Even though we had extensive experience with studying structure, and even though strategy research was based primarily on hypotheses concerning interaction structure, our initial work with strategy was entirely exploratory. It was not at all clear what sorts of strategy phenomena – if any – might emerge from the studies. Moreover, we had no definite ideas regarding what might be the most effective methods for uncovering these phenomena, only some guesses about where to start. After some initial groping and false starts, we developed a definite approach to method, and subsequently we began to encounter a range of strategy-related phenomena. Consequently, our notion of what strategy research might encompass expanded considerably. These developments, as well as more substantive results, will be apparent in this monograph.

Situation, the third element of interaction interlocking with the other two, is not considered in the present research. In fact, we continue to be uncertain about how to do a principled study of situation, although it is an exceptionally important, complex, and fascinating aspect of interaction. However that might be, we shall comment further on situation (in Chapter 2), only to suggest briefly how it fits into our general view of interaction.

The turn system

Chapter 3 describes the turn system, a set of structural hypotheses on which the strategy research is based. These hypotheses relate to various aspects of taking speaking turns and related phenomena in the two-person conversations we studied. The hypotheses involve, among other things, signals that can be displayed by speaker and auditor, and rules for appropriately responding to these signals. These hypotheses permit us to look at the ways in which individuals and groups in our conversations operate within the applicable interaction structure. This chapter, then, becomes the foundation for the subsequent strategy research.

Differentiating structure from strategy

The confusing thing about studying structure and strategy is that, in a sense, all that we see in an interaction (or in a game) is strategy. That is, we see participants taking actions by choosing from the alternatives available within the framework of structure. Nevertheless, except for human universals, these actions cannot be properly interpreted apart from knowledge of the structure within which they were chosen. How can we interpret the significance of a chess move (or even whether it is a permissible one) unless we know the rules for chess?

The ultimate aim of the investigator in exploratory research is to generate empirically based hypotheses. As in all exploratory research, initial discovery of promising regularities is followed by more systematic analyses. Through this empirical work, the definition of the regularity is progressively refined and elaborated. In the process, many apparently promising regularities will be found to be faulty in some way or other and discarded. Others will become candidates for hypotheses.

It is not enough, however, that a given regularity survive a careful empirical scrutiny. Eventually, the investigator will classify that regularity as being an element of either structure or strategy. This classification requires that a set of criteria be available. If the regularity is evaluated as stemming from strategy, then it becomes necessary to discover the underlying structural elements. If the regularity is regarded as structural in character, then one may well be interested in the strategies associated with it in the observed interactions.

Issues of research method therefore become critically important for our discussion. Before presenting some results relevant to the turn-system hypotheses, it seems appropriate to provide an overview of various approaches to doing structural research, followed by a formulation of our own research method. This is the subject of Chapter 4.

As in the discussion of external-variable research, we do not attempt a full review of the literature. Rather, the discussion focuses on several major types or schools of structural research, each exemplified by one or two prominent investigators. Thus, we shall consider Goffman's participant observation, ethnomethodology and conversation analysis, and context analysis. The discussion will be concerned entirely with methodology, as opposed to major findings, types of interactions studied, and the like. Concluding the chapter will be an extended discussion of the rationale and implementation of our own approach to structural research, including the major criteria for evaluating structural hypotheses.

The criteria we propose in Chapter 4 were used but not made explicit in Duncan and Fiske (1977). These criteria are another aspect of interaction research worthy of the most careful consideration by investigators. Our discussion of them is intended as an early entry in that discussion. The overall effectiveness and impact of the criteria may be evaluated in part through the total body of research described in Duncan and Fiske and in this monograph.

Method

Chapter 5 provides basic information on method for the chapters that follow. Participants, the interaction setting, and design issues are described. The processes of transcribing the interactions and transferring the transcription to the computer are recounted. There is also a discussion of our approach to breaking the stream of interaction into units for the purposes of analysis.

Preparatory structural research

It was necessary to do two structural studies to prepare for the strategy research, which is our main concern. These are the topic of Chapter 6. The first was termed a *structure-assessment* study. Its purpose was to determine whether or not the turn-system hypotheses applied to the conversations we planned to use in the strategy studies. Obviously, it makes little sense to base a strategy study on structure hypotheses when the hypothesized structure does not fit the interactions under study. For this reason, we evaluated the strength of the turn-system hypotheses in the new interactions.

The second preparatory study was required by the nature of the strategy work. Some of the strategy analyses became somewhat complex, requiring numerous partitions of the data. At the same time, the turn system itself was rather complex, having a number of signals, most composed of two or more cues. For this reason, use of the full turn system also imposed a number of partitions on the data. Considering the strategy and structure research together, the data often became excessively partitioned, even taking into account the relatively large number of data points that we had. For this reason, it became highly desirable to simplify the turn system as much as possible in order to permit a maximal elaboration of the strategy research. That is, we needed to permit the strategy research as many data partitions as possible. Therefore, we needed to minimize the partitions required by the structural hypotheses. To this end, we carried out a *turn-system simplification* study, resulting in three basic signals to be used in much of the strategy research. Each of these signals has only one cue.

Also included in Chapter 6 are some small-scale studies relating to certain modifications and elaborations of the turn system that have been developed since the publication of Duncan and Fiske (1977).

Strategy studies

Four strategy studies are reported in Chapters 7–10. We view each of these as contrasting with the others rather sharply in purpose and implication.

The first strategy study we carried out yielded perhaps the most surprising and unexpected results: the hypothesis of a set of *strategy signals*. Although a number of structure signals had been hypothesized and although we were gearing up for research on strategy, the notion of strategy signal was not anticipated in any way in the conceptual framework described in Duncan and Fiske (1977).

Briefly stated, a strategy signal seems to operate in conjunction with a structure signal, accentuating the effect of that structure signal. That is, the strategy signal, in conjunction with a structure–signal display, has some distinct effect on the probability of the partner's responding to the structure signal. Results on strategy signals include data both from the original conversations analyzed in Duncan and Fiske and from the new set of conversations used in other strategy analyses in this monograph. Strategy-signal results are reported in Chapter 7.

In Chapter 8, Denny reports a study that expands our understanding of turn-related phenomena in several ways. Focusing on the predictive power of various speaker actions on auditor response, the study has a distinct strategy orientation. Among other things, Denny's evidence suggests that the broader speech context in which speaker signals occur influences auditor response to these signals, and that different auditor responses are characterized by different temporal parameters. The work on speech context is innovative within the context of the turn system, whereas the work on temporal parameters constitutes a major departure in a major area of interest in the "nonverbal-communication" literature.

Denny's study differs from previous work in two important ways. First, the accuracy of measurement of pause durations is considerably greater (± 5 ms). The study includes measurement of each pause in the observed interactions longer than 65 ms. Second, the length of pause is related both to the speaker signal preceding the pause and to the type of auditor response. That is to say, pause-length parameters are embedded in and affected by the interactional context in which they occur. The research calls into question the large number of studies that focus exclusively on pauses alone, ignoring their interactional context.

In Chapter 9, Mokros reports several studies variously involving regularities in sequences of signal display by participants and/or subsequent response to these displays by the partner. Certain types of regularity emerge that seem directly related to neither structure nor strategy, but rather to cognitive and perceptual processes in the participants. These regularities appear to be a product of the interaction between cognitive and perceptual processing, and the structure within which the participant is operating. Sometimes presenting complex problems of data analysis, this general phenomenon nevertheless appears capable of producing regularities comparable in strength to the original structure results. Mokros's work is particularly exciting because it contributes to a highly promising research area that has only begun to be exploited: the study of cognitive processes based on interactional phenomena. Such a research area may be thought of as extending to interaction structure the traditional notion of psycholinguistic work based on linguistic structure.

A study of individual differences in interaction is presented in Chapter 10 by Kanki. This is the sort of study we had in mind when we first planned to do strategy research. The study seeks to characterize participants in terms of several aspects of their respective strategies within interaction structure and to group the participants in terms of similarities in these strategies. The work is substantially complicated by the fact that it no longer seems adequate to consider only the participant's actions when one is characterizing that participant's strategy. Because the participant is in interaction with a partner, any description of the participant's strategy would have also to include a description of the partner's strategy that provides part of the interactional context for the participant's action.

It would seem that the research we originally intended to do in a rather straightforward manner turned out to be the most complicated and perplexing of all. We developed an approach to work on individual differences, based on complex definition of variables and on grouping participants using log-linear analyses. Descriptions of a participant's strategy are formulated using information on both the participant's and the partner's actions. We hope that this study will present a constructive alternative to the external-variable studies of individual differences we criticize in Chapter 1.

Three of these four strategy studies (strategy signals, cognitive constraints, and individual differences) represent the first of its kind. The fourth (Denny's) is a significant new direction in a substantial research area. It is highly improbable that any of these present the last word for research in its area. However, each holds the promise of opening an entire area of research for investigators interested in interaction. The fourth study constitutes a major departure in a substantial research field.

Taken as a whole, the four studies suggest the multifaceted potential of research based on interaction structure. We are hoping that the studies suggest not only the possible fruitfulness of further research along those lines, but also the possible development of yet other sorts of strategy research. In this single, circumscribed project, we scarcely claim that we have exhausted the potential of strategy research, either as a whole or in the particular areas we have explored. This is a book about beginnings.

Concluding discussion

Finally, in Chapter 11, each of the strategy studies is considered from a broader perspective, and our experience in pursuing this research is summarized. Readers desiring an overview of the strategy research may wish to read this final chapter first. Those taking such a "the-butler-did-it" approach should be aware, however, that in Chapter 11, the material prior to Chapter 7 is considered in only the sketchiest outline.

Reflections on the project

The experience of doing this research has been striking. We continually encountered surprises. At first, there was the surprise of being abysmally at a loss for a coherent approach to doing strategy research despite years of experience in working on interaction structure. We never expected the research to be as truly exploratory as it was with respect to both method and phenomena.

Even though the research was entirely based on the preceding structure research, strategy proved to be very much its own area. It obstinately refused simply to be a mild modification or routine adaptation of structure research. We found that there was a great deal to be learned with respect to both strategy work and interaction itself. As with all exploratory research, there was that initial, dark period of mere groping when it appears that contact is made only with shifting, elusive ephemera.

The dawn began to emerge in our research when we adopted two key methodological tools: run-sequence variables and log-linear analysis. The run-sequence variable contains information not only on interaction sequences but also on the duration of actions in those sequences. This new type of variable, described in detail in Chapter 1, freed us from the complexities and noise involved in the rate variables that we had been using. The problems with rate variables in interaction research, even when the variables contain sequential information, was a second major surprise for us. But our results lost their ephemeral character as soon as we abandoned rate variables.

Log-linear analysis, widely used in other areas of social science such as survey analysis, is something less than a household term in psychology. Nevertheless, our data, which are essentially counts of the occurrence of various events (mainly sequences), are ideally suited for log-linear methods. Each of the three strategy studies involving log-linear analysis used a somewhat different application of it, so something of its versatility and power may be suggested. Nevertheless, we have exploited only a portion of its continually growing potential. We expect that log-linear methods will become increasingly used for dealing with a variety of types of research in psychology. It certainly should become the approach of choice in interaction research.

If there is any single, overarching lesson or principle to be gained from this research, it has to do with the interconnectedness of things in interaction. It would seem that interaction simply cannot be viewed as a series of messages, or a single message as a collection of separate components. Similarly, participants in an interaction cannot be analyzed separately. Interaction is an integrated, systematic process. Research on interaction will advance as investigators continue to develop approaches to studying the ways in which elements are interconnected.

To go at something in interaction – an action, a message, a participant – as a separate entity, analyzable in itself, is not to court serious error, but virtually to ensure it. In such a case, the most innocuous outcome would be excessive noise in the data, yielding marginal results. At its worst, substantive error in conclusions will be incurred. If error is avoided, it will be by chance alone.

Time and again we encountered aspects of our research procedures in which the closely woven fabric of interaction had not been sufficiently appreciated. Each time we moved to correct our shortcoming, our data seemed less of a matted tangle, results were substantially improved, and conclusions became more clear-cut.

As with almost all good things, there is, of course, a cost. The cost of greater appreciation of relatedness in interaction is complexity of both variables and analysis. There may be a way of avoiding this cost, but it is not apparent to us.

Throughout the study we repeatedly learned, usually the hard way, that interaction is a complicated, systematic thing, not particularly hospitable to attempts to study it piecemeal. We like the general shape of results presented in the chapters that follow. But the experienced investigator will appreciate the extent to which the road to these results was littered with abandoned approaches and fruitless "brilliant insights," some very costly of time and effort. Based on our experience so far, there is little reason to expect that this lesson will not continue to be forced upon us as we continue our work on interaction.

These comments are appropriately a part of any forthright account of the project we undertook. Certainly, they are not intended to discourage investigators from venturing into the domains of interaction structure or strategy. To the contrary, we hope that others will appreciate the potential of work in this area, which becomes all the more challenging because of its inherent complexity, the still formative nature of its research techniques, and the many phenomena waiting to be discovered. Like our work on structure, the study of strategy was a voyage of discovery; we scarcely returned with a thorough charting of the territory.

Terminology and abbreviations

From the preceding discussion, it may be seen that we shall frequently have occasion to refer to Duncan and Fiske (1977). As a convenience we have adopted the convention of abbreviating this reference to "D&F." No other reference will be abbreviated.

When we transcribed our videotapes, one of the actions we included was the head direction of the speaker and the auditor. Although we were actually interested in gaze direction, a major action in this research area, we used the term "head direction" instead because in some instances it was not possible to determine gaze direction accurately from the videotapes. Head direction is thus a more conservative term, used in D&F. However, to facilitate exposition we shall in this monograph use terms such as "gaze" and "gaze direction." It seems reasonable to believe that the phenomena we consider are associated with gaze rather than head direction.

Acknowledgments

This research was supported in part by Grant MH-30654 from the National Institute of Mental Health and by Grant BNS-8004434 from the National Science Foundation, awarded to Starkey Duncan, Jr. and Donald W. Fiske, and by Grant MH-38344 from the National Institute of Mental

Health, awarded to Starkey Duncan, Jr.; support was also awarded to Duncan from the Sloan Foundation and the Spencer Foundation grants to the University of Chicago.

R. Darrell Bock, Leo Goodman, and Shelby Haberman all gave instructive and patient advice indispensable to the log-linear analyses.

1. External-variable research

STARKEY DUNCAN, JR., AND DONALD W. FISKE

1.1. Introduction

In what now seems an antediluvian era, a review of research on "nonverbal communication" (Duncan, 1969) focused on actions observed in interaction, such as gestures and voice qualities, but not included in the traditional definition of language. A basic distinction was made between two broad types of studies in this area: external-variable studies and structural studies. This distinction was initially drawn to reflect a perceived difference in the aims of investigators.

External-variable studies were seen as using nonverbal actions as indexes of something else, as a way of getting at other, "external" variables or issues that the investigator was interested in, such as "the interaction situation, the personality characteristics of the interactants, or the reactions of judges to the interaction" (Duncan, 1969, p. 121). Later in the paper, other nonverbal actions were added to this list of variables in order to include studies in which investigators were concerned with relationships between nonverbal actions – for example, correlating rate of gazing with rate of smiling.

In contrast, structural studies were said to be concerned with "communication as a tightly organized and self-contained social system, like

1

language. This system operates according to a definite set of rules, and the task of the researcher is to explicate these rules" (Duncan, 1969, p. 121). In this case, the object of study is the process of interaction itself, approached from a particular point of view: that of rule-governed behavior. The goal is to explore the interrelations of nonverbal actions – and potentially of language as well – in order to discover the organization of interaction, where "organization" is understood very broadly in the same way that linguists speak of the grammar of a language.

At the time of the review there was at least a moderate number of external-variable studies in the literature. However, there were few structural studies, and these were mainly programmatic papers or exercises in careful behavior transcription (termed "descriptive studies" in the review).

In the years since the review, the trickle of external-variable studies has swelled to a flood. There are now, for example, a book-length review of external-variable research (Harper, Wiens, & Matarazzo, 1978); a book-length review devoted entirely to studies of a single action: gaze direction (Argyle & Cook, 1976); an edited book dealing with a single subarea: temporal parameters of speech (Siegman & Feldstein, 1978); a handbook of research methods dealing mainly, but not exclusively, with external-variable studies (Scherer & Ekman, 1982); and an edited monograph containing integrative or theoretical chapters on important topics, once again mainly, but not exclusively, concerned with external-variable studies (Siegman & Feldstein, 1978). These monographs are but examples of the many that have appeared. In addition to these monographs, the great preponderance of external-variable studies in the journals has continued.

In contrast, the structural-research literature has grown but slowly and remains relatively scattered throughout the literature. This work will be considered, beginning in the next chapter.

External-variable studies in "nonverbal-communication" research

There can be no doubt that external-variable studies have dominated the research literature. It seems reasonable to suppose that when most individuals think of "nonverbal-communication" research, they have external-variable studies in mind. Most of what we know about nonverbal communication comes from external-variable studies. Virtually all of these studies have been done by experimental social psychologists; these investigators have often been enterprising, prolific, and ingenious. The external-variable work on nonverbal communication must be considered with great care.

In addition, external-variable studies have played an important role in the development of the field as a whole. Many investigators of face-to-face interaction can recall an earlier time when nonverbal communication as an area of inquiry was not included in the existing definitions of any established academic field. Studies of nonverbal communication appeared to fall within the aegis of no journal. Submitted manuscripts might be returned with generally positive remarks by reviewers but with a regretful rejection by the editor, indicating that the paper, although of acceptable quality, might perhaps be more appropriately submitted to some other journal. Later, major social psychological journals (e.g., *Journal of Personality and Social Psychology, Journal of Experimental Social Psychology,* and *Sociometry*) started to accept studies of nonverbal communication, whether external-variable or otherwise. Subsequently, other journals followed suit. Now papers on face-to-face interaction have appeared in a wide spectrum of journals, from *Psychological Bulletin* to *Language.*

With full appreciation of its importance and historical contribution to the entire area of face-to-face interaction, we may consider some of the characteristics of external-variable research.

Characteristics of external-variable research

In reviewing his own seminal investigations of gaze, Exline (1971) posed the following questions: "Can visual behavior as a dependent variable be shown to be an indicator . . . of mood, state, or orientation toward another? Can it, on the other hand, be an independent variable, driving or shaping the nature of the interaction process?" (p. 172)

Exline's questions bring out the dual aspects of "nonverbal communication" that have attracted so many investigators. On the one hand, his second question asks whether nonverbal variables may be related to other actions by the participant or to actions by the partner, matters focusing on the interaction process. Such relationships can be studied from aggregate scores, such as the correlation between two rates, or from analyses of actions in sequence – a distinction that will be examined shortly. On the other hand, his first question involves relations between nonverbal actions and stable or transient characteristics of the participant. That is, nonverbal actions might serve as relatively direct indexes of personal attributes, such as dominance or anxiety, that are of great interest to personality, clinical, and social psychologists.

Thus, great interest centered on nonverbal actions as a vehicle for both individual-differences and interaction-process research. It was a significant bonus that these same actions made excellent data, easily and reliably observed, in many ways superior to standard psychological tests and the more diffuse, judgmental observations (Fiske, 1977, 1978).

These developments had two major consequences. First, use of non-verbal actions in experimental social psychology studies became extemely popular; the literature proliferated. Second, standard psychological thinking and research techniques – both geared primarily to the study of individuals – were applied to the use of nonverbal behaviors in this research.

In this type of research, the observation of nonverbal actions was and continues to be carried out within the context of a social psychological experiment. Hypotheses are presented, even in the earliest studies of a phenomenon. The use of nonverbal actions as either dependent or independent variables means that, for practical purposes, few actions can be included in a given study – typically one or two. Situations are constructed, often ingeniously, to induce various sorts of perceptions and reactions in the subjects. Because the study is cast in experimental form, relevant controls are necessary. Almost inevitably, these controls include use of a confederate, instructed to behave according to various specifi-cations, in order to control for the behavior of the subject's partner.

Simple-rate variables

There is a fairly standard technique for generating data in these studies. Nonverbal actions exhibited by the subject over some stretch of interaction, such as gaze direction or smiling, are counted or timed. These counts and timings are summed over that stretch and then converted into a rate variable by dividing them by some larger count or timing. For example, rate of smiling while speaking is calculated by dividing the number of smiles while speaking by total time with the speaking turn. We shall term nonverbal variables generated in this manner "simple-rate" variables. (Studies using such variables were termed "external-variable" studies in D&F, pp. 306, 315.)

While simple-rate variables have distinct advantages over standard psychological test scores, it is important to note that these variables are typically used in essentially the same manner as such test scores. (Barbara

Kanki first pointed out this parallelism to us.) The amount of, say, smiling is represented as a rate on some continuous scale, and this rate is interpreted as indexing relatively directly some internal characteristic of the subject.

External-variable research and interaction process

Our basic point regarding external-variable research is a simple one. In using standard psychological research techniques developed for the study of individuals, investigators using nonverbal actions insufficiently consider the fact that these actions are an integral part of the process of interaction. If that context is ignored, there are unexpected complications that generate error and noise in the data. The inferential links between results and concepts or conclusions may be either seriously impaired or severed altogether.

The basic source of these problems seems to be the strong interconnectedness of things in interaction. The essence of interaction is that events occur in ordered sequences. It seems obvious that a participant's action must appropriately take into account both the general social context and the preceding actions by both participant and partner. When sequential order is ignored in studies using interaction materials, serious error is almost inevitable. We shall attempt to identify the sources of imputed error as specifically as possible.

Well-functioning interaction cannot be viewed as merely a series of well-formed messages sent by the two participants. Imagine two television sets, each turned to a different channel for the five o'clock news. On each channel the news reader is appropriately dressed and groomed, enunciation is clear, language is syntactically well formed, and paralanguage and body motion are appropriate. Now imagine turning the two sets so that they face each other. An interaction does not result. The respective messages are virtually perfect, but neither is in the slightest way contingent on the other. There is no trace of sequential ordering, hence no interaction.

Research that uses interaction materials but ignores sequential ordering does so at its own peril. In this sense, research procedures that are widely used for studying individuals may in some respects be ill-suited for application to interaction process. We shall argue that this is, in fact, the case. The argument will center on three issues: (a) controlling the behavior of confederates in experimental situations, (b) use of simple-rate variables in the study of interaction process, and (c) use of simple-rate variables in the study of individual differences in interaction.

1.2. Use of confederates

It was undoubtedly a concern with the connectedness of things in interaction that led to the use of confederates in external-variable research. Ironically, it is precisely this connectedness that tends to undermine the rationale for using confederates.

Consider an investigator planning a study of individual differences in subjects' use of certain nonverbal actions. In uncontrolled interactions there is the high probability – indeed, certainty – that the behavior of the partner will not be constant across subjects. Variability in the partner will occur regardless of whether each subject has a different partner, or all subjects have the same partner. This variability may reasonably be expected to lead to corresponding variability in the subjects' responses to the partner. For this reason, one cannot be sure whether observed differences in the subjects' behavior stem from partner variation, or from subject variation which is the object of study.

For example, a study might be designed to test for sex differences in smiling in conversations. All subjects interact with the same partner, but that partner's actions are uncontrolled. It is possible that there is no sex difference in the subjects' smiling per se, but the partners happen to smile more with females than with males. The females respond by smiling in return, as might be expected in a conversation. The results would show that females smiled more than males in the interactions. But this apparent sex difference is an artifact, traceable to a systematic difference in the partner's, not the subject's, behavior. (Notice that in a study using simple-rate variables, this possibility could never be detected in the data, because there would be no information on which participant, the partner or the subject, smiled first, or on the extent to which smile initiations by the partner were responded to by the subject.)

Concern with this sort of artifact, not at all unreasonable, gave rise to the use of confederates in experimental studies. The confederates are instructed to control their actions in certain relevant ways, so that each subject would receive the same interactional "treatment." In the example just cited, the confederate might be instructed never to initiate a smile, but if the subject smiled, to smile back for a brief period.

Various approaches have been taken to the problem of controlling the actions of confederates. Perhaps most common, especially in the earlier studies, was the holding constant of some action or actions thought to be relevant. In studies of gaze direction, the confederate might be instructed to maintain constant gaze at the subject.

Other studies attempted to achieve a more natural pattern. For example,

Mehrabian and Ksionzky (1972) report the following, which is only part of a more complex experimental procedure:

> As [the confederate and subject] entered the room, the confederate smiled once at the subject, and during the waiting period he looked in the subject's direction 30% of the time, which included eye contact when the subject spoke to him. When the subject made a statement or asked a question, the confederate responded with a statement of about five words. For every three such initiations by the subject, the confederate initiated one topic himself. (p. 595)

Still other studies involve confederates who are instructed to establish some more global attitude toward the subject, such as "warm" or "distant."

Whatever the general approach, in virtually all of the studies using confederates the procedure has been to train confederates until they meet stated criteria. Once the study has begun, however, attention becomes focused entirely on the subjects' behavior. We are not aware of a study in which confederates' behavior was actually checked during or after the study to verify that the instructions continued to be adequately followed.

We wish to raise three objections to the use of confederates in interaction research. The practice (a) assumes adequate knowledge of both what is to be controlled and the manner in which it should be controlled, (b) assumes the ability of the confederate actually to achieve the desired control, and (c) appears to involve a fundamental paradox with respect to interaction process.

Adequate knowledge

Many studies have controlled a confederate's action even though there has not been systematic research on the action in question as it occurs in interaction. For example, in many studies concerned with subjects' gaze as speaker, just the confederate's gaze is controlled, not other actions such as auditor back channels and smiles. Until there is more substantive information on the interrelation of various actions in interaction, the selection of actions to be controlled by the confederate will be mainly a matter of guesswork. To the extent that guesses are inaccurate, artifactual variation in the subjects' actions will be produced.

Furthermore, the problem of accurate knowledge obviously extends to the manner in which actions are to be controlled. It is important not only that relevant actions are known, but also that the specified patterns for these actions are appropriate within the type of interaction studied. The confederate's use of inappropriate or unnatural interaction patterns is another source of artifact in the data.

We conclude that, given the present state of knowledge of interaction process, specifying both the relevant actions to be controlled and the manner in which they are to be controlled is a distinctly chancy matter. It is possible that an unlucky choice of actions and patterns for control through the confederate can actually introduce artifactual variability in the subjects, rather than reducing it as intended. This source of error becomes difficult to detect because the use of confederates is presumed to minimize it, with the result that investigators do not consider it necessary to check carefully for it. This brings us to our second point: the ability of the confederate to achieve the desired control.

Ability to control actions

Even if there were sufficient knowledge of face-to-face interaction to enable investigators to develop natural and relevant instructions, the effective use of confederates requires that the instructions be followed accurately and consistently. Experiences in our laboratory have caused us to have considerable concern about the confederates ability to achieve adequate control over interaction behavior. This concern stems from Rosenthal's work on experimenter bias in social science studies (e.g., Rosenthal, 1966; Rosenthal & Rosnow, 1969).

Rosenthal's extensive research showed a dismaying tendency for experimenters to obtain results from subjects that were in line with the experimenters' expectations of the subjects' performance. This effect could be manipulated from subject to subject within a single study.

An exploratory study was designed by Duncan and Rosenthal (1968) to discover the mechanism by which this biasing effect was being communicated by the experimenters. The standard Rosenthal task was used: subjects were asked to rate each of a series of photographs of men as to whether the man had experienced success or failure in life. Ratings were on a scale of -10 (extreme failure) to +10 (extreme success). The series had been standardized to yield an average rating of zero under neutral conditions. Systematic deviations from zero had been found in conformity with expectations that had been imparted on a random basis to experimenters who were administering the task.

In the Duncan and Rosenthal study, a careful analysis was made of patterns of intonational and paralinguistic stress in the experimenter's reading of certain critical portions of the experimental instructions. A *differential-emphasis* score based on these stresses was developed that yielded a correlation of .72 with the subjects' rating of the photos. Because both experimenter expectancy and the differential emphasis in instruction reading were potential contributors to the bias effect, a partial correlation was calculated between the subjects' ratings and the differential-emphasis score, with the expectancy held constant. The partial r between ratings and differential emphasis was .74. The correlation between experimenter's expectancy and differential emphasis was only .24. It appeared that the manner in which the experimenter read the standard instructions accounted for half the variance in the subjects' performance in this study.

A highly controlled cross-validation of these results was carried out by Duncan, Rosenberg, and Finkelstein (1969). Also introduced in the design was the factor of evaluation apprehension (Rosenberg, 1969). In this study, there was no face-to-face interaction between experimenter and subject. Subjects were brought in groups into a language laboratory with a number of listening booths separated by dividers. At some booths was a set of instructions intended either to raise or to lower evaluation apprehension (EA); a third group of subjects received no instructions relative to EA. All three EA conditions (high, low, and control) were present in each session.

Nine audiotapes of the standard instructions were prepared, consisting of three readings each by three individuals. These tapes contained for each individual a range of differential-emphasis scores; very generally, there was a positive, neutral, and negative reading for each. Different tapes were played to different subjects in each subject group, so that there was a mixture of both tapes and EA conditions in each group. After some subjects had read their brief EA instuctions and all had heard a tape of the experimental instructions (to rate the success or failure of the individuals pictured), slides of the pictures were projected on a screen, and all subjects rated each picture.

Results confirmed the differential-emphasis hypothesis: the bias effect was obtained on the basis of the taped instructions alone. This effect interacted with EA in the predicted manner: High EA produced the greatest positive and negative bias effects, control EA produced the next greatest bias effects, and low EA produced negligible bias effects. By combining these EA-differential-emphasis groups in the predicted order, a significant linear trend was obtained for the data.

Although it was gratifying to obtain some validation for the original differential-emphasis hypothesis, the most stiking aspect of the study had to do with the preparation of the tapes – the sort of thing that is rarely described in journal articles. Two of the readers (or "experimenters") were friends of Duncan and were in the last stages of writing their dissertations in psychology; the third was Rosenthal. The first two readers made their tapes in sessions with Duncan in which they were asked to produce contrasting readings of the instructions. They were first asked to produce one or two readings that were entirely neutral and unbiased. Then they were asked for readings "very subtly shaded" in a positive or negative direction. After the "subtle" readings, they were asked for readings with heavy emphasis in a positive or negative direction. Rosenthal produced his readings in accordance with written instructions of the same sort. Using this procedure, a set of tapes was obtained with which all three readers were highly pleased. They reported that they had done an excellent job in producing the type of reading requested.

It was a matter of considerable surprise, then, when the tapes were analyzed for differential emphasis. It was found that, for each of the readers, there was little or no relation between the differential emphasis (neutral, subtle, or heavy) requested and the differential emphasis actually produced. Further, there was not even a relation between the direction (positive or negative) requested and that actually produced. For example, if a "heavy negative" reading was requested, a subtle, positive reading might be produced. Of course, the subsequent study used only the actual differential-emphasis score of the reading, not the type of reading requested.

If the two studies (Duncan & Rosenthal, 1968; Duncan et al., 1969) are accorded some degree of validity, they yield a startling and somewhat unsettling picture. The results suggest that, although striving for consistency and neutrality in dealing with subjects, an experimenter nevertheless varies specified actions appreciably between subjects and that these actions can account for 50% of the variance in the subjects' responses. Recall that this last result was obtained by analyzing only the experimenters' intonation and voice quality with respect to word stress. Content was constant in the standard instructions, and body motion was not considered. It would appear that relatively powerful interactional effects can be transmitted through subtle and small-scale actions. There is no evidence that the experimenters in the first study had the slightest awareness of their differential treatment of subjects or of the effects of these differences on the subjects.

The experience with consciously manipulated readings suggests that individuals not only are potentially unaware of their differential actions but also in some situations may be unable effectively to control these actions on a volitional basis. Action may deviate significantly from instructions, and confederates may not be aware that such deviations occurred. Nevertheless, these deviations, in conjunction with other experimental factors, can produce significant variation in the subjects' task performance. As might be imagined, this was a decidedly sobering experience that left a deep impression on those involved in the study.

Paradoxical control

A final point remains to be noted regarding the use of confederates. This point is not directly related to the pragmatic considerations of knowledge of patterns and ability of the confederate to carry them out. Let us assume for the moment that neither of these problems obtains. Even if investigators had extensive knowledge of appropriate behavior patterns and confederates were able to carry out instructions with satisfactory fidelity and constancy, there would still be a serious problem with the use of confederates in experimental interactions.

Appropriate conduct in interaction is not a simple matter of carrying out certain actions. The nature of interaction requires that each participant respond appropriately to the actions of the partner. A participant cannot simply be programmed to act in certain ways independently of the actions of the partner. In this sense, a participant's action must be tied in part to the action of the partner. For this reason, full control of a confederate's actions – thus insuring the confederate's constancy between subjects – would necessarily require that variations in the subjects' actions be ignored. Conversely, if the confederate responds appropriately to the actions of the subjects, then constancy between subjects will be lost to the extent that subjects vary in their interactions with the confederate.

It follows, then, that to achieve true constancy in the confederate's treatment of different subjects, control would have to be obtained not only over the confederate's actions but also over the subjects' actions. If the subjects' actions were not controlled, then each interaction would proceed to take its own course, based in part on the individual style of the respective subjects. Thus, the investigator seeking true interactional control through the use of confederates would appear to confront a distinctly paradoxical situation. Once again, the interconnectedness of things in interaction would appear to compromise procedures developed for use in research with individuals.

A simple example may illustrate this paradox. Let us say that an investigator, seeking to maintain some sort of normal pattern for the confederate, instructs the confederate to smile in response to every third smile by the subject. Obviously, the confederate's smiling behavior could vary widely between subjects. There will be much smiling with subjects who smile frequently, little smiling with those who smile infrequently, and no smiling (a) with subjects who initiate no smiling, (b) with subjects who smile all the way through the interaction, and (c) with subjects who smile once or twice. Further, the more extensive smiling in some interactions may lend them an entirely different cast from those in which there is little smiling. All in all, it would seem that the notion of constant treatment of subjects has been lost.

Taken as a whole, then, it would seem that attempts to exert experimental control through the use of confederates may encounter formidable difficulties when applied to interaction phenomena. Use of confederates may, in many cases, create more difficulties than it solves, providing a source of uncontrolled variance between subjects rather than eliminating such variance. This uncontrolled variance may result from the use of unnatural patterns, from the inability of the confederate to achieve adequate constancy of action, or from the confederate's response (in accordance with instructions) to differences in subjects' actions.

For these reasons, use of confederates in studies of interaction would not appear to be a productive technique. However, if an investigator deems the use of confederates to be a necessary element of experimental design, then it would seem necessary – and definitely in the best interests of the investigator – to record and examine the actions of the confederate as carefully as the actions of the subject.

Control not involving confederates

We hasten to add, as was pointed out in D&F, that we are not questioning the notion of control itself, only the use of confederates as part of the controls in an experiment. Other elements of control seem entirely straightforward and generally unproblematic. One can control the physical setting of the interaction, the positioning of the subjects with respect to each other, the type of interaction or task that the subjects engage in, and the type of subjects that interact with each other. For example, one can arrange for the subjects to be seated in chairs at a 45-degree angle one meter apart, discussing the solution to a problem presented to them, and for all subjects to be female high-school students.

Reasonable approaches to controlling elements such as these should generate none of the complications that we have been discussing with respect to confederates.

Conclusions

Stated briefly, we draw the following conclusions on using confederates.

1. Interaction is a complex and subtle process. Attempting to control merely for one or two major actions, such as gaze, may be woefully insufficient.
2. Unfortunately for the experimenter seeking to develop more sophisticated instructions for confederates, appropriate or natural patterns for a wide variety of actions are simply not known in most cases.
3. If the patterns were known, the confederates in the actual press of interaction with subjects may not be able to conform to such patterns.
4. One cannot be assured that the confederates are able to monitor accurately whether or not they are successfully performing the patterns. For this reason, if the experimenter chooses to use confederates, it seems absolutely essential that their actual performance in the study be at least as carefully observed as the subjects' actions.
5. Finally, because interaction is sequentially ordered, each participant's action is apppropriately contingent on the partner's action. For this reason, full control over the confederate's action may require control over the subject's action. This paradox brings into question the very concept of using confederates as part of the controls in studies of interaction.

1.3. Simple-rate variables

Although use of confederates is a common practice in external-variable studies, it is not a necessary element of them. In contrast, use of *simple-rate variables* is the defining feature of external-variable studies. It is important, therefore, to examine in some detail the characteristics of simple-rate variables.

It will be recalled that simple-rate variables are those that are generated by counting or timing an action by a participant in interaction. Because the counting or timing involves no information on the sequences in which actions occur in interaction, the variable is said to be "simple," as opposed to "sequential." That count or timing is then typically converted into a rate by dividing it by some broader, more encompassing value, such as time with the speaking turn or number of turns, that reflects the extent of interaction over which the count or timing could have occurred.

For example, in the external-variable study reported in D&F (Part II), three types of simple-rate variables were used: rate, extent, and mean length. These three types can be illustrated using speaker gaze as the action in question. Rate of gazing while speaking would be calculated by dividing a speaker's total number of gazes by the total duration of his or her speaking. For extent of speaker gaze, the total duration of speaker gazes would be divided by the total duration of speaking. Mean length of speaker gazing is obtained by dividing the total duration of speaker gazes by the total number of speaker gazes. A comparable set of variables was generated for auditor gaze. These, of course, are standard rate variables, entirely familiar in a variety of types of psychological research.

Based on experience in our laboratory, we believe that simple-rate variables have two apparently independent characteristics, either one of which is sufficient to render them unusable in research on interaction. These two characteristics relate to the two aspects of the definition of the variable.

1. The "simple" aspect of the variable means that the variable contains no information on the sequences in which actions occur in interaction. We shall argue that this undermines both inferences regarding interaction process, and the identification of a variable with a specific participant, even though the variable is intended to describe the actions of that participant. That is to say, lack of sequential information essentially negates the usefulness of the variable for research on either interaction process or individual differences.
2. The "rate" aspect of the variable may introduce noise and indeterminacy with respect to which participant's action is influencing the value of the variable. In addition, in interaction research where sequences are studied, a single rate variable may be viewed as only a partial picture of the data situation and thus may almost always be improved upon.

These two points will be carefully examined in this section. The discussion will be organized in terms of the two major concerns of external-variable research: interaction process and individual differences.

Interaction process

An essential property of interaction is that it is sequentially ordered. It is important not only whether certain actions occur, but also where they occur in the stream in interaction. Description of interaction processes must be based on observed sequences of actions between participants. For this reason, results based on simple-rate variables, which lack sequential information, cannot be used to draw direct inferences concerning interaction processes.

An example may illustrate this position. Imagine that, observing a number of interactions, an investigator found a significant correlation between the extent of smiling by one participant and that by the partner. The obvious, intuitive interpretation is that there is a strong tendency toward mutual smiling in the observed dyads. But this, of course, is an unjustified inference from the simple-rate data because there is no information on smiling sequences in the variables. The same correlation could have been obtained if all of one participant's smiling was during the first half of the interaction, all of the partner's smiling was during the second half, and the amounts of these respective smilings were consistently proportional for the two participants in each interaction. Although this interpretation is improbable to say the least, the point is that it cannot be ruled out as a possible source of the correlation, based on the information available in the variable.

We therefore conclude that simple-rate variables cannot support hypotheses concerning interaction processes. The variables simply do not contain the necessary information. In the external-variable study reported in Part II of D&F, this problem was pandemic in the results. Let us examine a specific case.

In Table 5.1 (pp. 66-67) in D&F, correlations are reported between a participant's total time with the speaking turn and a number of simple-rate variables. One pair of variables provided a particularly interesting set of correlations: gaze rate when speaking, and gaze rate when not speaking. The correlations for the two variables were in opposite directions. Gaze rate when speaking was negatively correlated with speaking time, whereas gaze rate when not speaking (i.e., when the participant was auditor) was positively correlated with speaking time. That is, the more a participant as speaker looked back and forth at the auditor, the less total speaking time that participant had in the conversation. In contrast, when a participant was auditor, the more looking back and forth toward the speaker, the more speaking time that participant had.

These correlations were just the sort of highly patterned and differentiated results that we were seeking in the study. However, when we began to consider possible interpretations, we became aware that we were lacking some centrally important information on the relationship between gaze and turn time.

First, the data contained no information on how close the relationship was between gaze and turns. In order for gazing to be related to turn time, we have to assume that gazing is somehow related to the exchange of speaking turns. But the data provide us with no information on whether turn exchanges tended to follow closely on gazing, or gazes tended to follow closely on turn exchanges. Alternatively, the gazes might have tended to occur somewhere during the middle of the turn, so that the relationship between gazing and turn exchanges was more distal than proximate. Information on the order and proximity of gazing and turn exchanges was not available.

Second, what was it about gazing that linked it to longer or shorter turns? In a series of gazes, there are two things a participant must do in order to receive a count of one gaze toward the partner: shift gaze toward the partner, and then shift gaze away. There are, then, four aspects of gaze that might be relevant to the relationship: shifting toward the partner, actual gazing at the partner, shifting away, and gazing away. These distinguishable aspects of gaze seemed of potential importance because the correlations of speaker gaze and auditor gaze with turn time were in opposite directions. The data contained no information on these distinguishable aspects of gaze that may be differentially related to turn time.

One might argue that distinguishing shifts of gaze toward the partner from shifts away is largely irrelevant because, after all, the number of shifts toward is essentially the same as the number of shifts away. However, it is possible, for example, that turn exchanges tend to occur shortly after the speaker shifts gaze toward the auditor and is gazing at the auditor. (This, in fact, is the case in our data.) In this manner, information on such aspects of actions permits a more differentiated examination of action sequences.

It happened that structural research on turn taking, based on analysis of interaction sequences and carried out both before and after the external-variable study, can shed some light on the correlations in question. First, the speaker's shifting gaze toward the auditor, when co-occurring with a speaker turn signal, was hypothesized as a *strategy signal* (Chapter 7), increasing the probability of the auditor's acting to take the turn in response to that turn signal. This effect is consistent with the negative relationship between speaker gaze and turn time.

Second, when the auditor shifts gaze away from the speaker in conjunction with an utterance, that gaze shift was hypothesized to be a *speaker-state* signal (D&F; cf. Chapter 3), indicating that the utterance was the beginning of a speaking turn, as opposed to an auditor back channel. Thus, it signaled that the auditor was at that moment acting to take the speaking turn. This element of interaction structure is consistent with the negative correlation between auditor gazing and speaker's turn time.

It would seem, then, that the negative correlation between speaker gaze rate and turn time is related to the speaker's shifting gaze toward the auditor, thereby increasing the probability of the auditor's taking the turn. In contrast, the positive correlation between a participant's gaze rate as auditor and the participant's turn time is related to the auditor's shifting gaze away from the speaker in connection with auditor turn beginnings. These relationships are suggested by structural research based on extensive information on both interaction sequences and aspects of actions.

This example shows why simple-rate variables are inappropriate for research on interaction process. These variables contain no information on interaction sequences, and sequential ordering is an essential property of interaction. One cannot interpret results from analyses of simple-rate variables in terms of interaction process. Therefore, simple-rate variables cannot support inferences regarding interaction process.

1.4. Pseudounilaterality

The arguments just presented focused on difficulties in using simple-rate variables in reseach on interaction process. These arguments might appear limited because much – probably most – external-variable research is concerned with individual differences, rather than with interaction process. It does not necessarily follow that simple-rate variables are similarly problematic in individual-differences research.

Consideration of individual-differences research brings us to a convenient point for discussing the second characteristic of simple-rate variables: the use of rates. Much to our surprise, it appears that rate variables, seemingly essential in much of psychological research, can, when improperly used, become a source of significant confusion and potential error when they are applied to interaction phenomena. In individual-differences research, these problems serve only to compound those already mentioned with respect to lack of information in interaction sequences.

Let us begin the discussion with a single, prototypical simple-rate variable, *extent of gazing while speaking:* number of seconds gazing while speaking, divided by number of seconds with the speaking turn, both summed over an interaction.

(As already mentioned,in many studies of individual differences a variable of this sort is treated very much like a test score, strongly analogous to a rate of correct or keyed responses to an inventory. The variable is considered to index fairly directly some dimension such as "affiliativeness," "dominance," or the like. Alternatively, the variable is used to measure some major group difference such as sex differences.)

Because the values entered into the computations of a simple-rate variable are obtained directly from measuring the actions of the participant, it has seemed safe to assume that the variable should be attributed to that participant. Certainly, we had no inclination to doubt that assumption. It therefore came as a considerable surprise to us that, because of the characteristics of interaction process, such a variable may instead reflect either a pattern of action by the partner, or (more likely) a product of the actions of both participant and partner. That is, the variable simply does not "belong" exclusively to the participant.

The fact that both participants can influence the value of a variable designed to describe the action of only one participant obviously undermines the chain of inference linking the variable directly to some internal characteristic or interactional tendency of the participant. Serious error may occur when interpretation of results is based on the assumption that the value of the variable is affected only by the single participant.Once again, it would seem that the interconnectedness of things in interaction intrudes itself, disrupting standard research techniques designed for the study of individuals.

If this claim is true, then interpreting results from simple-rate variables strictly in terms of the individual participant involves an interpretive error. To refer to this sort of interpretive error, we have proposed the term *pseudounilaterality* (PU) (Duncan et al., 1984). Pseudounilaterality refers to the false assumption that the variable is necessarily determined unilaterally, only by the actions of the single participant.

This problem is not at all confined to simple-rate variables. It may occur as well with any other currently formulated interaction variable. This situation will be explored carefully in a later section. The PU error, however, seems to occur in its most extreme form in connection with simple-rate variables. Because such variables have predominated in the literature, we shall begin the discussion with them.

A typical use of simple-rate variables in individual-differences research would be to study the extent of use of some action, such as gaze or gestures, for different groups of subjects. For example, one might observe the extent of gazing while speaking by males and by females in two-person conversations. If extent of gazing is found to be greater for females than for males, then the investigator would straightforwardly interpret these results as indicating that the females in the conversations actually gazed more at the partner than did the males.

Similarly, one might study some action by participants in each of two interactions. Change in the simple-rate variable for a participant from one interaction to the next would be interpreted as change in the participant's actions between the two interactions; and conversely, lack of change in the variable would be interpreted as constancy in the participant's actions.

Regardless of the intuitive appeal of these inferences, we hold that they are not necessarily justified when natural or uncontrolled interactions are involved. Although it may seem counterintuitive, we hope to show that the information available in the variable is insufficient to support direct inference about the behavior of the participant from the value of the variable. It is entirely possible that more extensive use of all available information on the interaction may reveal a much more complex state of affairs.

The classical proposition that behavior is a function of the person and the situation is so vague that no one questions it. In work on individual differences, the proposition is invoked to account for the annoying observation of changes in a person's actions from one situation to another. Consider, however, an instance in which two individuals talk at length about themselves in separate interactions. We do not attribute self-centeredness to both of them if we know that one interaction was an interview in which the individual was asked a long string of personal questions, the interviewer largely determining what the individual talked about. Similarly, a simple-rate variable may be determined primarily by the actions of the partner.

As mentioned above, in a simple-rate variable the numerator is the action on which the variable is focused, such as number or duration of gazes or gestures. The denominator is a broader, more encompassing value, such as time with the speaking turn or number of turns, that reflects the extent of interaction over which the target action might have occurred.

Interpretive error may arise in interaction research because both the numerator and the denominator may reflect the actions not only of the participant in question, but also of the partner. A given variable may be deeply influenced by the actions of both participants. It becomes extremely difficult to claim that a variable is the "property" of either participant, even though it is defined in terms of the actions of only one participant.

Examples may clarify the potential interactive character of both numerator and denominator in simple-rate variables. In order to achieve a direct illustration of the point, these examples have been drastically simplified. They are not intended to represent typical process in observed interactions. They may, however, suggest how both participants can influence the value of supposedly unilateral variables.

Numerator affected

Consider a variable concerned with speaker gaze. For the sake of example, let us say that the participant has an entirely uniform gaze pattern while speaking: an alternation of three seconds gazing away from the partner, followed by three seconds gazing toward the partner. That is, from the beginning of the speaking turn and continuing throughout its duration, there is a regular six-second gaze cycle, consisting of a three-second gaze-toward phase. The participant never deviates from this pattern either within an interaction or between interactions. The simple-rate variable is extent of gaze while speaking: number of seconds gazing at the partner while speaking, divided by number of seconds speaking, summed over the interaction. The study is concerned with the amount of change in this variable for the participant from one interaction to another.

In the first interaction, it happens that the partner typically takes the speaking turn at the end of the first gaze cycle, after the third second of gaze toward the partner – just before the speaker would have begun the second gaze cycle. In this interaction, the gaze-extent variable would be about .50 (3/6). In the second interaction, the partner typically takes the speaking turn during the first cycle no more than one second after gaze toward the partner begins. Here the gaze-extent variable would be about .25 (1/4).

In each case, the partner's pattern of taking the turn directly affects the length of the participant's gaze as speaker (the numerator of the variable). (The denominator is also affected because the second partner takes the turn sooner.) In this example, there has been no change in the participant's gaze pattern, but there is a substantial difference in the behavior patterns of the respective partners. Nevertheless, results of this sort might be interpreted as reflecting a major, unilateral change in the participant's gazing between the two interactions.

More subtle actions than the partner's turn taking can affect the duration of the participant's actions. Staying with the example of gaze extent while speaking, imagine an interaction pattern in which, during the speaker's gaze, there is a tendency for the gaze to be shifted away after an auditor back channel. Once again, different rates of auditor back channels in different interactions will affect measures of speaker gaze duration.

Taken together, the two examples using gaze suggest the possibility that a given action by the participant may be affected by more than one action by the partner, making the total effect more complex.

Denominator affected

Continuing the case of stability of actions between interactions, let the action of interest be gesticulation. Once again, the simple-rate variable will be extent: duration of gesturing divided by duration of speaking, summed over the interaction. The participant in question has a completely stable pattern of gesturing. At the beginning of each speaking turn, the participant gestures for five seconds and then stops, having no further gestures for the remainder of the turn. The pattern does not change, either within each interaction or between interactions.

You will anticipate the scenario. In the first interaction, the auditor always waits for five seconds after the end of the gesture and then takes the turn, resulting in a value for extent of gesturing of .50 (5/10). In the second interaction, the auditor is more active, taking the turn one second after the end of each gesture. Gesture extent for the second interaction is .83 (5/6). The results suggest a 66% increase in extent of gesturing by the speaker, but the gesturing pattern and the total number of seconds of gesturing within each turn have remained constant. The change is entirely due to the difference in the auditors' respective responsiveness – that is, in the relative duration of the participant's speaking turns.

These examples illustrate how false interpretations of a participant's change from one interaction to another may arise. Obviously, the opposite false interpretation is also possible. A participant may appear to be relatively stable in some action from one interaction to the next but is actually producing rather different action patterns that are being counter-balanced by the partner's responses.

Despite the artificiality of the examples, the principle should be clear and clearly applicable to more complex natural interactions. Speaking time, number of turns, and an undetermined number of "nonverbal" actions by a participant are not unilateral, but interactively determined. A variable involving turns or any affected action cannot be said to "belong" exclusively to the participant producing the actions; it is, rather, a product of the joint action of both participants in a way that cannot be determined on the basis of the simple-rate variable alone. Variables based on such interactively determined elements cannot legitimately be interpreted as reflecting unilateral individual performance.

Investigators may be surprised to find total time speaking, one of the most natural and commonly used denominators for simple-rate variables, to be a prime culprit in these examples. Total time speaking is, unfortunately, one of the most interactive of measures. In many cases, one may view participant's speaking time as a property more of the partner as auditor than of the participant as speaker.

Further examples

It is clear that the interpretation of results from many studies of individual differences in "nonverbal communication" may be subject to the PU error. A simple example is the early and frequently replicated result that female interactants gaze more at the partner than do male interactants. On the basis of results from simple-rate variables in natural interactions, it cannot be determined which of the following five possibilities is responsible for the phenomenon: (a) the females are actually gazing more, (b) the males are gazing away more, (c) the partners of the males are taking the turn sooner after the onset of the males' gazing, (d) the partners of the females are taking the turn more during the females' gazing away, or (e) some combination of these factors is occurring.

Based on the information contained in simple-rate variables, one cannot dismiss the possibility that the entire effect has nothing at all to do with actual gaze patterns by males and females, but rather with differential patterns of turn-taking in response to gaze or nongaze by partners of males, as opposed to partners of females.

In the D&F external-variable study, one perplexing set of results was the low stability in the various simple-rate variables for participants (professional-school students) from the first to the second interaction, where the second interaction followed immediately upon the first. Although the partner in the second interaction was always of the opposite sex from that in the first, gross changes in participants' behavior were not readily observable on the videotapes. Nevertheless, consistency across interactions, as indexed by the simple-rate variables was, in general, quite low. The median correlation of participants' rates on simple-rate variables from first to second interaction was .40, with a range from .80 to .00 (D&F, p. 49). Based on the median value, a major part of the variance in the participants' action was shifting from one interaction to the next. And for many variables, virtually all of the variance was shifting in this way. These results seemed counterintuitive and not well supported by general impressions from the tapes.

It may now be seen that such low stability may be expected because the partner can actually be a major contributor to the value of such variables. Our viewing of the tapes suggested no striking consistency in a participant's partners from one interaction to the next; therefore, the values of the simple-rate variables may be expected to vary accordingly.

Discussion: simple-rate variables

It was recommended in D&F (p. 315) that simple-rate variables be abandoned altogether in studies of interaction process, and that they be replaced with variables containing information on action sequences. Variables of this sort are considered in the next section. Considering that most studies in the area used simple-rate variables, we did not expect that this recommendation would be a popular one. It should be pointed out that at the very least it was not a "holier-than-thou" sort of position; rather, it resulted from our own painful experience with a major research project. After carrying out a large-scale study, we recognized a fundamental flaw in its conceptualization when we were interpreting the results.

Two frequently encountered misunderstandings of the recommendation are worth mentioning. Some colleagues have alleged that our argument against simple-rate variables was based on sour grapes because we failed to obtain as many significant results in our study as we had expected. Others have understood the recommendation as stemming from the observation that simple-rate variables contain less information than action-sequence variables and therefore are to be preferred. From this perspective, our recommendation that simple-rate variables be abandoned altogether is an instance of taking a possibly useful point to extremes.

The discussion so far should have made clear that the argument against simple-rate variables is based on principle, rather than resentment or degree of usefulness. If ordered sequences of action are an essential characteristic of interaction, and if simple-rate variables by definition contain no information on action sequences, the results based on simple-rate variables cannot be applied to interaction without problematic results.

Conclusions: simple-rate variables

Consideration of the problems attached to simple-rate variables leads us to the following conclusions, briefly stated. Beyond the examples given in this chapter, these ideas will be exemplified in analyses in later chapters.

1. Interaction sequences, not single actions, should be subjected to analysis. This may be accomplished either by incorporating sequential information in the variables used, or by analyzing tables in which rows represent preceding actions, and columns represent succeeding actions, or the like. The discussion of action-sequence variables in the next section will provide examples of variables carrying sequential information.
2. Although rate variables are standard in psychological research and can be valuable in studies of actions under essentially fixed conditions, they should be used with caution in studies of interaction. It would appear that any variable in interaction research can be quite tricky and complex in the best of cases, and the denominator of a rate variable may in some cases provide an additional element of complexity. In addition, focusing on only one or two rate variables may in some cases unnecessarily limit the investigator's view of the data. This is not to say, however, that rate variables should not be used at all – only that they should be used carefully. Rates will be found in some of the studies reported in Chapters 7-10. (Their use in those chapters may be considered in terms of the PU considerations we have outlined.) To minimize potential difficulties with rate variables, we suggest that variables be concerned with interactional sequences, rather than properties of individual participants. In any event, the main point

here is that rate variables cannot be imported wholesale from individual-differences research in psychology.

3. Variables should include as much differentiated information as possible on the actions in question. We referred to this as information on the aspects of actions. We used gaze as an example to show how information on the beginning, duration, and ending of gazing in the stream of interaction seems preferable to simply measuring gazing itself.

4. Instead of focusing on a single variable, such as gaze extent, one should seek maximal leverage by analyzing multiple, related variables. Such an approach may permit viewing the action simultaneously from a number of perspectives, or placing it within the context of a more complex stream of interaction.

These points will be elaborated in the next section.

1.5. Sequence variables

As an alternative to simple-rate variables, we propose variables containing information on the sequences of actions occurring in interaction. These variables are extensively used in the structure research (Chapter 6) in the strategy studies (Chapters 7-10), including a special form – the *run-sequence* variable – which is the most information-packed variable that we have been able to devise. The description of strategy research will be based on the discussion in this section of sequence variables and of the properties of interaction that must be considered in devising appropriate variables.

Sequence variables are designed to provide information on the location in the stream of interaction of each occurrence (or nonoccurrence) of the target action (such as speaker gaze). In their simplest form, sequence variables contain information on a participant's action (e.g., speaker gaze) and some other preceding, subsequent, or concurrent action by the partner (e.g, taking the turn). To this simple, two-action sequence may be added further information on other actions by both participants.

Sequence variables are described in terms of (a) the *participants* involved, (b) the *aspects* of actions relevant to the variable (e.g., onset, offset, or duration of an action), and (c) the type of *linkage* between the sequential actions (temporal or event based, as explained below).

We may illustrate these elements of a sequence variable, staying with speaker gaze as the example. Let the variable be concerned with a two-action sequence: the auditor's taking the turn during the speaker's gaze toward the auditor. That is, we wish to count the number of times that the auditor acts to take the turn while the speaker is gazing at the auditor. With respect to aspects of actions, the variable involves duration for speaker gaze (the speaker must be looking toward the auditor and onset of taking the turn for the auditor). The linkage between gazing and turn taking is

Table 1.1. *Speaker gaze and auditor turn attempts*

	Speaker gaze	No speaker gaze	Total
Turn attempt	a	b	a + b
No turn attempt	c	d	c + d
Total	a + c	b + d	a + b + c + d

event based (rather than temporal): The speaker must be gazing during the turn attempt.

It is not necessary to limit one's analysis to the single relation between speaker gaze and auditor turn taking. It is obvious that the data contain further, potentially useful information on the relation between speaker gaze and turn exchanges. We might supplement the original rate variable by counting the number of times the auditor acted to take the turn while the speaker was not gazing at the auditor. (For brevity, we shall call this *speaker nongaze*.)

The nonoccurrence of events can be observed if the interaction materials are divided into units for the purpose of analysis. These units may be constructed either temporally or via some behaviorally defined unit. For analyzing conversations, we have divided the stream of interaction into *units of analysis*, a complex event defined in terms of the actions of the speaker. The procedure for identifying units of analysis is described both in D&F and in Chapter 5. Units of analysis tend to be two to four words in length.

By observing both gaze and turn taking in each unit of analysis, we can construct a 2 × 2 table as in Table 1.1. This table contains appreciably more information than was available in the single rate variable. It permits calculating a set of both row and column rates (and ratios), the interaction between gaze and turn taking [(a × d)/(b × c)] and rates and ratios relating the four marginal terms (a + c, etc.) to each other and to the total. The table thus gives us a broader basis on which to evaluate the relation between gaze and turn-taking than does any single rate.

Apart from the various rates and ratios that can be calculated, Table 1.1 presents information on four action sequences: speaker gazes during which the auditor took the turn (cell a), turn attempts in the absence of speaker gaze (cell b), and so forth.

Of course, it is not necessary to limit our inquiry to the data in Table 1.1. We may add further information on whether the speaker's gaze or nongaze occurred at the very beginning of the speaking turn, or during the

Table 1.2. *A group of related sequential variables*

Location		Speaker		Turn		Sequence number
Initial	Internal	Gaze	Nongaze	Taken	Not taken	
+			+		+	1
+			+	+		2
+		+			+	3
+		+		+		4
	+		+		+	5
	+		+	+		6
	+	+			+	7
	+	+		+		8

course of the turn. Thus, we have both turn-initial gazes and turn-internal gazes, and turn-initial nongazes and turn-internal nongazes.

We have by this time defined eight action sequences: (a) initial speaker nongazes during which the auditor did not take the turn; (b) initial speaker nongazes during which the auditor took the turn; (c) initial speaker gazes during which the auditor did not take the turn; (d) initial speaker gazes during which the auditor took the turn; and four comparable sequences for internal gazes and nongazes. Table 1.2 diagrams this set of related sequence variables. It will be apparent that multiple, related sequence variables can be generated rather easily in this manner.

Run-sequence variables

To this point, we have stayed entirely within the action-sequence framework described by D&F. We wish now to consider a further element: the duration of events in the sequence. This information seems important because it is often useful to know not only how many times an event occurred, but also the duration of each occurrence. It obviously makes a difference whether, for example, a gaze was very brief or occupied most of an interaction. A participant's total gazing in an interaction may be made up of many short gazes, a few long gazes, or some combination of these. The composition of gaze lengths may have important interactional consequences or be a result of important interactional events. Thus we may speak of the duration or length of each gaze. We shall term the occurrence of some action a *run* of that action. In a *run-sequence variable*, information on the length or duration of each run is part of the variable.

For present purposes, we shall measure the length of runs in units of analysis, as outlined above.

Table 1.3. *Distribution of run lengths for males and females on eight speaker-gaze run sequences*

	Run length														Total runs
	1	2	3	4	5	6	7	8	9	0	11	12	13	>13	
1-Initial, speaker-ended nongaze															
Males	55	19	21	20	15[a]	8	4	2	2	0	1	1	1		149
Females	46	35	18	17	7[a]	4	0	2	0	1	0	0	0		130
2-Initial, auditor-ended nongaze															
Males	7	8	3	3[a]	1	1	0	0	0	0	0	0	0	1	24
Females	13	4	2	1[a]	0	0	0	1	1	0	0	0	0	0	22
3-Initial, speaker-ended gaze															
Males	15	12	10	2	3[a]	0	1	1	0	3					47
Females	22	5	9	6	3[a]	2	1	2	1	0					51
4-Initial, auditor-ended gaze															
Males	42	31	20	8[a]	4	0	1	1	1	2					110
Females	60	41	23	14[a]	6	8	4	2	3	0					161
5-Internal, speaker-ended nongaze															
Males	91	80	33	24[a]	13	6	5	3	4	2	0	0	0	2	263
Females	81	67	44	20[a]	14	8	1	1	2	2	0	0	1	0	250
6-Internal, auditor-ended nongaze															
Males	10	5	3[a]	2	0	1	2	1							24
Females	26	5	4[a]	0	1	0	0	1							37
7-Internal, speaker-ended gaze															
Males	81	66	41	22[a]	13	3	7	3	2	0	0	1	1		240
Females	84	55	37	27[a]	8	13	3	2	2	4	2	0	0		237
8-Internal, auditor-ended gaze															
Males	34	39	26	21	24	4	15[a]	1	5	2	0	0	0	1	172
Females	39	25	16	13	12	8	9[a]	7	2	5	0	2	2	3	143

[a]Cutoff point for analysis.

Returning to the example of speaker gaze, we may obtain a distribution of run lengths for each of the four gaze and four nongaze action sequences for each participant in the interactions being studied. That is, for each gaze or nongaze sequence, we can count how many runs were one unit long, two units long, etc. In this manner, analyses of the eight speaker-gaze sequences can be based on distributions of run lengths.

Table 1.3 presents data on the set of run-sequence variables just outlined. These data are taken from Table 1 in Duncan, Kanki, Mokros, and Fiske (1984). They are based on the 16 two-person conversations between adults used in our strategy studies. Variables are arranged and numbered as in Table 1.2.

Table 1.3 adds yet another partition to the sequences contained in Table 1.2: the sex of the speaker. Thus, there are actually 16 sequences presented in Table 1.3, as opposed to the eight in Table 1.2.

Table 1.3 illustrates how run-sequence variables may be expressed in terms of contingency tables. Both sequence and run-sequence variables can be used to generate cross-tabulated data arrays. These arrays can be analyzed using log-linear methods, as exemplified in Chapter 9.

Inspection of Table 1.3 reveals several fairly obvious effects. For example, looking across the table as a whole, auditors tend strongly to take the turn during speaker gaze, as opposed to nongaze. (This phenomenon is also examined in Chapter 7, but not in terms of runs.) Initial runs of gaze (sequences 3 & 4) are more likely to be auditor ended than are internal runs (7 & 8). Initial auditor-ended runs of gaze (4) tend to be shorter than internal, auditor-ended runs (8). Log-linear analyses of sex differences in Table 1.3 (not a strong phenomenon in these data) were presented in Duncan et al. (1984), but these analyses are not necessary for the purposes of this discussion.

The run-sequence approach seems to embody the suggestions proposed in the concluding discussion of simple-rate variables. First, counts were made of sequences, such as speaker gaze and auditor turn taking, rather than of single actions. Sequential information was also used in defining turn-initial and turn-internal gazes. Second, it was possible in this case to avoid rates. Third, the aspect of the action (in this case, duration) is specified. A more thorough analysis might include further aspects of gaze. Finally, multiple, related variables were generated – eight in this case – in order to analyze the issue in question: sex differences in gazing. The run-sequence variables may be useful in many cases, in that they contain the additional distributional information on length of action.

1.6. Discussion

The underlying point of this chapter seems straightforward: Interaction is a complex process whose properties are only beginning to be appreciated by investigators.

It is perhaps both a curse and a blessing that most of the work on nonverbal communication and other aspects of interaction has been done by psychologists. On the positive side, psychological investigators have brought their characteristic energy, enterprise, and ingenuity to research in this area.

The negative aspect is that many of the procedures commonly used in psychological studies have been applied routinely to studies of interaction phenomena. However, it appears that these procedures may be inappropriate when applied to interaction research. The "psychologizing" of interaction research certainly applies to our own early work with individual differences in interaction (reported in D&F, Part II), which resulted in a mixture of unpleasant surprises and quixotic or frustratingly slippery results.

The problem with many psychological techniques (designed for studying individuals) in this context seems to be the deep interconnectedness of things in interaction: the major theme of this monograph. The challenge that interaction phenomena pose to investigators is to develop effective methods for better understanding the nature and extent of this interconnectedness.

The strategy research described in Chapters 7 through 10 represents our initial efforts at dealing with interactional interconnectedness in the context of strategy research. We do not propose that the research constitutes ultimate solutions, but we hope that the studies will provide constructive responses to the interactional problems they address. The issue of interconnectedness will be further developed in Chapter 11.

It simply does not seem possible that meaningful results can be obtained by investigators whose methods either ignore interactional interconnectedness or assume that it does not exist. We have tried to provide specific examples of such methods in this chapter. Unfortunately, these methods appear to be widespread in the literature, including Part II of D&F.

In questioning many received research methods, we do not expect our position to be a popular one, accepted with open arms by other investigators. Nevertheless, we hope that investigators will appreciate the import of our arguments and be stimulated both to vigorous debate of the issues and to development of methodologies designed to capture and capitalize on the rich network of relatedness that interaction offers.

2. Structure and strategy in interaction

STARKEY DUNCAN, JR., AND DONALD W. FISKE

2.1. Introduction

Having dealt with problems we perceive in the research literature, and having outlined the kind of variable we shall be using in all the work reported here, it is time to turn to more conceptual issues. The studies reported in this monograph were designed to focus primarily on interaction strategy, as manifested in some two-person conversations between adults. We need, then, to consider what we mean by "interaction strategy."

It is difficult, however, to approach the notion of strategy directly. For us, strategy is defined in terms of, and derives its meaning from, interaction structure. That is, we regard strategy research on interaction as being based in one way or another on hypotheses concerning interaction structure. For this reason, we must begin with a discussion of structure. We see interaction as structured in part by the operation of rules applying to the participants' conduct. That is, we view face-to-face interaction as being, in part, a rule-governed process.

It will be immediately apparent that the notion of rule-governed interaction is scarcely a novel one in social science. In fact, it is the dominant idea in much of social science. Terms such as "norm," "custom," and "convention" refer to this notion. Linguistics centers on hypothesizing rules for that important social activity: language. In this monograph we shall use "structure" and "convention" interchangeably. The general structural perspective, considered in this chapter and in Chapter 4, is one that proceeds from the notion of conventions – that is, rule-governed behavior – operating in interaction.

In contrast, it happens that rules are not traditionally a primary concern in psychology. Because much of the research on "nonverbal communication" has been done by psychologists, the notion of rules has not been prominent in the research literature relevant to the work reported here. It seems appropriate, therefore, that some consideration be given to rules, strategy, and the specific application of these ideas to our research.

Interaction rules have to do with appropriate action sequences between participants in a given social context. That is, within the particular context, the rules specify appropriate actions to take and the locations in the stream of interaction where they should or may be taken. (In the same way, of course, rules may also specify actions that should not be taken and where they should not occur.) As we showed in D&F, the rule-governed aspect of interaction can be a source of strong regularities in participants' conduct.

Given the operation of structure in interaction, the relation of strategy to structure is simple and straightforward at the most general and intuitive level. If structure constitutes the "rules for the game" in interaction, then strategy is the manner in which a participant or group of participants actually plays the game.

In a game, we can identify and describe a strategy only when we know what the rules are. By the same token, variations in behavior are not meaningful if they are not related to some aspect of structure. (An exception to the relation between meaning and structure would be human universals of action or expression, such as the facial expressions hypothesized by Ekman and his colleagues (e.g., Ekman, Friesen, & Ellsworth, 1972). Such human universals of action or expression as may exist would also be meaningful but are not convention based, although their use may be constrained by convention.

Just as strategy is meaningful only in relation to structure, it is impossible to act within a given structure without simultaneously engaging in a strategy. That is, when rules are applicable to action, then acting within those rules necessarily involves some strategy. Even refusing to act within the applicable rules is itself a possible strategy. In this manner, interaction structure and strategy are joined and complementary as the two sides of a coin. Either element necessarily entails the other. It therefore becomes apparent that a full description of interaction cannot be confined to structure alone; strategy would also have to be included. Our research on strategy was motivated by our appreciation of it as an integral part of a full description of interaction. Our pursuit of strategy research has led to our realization of its considerable potential in a variety of areas.

Stated in these terms, the notions of structure and strategy seem entirely familiar and unexceptional. It would be surprising if these notions were not part of every culture on earth. They would be involved wherever everyday life is constrained by structural considerations, such as ethical norms, religious rituals, rules for everyday conduct, standards for "fair play," "good sportsmanship" and other social values, or games.

It will be apparent that, as in D&F (pp. 290-291), we are using "strategy" here strictly in the sense of some pattern of action within a framework of rules. We shall not be concerned with other senses of strategy, such as plans of action, goals, or motivations, although these senses are commonly intended when the term is used. That is, we speak of strategy in terms of action patterns without speculating or hypothesizing about the cognitive processes that underlie those patterns. Certainly, we do not wish to deny that cognitive/motivational processes give rise to the patterns of strategy that we observe. It is in terms of cognition that the notion of strategy, as it derives from structure, becomes meaningful. Nevertheless, our use of the term entails only strictly observable action patterns.

2.2. Linkages between structure and strategy

Choice

As we began this research, we saw the link between structure and strategy as lying in the exercise of choice. We believe that operating within a structure always involves a series of choice points. The process of making the required choices results in the action patterns that we term strategy. There seem to be two types of choice relating to structure; one type is always present, and the other may be.

Always present is the possibility of violating the relevant structure. One may choose to break the rules of the game, violate ethical norms, refuse to show proper respect for one in authority, and the like. Whenever structure applies to interaction, it is possible to violate it. Of course, such a violation elicits sanctions that may carry distinct consequences for the course and outcome of the interaction and for the relationship between the participants. In any event, the possibility of violation is always an option. One should not discount violation in an interaction simply because it is never observed to occur. In such an interaction, we would regard the participants, in effect, as continually choosing not to violate the structure – a significant element of their strategy.

While rule violation is always an option in rule-governed behavior, the prevailing structure may also provide options for one's action and allow a choice between them. For example, in baseball the batter has the option of swinging at a given pitch or not. Given the options provided by the rules, the batter is forced to choose which alternative to exercise. Upon the pitcher's delivery, the batter cannot avoid choosing either one course of action or the other. Either action is a legitimate alternative; neither involves violation. However, on a given pitch, each alternative has distinct implications, depending on the current circumstances of the game. Thus, when the prevailing structure provides for the option of alternative actions, the participant must choose between the alternatives, and this choice is an element of strategy.

Notice that the exercise of choice is crucial in the everyday interpretation of strategy. Imagine a participant's violating some rule of everyday conduct. When confronted with adverse reaction by others, the participant may plead that the violation was inadvertant rather than a deliberate choice. If such an excuse is accepted, then the action is regarded as an accident, not part of the participant's strategy, and may be disregarded. As Goffman points out (1971, pp. 102n-103n), special pleadings with regard to structure violations may be quite varied.

Cognitive constraints

In addition to choice, Mokros's research (Chapter 9) suggests another source of "strategy": cognitive constraints on a participant's actions within the framework of convention. That is, it appears that the processing of one's interactive behavior is subject to cognitive constraints, just as the processing of one's linguistic utterances is constrained. This possibility, entirely unanticipated at the beginning of our work on strategy, raises the possibility of studying cognition through analysis of interaction processes, analogous to the psycholinguistic study of cognition based on language production. Such an area of study does not even have a name at present. But the potentiality of a truly new approach to cognitive research, based on interaction structure, appears to be present.

This, as we see it, is the broad outline of the relation between interaction structure and strategy. The notions of structure and strategy are considered in some detail in D&F. In this chapter, we shall sketch some of the more general points essential to understanding the reported research, confining our discussion to issues having a relatively direct relation to the interactions we have studied and the phenomena we have hypothesized.

In D&F, it was said that an interaction could not be fully described solely in terms of the social practices, or conventions, used in that interaction. At least two other elements would be necessarily included: situation and strategy.

Each participant's defining the situation is an element of interaction because such a definition is required in order to choose appropriate conventions. The relation between situation and convention is itself conventional, so that both are elements of the conventional conduct of the interaction. However, we shall continue to use "convention" for the actual social practices, and to say that these are chosen in light of one's definition of the situation.

The third element of the description of an interaction would be strategy. Strategy is manifested both in the definition of the situation and in the enactment of the conventions. For this reason, both convention and situation must be considered before we turn to strategy. The discussion will start with and emphasize convention, however, because our strategy research is based entirely on hypotheses concerning convention.

2.3. Convention

Following Lewis (1969), we regard conventions as solutions to recurring coordination problems. A coordination problem is one that requires the coordinated action of two or more participants for its solution. In order for the solution to be conventional, there must be more than one possible solution. If one of these possible solutions is preferred or seen as mutually beneficial for any reason, it may become the solution generally adopted for dealing with the coordination problem, and thus the convention that holds for the interaction.

Conventions are established and maintained through the coordination of expectations of the participants. When a convention is appropriate within a situation, each participant expects the partner to take the actions that are part of the convention; each participant expects the partner to expect the participant to take the conventional action; and so on.

Note that coordination problems do not have to involve pure coordination. Conventions are used by the antagonists in many types of conflict, such as political elections, games, and even war. In these sorts of interactions, each side, while seeking to defeat the other, still finds it beneficial to constrain its actions in terms of the appropriate conventions. Games and other sorts of interactions are constituted by conventions; they cannot exist apart from the conventions that define them.

Signals

Signals are used to facilitate the coordination of actions within a convention and are themselves a part of the convention, aside from the possible cases in which the signals involve human universals as mentioned previously. As Lewis (1969) points out, signals transmit information that the signaler, but not the audience, is in a good position to observe.

A simple example would be the conductor and the engineer of a passenger train. When the train is in a station, one of their jobs is to get the train underway only when it is safe and all appropriate passengers have either boarded or detrained. The conductor stands in a good position to observe the necessary circumstances and, when the appropriate conditions are met, signals to the engineer, who is not in a good position to observe these matters, that it is safe to get underway. The whole process is a convention, involving, in Lewis's terms, both signals and a contingency plan indicating what actions to take in response to the signals. The convention exists as a solution to a coordination problem requiring both the conductor and engineer: the safe and effective operation of the train in departing the station.

A special – and very important – kind of information that one participant, but not the other, is in a position to observe is the internal states of that participant. Many conventions may involve signaling concerning any number of these internal states, so that other participants may act appropriately. This would appear to be the case with the conventions that we have hypothesized in connection with speaking turns in the conversations we have observed (cf. Chapter 3). Some possibilities along this line are discussed in terms of *transition readiness* (e.g., D&F, pp. 178-179; 196-198).

Moves

It is useful to distinguish signals from what we have termed *moves* (D&F, p. 182). An example of this distinction would be a turn indicator in a car. The driver may signal, for example, a left turn and, in addition, may also turn left. The actual turn would be the move. Obviously, the driver may either signal or turn in either direction or do one without the other, although optimally the signal precedes the move and is congruent with it. Notice that the signal in this case is used to inform other motorists of an internal state of the driver: the intention to turn. Signals and moves are not invariably paired in conventions. Some conventions may involve moves without signals or signals without moves.

Sanctions

Because conventions represent preferable solutions to coordination problems, Lewis (1969) points out that the violation of a convention will always incur negative reactions from those adhering to it. Thus, the sanctions attaching to violation should be a part of the description of each convention. Of course, conventions may vary greatly in the strength of their sanctions. For some conventions a single violation may incur a death penalty or other severe punishment; for others, repeated violations may only result in a somewhat negative shift of observers' opinions of the violator. Although all conventions carry a normative aspect, there is a great deal more to the description of conventions than this single aspect.

For the conversational conventions we hypothesized, it would seem that violations, such as interruptions, occurring in isolation were not considered as particularly serious. It may be that a participant's repeated violations would at the least be irritating to the partner, but we did not observe such chronic violation in our conversations. For this reason, we had little to say about sanctions attached to the hypothesized conventions, except to observe that isolated violations incurred minimal reaction.

2.4. Sources of regularity in interaction

In the structural studies of two-person conversations reported in D&F, a set of strong regularities in interaction was described. For example, if there was a smooth exchange of the speaking turn in the conversations we observed, there was a strong tendency for it to occur after certain actions by the speaker. Because the studies dealt with conversations between adults, and because the regularities conformed to a carefully defined notion of conventional regularity, we ascribed them to the operation of convention in those interactions. Note that we do not assume that all strong interactional regularities reflect the operation of convention. Granting the importance of convention-based regularities, it is clear that other types of regularity will be found that either are not related to convention or represent special cases. The present research itself was designed to explore one of these sources of regularity: interaction strategy. Some examples may illustrate regularities that are not convention based.

Lewis points out that there are a number of sources of strong behavioral regularity that are not conventional. He provides the example of a concentration camp. At this camp, there is a strong behavioral regularity among the prisoners that escape attempts are extremely infrequent. This regularity does not stem from a convention, however. It is a result of the fact that the guards' practice is to shoot to kill all prisoners attempting to escape. Other examples of nonconventional regularities may be found in Lewis and in D&F (p. 254).

A more complex example confronts investigators studying mother-infant interaction. It has been suggested (e.g., Newson, 1978; Schaffer, 1979; Kaye, 1982) that much of young infants' actions during interaction may be physiologically determined, but that mothers' actions are framed as if the infant were interacting on the basis of convention. If something like this is the case, then it would present an example of what Lewis (1969) calls one-sided signalling, where the convention is observed either by the signaller or by the audience, but not both. However, as the infant gains more control over his or her own action, then the mother's regular actions provide a conventional framework into which the infant can guide his or her actions as part of the socializing process.

This general picture, which does not seem unreasonable in terms of the available evidence, presents a particularly difficult and complicated task to the investigator. It is not clear to us exactly how to identify true conventional action, differentiating such patterns from those in which the mother is responding in a conventional pattern to the infant's physiological reactions. In any event, this situation suggests another way in which strong patterning in interaction may not lead directly to the hypothesis of fully conventional action. With this caveat, we may return to the discussion of interaction structure based on convention.

2.5. Sources of strategy

Strategy must be defined in terms of the specifics of the particular conventions from which it is derived. For example, the possible strategies in chess are strictly delimited by the rules for the game. For this reason, strategies within the conventions hypothesized for speaking-turn phenomena must be elaborated in terms of the details of those conventions. However, in this section we shall consider in more general terms the sources of interaction strategy. Within rule-governed action, what are the elements from which participants fashion their strategies? The two elemental sources are convention and situation.

Convention

It will be apparent that strategies are constructed from variations possible in signal display and in the moves specified by the convention. These variations are framed in terms of the two components already discussed: violation of convention (always a possibility), and exercise of legitimate options (when those options are available within the convention).

Options may be exercised with respect to moves, display of signals, and response to those signals. All of these have to do with the way the convention is enacted by a participant in a specific interaction. One may smile or interrupt more or less during a conversation, attempt to steal bases in baseball, or drive over the speed limit. Each element of action constrained (and thereby rendered meaningful) by convention becomes an element of strategy because the participant exercises an option regarding it. Minimally, there is an option to violate the convention. Often there are options with respect to permissible variations in action.

In describing strategies, we shall be referring exclusively to patterns of action within the framework of convention. As pointed out in an earlier section, we specifically avoid reference to cognitive processes underlying and directing strategies, although "strategy" is often used in this sense. Thus, we shall not be describing general plans of action or the motivation or goals that give rise to those plans. Instead, we shall be sticking close to observables: the specific convention-based actions taken by participants. These actions will be analyzed to discover larger patterns. It seems entirely possible, however, that extended research on interaction strategy will suggest hypotheses concerning the goals, intentions, motivations, or cognitive processes of participants.

Situation

The other aspect of interaction structure, intimately connected to convention and providing a source for strategy, is situation or context. It is possible that situation, together with its attendant strategies, is the source of much of the richness and subtlety that we experience in interaction. However, relatively little direct research has been done on situation, and we have done none at all. In fact, it is quite difficult to formulate a study of situation that retains reasonable objectivity in its methods, and that eventuates in straightforwardly disconfirmable conclusions. For these reasons, we shall touch only lightly on situation here. A more detailed treatment may be found in D&F, together with a more elaborated terminology than will be used here.

Just as convention arises when there are two or more possible solutions to a coordination problem, situation arises when there are two or more conventions for solving a coordination problem but the available conventions are not interchangeable – that is, equally appropriate for all interactions. Situation provides a mechanism whereby an appropriate match can be achieved between convention and a specific interaction.

We shall say that each convention has a set of situational requirements that specifies the types of interactions in which the convention may be appropriately used. These situational requirements are framed in terms of social categories that may apply to the participant, the partner, various aspects of the relationship between them, the setting in which the interaction is taking place, and so forth.

An example of multiple conventions for a single coordination problem would be the case of forms of address, interestingly studied by Ervin-Tripp (1972). We shall illustrate our discussion of situation with data from her study. Building on the Brown and Ford (1961) study by observing her own rules of address, Erving-Tripp sought to identify situational factors underlying the use of the forms: title plus last name, Mr. plus last name, Mrs. plus last name, Miss plus last name, kin title plus first name (e.g., Uncle George), first name, and zero (no address form used). Examples of the social categories that Ervin-Tripp suggested as relevant to the choice of address form were whether or not the interaction took place in a status-marked setting, and whether or not the partner (addressee) was kin to the participant, was a friend or colleague, was of higher rank, was 15 years older than the participant, and was married.

It appears that, in order to choose an appropriate convention in an interaction, a two-step process is required. First, one must categorize various aspects of the participants (including oneself), of one's relation to the partner, and of the interaction setting. Then one must choose conventions whose situational requirements are compatible with those classifications. We shall term this initial process of categorizing *defining the situation*.

Disclosure and ratification. In any given convention used in an interaction, such as an address form, it would appear that one participant would have to introduce the convention by taking the first action(s) that are identifiably part of that convention. Once the convention is recognized as such by the partner, then at least some of the participant's definition of the situation is disclosed to the partner via the convention's situational requirements. At that point, the partner is in a position to agree tacitly with the participant's revealed situational definition by responding appropriately within the convention, or to disagree with the revealed situation by refusing to respond within the convention. This process of disclosure and ratification of situational definitions via the mediation of convention has been considered extensively by Goffman (e.g., 1967, 1971).

It will be apparent that definitions of the situation are formulated by each participant, but they become manifest only through the enactment of conventions. However, through successive introduction and ratification – or lack thereof – of conventions, participants can make known to each other a potentially rich and subtle variety of information couched in terms of social categories. Further, the disclosure of this information is unavoidable once one engages in convention-based action. This relation between convention and situational categories, presumably a characteristic of all conventions, is the property of *indexicality* (usefully discussed in relation to language by Silverstein, 1976). Use of a convention, such as a certain form of address, indexes – or assigns values to – certain situational categories, such as kinship, relative rank, marriage status, and the like. Thus, within Ervin-Tripp's scheme, the use of title plus last name assigns the value of "yes" or "one" to the categories of, for example, "adult" and "status-marked setting" and a value of "no" or "zero" to "friend or colleague" and "kin." In this manner, use of a convention indexes some set of social categories that may range from the stable, such as age differences and kinship, through relatively stable, such as colleagueship or friendship, to the highly labile, such as emotions.

2.6. Strategy and situation

Once the general processes of situational definition, disclosure, and ratification are outlined, a variety of sources of strategy based on situation is suggested. As indicated above, there is always the possibility of violation: the choice of conventions that index social categories that do not appropriately apply to the interaction. For example, referring to Ervin-Tripp's results, one might use a first-name greeting with a partner who is older and of higher rank and in a status-marked setting to boot.

In addition, the exercise of options would appear to apply to both the definition of situation and the choice of conventions in light of that definition. For example, after a sharp dispute with someone, a participant might choose a convention that evinces continued anger or conflict, or one that indicates a desire for rapprochement.

Finally, given the disclosure and ratification of a convention, a participant may subsequently introduce a change in the prevailing situation by initiating a new or different convention. This proffered change requires, of course, ratification by the partner.

It should be emphasized here that a change in behavior by a participant does not necessarily indicate a change in the situation. Only a change in the prevailing convention indicates such a change. As mentioned in the preceding section on convention and strategy, by exercising different options within a single convention, a participant can engage in behavioral change without any change in the convention being used. To construct a simple example, let us say that smiling on greeting another indexes a social category of friendliness in the relationship. It is possible to smile more broadly with one partner and less broadly with another, thereby indicating greater or less friendliness. However, the basic category of friendliness applies to both interactions, and in this respect both situations are the same.

Similarly, let us say that the turn system as we have hypothesized it is appropriately used in some situations and not in others. (This is almost certainly the case, although we have no confirming data.) Thus, using the turn system would index a certain type of situation. However, within the system there are a number of options available to participants. For example, one can choose either to violate the system by interrupting, or to avoid such violation. Within the legitimate alternatives, one can choose to gesture to a greater or lesser degree, respond more or less frequently to the turn signal, and the like. In these ways a participant's actions may vary from one conversation to another strictly within the framework of a single convention, and, therefore, with no change in situation.

Despite its great fascination and complexity, we shall not consider situation further because our studies of strategy within the framework of single conventions do not bear on it. Needless to say, situation is an area greatly in need of development. An account of interaction will always be incomplete without a full treatment of situation. Similarly, a description of a specific interaction will be incomplete without a treatment of its situation.

2.7. Studying interaction structure and strategy

We have emphasized that the notion of strategy derives its meaning from the notion of structure. In this way, it is impossible to interpret a participant's strategy in a given interaction unless one knows what rules (structure) are being used. This priority of structure over strategy is, however, entirely conceptual. It does not seem necessary to observe it rigidly in empirical studies. When studying interactions in which the conventions are not known, one might discover some set of strong regularities. Further investigation would lead to identifying those regularities as having a source in either structure or strategy. If the source proved to be structure, then those results would directly indicate where one might look for the complementary elements of strategy, and vice versa. These connections are natural because structure and strategy are so intimately related.

Distinguishing structure from strategy in empirical work is possible insofar as criteria are available for identifying patterns of results as reflecting structure, as opposed to strategy. This is obviously a point of great importance in interaction research. It will be considered in detail in Chapters 4 and 7. The issues are somewhat complex, and it seems important that careful consideration of these issues continue. Distinguishing structure from strategy is central to our research, both in conceptualization and method. Both the advantages and the potential problems in this approach will be evident as the story of the research unfolds.

3. The turn system

STARKEY DUNCAN, JR., AND DONALD W. FISKE

Having considered the broader framework for our structural research, we may address more specifically our studies of structure in two-person conversations between adults. The hypotheses emerging from this research form the basis for the subsequent strategy research described in the following chapters. Although most of this work was reported in D&F, we summarize the hypotheses here because they are necessary for understanding the subsequent chapters and because some refinements have been made in the hypotheses.

The various hypotheses are interpreted as relating to each other in a systematic manner, so that the full set has been termed the "turn system." The turn system appears to provide the participants in a conversation with a set of procedures for such things as accomplishing exchanges of the speaking turn, exchanging information on the current status of the speaker's message, and indicating how well the auditor is following what the speaker is saying. In other words, the turn system appears to be a mechanism for achieving the ongoing coordination of the participants' actions.

We shall describe the system itself in two phases. First, various elements of the system will be described in very general terms. This will be followed by a more detailed description, including a set of modifications and elaborations that has resulted from work done after the completion of D&F. Because certain distinctions and details are omitted from the general account, the second, detailed description should be considered the definitive one.

Evidence obtained in several studies relevant to the turn-system hypothesis will be presented in Chapter 6.

3.1. Overview

Broadly speaking, the turn system involves hypotheses regarding a number of signals, rules, and other elements that permit participants in a conversation to coordinate their respective actions on both the ongoing management of individual speaking turns and the exchange of turns. Through proper use of the turn system, participants are able collaboratively to create *units of interaction*. These units are viewed as structural building blocks of the conversations we studied. Analogous would be describing via a linguistic grammar the units of a language, whether these units be phonological (e.g., syllables) or syntactic (e.g., grammatical phrases or clauses). The turn system describes interaction units on two hierarchical levels: *speaking-turn units*, and *within-turn units* that combine to form turns.

An interesting attribute of the turn-system units is that they can be created only interactively through coordinated sequences of action involving both participants. A participant cannot unilaterally create one of these units. Thus, the turn system hypothesizes units of interaction, rather than units of individual messages. This is as true of phenomena occurring within a given speaking turn, as of the exchange of turns.

Speaking turns

We hypothesize that the boundary of a speaking-turn unit – that is, an exchange of the speaking turn – is properly created through the following sequence of three actions: (a) The speaker displays a *turn signal* and does not concurrently display a *gesticulation signal*; (b) the auditor displays a *speaker-state signal* while beginning an utterance; and (c) the original speaker yields the speaking turn.

A display of the speaker turn signal is accomplished through the occurrence of any one of the following five actions: (a) the use of a certain set of intonation contours, (b) the utterance of a *sociocentric sequence*

(Bernstein, 1962), that is, stereotyped phrases such as "you know," (c) the completion of a grammatical clause, (d) paralinguistic drawl on certain syllables, and (e) completing a hand gesticulation or relaxing a tensed hand position. Although the use of any one of these actions by the speaker is sufficient to constitute the display of a complete turn signal, it was typical in the conversations we observed for two or more of the actions to occur together in clusters.

The auditor is not obliged to take the turn when the signal is displayed. Rather, the signal is hypothesized to mark points in the stream of interaction at which the auditor may appropriately act to take the turn if so inclined. That is, optionality is an important aspect of the signal. For this reason, we said that the signal has to do with the *optional*, as opposed to *obligatory*, response by the auditor. We shall refer repeatedly to the optional/obligatory distinction in discussing the turn system.

Another signal – the speaker gesticulation signal – is said to have a strong effect on the auditor's response to the speaker turn signal. If the speaker is gesticulating or maintaining a tensed hand position at the same time as the turn signal is being displayed, that display is said to be inhibited or "turned off." Auditors very rarely acted to take the turn in response to the turn signal when the gesticulation signal was being concurrently displayed. This effect was so strong that we said that the gesticulation signal has an obligatory effect on the auditor; that is, the auditor should not take the turn in the presence of the gesticulation signal. In this case, the obligatory effect is a negative one, specifying something the auditor should not do.

The auditor acts to take the turn by displaying the speaker-state signal as he or she begins speaking. Although the auditor's response to the speaker turn signal is said to be optional, if the auditor does act to take the turn in response to the turn signal (in the absence of the gesticulation signal), then the speaker is obliged to yield the turn. If this happens with no overlap in the speech of the two participants, a smooth exchange of the turn is said to occur. The turn system provides a routine procedure for accomplishing such smooth exchanges.

In the conversations we studied, instances of simultaneous turns typically occurred when (a) the auditor attempted to take the turn in the absence of the turn signal or while the gesticulation signal was being displayed, and (b) the speaker failed to yield the turn when the auditor appropriately responded to a turn-signal display. The occurrence of simultaneous turns is considered to be a momentary breakdown of the turn system.

Auditor back channels

Taking the speaking turn is not the only action available to the auditor. Alternatively, the auditor may respond in the *back channel* (Yngve, 1970). Auditor back channels may be vocal (e.g., "yeah" or "m-hm"), visual (e.g., head nods or shakes), or both. Auditor back channels are not considered to be speaking turns or claims of the turn.

The *speaker within-turn signal* appears to be related to auditor back channels much as the speaker turn signal is related to auditor attempts to take the speaking turn. The within-turn signal marks points in the stream of interaction at which the auditor may, but is not obliged to, respond with a back channel. The signal itself is composed of the occurrence of at least one of two actions: (a) completion of a syntactic clause (the same as in the turn signal), and (b) shift of speaker gaze toward the auditor. (Speaker head direction, rather than gaze, was actually observed and was so reported in D&F. However, head direction is thought to reflect the operation of gaze. The term *gaze* is used in this monograph in place of *head direction* for ease of exposition.)

After a speaker within-turn signal and an auditor back-channel response, the speaker would typically shift gaze away from the auditor. This action is termed the *speaker continuation signal*.

There was also a strong relationship between a so-called *early* auditor back channel and a subsequent speaker continuation signal. An early auditor back channel overlaps with the speaker's speech, often occurring before a speaker within-turn signal. There was a strong tendency for the speaker to follow an early auditor back channel with a speaker continuation signal.

A *within-turn interaction unit* can be created in two ways. The first way involves a three-action sequence: (a) a speaker within-turn signal, (b) a auditor back channel (not early), and (c) a speaker continuation signal. The second way involves a two-action sequence: (a) an early auditor back channel, and (b) a speaker continuation signal. These sequences are considered to define boundaries between within-turn units. The final unit in a turn is always ended by a turn exchange, rather than a back channel. However, that last unit is also considered to be a within-turn unit. Thus, for example, a turn may have one speaker-auditor sequence defining a within-turn unit boundary. That turn would be considered to have two within-turn units: one before the boundary, and one after, even though the second unit is ended by a turn exchange. In the case of a turn (presumably a brief one) during which the auditor does not give a back channel, that turn is obviously not divided into within-turn units.

Table 3.1. *Elements in the description of the turn system*

I.	Postulated states
	A. Participant states
	B. Interaction states
II.	Hypothesized participant states
III.	Signals: display and activity
	A. Speaker-auditor state(s) required for signal display
	B. Cues
	1. Actions comprising the cue
	2. Location restrictions (where the actions must occur in order to be considered a cue)
	3. Active period (stretch of interaction over which a cue is considered to be active,once it is displayed)
IV.	Rules (statements of relationships between two elements of the turn system)
	A. Signal-definition rules (relationships of a given signal to a turn-system state, a move, or another signal)
	B. Interaction rules (permissible sequences of action within the system, given some specified states of affairs)
V.	Moves
VI.	Units of interaction

The within-turn interaction unit is like the turn unit in that it can be created only through sequences of action involving both participants. In this way, both units are interactively defined; neither can be created through the unilateral action of a single participant.

Back channels appear to provide the auditor with a means of communicating to the speaker how well the speaker's message is being followed. In some cases, the auditor back channels can also show agreement or disagreement with the speaker's message. An early back channel apparently indicates that the auditor not only is following the speaker's message but also is actually somewhat ahead, anticipating what will be said. In this case, the speaker may adjust the message accordingly by displaying a continuation signal and moving to the next within-turn interaction unit.

3.2. Turn system in detail: preliminary considerations

The question of how best to describe a convention is of central importance in structural research. Unlike the extensive debate and controversy between competing approaches to describing aspects of language, this issue has received minimal attention in interaction research.

In D&F, we proposed a general descriptive scheme that was the most comprehensive that we could devise. Table 3.1 shows the main elements of that scheme.

The actual description of the turn system in D&F included only those aspects of the comprehensive scheme on which we had some results. In the discussion that follows, we shall adopt this same practice. In this section, we shall state some presuppositions and define some basic terms. In the next section, the elements of the turn system will be described as concisely as possible. Further detail and the more comprehensive descriptive scheme may be found in D&F.

Turn-system states

Postulated participant states. In order to render the turn-system research meaningful, it was necessary to postulate that each participant consider him- or herself to be either a *speaker* or an *auditor* at each moment in the conversation. A participant is a speaker if he or she claims the speaking turn at a given moment; a participant is an auditor if he or she does not claim the speaking turn. These two postulated states are considered to be discrete and, within each participant, mutually exclusive. The speaker and auditor states are clearly classifications that participants apply to themselves and can be known to others only through the participants' actions.

Postulated interaction states. Given the two participant states, one can describe the state of the interaction at a given moment in terms of the respective states of the participants. In a two-person interaction, there are four possible speaking-turn interaction states: speaker-auditor, auditor-speaker, speaker-speaker, and auditor-auditor.

In the *speaker-auditor state*, one participant claims the speaking turn, and no such claim is made by the partner. In this interaction state, the current speaker continues the turn, neither yielding it to the partner, nor being interrupted. The *auditor-speaker state* is the same, except that the participants have exchanged the speaking turn. The participant who had previously been the speaker has now switched to the auditor state, and vice versa. When this exchange is accomplished without passing through the interaction state of simultaneous turns, a smooth exchange of the speaking turn is said to have occurred.

In the *speaker-speaker state*, both participants are in the speaker state, simultaneously claiming the turn. This constitutes an instance of *simultaneous turns* and represents a breakdown of the turn system for the duration of the state. It is important to distinguish an occurrence of simultaneous turns from an occurrence of *simultaneous talking*. If the two turns overlap by any perceptible amount, even a fraction of a syllable, that overlap is considered to be an instance of simultaneous turns.

There are two types of speech overlap that are not considered simultaneous turns: (a) an auditor's vocal back channel that overlaps with the speaker's speech, and (b) a new speaking turn that overlaps with a sociocentric sequence, filled pause, or audible inhalation at the end of the previous speaker's . Both of these cases would be considered an instance of simultaneous talking by the two participants but not of simultaneous turns.

In the *auditor-auditor state*, both participants become auditors, with the obvious result of silence for the duration of that state. Although experience suggests that this interaction state occurs in conversations – sometimes with accompanying embarrassment – it does not appear to have occurred in the conversations we have studied. Accordingly, we have no data on it. The process by which it occurs may be conjectured, however. The previous speaker may display a turn signal and cease talking, thereby apparently relinquishing the turn, but the previous auditor may fail to claim the turn.

In many conversations, perhaps especially between participants who know each other well, there seems to be no constraint on stretches of silence. With someone like a close friend or members of one's family, one simply does not have to keep talking all the time. However, in the conversations we have analyzed, appreciable stretches of silence are conspicuously avoided by the participants. Many readers may be familiar with the sense of embarrassment that occurs during undesired lapses in conversations at parties or other situations, especially with those we do not know well. It is a tribute to the social adroitness of our participants that they managed to avoid these lapses altogether in the taped conversations.

Hypothesized participant transition readiness. The signals of the turn system are hypothesized to facilitate coordinated and appropriate action by the participants in a conversation. This is accomplished in part by the participants' ability to indicate their respective states via the signals. In addition, it is hypothesized that both the structure signals and the strategy signals (described in Chapter 7) permit the participants to indicate relative degree of *transition readiness*: the inclination or lack thereof to move to the next unit of interaction – the next speaking turn, for example. At any given point in the conversation, each participant's reading both of his or her own transition readiness and of the partner's transition readiness is considered to be an essential factor in the process of framing a course of action with respect to speaking-turn phenomena.

In contrast to the discrete, mutually exclusive participant states, transition readiness is hypothesized to be a single state continuously operative throughout the interaction within each participant, and to have values on a continuous scale. The value of a participant's transition readiness is presumably free to vary from moment to moment in the interaction and may be influenced by many factors.

Definition of signal display and activity

Within the turn system, signals displayed by a participant provide the partner with various sorts of information that facilitate the successful carrying out of the convention. The structure signals in the turn system are hypothesized to be discrete; that is, each signal is considered to be either displayed or not displayed at any given point in the interaction. In general, each signal is defined in terms of two elements: (a) the state (speaker or auditor) of the participant eligible to display the signal, and (b) a set of cues based on actions.

With regard to speaker-auditor state, a given signal may be defined as being displayable only by speakers, only by auditors, or by either speakers or auditors.

Each signal is defined as being composed of a set of one or more action-based cues. The display of a turn-system signal is defined as the display of at least one of its constituent cues. Like the signals themselves, the display of each cue is considered to be discrete. There are, in general, three elements in the definition of a given cue: (a) the actions comprising the cue, (b) those locations in the stream of interaction at which the indicated actions must occur in order to be considered a cue display, and (c) the stretch of interaction over which the cue is considered to be active once it has been displayed.

1. *Actions*. Of the three elements of cue definition, the first seems self-evident. The actions comprising the cue will be termed *cue-relevant actions*.
2. *Location restrictions*. Some cue-relevant actions are considered to be cues only when they occur at certain specified points in the stream of interaction. For other cue-relevant actions, such location restrictions are not included in the definition.
3. *Cue activity*. Each occasion of an appropriately located cue-relevant action is considered a display, both of the relevant cue and of the signal of which the cue is a constituent. Beyond the physical display of a cue, it is necessary to consider

the stretch of interaction over which the display is considered to possess the property of a signal.

In anticipation of the signals to be described in the next section, it may be noted that there is variety in the duration of cue displays. Some actions, such as gesticulation, can continue over a substantial stretch of interaction. Other actions, such as paralinguistic drawl, can by definition occur only over a single syllable. Still other actions, such as termination of a gesticulation or completion of a grammatical clause, are defined as occurring only at some instantaneous point in the interaction.

The structure results suggest that the effects on the interaction of a cue display can extend beyond its actual display. This is especially important for actions of brief or instantaneous duration. It thus becomes necessary to define some period, longer than the display itself, over which each cue is considered to be active in the interaction. This active period for a cue is considered to begin at the point at which the cue is displayed. Because the cue displays are considered to be discrete, it will be said that the cue is *switched on* or *activated* at the moment of its display, and that the cue is *switched off* at that later point at which it is considered to be no longer active in the interaction. The stretch of interaction over which the cue is switched on is termed its *active period*.

The concept of active period is necessary to prevent viewing each signal as active indefinitely, even after it recurs later – an unlikely and unwieldy condition. Yet a signal must often be seen as remaining active after its physical termination. For example, the effect of completing a syntactic unit such as a sentence may extend in the interaction beyond the instant at which the completion occurs.

Rules

A *rule* is a statement defining the hypothesized relationship between two or more elements of the turn system. A rule may relate a signal to a state of the participant displaying the signal, describe the effect of one signal upon another signal concurrently being displayed, or describe the relationship between activation of a signal by one participant and some subsequent action by the partner.

For purposes of description, signal-definition rules will be distinguished from interaction rules. A *signal-definition rule* specifies the relationship between (a) a given signal, and (b) either a turn-system state or another signal. An *interaction rule* specifies permissible sequences of action within the turn system, given (a) the currently active signal(s), and in some cases (b) certain preceding moves by one or both participants.

Moves

Moves are actions that play a part in the turn system but are not defined as signals. A simple example may clarify this distinction. In driving, one may activate the left- or right-turn signal in one's car. One may also actually make a left or right turn; this would be a move. Typically, the signal and the move go together, but one can obviously do either one without the other. In the turn system, moves may or may not have signals associated with them.

Having considered these basic definitions, we are now in a position to describe the specific turn-system signals, rules, and other elements hypothesized in D&F.

3.3. Turn-system hypotheses

Most of the turn-system hypotheses described here appeared in D&F, where they were considered in more detail. Also discussed in D&F were various rejected hypotheses. Structural hypotheses developed since D&F are marked in this discussion by the pound sign (#). A variety of results that both support these hypotheses and are required for the strategy research may be found in Chapter 6.

Speaker turn signal

Interaction rules. The auditor may claim the speaking turn during the active period of the turn signal, subject to the verbal-overlap restrictions described below, provided the gesticulation signal is not concurrently active. In proper operation of the turn system, if the auditor so claims the turn in response to the signal, the speaker is obliged to relinquish immediately his or or her claim of the turn. When the turn signal is not active, auditor claims of the turn are inappropriate and typically leading to simultaneous turns.

The turn signal is permissive, not coercive. The auditor is not obliged to claim the speaking turn in response to the display of the signal by the speaker. The auditor may always remain silent. For some turn-signal displays, the auditor has the alternative of communicating in the back channel. In this sense, the auditor possesses real options with respect to the appropriate response to the speaker's display of the turn signal.

During the active period of the turn signal, an auditor claim of the speaking turn must be made in such a way that the syllables of the new turn do not overlap with the syllables of the preceding turn. Any perceptible overlap of the two turns, even when the overlap occurs over only a portion of a single syllable, is treated as an instance of simultaneous claiming of the turn (simultaneous turns) by the two participants and is so indicated in the data. An exception to the no-overlap rule is made with sociocentric sequences. When syllables of the new turn overlap with syllables of a sociocentric sequence, the overlap is not considered to be an instance of simultaneous turns, but rather an instance of permissible simultaneous talking. Similarly, overlap of the new turn with the previous speaker's filled pauses and audible inhalations is considered to be permissible simultaneous talking. Another instance of simultaneous talking considered to be permissible within the turn system has to do with vocal auditor back channels. Because these back channels are not considered to be speaking turns, the overlap of these back channels with syllables of the previous speaker's turn is not treated as an instance of simultaneous turns.

Signal display and activity. In this section, the turn-signal cues are described just as they were in D&F. For the purposes of strategy research, the signal was modified twice. In the structure-assessment study (Chapter 6) and the strategy-signal study (Chapter 7), several relatively minor modifications in cue definition were made. For most of the strategy research (Chapters 8-10), the signal was drastically reduced. These changes will be described later in this chapter.

This account uses the notion of a unit of analysis. These units were used to break the stream of interaction into brief stretches for the purposes of analysis. Units are defined in terms of the actions of participants, and most are two to five syllables long. Units of analysis are described in more detail in Chapter 5.

The turn signal is switched on when the speaker displays at least one of five constituent cues. Following a display of one or more turn cues, the signal is switched off when all displayed cues are switched off. Thus, for any single occurrence of the turn signal, its active period lasts from the display of the first cue in that occurrence, until all cues in that occurrence are switched off. Each cue will be briefly described, together with applicable location restrictions and its active period.

1. *Intonation-marked phonemic clause.* An intonation-marked clause is defined as one in which there is a deviation from the 2 2 | pitch/terminal-contour pattern (Trager & Smith, 1957). In this pattern, the vocal pitch remains level with no rise or fall throughout the phonemic clause. Location restriction: The deviation must occur no earlier than the last two syllables of a phonemic clause. Switch-off point: This cue is switched off at the onset of the first syllable of the next unit of analysis following its display.
2. *Sociocentric sequence.* This cue consists of one of several stereotyped expressions, such as "you know," and "or something." Switch-off point: the onset of the first syllable of the next unit of analysis following its display. Location restriction: none.
3. *Decrease of paralinguistic pitch or loudness on a sociocentric sequence.* This decrease must be in contrast to the comparable paralinguistic actions on the syllable(s) immediately preceding the sociocentric sequence. Location restriction: The decrease must occur either across the entire sociocentric sequence, or during its final syllable or syllables. Switch-off point: the onset of the first syllable of the next unit of analysis following its display. #This turn cue is dependent on the sociocentric-sequence cue and was therefore dropped, reducing the total number of turn cues to five.#
4. *Paralinguistic drawl.* Drawl involves a distinct prolongation in the utterance of a single syllable. Location restriction: The drawl must occur on the final syllable or on the stressed syllable of a phonemic clause. Switch-off point: the onset of the first syllable of the next unit of analysis following its display.
5. *Termination of any hand gesticulation or the relaxation of a tensed hand position* (e.g., a fist). This cue was not considered displayed unless both hands were at rest and relaxed following a gesture or tensed hand position. Location restriction: none. Switch-off point: the onset of the first syllable of the third unit of analysis following its display. #The switch-off point was subsequently changed to the onset of the first syllable of the next unit of analysis following its display, making the cue consistent in this regard with the other turn cues.#
6. *Completion of a grammatical clause.* Location restrictions: none. Switch-off point: the onset of the first syllable of the next unit of analysis following its display.

#The grammatical-completion cue was originally defined as the "completion of a grammatical clause, involving a subject-predicate combination" (D&F, p. 171). It is desirable to expand on this rather cryptic definition, making more explicit the definition used in the strategy studies reported later. This expanded definition was developed primarily by Denny. We wish to include three distinguishable types of grammatical completion as components of the basic definition.

1. Phrases or dependent clauses following independent clauses were considered to be grammatically complete when those phrases or clauses were not presupposed by the preceding clause. This type of grammatical completion may be clarified by some counter examples taken from our data. The initial clauses in each of the following examples (a, b, c) would

not have been considered an instance of grammatical completion in our data. (Of course, other turn cues could have appeared in conjunction with these clauses.)

(a) But you know if we were interested, we could get the results of what she was working on.
(b) If they beat uh, uh, Texas, they consider it a winning season.
(c) And then in the process of running away, th- they may get a car.

In (a), the first clause ("if we were interested") presupposes a continuation of the if-then construction that is in fact realized in "we could get the results of what she was working on." If the clauses of this sentence had occurred in reverse order ("We could get the results of what she was working on if we were interested"), there would have been two grammatical completions: after "on" and "interested." In (b), there is a similar if-then construction in which the first clause presupposes the second. In (c) "in the process of running away" introduces an expectation of further explication by the speaker.

2. A grammatical completion was considered to occur at the end of an independent clause and at the end of subsequent independent clauses linked to it by a relative pronoun. An important exception to this rule occurred when a subsequent dependent clause or phrase was presupposed by the preceding independent clause; in this case, the grammatical completion was considered to occur at end of the dependent clause or phrase. An example would be:

(d) In every course I play with the idea of going into that sort of law.

Here grammatical completion would be considered to occur at the end of "law," not "idea," because of the preceding definite article "the."

3. Finally, grammatical completion was considered to be achieved through elliptical utterances. In D&F, the definition of grammatical completion relied entirely on the formal presence of subject and predicate. Not taken into account were utterances in which grammatical completion occurred by virtue of ellipsis. The general notion of ellipsis was considered by Halliday and Hasan (1976):

> When giving a direct response in its simplest form the speaker makes explicit just one thing, the information that the question calls for, and leaves all the rest to be presupposed by ellipsis. With a yes/no question, this information is the polarity, so the answer specifies the

polarity and presupposes all else. In the WH- question, the information required is the item occupying a particular function . . . in the
structure; the answer specifies this and presupposes the remainder of
the clause. (p. 211)

Some examples of exchanges involving elliptical utterances are shown in
(e)-(i). In each case, the second speaker (S2) provides the elliptical
response. None of these responses would have been considered grammatically complete in D&F, but all were considered complete in the present
research. Utterances were considered complete independent clauses by
ellipsis if the presupposed clause was found in the preceding speaking
turn.

(e) S1: Did you do your undergraduate work in Oklahoma?
   S2: Yeah.
(f) S1: Well, what's your name?
   S2: Susan Rolfe.
(g) S1: My name is Don Smith.
   S2: Jim Wesson.
(h) S1: Where're you from originally?
   S2: Chicago.
(i) S1: Which two are you choosing?
   S2: Uh, the group work and case work.#

Speaker gesticulation signal

Signal-definition rule. The gesticulation signal serves to inhibit any turn
signal being concurrently displayed. When the gesticulation signal is
displayed during the active period of a turn signal, auditor claims of the
turn are strikingly reduced.

Signal display and activity. The speaker gesticulation signal is hypothesized to be composed of a single cue: one or both of the speaker's hands
being engaged in gesticulation or in a tensed hand position. Self- and
object-adaptors (Ekman & Friesen, 1969) are not considered to be elements
of the gesticulation signal. There are no location restrictions applying to the
gesticulation signal. The signal is switched on at the point of its display and
is switched off when neither hand is gesticulating or tensed. Thus, the
active period for the signal is identical to its display.

Speaker-state signal

Signal-definition rule. The speaker-state signal is hypothesized to be
displayed at the point at which the auditor is shifting to the speaker state.

The signal indicates that the vocalization accompanying the signal is the beginning of a new speaking turn, differentiating that vocalization from various types of auditor back-channel responses (described later).

When a speaker-state signal accompanies the beginning of a new speaking turn, that turn will be said to be *claimed* by the speaker. The phrase "attempt to take the speaking turn" will be used to refer to all new turn beginnings, whether or not they are marked by the speaker-state signal – that is, claimed. For purposes of exposition, we shall say that it is the erstwhile auditor who displays the speaker-state signal, despite the fact that the signal is hypothesized to indicate, at the moment of its display, a shift to the speaker state.

Signal display and activity. The speaker-state signal is considered to be switched on when the auditor displays at least one of two constituent cues, in connection with a vocalization: (a) shift away in gaze, and (b) beginning a gesticulation. Once switched on, the signal is considered to be switched off only at that point at which the participant displaying the signal switches to the auditor state.

Location restrictions are the same for both cues. To be considered a speaker-state signal, the indicated cues must occur within a stretch of speech extending from one unit of analysis (of the partner's speech) preceding a verbalization by the auditor to the onset of the first word following the syllable carrying the primary intonation stress within the first phonemic clause of that verbalization.

In a few cases, the first phonemic clause of an auditor verbalization consisted entirely of a phrase such as "well, uh." When this occurred, the location restriction was relaxed so as to extend through the primary stressed syllable of the second phonemic clause of the verbalization. However, this relaxation was not applied when the first syllables of a new turn were a back channel.

In the case of a back channel, the speaker-state signal had to occur before or during the back channel itself. It should be noted that, because the signal is hypothesized to differentiate the two types of auditor verbalization – auditor back channels and speaker turn beginnings – the location restrictions require that the signal closely accompany any auditor verbalization. Cue actions by the auditor, such as looking away, that do not accompany such a verbalization, are not considered to be speaker-state cue displays.

Smooth exchange of the speaking turn
Within the turn system, a smooth exchange of the turn is appropriately accomplished by a three-step sequence of actions involving both partici-

pants: (a) The speaker displays a turn signal in the absence of a gesticulation signal; (b) during the active period of the turn signal and without overlapping the speaker's turn, the auditor displays a speaker-state signal and begins a new turn; and (c) the original speaker yields the speaking turn, becoming quiet except for auditor back channels.

Auditor back-channel responses

Auditor back channels (a term suggested by Yngve, 1970) appear to represent a class of responses by which the auditor can communicate with the speaker without actually taking the turn. Analyses presented in D&F suggested that the several apparent forms of auditor response may be considered as a single "back-channel" class. More recently, analyses by Brunner (1979) led to the addition of smiles to the list of auditor back channels.

Signal-definition rules. Auditor back channels not marked by a speaker-state signal do not constitute speaking turns or claims of the speaking turn. They appear to indicate continuing attentiveness and responsiveness of one sort or another to the speaker's message. The back channel appears to provide the auditor with a way of actively participating in the conversation, thus facilitating the general coordination of action by both participants within the structure of the interaction.

Signal display and activity. The following six types of back-channel responses have been differentiated in the turn system. A back-channel signal is defined as the display of at least one of its constituent forms. In the examples that follow, "S" stands for "speaker," and "A," for "auditor."

1. *M-hm.* This expression is used to stand for a group of readily identified verbalizations, such as "m-hm," "yeah," "right," and Kendon's (1967) examples from British English of "yes quite," "surely," "I see," and "that's true." Most of the m-hm back channels may be used singly, in combination, or repeatedly in groups, such as "yeah, yeah."
2. *Sentence completion.* Not infrequently, in our materials an auditor would complete a sentence that a speaker had begun. In such a case, the auditor would not continue beyond the brief completion, and the speaker would continue the turn as if uninterrupted. The entire exchange appeared quite seamless. An example would be, S: "eventually, it will come down to more concrete issues," A: "as she gets more comfortable;" S: "and I felt that . . . ."
3. *Request for clarification.* Contrasting with sentence completions are brief requests for clarification. Such requests were usually accomplished in a few words or in a phrase. Example: S: " . . . somehow they're better able to cope with it." A: "you mean these anxieties, concern with it?"

4. *Brief restatement.* This back-channel response is similar to the sentence completion, except that it restates in a few words an immediately preceding thought expressed by the speaker. Example: S: " . . . having to pick up the pieces"; A: "the broken dishes, yeah"; S: "but then a very . . . ."

5. *Head nods and shakes.* Head nods and shakes may be used alone or in company with the verbalized back channels. Head nods may vary in duration from a single nod to a rather protracted, continuous series of nods.

#6. *Smiles.* Based on Brunner's (1979) research, we now consider auditor smiles as an auditor back channel. Like head nods and shakes, the length of smiles may vary from very brief to protracted. Interactional factors affecting the length of smiles are considered in Chapter 9.#

Location restrictions and active period. No location restrictions are placed on the occurrence of auditor back-channel signals. The active period for back channels is considered to be coincident with their display. The back channel is considered to be switched on at the beginning of the vocal or visual display and switched off when that display is ended. When m-hm back channels are used repeatedly in groups and each successive vocalization immediately follows upon the preceding one (as in "yeah, yeah"), the sequence is considered to be a single display.

While no location restrictions were placed on auditor back channels, four different locations for the occurrence of back channels were differentiated for the purposes of both structure and strategy research.

1. *Postboundary.* The auditor back channel occurs on or soon after the first syllable of a unit of analysis.

2. *Speech overlap.* The auditor back channel overlaps with one or more syllables of the substantive speech of a unit of analysis, other than those first syllables defined as being in the postboundary position. The term "substantive" is used here merely to exclude sociocentric sequences.

3. *Sociocentric sequence.* The onset of the back channel overlaps with one or more syllables of a sociocentric sequence; or the back channel occurs in the brief pause, if any, between the final substantive syllable of unit of analysis and a sociocentric sequence.

4. *Pause.* The back channel occurs during the brief pause, if any, between the final syllable (regardless of whether it is substantive speech or a sociocentric sequence) of a unit of analysis, and the first syllable of the next unit. This location is the same as that required for a smooth exchange of the turn that has no simultaneous talking.

Speaker within-turn signal

Interaction rules. Both visual and vocal auditor back channels occurring in the pause and postboundary positions tended to follow the speaker within-turn signal. Like the turn signal, the within-turn signal is permissive, not coercive. The auditor is not obliged to respond in the back channel upon display of the within-turn signal.

Signal display and activity. The within-turn signal is considered to be switched on when the speaker displays at least one of a set of two constituent cues. Following a display of one or both within-turn cues, the signal is considered to be switched off when all displayed cues are switched off. Thus, for any single occurrence of the within-turn signal, its active period lasts from the display of the first cue in that occurrence until all cues in that occurrence are switched off.

The two within-turn cues are: (a) shift of the speaker's gaze toward the partner, and (b) completion of a grammatical clause. Neither cue has location restrictions. The gaze cue is switched off at the boundary of the third unit of analysis following its display if the gaze is maintained toward the auditor for at least that long, or upon shifting gaze away from the auditor if that occurs in less than three units. The grammatical-completion cue is the same as that in the speaker turn signal. Its switch-off point is the onset of the first syllable of the next unit of analysis following its display.

Speaker continuation signal

Signal-definition rule. The speaker continuation signal is hypothesized to mark the beginnings of new units of interaction within a single speaking turn when the signal follows an auditor back channel. Units of interaction will be described in the following section.

Signal display and activity. The continuation signal is considered to be switched on when the speaker displays a single cue: a shift of gaze away from the auditor. The cue is identical to the gaze cue in the speaker-state signal. To be considered a continuation signal, the speaker's looking away must occur within a stretch of interaction extending from one phonemic clause preceding a boundary of a unit of analysis, to the onset of the first word following the first stressed syllable following that boundary. The active period for the signal is coincident with its display. The signal may be said to mark the beginning of a new interaction unit within a single speaking turn, and that new unit may be said to be in effect either until the beginning of another such unit, or until the exchange of the speaking turn.

Units of interaction

One aim of the structural study was to discover *units* within the process of interaction. These units would be basic building blocks out of which the interaction is constructed. Because the focus of the study is on interaction, these units would, for the most part, be constructed through the joint, coordinated action of both participants, and not through the unilateral action of a single participant. On the basis of the results, two such units are hypothesized.

Speaking turn unit. Results suggested that the *speaking-turn interaction unit* is constructed through an ordered sequence of three actions involving both participants. (a) The speaker activates the turn signal (and does not concurrently activate the gesticulation signal). (b) The auditor switches to the speaker state, activating the speaker-state signal, and takes the turn without overlapping the previous speaker's turn. (c) The previous speaker switches to the auditor state, thereby relinquishing the turn. The omission of any one of these three steps results either in no exchange of the turn or in the occurrence of simultaneous turns. Viewed from a slightly different perspective, this sequence of actions may be said to define the boundaries between successive speaking turns.

Within-turn unit. Also hypothesized is the *within-turn interaction unit.* In this case, the auditor contributes to the unit by communicating in the back channel, rather than taking the turn. Results suggest that the within-turn unit may be constructed in two ways, both involving the action of both participants. The first way involves an ordered sequence of three actions: (a) speaker within-turn signal, (b) auditor back channel in the pause position, and (c) speaker continuation signal. The second way involves an ordered sequence of two steps: (a) early auditor back channel, and (b) speaker continuation signal. The within-turn unit provides speaker and auditor with a means of segmenting speaking turns into two or more smaller interaction units, if desired by the participants.

The action sequences described above create boundaries of within-turn units in a manner strictly comparable to the creation of boundaries between speaking turns outlined in the preceding section. Each new within-turn unit would begin with the onset of the next unit of analysis following the auditor back channel. If the prescribed sequences did not occur during a turn, that turn would have no within-turn units. A turn having one such sequence would have two within-turn units: one before the sequence and one after, and so forth.

3.4. Generality of results

In this chapter, we have described some hypotheses resulting from our exploratory studies of conversations. Our position on the generality of the turn-system hypotheses has been misunderstood by some investigators, perhaps because it is somewhat different from that frequently encountered in the psychological literature. This issue was discussed in two sections in D&F (pp. 232-233 & 336-337).

Our position is this: We know of no way to generalize a priori the results of studies of convention-based phenomena. Please note that this is not to claim that the results have no generality; rather, that degree of generality is regarded as entirely an empirical issue.

Until compelling evidence and arguments to the contrary are produced, the turn-system regularities are regarded as conventions. Although there is always the possibility that some aspects of interaction are true universals (and the use of these universals is unaffected by convention), it seems more likely in most cases that behavioral regularities such as those evidenced by the turn-system phenomena stem from the operation of conventions. Once a convention is hypothesized to be operating in an observed interaction or set of interactions, the extent to which it is used in other interactions is simply an empirical issue.

When two studies obtain different results with regard to some hypothesized convention, it is entirely possible that neither study is actually "wrong" or faulty in its execution or in the inferences drawn from it. The use of social practices is much too complex to permit such an immediate, direct interpretation of the discrepancy. This is the point that has been missed entirely by some authors who have criticized or dismissed the hypothesized turn system by citing studies that have produced results apparently divergent from those reported in D&F. (Another issue is whether or not the cited studies included an adequate set of turn-system actions or even asked the same questions of the data. These are empirical issues that we shall not pursue here.)

What might be the source of discrepancy when different results are obtained from two different studies of ostensibly the same sort of interaction? An obvious source of difference is the possibility that the participants in the two studies were using different conventions. This might occur for at least two reasons: (a) the two studies used participants from different cultures or subcultures, and (b) different definitions of the situation were somehow developed by the participants in the two studies.

Different conventions

Participants belonging to different cultures or subcultures may have different procedures (conventions) for handling the aspects of the interaction (such as greeting or turn taking) under study, just as they may have different languages or dialects.

Different situations

Even when the two sets of participants belong to the same subculture and therefore have access to and subscribe to the same repertoire of conventions, something about the way the studies were set up may have led the two sets of participants to define the situation differently, and therefore to use a different set of conventions. The significance of a change in the definition of the situation is that there is at least some change in the conventions considered appropriate for use. This change may have affected the particular conventions under study.

A given convention may prove to be used in all situations by every member of the relevant culture; on the other extreme, it may be unique to the participants in the observed interaction, and only in a highly specific situation at that. (This is the distinction between general and local conventions made in D&F, e.g., pp. 270-272.) It is more likely, of course, that the observed convention occupies some intermediate position, used by some subgroups and not by others, in some situations and not in others. This is the case, for example, with many familiar greetings. In any event, only empirical research can establish the extent of use of a given convention.

It will be apparent that straightforward replication is not a simple task in interaction research. But this seems to follow from the nature of convention-based action. An adequate replication of a structural study would have to include full replication of the situation. This task would seem to be possible in principle but far beyond the capabilities of research in its present state.

Structure-assessment studies

With this view of convention (certainly not a novel one), it becomes clear that, in studying new interactions, one cannot assume that previously hypothesized conventions will be operating within those new interactions. This caveat applies equally to studies of both convention and strategy. It is necessary to verify that the previously hypothesized conventions are operating in the new set of interactions.

This understanding of the generality of results based on conventional action lay behind the *structure-assessment* study described in Chapter 6. Consideration of generality issues is continued in the discussion of that study.

4. Approaches to structural research

STARKEY DUNCAN, JR., AND DONALD W. FISKE

4.1. Introduction

Having described the turn system, it is appropriate to consider our results relevant to it. However, before we present these results in the next chapter, it may be useful to consider briefly some broader methodological issues concerning the conduct of research on interaction structure. We shall be describing our own approach to structural research, as well as the approaches of several other investigators of structure. It will be seen that, although there is considerable communality among these investigators in their general view of interaction, there is also great diversity in their approaches to studying it. This more general discussion of methodology provides a useful context for considering the research presented in the following chapters.

Since the area of interaction research lies at the intersection of most, if not all, of the social sciences, its investigators have been drawn from a number of traditional disciplines: anthropological linguistics, sociology, psychiatry, and a number of different areas in psychology, such as social psychology, clinical psychology, developmental psychology, and psycholinguistics. Because some very different research methods are used in these disciplines, even investigators sharing a common concern with interaction structure have employed a variety of research methods. The result is that, while the area is quite fascinating in its variegated activity, different lines of research often appear incommensurate, and different sets of results seem difficult to compare or integrate.

Perhaps a more serious problem is that investigators in one methodological mode or tradition often pay little or no attention to the work being done in another mode. Or, to the extent that notice is taken at all, the "alien" work is summarily dismissed or seen as a threat. This is especially unfortunate in the case of work on interaction structure because there are relatively so few investigators doing research of this sort.

It seems appropriate, therefore, to consider at least briefly some of the major approaches to doing work on interaction structure, focusing on issues of research method. Without reviewing all currently active research methods, we shall consider certain basic contrasts in some of the approaches to structural research. Despite the methodological heterogeneity, investigators considered here share an essentially common vision of interaction as being structured in part by the operation of rules and related phenomena.

We hope that this discussion will contribute to the ongoing consideration of research issues in this area, as well as reaffirm the basic conceptual communalities that exist despite the various procedural differences. We shall not undertake a review of all relevant research done within the framework of each of the approaches considered. Rather, we shall discuss each approach in terms of one or two exemplary papers or investigators.

(We have already begun a more general methodological discussion by considering in detail issues arising in some of the research being done primarily by social psychologists. This discussion in Chapter 1 focused on problems arising in interaction research from using methods devised for work on individuals. However, few of the investigators doing external-variable research have a structural view of interaction.)

4.2. Goffman's participant observation

A major contribution to the research literature is the work based on participant observation. In this area, Goffman (e.g., 1974; 1981) was the most prominent and prolific investigator.

Goffman's view of interaction is altogether structural, but the necessary presuppositions are virtually taken for granted; he does not belabor them.

In *Relations in Public* (1971), he briefly observes that in public places, even on streets:

> Voluntary coordination of action is achieved in which each of two parties has a conception of how matters ought to be handled between them, the two conceptions agree, each party believes this agreement exists, and each appreciates that this knowledge about the agreement is possessed by the other. In brief, the structural prerequisites for rule by convention are found. (p. 17; cf. Lewis, 1969)

But Goffman's interest is clearly in the phenomena to be found in occasions of interaction, and not in extensive theoretical development of these presuppositions.

With respect to method, Goffman (1971) holds no illusions concerning his participant observation:

> Throughout the papers in this volume unsubtantiated assertions are made regarding the occurrence of certain social practices in certain times and among peoples of various kinds. This description by pronouncement is claimed to be a necessary evil. I assume that if a broad attempt is made to tie together bits and pieces of contemporary social life in exploratory analysis, then a great number of assertions must be made without solid quantitative evidence. (Admittedly this license has greater warrant in traditional ethnographic work than in the study of "small behaviors." Face-to-face interaction generates many natural indicators nicely subject to measure and count. Further, much of expressive behavior disappears from mind as soon as it is observed, and only a randomly scheduled use of appropriate recording equipment is likely to be fully successful in sampling it.) (pp. xiii–xiv)

That is, Goffman's research agenda precludes taking the time to stop and check out carefully each of the many proposals that he makes, even though, strictly speaking, this ought to be done, especially when "small behaviors" are involved. The issue of methodology is, then, essentially moot in the case of Goffman's brand of participant observation. Goffman claims no particular method or substantiation of the interactional regularities he describes. He relies entirely on his acute powers of observation and intuition, and on his cognitive "soft computer."

As a pioneering investigator of startling scope and originality, Goffman continues as an inspiration to many of us in the area. And the sheer volume of insights and proposed phenomena, quite apart from the theoretical contributions, is decidedly intimidating to more plodding empirical investigators. There is surely more than a century's worth of work lying ahead for any large-scale, systematic attempt to verify the innumerable, convention-based interactional regularities that Goffman proposed. (Understandably, there is no present indication of any such research program being planned.) In any event, there is plenty of grist for the research mill for investigators with a more traditional research orientation.

We remain forever in Goffman's debt for both his specific observations and his broad conceptualizations of the research area. No other investigator has so compellingly illuminated the subtlety and complexity of interaction processes. Nevertheless, it remains true that his many accounts of specific regularities remain to be verified, refined, and elaborated.

4.3. Conversation analysis in ethnomethodology

Among many workers in this area, it seems that the term *conversation analysis* is taken as a subarea of the larger field of ethnomethodology. In any event, our concern will be with investigators who focus on conversation processes, as opposed to other types of interaction. The discussion will center primarily on three studies: "Opening up closings" (Schegloff & Sacks, 1973), "A simplest systematics for the organization of turn-taking for conversation" (Sacks, Schegloff, & Jefferson, 1974), and *Conversational Organization* (Goodwin, 1981). For convenience, we shall refer to this general area as conversation analysis.

Although some writers within the ethnomethodological mode appear to take a radical approach to understanding interaction process (cf. Duncan, 1983), the investigators considered here seem to operate from a straightforward structural perspective. For example, Schegloff and Sacks (1973) state, "Our analysis has sought to explicate the ways in which materials [of conversations] are produced by members in orderly ways that exhibit their orderliness, have their orderliness appreciated and used, and have that appreciation displayed and treated as a basis for subsequent action" (p. 290). Their study was designed to find the "institutionalized solution[s]" (p. 298) used by conversationalists in dealing with various problems of coordination that arise in conversations. Goodwin's monograph appears to be congruent with this general perspective. (In the "simplest systematics" paper, Sacks, Schegloff, and Jefferson are more concerned with an underlying framework for the operation of turn-taking systems than with specific conventions.)

As in the discussion of Goffman, the present discussion will focus entirely on issues of methodology, as opposed to the considerable substantive contributions of the investigators.

Like most other investigators of interaction structure, workers in conversation analysis are primarily concerned with exploratory research aimed at discovering significant patterns or *procedures* (i.e., in our terms, conventions and strategies) used by participants. Unlike Goffman, conversation analysts work from audio- or videotapes of interactions; hypotheses are proposed on the basis of detailed scrutiny of these tapes. Unlike some other structural investigators, there tends to be a primary emphasis, especially in earlier studies, on the linguistic aspect of conversation, with no or negligible inclusion of information on paralanguage, body motion, and the like. (Goodwin's work is an excellent example of an attempt to extend conversation analysis beyond speech to include body-motion actions such as gaze direction.) Thus, systematic observation of recorded interactions, typically including careful transcription of speech and sometimes other actions, is a basic technique in this area.

At issue in this discussion is the general tendency of conversation analysts to avoid systematic analysis of data based on their transcribed materials. We shall be considering, then, the manner in which conversation analysts present evidence in support of their proposed hypotheses.

It seems fair to say that a common approach of conversation analysts to presenting evidence is simply to provide examples from their transcriptions that are consistent with their hypotheses. One or two examples of a given phenomenon are typically considered sufficient. Schegloff and Sacks deal with this in a humorous manner, using the case of a greeting between two participants (A and B), such as A: "hello"; B: "hello." They observe that "it would be redundant to cite multiple instances of such exchanges, or minor variants of them (though some variants would require separate treatment)" (p. 291n). Certainly, it would be difficult to quarrel with this judgment. One can imagine papers on greetings bulging with hundreds of instances of "hello; hello" and the like. Surely, they seem to suggest, one or two examples should suffice.

There can be no doubt that examples are a critically important element in the description of any interactional phenomenon. Conversation analysis papers typically provide a wealth of anecdotes and examples that significantly clarify the ideas and phenomena being described. But we believe that this sort of clarification is the prime value of examples. They do not contain the kind of information needed by other investigators to make an independent evaluation of the strength of the proposed phenomenon in the corpus being studied.

A case in point would be the report by Sacks, Schegloff, and Jefferson that "examination of WHERE such 'next-turn starts' occur in current turns shows them to occur at 'possible completion points'" (p. 721, original emphasis). This statement is immediately followed by a sentence further specifying the notion of possible completion points, followed by a series of relevant examples from transcripts.

To avoid excessive concentration on the particulars of a single instance, that statement of Sacks et al. may be generalized to the following form: Event A (next-turn starts) tends strongly to occur at location X (possible completion points), at least within a given corpus of transcribed material. But this statement can be evaluated only on the basis of knowing the proportion of all A's occurring at location X, together with the rate of occurrence of location X within the corpus. To generate these proportions, it is necessary merely to obtain from the corpus the frequency of occurrence of (1) event A at location X; (2) event A not at location X; (3) location X without event A; and (4) neither event A nor location X.

Clearly, none of this information can be derived from a set of examples. At the most, two examples show that event A does occur at location X at least two times. It seems reasonable to expect investigators to provide each other with more complete and systematic information in substantiating their claimed findings when the findings relate to patterns of action sequences.

Goodwin takes a somewhat stronger position on this issue than do Sacks and Schegloff, and one gains the impression that his position is not unique among his colleagues in conversation analysis. He expresses a distinct and seemingly principled aversion to systematic data analysis. In his monograph, only one ten-minute, two-person conversation was transcribed and treated in its entirety, although he considers portions of a number of other interactions in developing his hypotheses. On the basis of the data so generated, Goodwin presents two 2×2 contingency tables, which he analyzes by chi-square. Goodwin is at pains to distance himself from this quantitative endeavor. Introducing this section, he grumbles that:

> One frequent request that has been made by readers of this analysis who are not themselves conversation analysts is for some quantitative measurement of the processes being investigated. I myself consider quantitative methodology not only premature but inappropriate to the type of phenomena here being investigated. However, to deal with questions that readers from other research backgrounds find both troublesome and legitimate, I will here attempt to provide at least some quantitative description. (p. 77)

The monograph being based on Goodwin's dissertation at the University of

Pennsylvania, one can only surmise that the quantitative material was provided at the behest of a committee member.

Paradoxically, Goodwin considers it neither premature nor inappropriate to base conclusions on one example or a few examples whose representativeness for the full interaction is never established. Except in the case of the two chi-squares, this is the standard procedure throughout the monograph.

At issue in the contingency tables that Goodwin produces is his proposal that, when the speaker's gaze is shifted toward the auditor, the speaker will restart the sentence in progress if the auditor is not gazing toward the speaker. Goodwin cross-tabulates his data in the way outlined in the last paragraph. When the speaker's gaze arrives, auditor is (a) gazing, or (b) not gazing; and speaker (a) restarts, or (b) does not restart. One table presents data for the entire conversation; the other table, only for turn beginnings. Goodwin seeks to show that most restarts occur in connection with the auditor's not gazing.

It will be apparent, however, that the tables represent an inexact test of Goodwin's hypothesis, which is concerned only with the prediction that a restart will occur if the auditor is not gazing when the speaker shifts gaze toward the auditor. Goodwin is careful to acknowledge the literature that exists on speech nonfluencies, many of which are not at the interactional location he designates. He, of course, makes no claim that all restarts are a product of interaction processes, and therefore he need make no prediction concerning the rate of restarts not occurring at the designated location.

Nevertheless, Goodwin analyzes his tables and obtains significant chi-squares. He then suggests that, given such significant results, quantitatively oriented investigators would consider the hypothesis supported by the data and proceed to sweep the aberrant cases under the rug: "Exceptions and examples that do not support the point being argued can be disregarded as 'noise' if an acceptable level of significance is obtained" (p. 79). This, of course, is a parody of standard research process. Goodwin notices that in the turn-beginning table, for example, only six out of seventeen instances of the auditor's not gazing are accompanied by predicted speaker restarts. That is, the hypothesis holds in only 35% of the cases. In work on interaction structure, this result calls either for rejection or revision of the hypothesis, regardless of the statistical significance obtained. Just as a quantitative researcher might do, Goodwin returns to his transcribed materials and develops in a reasonable way an elaborated version of his hypothesis that eventually accounts for ten of the eleven failed predictions. (Unfortunately, there was a total of only seven restarts at turn beginnings in the one conversation analyzed, making it less than optimal for studying this phenomenon.)

Thus, through comprehensive treatment of an entire conversation, Goodwin is led to an improved version of his hypothesis, something that might not have happened if he had focused only on some subset of examples. Goodwin's hypothesis in this case is eminently testable; it is difficult to see why quantitative analysis here is either "premature" or "inappropriate." Rather, such analysis led Goodwin to a sharpened statement of the proposed procedures. The effect of the noisome data analysis seems salutary.

It bears mentioning that, although most of Goodwin's proposals are straightforwardly testable, this is not always the case in his study and in some other conversation analysis studies. For example, Goodwin analyzes the following statement, addressed to three recipients: "I gave, I gave up smoking cigarettes – I, uh, one – one week ago today, actually" (p. 160). (We do not use here Goodwin's transcribing conventions.) He seeks to show that the utterance is made up of three sections, each of which is addressed to a different participant (as indexed by gaze direction) and is appropriately modified for that participant's degree of knowledge concerning the event in question. The argument, however, turns on the premise that the speaker's wife should not be "expected" to know that this is the one-week anniversary of the speaker's abstinence. This claim, relating to what is inside the wife's head, is not otherwise supported. Hypotheses concerning the knowledge held by participants may in many cases be unfalsifiable; such hypotheses may be sharply contrasted in this respect with hypotheses concerning actions sequences (for example, auditor gaze and speaker restart).

The practice of using examples in conversation analysis is similar to, and may be derived from, linguistics. Beyond merely illustrating a point, examples are often offered in support of linguistic hypotheses, although hypotheses may also be based on extensive analysis of transcribed materials. In the case of linguistics, when arguments are directed toward speakers of the language (as in the case of English), examples may be used to show that a given construction is either permissible or inappropriate, based on the readers' intuitions as native speakers. For example, we could all agree that the following sentence is inadmissible in English: The clouds is drifting across the sky. (It might be noted in passing that not all examples are equally unambiguous as to admissibility.)

The situation does not appear so clear-cut when one is dealing with "nonverbal" or interactional phenomena. Consider a judgment on the appropriateness of the following interactional sequence: The auditor acts to take the speaking turn after a 2 2 # (i.e., downward curving terminal juncture) intonation pattern, in the absence of a grammatically complete utterance and while the speaker is gazing away from the auditor. One might experience difficulty in forming a firm opinion as to whether the sequence is appropriate or not. (It is appropriate within the turn system that we have hypothesized, providing the speaker is not gesticulating at the time.)

Goodwin's hypothesis just described would be another case in point. Is it appropriate for a speaker to restart an utterance when the auditor is not gazing at the speaker? Goodwin suggests that a restart at such a point is a device to regain the speaker's visual regard. An informant might say that there seems to be nothing wrong with it, but that he or she is unable to recall having seen it. Thus, it may be that fully conventional interaction sequences are not readily susceptible to critical evaluation via examples. For this reason, generalizing the use of examples in linguistics to research on interaction may be problematic. We recommend that hypotheses concerning interaction sequences be supported with systematic data analyses.

4.4. Context analysis

Context analysis is the term Scheflen (e.g., 1966) gave to his formulation of an approach to structural research. This approach gains further importance because it is used by Kendon (e.g., 1977; 1982), a leading structural investigator. Both Scheflen and Kendon have been prominent spokesmen for structural research, contributing substantially to its establishment as a research area.

The late Albert Scheflen was a pioneering and prolific structural investigator, contributing some of the earliest studies of this sort. A psychiatrist, his interest initially was in psychotherapy process (e.g., 1961; 1963; 1965; 1973a). As his work continued, he began writing on broader communication issues and on other aspects of interaction (e.g., 1966; 1967; 1968; 1971; 1972; 1973b; 1975). Clearly, Scheflen's efforts played a major role both in bringing structural research on interaction to the attention of a broad spectrum of investigators, and in stimulating and encouraging active workers in the area.

Kendon is one of the two or three best-known investigators of face-to-face interaction. No other researcher has studied so intensively such a wide variety of communication phenomena and types of interaction. Kendon's published studies have included greetings at a birthday party, a conversation in an English pub, gazing and turn taking in conversations, spatial arrangement of participants in a conversation while standing, a "kissing round" between a couple on a park bench, and sign language in an Australian aborigine group. Many of these studies can be found in a volume of his collected works (1977). In addition, he was an editor in an early volume devoted to structural research (Kendon, Harris, & Key, 1975). More recently, he has studied sign language in several unusual situations, such as a fully developed sign language used by the hearing (1980).

Few investigators have involved themselves so deeply in interaction in an empirical sense. Kendon has the remarkable ability to immerse himself in a welter of complex, highly detailed data and emerge with a coherent, convincing picture of interaction process, which he then describes in a clear and comprehensive manner. An excellent, extended discussion of Kendon's perspective on context analysis may be found in his 1982 paper.

The most succinct description of the context-analysis method is provided by Scheflen (1966). (An excellent, extended discussion of Kendon's perspective on context analysis may be found in his 1982 paper.) After considering techniques of recording and transcribing, Scheflen considers the nature of the *structural unit*, which he defines as a

> regular organization or complex of components occurring in specific situations or contexts. A structural unit, then, has: (1) a given set of component parts; (2) a definite organization; and (3) specific location in a larger system. For example, an immediate family consists of a mother, father, and children with prescribed relationships and a definite position in a larger family or kinship system. Morphemes (words) consist of given phonemes arranged in regular ways and having set locations in the sentence . . . .Structural units, then, are parts of larger units, which are parts of still larger units, and so on. (pp. 271-272)

These units are arranged in a hierarchy of levels. This is certainly a structural view of the organization of interaction.

Our concern in this discussion is Scheflen's approach to research method in structural research. In the same 1966 paper, he proposes the following formula:

> the method for ascertaining or identifying the structural unit is based

upon its three characteristics, i.e., its components, their organization, and the context(s) in which they occur. We begin by inspecting the behaviors and grouping, as a tentative unit, those that occur together in time. We then test this tentative formulation by three tests, reformulating the unit over and over by trial and error until we have determined the relations of components. When we have found the combination that is a structural unit each of its components will occur together every time. They will have consistent arrangement and appear invariably in the same context. If not we must begin again.(pp. 272-273)

The relations between potential behavioral components of a unit
> are determined by what in mathematics is called the *Method of Agreement and Difference* (also formulated as *Mill's canons*). Simply stated, if *A* appears every time *B* appears, and vice versa, and if *A* does not appear when *B* is absent, then *A* and *B* have relations of interdependence and represent an entity. (p. 273, original emphasis)

In D&F, we criticized Scheflen's approach on the basis of two, essentially independent considerations: (a) that it is overly rigid, and (b) that it presupposes the nature of the relationship between actions in interaction.

Rigidity

Experienced investigators may blanch at the requirement that relationships between actions be invariant in their data. If we take Scheflen at his word, a promising hypothesis of a structural relationship between actions would be irremediably destroyed, either if a participant made a single error in interaction performance, or if an investigator made a single error in transcribing or analyzing data. In the dust and confusion of both interaction and investigation, error will almost certainly occur; single exceptions to otherwise strong relationships should not be permitted to disrupt the research process. As we pointed out in D&F, if Scheflen's statement of his approach were taken seriously, a single grammatical error in speech, say a disagreement in number between subject and verb, would be sufficient to destroy the proposed grammatical rule of agreement in number between subject and verb. Similarly, a single mistake in transcribing could wreak the same damage. Surely, a more flexible approach can be found. Significantly, Kendon's (1982) extended discussion of context analysis does not emphasize this aspect of Scheflen's formulation.

As McQuown (1959) points out, context analysis is an application to communication research of the more general natural-history method in science. McQuown suggests that Scheflen's formulation is a partial articulation of the analytic methods in wide use at that time by linguists (that is, those linguists involved with intensive analyses of data corpora, as opposed to the positing of examples). McQuown provides a more complete, if highly condensed, account of the general appproach.

Presupposed relation between actions

There is another problem with Scheflen's formulation of context analysis that is both more subtle amd more significant than the methodological rigidity just mentioned. Scheflen requires that the relation between actions be an invariant one. That is, *A* must always be followed by *B*, and *B* must always be preceded by *A*. This type of relationship is what we have called an *obligatory interaction* sequence. If one participant does *A*, then the partner must do *B*; and *B* never occurs unless preceded by *A*.

A simple example of an obligatory interaction sequence might be a handshake. If one offers to shake hands with another, there is a strong obligation to respond, except for unusual circumstances, such as dirty hands, for which apologies are made. In the hypotheses concerning turn-system signals, an obligatory relationship was posited between the speaker's gesticulating and the auditor's attempting to take the turn. The evidence suggests that, if the speaker is gesticulating, the auditor is obliged not to take the turn. This seems to be the sort of relation between actions that Scheflen had in mind, even though the relation is between *A* and not −*B*.

However, it seems important to allow for the possibility of at least one other sort of basic relation: what we call an *optional sequence*. In an optional sequence, an action *A* by a participant marks a point at which the partner may appropriately do *B*, but at which *B* is not required. That is, upon the occurrence of *A*, the partner chooses whether or not to do *B*. However, the action *B* appropriately occurs only after *A*.

Examples of optional action sequences occur in games. For example, in baseball the batter has the option of either swinging or not swinging at a pitch. There is certainly no obligation to swing; however, the choice has significant consequences for the progress of the game, depending on the circumstances prevailing at the time of the pitch. Further, given the existence of the option, the batter cannot avoid making a choice when the pitch is delivered. Because the option applies, not swinging is just as significant as swinging.

In the turn system, a number of optional relationships are hypothesized. One is between the speaker turn signal and the auditor's acting to take the speaking turn. The proposed rule is that the auditor may appropriately act to take the turn only when the turn signal is displayed (and the speaker is not concurrently gesticulating). However, given the display of the turn signal, the auditor is not obliged to take the turn but rather exercises an option in this regard.

Many examples of optional relationships between actions can be imagined in games and in face-to-face interaction. It seems to be a mistake to set up a method that does not provide for the existence of such options. In this sense, also, it seems desirable to seek a more flexible approach.

Kendon's approach to transcription

Kendon's extensive structural research bears a complex relation to Scheflen's formulations. In some respects, there is a close correspondence, while in others, a distinct divergence. These matters are well covered in Kendon's (1982) paper. Of particular relevance to our discussion is Kendon's approach to transcribing. Because Kendon's approach is sharply different from the one used in our studies, this seems an appropriate point to consider, in general, some of the complexities and paradoxes of transcribing in exploratory structural research.

Scheflen advocates a position essentially identical to ours. Initial exploratory studies of interaction require as extensive a transcription as possible. Once hypotheses are generated by exploratory research, subsequent work based on hypotheses generated by that exploratory research need include transcription of only those behavioral elements involved in the hypotheses.

In contrast, Kendon regards the transcription in exploratory studies as "a form of *conclusion* to one's investigation, not as a starting point" (p. 479, original emphasis). In Kendon's view:

> The transcription system one adopts itself embodies a set of hypotheses and assumptions that will thereafter structure one's inquiry. It is of the greatest importance to know what these hypotheses and assumptions are, and whether they are appropriate to the question one is engaged upon, before adopting any system of transcription. It is a mistake to think that there can be a truly neutral transcription system, which, if only we had it, we could then use to produce transcriptions suitable for any kind of investigation. (p. 478)

More specifically, transcribing at the onset of a study incurs "the danger of becoming irrevocably committed to a set of assumptions about the organization of behavior that will almost certainly not be correct" (p. 478).

Rather than beginning an exploratory study with a transcription and basing all subsequent analyses on it, Kendon proposes a more reciprocal relationship between transcription and hypotheses. One begins with a close inspection of the interaction materials under study, fully acknowledging the initial and relatively primitive expectations one has concerning the structure of those materials. As the investigator's immersion in the materials continues, the current notion of their structure may be committed to paper. This representation is, in a sense, both the first transcription and the first, tentative set of structural hypotheses.

As one returns to the materials, however, it becomes apparent that the initial transcription is limited or in error, so that in time a revised transcription is prepared. In this manner, the study proceeds "in continual dialogue with the [materials], stopping only at that point where one's current 'irritation of doubt' (to adopt an expression from C. S. Pierce) about the issue at hand has been laid to rest" (p. 479).

We shall consider, then, the characteristics and the relative strengths and weaknesses of the two approaches, which in this discussion we shall call the *evolving-hypothesis* approach (Kendon's) and the *initially-detailed* approach (the one we have used).

The general goals of initially-detailed transcribing are to include all possibly relevant actions, and to describe these actions in greater detail than will be required by the hypotheses resulting from data analysis. This process may be distinguished from evolving-hypothesis transcribing, in which only those actions are included in the transcription that are believed to be part of the organization under study.

As we pointed out in D&F (p. 162), using the initially-detailed approach involves the paradox of having to make choices regarding what actions to include in the transcription before one knows what the significant elements of the interaction structure will be. This situation has led some investigators, such as Scheflen and McQuown, to suggest that initial transcriptions be as detailed and comprehensive as practical, in order to avoid excluding actions that may be essential to the ultimate structural hypotheses. This practice is one that has been well established in linguistics for decades.

For example, in beginning study of a heretofore unknown language, an anthropological linguist would attempt to make an exhaustive phonetic recording of the speech sounds of native speakers because there would be no way of knowing which of these sounds would prove to be part of the phonological system of the language. Imagine the plight of linguists studying certain languages of southern Africa if they had decided to ignore clicks just because clicks, although used by English speakers, are not part of the sound system of English.

In the face of ignorance of the phenomenon in question – or even of what the phenomenon in question is – (which is a defining characteristic of exploratory research), excluding potential data is always risky. It is altogether possible to omit transcribing some action or set of actions that may be crucially important to the phenomena that are eventually discovered. Similarly, one might transcribe actions in an excessively gross manner that omits critical detail. In either case, missing information may well prevent the results from cohering, and one may never know or be able to guess just what actions or details of actions are missing. Of course, it is always possible to add to the transcription at any time in the course of the research. But in supplementing the transcription, the basic problem simply recurs: what to transcribe and in what detail? Considerations such as these have led to the recommendation that transcriptions for exploratory research be as comprehensive and detailed as possible.

Nevertheless, time, research funds, and patience all impose real limits on the inclusiveness and detail of what is transcribed. The transcribing process can become a quagmire for the investigator. As Kendon points out, "no transcription, no matter how fine grained, can ever be complete. One must inevitably make a selection" (p. 479). I believe that no experienced investigator in this area would challenge this view. The more one works on a videotape or film, the more one becomes aware of the many actions occurring that were not at first noticed. We have never known an investigator who, while working on a given film or videotape, has arrived at the point of not noticing new movements or vocal variations. In this sense, a film or videotape of interaction is an inexhaustible source of data.

For these reasons, decisions obviously have to be made concerning what actions to transcribe and in what detail. In other words, it is crucially important to decide, not only when to stop transcribing further detail, but also what actions to include before stopping. These decisions are an integral part of the initially-detailed approach to transcribing.

Given the nature of exploratory work, decisions on transcribing necessarily have a heavily intuitive aspect. Kendon characterizes these decisions as "hypotheses." But given the absence of knowledge concerning the phenomena to be discovered, the notion of hypothesis in this context seems overextended. The decision process seems more aptly described as an exercise in risk taking. With each decision to exclude an action from the transcription, or to combine several aspects of an action into a single transcribing category, the investigator is, in effect, gambling that that decision will not sabotage the results. It is, obviously, a research phase during which the investigator must have at least some confidence in his or her experience and intuition.

Similarly, it does not seem accurate to say that the initially-detailed approach commits the investigator "to a set of assumptions about the organization of behavior" (Kendon, 1982, p. 478). In this case, Kendon would seem to overgeneralize from his own approach. The decisions one makes in devising a fairly comprehensive transcription have perhaps nothing to say about the way the observed interaction is organized. They do have considerable bearing on what actions may be discovered to play a part in that organization, and thus on the completeness with which the organization can be described. For example, the turn system would have been much less effective in accounting for turn-taking phenomena if we had decided to ignore the hands and arms altogether.

Beyond the risk-taking aspect, a second problematic characteristic of the initially-detailed approach is that it is slow, tedious, expensive, and inefficient. One cannot avoid transcribing a considerable amount of detail that almost certainly will never be used in the final results of the study. For example, as described in D&F, in our earliest exploratory work we transcribed hand and arm movements in great detail. However, our hypothesized gesticulation signal was defined only in terms of whether or not the hand was gesticulating in any way or tensed. This definition rendered superfluous all the fine detail, so laboriously obtained, on hand and arm movement and position. (At least some of the difficulty of detailed transcribing may be lifted as technology provides more rapid and efficient techniques.)

In this respect, the evolving-hypothesis approach seems more focused and efficient. Although early versions of the transcription will almost certainly need to be replaced or supplemented, the investigator is nevertheless in the process of homing in on the final set of hypotheses, as opposed to squandering time in transcribing a broad array of irrelevant actions.

It is perhaps some consolation for the initially-detailed approach that an extensive transcription, once completed, remains a resource that may be mined in any further study for which it is relevant. Thus it was that we continued to return to our early detailed transcriptions as we explored further structure and strategy signals relating to turn taking. And other investigators (e.g., McNeill, 1979) have used our transcriptions, including the fine detail on gestures, to explore other phenomena.

For its part, the evolving-hypothesis approach seems to be limited in that it is poorly adapted to systematic, exploratory data analyses. As indicated in the discussion of conversation analysis, systematic analyses require data containing information on each occurrence – and nonoccurrence – of both the phenomenon in question and the behavioral elements one is testing in relation to that phenomenon. For example, with respect to turn exchange, one needs to know when such exchange did and did not occur and what actions were present at both the occurrences and nonoccurrences. This sort of analysis is required to validate the investigator's initial insights.

Relatively speaking, in using the evolving-hypothesis approach, the investigator is limited to the power of his or her own skill in perceiving critical relationships in the data. Once again, heavy emphasis is placed on one's "soft computer." This fact becomes even more critical when heavy emphasis is placed on the backwards-going sort of analysis we advocate in the next section of this chapter. This analysis, focusing on the antecedents of actions, as opposed to their consequents, may be particularly difficult to conduct effectively on the basis of intuition alone.

We suggest there is a place both for systematic sweeps of the comprehensive transcription that may turn up relationships not imme- diately apparent to the investigator, and for thorough data analyses designed to highlight critical elements of the organization, differentiating these from elements that are merely concomitants of the organization.

Conclusion

The chief proponents of context analysis have made major contributions to research on face-to-face interaction: Scheflen as a pioneer whose work gave impetus to the field, and Kendon as a preeminent investigator of interaction structure. Although the method itself, as outlined by Scheflen, usefully articulates many aspects of the structural approach to under- standing interaction, his formulation of the method has both conceptual and pragmatic shortcomings.

Kendon has long used an approach to transcribing (which we have termed the evolving-hypothesis approach) that contrasts in many ways with with the one we have used (termed the initially-detailed approach). It is probably a mistake to think of either approach in absolute terms. Each has distinct advantages, depending on the study at hand and the investigator's skills and preferences.

For example, when we began our initial exploratory studies of conversations, we did not even have the notion of speaking turns in mind; we were simply looking for some sort of structure in the conversations. In this context, the evolving-hypothesis approach would probably not have been usable. On the other hand, if one approaches some filmed or videotaped materials with an interest in greetings (which Kendon uses as the example in his [1982] paper), then, *depending on the skill and experience of the investigator*, the evolving-hypothesis approach may prove effective. Inevitably, choice of one of the two approaches will depend heavily on the investigator's preference and personal style. It is perhaps an advantage in the developing field of structural research on interaction that such methodological alternatives exist.

4.5. Considerations relevant to hypothesizing structural relationships

A major concern in our own research has been with the sorts of evidence that would be appropriately presented in support of structural hypotheses. In this section we shall describe our approach as it is currently formulated. We anticipate that, as further experience with structural research is gained and more diverse phenomena are discovered, this approach will have to be further developed. However, it seems adequate for the phenomena currently hypothesized.

It will be seen that the approach in no way works at cross-purposes with the research done by the investigators or research programs already considered in this chapter. Rather, we see the approach as providing a relatively more comprehensive way of documenting (and potentially elaborating or refining) the various hypotheses proposed by these investigators. We have already made it clear that, from our perspective, structural research can only gain from a rigorous and flexible approach to data analysis.

Four considerations were taken into account in developing the structural hypotheses in D&F, on which the strategy research was based: (a) the probability of an antecedent; (b) the probability of a consequent; (c) differentiating actions; and (d) parsimony. Although underlying the structural research, these considerations, were never made fully explicit in D&F. It will be useful, therefore, to enumerate them here, and to discuss the manner in which they were used to evaluate structural hypotheses.

Sequential probabilities

Most research on interaction structure is concerned with sequences of actions involving minimally an action by a participant and a subsequent action by the partner. For purposes of discussion, we shall consider only these two-part interaction sequences, although three-part sequences were hypothesized in the turn system and longer sequences are certainly analyzable. Let us term the first action, A, and the second action, B.

Given a body of data on interaction sequences, two sequential probabilities are always available: the probability of a consequent (the probability of B following an occurrence of A), and the probability of an antecedent (the probability of A preceding an occurrence of B).

As was pointed out in Chapter 1, much research on "nonverbal communication" has not used information on interaction sequences. The external-variable research reported in Part II of D&F is an example of such work. When sequential information has been used, it has almost invariably been confined to the forward-going probability of a consequent. This practice is understandable, in that the consequent probability follows the natural flow of events in time. Further, it provides critical information when one is concerned with predicting behavior, whether of persons or, say, the stock market.

Nevertheless, data containing sequential information always permit calculation of the probability of an antecedent. In contrast to the consequent probability, the antecedent probability may seem unnatural, flowing as it does against the stream of interaction. It is a kind of backwards probability. Moreover, investigators must become accustomed to working their way backwards through a set of data sequences – not an intuitively natural process for all. They may be surprised at the regularities to be found in interaction sequences considered from this perspective. We regard antecedent probabilities as the sine qua non of structural research.

Strictly speaking, the antecedent and consequent probabilities for a given action sequence are not independent. They may, however, vary broadly in interesting ways that are useful in developing hypotheses. Although the probability of an antecedent would seem to have nothing to do with prediction, it should not be concluded that it is irrelevant to predicting behavior. Structural hypotheses based on the antecedent probability permit useful predictions of one sort, as will be discussed later in this section.

Differentiating actions

In addition to the antecedent and consequent probabilities, other considerations are relevant to structural hypotheses. Whenever possible, it is highly convenient to be able to test a hypothesized signal in terms of its ability to differentiate types of action. For example, as described later, the speaker turn signal was tested for the extent to which it preceded smooth exchanges of the turn in our data and was absent prior to instances of simultaneous claiming of the turn by the two participants in a conversation. Similarly, the speaker-state signal was tested in terms of its appearance at the beginnings of speaking turns, as opposed to the utterance of auditor back channels.

Tests of this sort provide the investigator with considerable analytic power. However, it is not always possible to define a relevant test of this sort for a signal. For example, we did not succeed in formulating such a test for analyzing the relation between the speaker within-turn signal and auditor back channels.

Parsimony

Finally, in cases of alternative hypotheses competing as candidates for describing a structural relationship, investigators may invoke the principle of parsimony. Although this may appear an obvious consideration, it raises complex issues both in the formulation of structural signals and in the differentiating of strategy signals from structural signals. We shall consider the complicating issues in later chapters in dealing with specific analyses. Parsimony has played a critical role in our work.

Optional and obligatory interaction sequences

The basic distinction between optional sequences and obligatory sequences was introduced in the last chapter and expanded in this one in the discussion of context analysis in Section 4.4. In an obligatory sequence at some specified point(s) in the stream of interaction, a given participant must (or must not) appropriately take some action.

A convenient example of an obligatory situation is the traffic light. Motorists must stop when it is red and similarly must go when it is green. Within the turn system the speaker gesticulation signal, which inhibits auditor attempts to take the turn, was hypothesized as an obligatory signal.

In an ideal obligatory sequence involving two actions, the first action would always be followed by the second, and the second would always be preceded by the first. (Note that "action" is used here to include "non-action," as in not attempting to take the turn.)

Distinguished from the obligatory sequence is the optional sequence. In an optional sequence, at some specified point(s) in the stream of interaction, a given participant may appropriately take some action. Thus, the participant has, at those points, the option of taking the action or not. However, the action may be appropriately taken only at those designated points. In a properly operating optional sequence, the second action is always preceded by the first, but the first is followed by the second to a lesser and unspecified extent.

Within the turn system, the speaker turn signal is hypothesized to indicate points at which the auditor may appropriately act to take the turn. At some proportion of the turn-signal displays (in our data, typically 20-25%), the auditor chooses to exercise the option of taking the turn. Such attempts, when the turn signal was active, typically resulted in smooth exchanges of the turn. That is, there was no overlap in the respective turns.

It will have become apparent that obligatory sequences, such as may be found to exist in interactions, involve strongly paired actions. In proper operation of the sequence, the first action is always followed by the second, and the second is always preceded by the first. Optional sequences – which appear to be quite common in interactions – are somewhat more elusive, particularly if one attends only to the forward-going consequent probability. An adequate evaluation of an interaction sequence involves a certain amount of looking backward. We must know not only how frequently the first action is followed by the second, but also how frequently the second action is preceded by the first.

In the case of an ideal obligatory sequence, both the probability of a consequent and the probability of an antecedent would be 1.00. That is, each A is followed by a B, and each B is preceded by an A.

In the case of an optional sequence, the probability of an antecedent would ideally be 1.00, while the probability of a consequent is not directly specified but is appreciably lower than 1.00. Here each B is preceded by an A, but A's are followed by B's at a rate that is the result of the partner's inclination to exercise the available option.

Within our analytic approach, an interaction sequence can be properly evaluated only through simultaneous consideration of both the antecedent and consequent probabilities.

The meaning, in interaction terms, of the antecedent probability becomes apparent. The initial action (A) marks those points at which the second action (B) either must (obligatory) or may (optional) appropriately be taken. The antecedent probability is essential to discovering these markers. The consequent probability is essential to differentiating the optional from the obligatory sequences.

Investigators focusing only on consequent probabilities may be able to find potential obligatory sequences but would be unable to evaluate them properly. For example, in a data set it might be that all A's are followed by B's, but that a number of B's are not preceded by A's. In this case, we would conclude that we might be close to defining an obligatory sequence, but that the definition of A must be further developed, so that A's preceded virtually all B's.

When only consequent probabilities are used, optional sequences are likely to be missed altogether. Let us consider a simple but not unrepresentative example. Let us say that there are 50 A's in a data corpus and only 5 B's, but each of these B's occurs immediately after an A. The probability of a consequent B, given A, is only .10; but the probabilty of an antecedent A, given B, is 1.00. Here is a real lead that might be pursued in data from other interactions containing more B's, but it would be noticed only by those bothering to calculate the probability of the antecedent A. The .10 consequent probability of B's following A's would, in itself, be likely to inspire little enthusiasm.

Conclusion

In our approach to structural research, then, all hypotheses of regularities in interaction sequences involve a substantial probability of an antecedent. Thus, in exploratory research the search often begins there. One need only become accustomed to working one's way backward through the action sequences, listing recurrent actions, and testing and refining the definition of potential relationships. Investigators looking for the first time at probabilities of antecedents may be surprised at the regularities to be found. Ignoring such probabilties would appear to involve considerable loss of information on interaction sequences.

Special considerations

The four criteria – consequent and antecedent probabilities, differentiating actions, and parsimony – are used whenever possible in structural research on interaction. However, various circumstances sometimes render one or more of these criteria irrelevant or unobtainable. These circumstances deserve mention.

Already discussed is the case in which the investigator cannot formulate a set of actions that the signal should be differentiating. The speaker within-turn signal is a case in point. It was hypothesized as an optional signal preceding auditor back channels. We were unable in this case to suggest some other action that should be differentiated from back channels by the within-turn signal. Analysis therefore focused on consequent and antecedent probabilities, and parsimony.

The speaker-state signal is an unusual case. In itself, it does not involve interaction sequences. It is hypothesized to differentiate two kinds of auditor utterances: back channels and turn beginnings. The speaker-state signal is supposed to accompany turn beginnings but not back channels. Use of the signal is said to indicate that the auditor is, at that moment, switching to the speaker state. In this way, it is said to help clarify for the speaker what the auditor's utterance is. For this reason, we did not use sequential information in deriving and testing the hypothesis. The signal's ability to differentiate turn beginnings from back channels was critical, and parsimony was considered.

The speaker gesticulation signal represents the most complex case. It is hypothesized to inhibit – or "turn off" – the speaker turn signal, so that when the two signals occur concurrently, auditor attempts to take the speaking turn are sharply reduced. Because of its strong suppressing effect, we hypothesized it as an obligatory signal, but a negative one.

The negative aspect of the signal seems to create a special problem for analysis. In considering interaction sequences, the probability of a consequent shows a strong effect: When the gesticulation signal is active, there is minimal probability of a subsequent auditor turn attempt. However, the probability of an antecedent cannot be meaningfully calculated. The gesticulation signal has to do with not responding, and there are innumerable places throughout the interaction where the auditor does not respond with a turn attempt when there is no gesticulation signal. We certainly did not hypothesize that, whenever the signal is absent, the auditor must respond. For this reason, in formulating the signal, we considered the probability of a consequent, the differentiation of actions (rate of responding to the turn signal in the presence versus absence of the gesticulation signal), and parsimony, but we did not consider the probability of an antecedent.

The problem here is compounded by the fact that the signal's action is in conjunction with the speaker turn signal – an optional signal. When the turn signal is displayed in the absence of the gesticulation signal, the auditor is not obliged to take the turn. Thus, there were many such points in the conversations we observed where the auditor did not respond. We have the situation, then, in which auditor response to the turn signal alone is rather low (20-25%), but response to the turn signal plus gesticulation is distinctly lower still.

One way of handling this problem would be to hypothesize the gesticulation signal as a strategy signal – something we had not formulated when the gesticulation signal was originally developed. Discussion of this possibility will have to be taken up in the section on strategy signals. In any event, the general issue is how to conceptualize the action of a negative obligatory signal in conjunction with an optional signal. Should it be considered a structure signal or a strategy signal?

4.6. Summary

It may be seen that interaction phenomena are variegated, requiring a generally flexible approach to analysis. And it seems virtually certain that new kinds of structural phenomena will be discovered, calling for further modifications. We believe, however, that these complications and special cases should not obscure some basic points.

1. Information on interaction sequences is essential to research on interaction.
2. Thorough data analysis is essential to evaluate hypotheses. A few selected examples do not supply sufficient information to permit independent evaluation of proposed interaction phenomena.
3. An orderly approach to data analysis can be developed within the framework of structural research.
4. Maximal use should be made of information on both antecedent and consequent probabilities in interaction sequences, in addition to other standard research criteria.
5. These methodological issues require further consideration, debate, modification, and elaboration by investigators. Vigorous debate of methodological issues would be a healthy and welcome development in the field.

5. Strategy research: method

STARKEY DUNCAN, JR., AND DONALD W. FISKE

Having considered some of the more general issues in structural research on face-to-face interaction, we are in a position to present the strategy research that is a main focus of this monograph. In this chapter, we shall describe some basic material on participants and transcription that is relevant to the studies reported in Chapters 6 to 10.

In the structural research reported in D&F, there was a sharp distinction between the initial, exploratory research designed to generate empirically based hypotheses and subsequent work (the "replication" study) aimed at evaluating the operation of hypothesized phenomena in further inter-actions. The exploratory research used a variety of techniques designed to maximize the discovery of interaction phenomena. The subsequent replication study was essentially a direct, mechanical application of hypotheses to new interaction materials.

The strategy research is curious in that it occupies a more complex position, having elements characteristic of both exploratory and replication structural studies. On the one hand, it is like the replication study in that it is based almost entirely on hypotheses generated in the exploratory research. On the other hand, although drawing on those structural hypotheses, it is wholly exploratory research, seeking to discover phenomena relating to interaction strategy. Thus, the research is constrained by the structural hypotheses, but quite free to be exploratory within those constraints. These characteristics render the strategy research something of a hybrid. This is reflected in the methods used, as detailed in this chapter.We hoped, of course, that the strategy research would possess more generativity than less metaphorical hybrids.

5.1. Participants

Videotapes used in this study were taken from a larger set of tapes recorded for a study of individual differences in interaction reported in Part II of D&F. In that study, the general aim was to have brief (seven- to eight-minute) conversations between unacquainted participants. Accordingly, participants were recruited from the Law School and from the School of Social Service Administration (SSA) at the University of Chicago. We assumed – correctly, as it turned out – that students at the two schools would not know each other. At the same time, the schools were located only about a block apart, offering convenient access for participants. Each participant was to have two conversations.

   Names of participants were randomly selected from student directories. Participants were recruited by a letter and a subsequent telephone call describing the research as "an exploratory study of human conversations." The refusal rate was very low. Of those who agreed to participate, most appeared at the appointed time. Hence, there was little self-selection. Participants were paid $3.00 for the 90-minute session. All were white, except for two black women, one from each school. The ages of the participants ranged from 22 to 36 years, with a mean of 25.

   All conversations were held in the Law School. It happened that there were two lounges, identical in size, shape, and furnishings, one on each side of the moot-court room. A videocamera was set up in each lounge. Participants were seated in adjacent chairs turned slightly towards each other. Each participant had a small lavaliere microphone suspended around his or her neck. A female experimenter gave the following instruction: "I would like the two of you to have a conversation for the next seven minutes or so. You can use the time to get acquainted with each other, or to talk about anything else that interests you." She then left the room. When the first conversation was completed, one member of each pair exchanged places, the instructions were repeated, and a second conversation was recorded for each of the new pairings. (In addition to the conversations, participants completed personality inventories before interacting, and postexperimental questionnaires afterwards. These data are not considered in our study of strategy.)

We arranged for participants to arrive in groups of four: one male and one female from the Law School, and one male and one female from SSA. We shall term each group of four, a *block* of participants.

In each conversation, a Law School student talked with an SSA student. Half the conversations were between participants of the same sex, and half were between participants of the opposite sex. The order of same-sex and opposite-sex conversations was balanced across the study. The second conversation followed immediately upon the first.

In the individual-differences study reported in D&F, there were 88 participants; because each was in two conversations, there were 88 conversations. The present study used four blocks of participants, yielding 16 participants and 16 conversations, or data on 32 participant-conversations.

The four blocks of participants were chosen for this study on a somewhat indirect basis. As part of a "replication" study of hypothesized interaction structure reported in D&F, four conversations were selected from the larger pool of 88. (There were also some conversations from other sources used in the replication study.) These four conversations were chosen using two criteria: (a) adequate sound and video on technical grounds, and (b) a reasonably large number of speaking turns in each conversation. This was important because the structural analyses heavily emphasized speaking-turn phenomena. In the four conversations, the number of attempted exchanges of the speaking turn ranged from 30 to 45 (counting both smooth exchanges of the turn and instances of simultaneous turns).

Because these four conversations had been extensively transcribed for the purposes of the replication study, it was decided to use them, plus the other conversations in their respective blocks. It happened that each of the four replication conversations was from a different block, so these four blocks were used in the study. The number of smooth exchanges of the turn plus instances of simultaneous turns in the 12 new conversations ranged from 27 to 55; these values are above the mean for the entire set of conversations.

Identifying interactions and participants

In a series of papers (e.g., Duncan, 1972; D&F; Duncan, Brunner, & Fiske, 1979), results on interaction structure and on strategy signals have been reported. These studies used different, though sometimes overlapping, sets of conversations. D&F reported three studies (an individual-differences study, and two structure studies: an exploratory study and a "replication" study); once again, the conversations used were different but partially overlapping.

This situation is repeated in the studies reported in this monograph. As just described, the 16 conversations used for the strategy study were drawn from the 88 recorded for the D&F individual-differences study. Denny's research (Chapter 8) uses eight of these 16. Some of these conversations, then, were used in the individual-differences study, in the replication study, and in the strategy studies reported here, including Denny's subset.

Whereas the conversations used for each study are described in conjunction with that study, the use – or nonuse – of conversations in successive studies has nowhere been detailed. It also happens that a different numbering or identification system has been used in each of these studies. The D&F structural studies and the strategy-signal study used the same conversations, but in D&F the numbering referred only to full conversations, whereas in the strategy-signal study numbering identified individual participants. In addition, Denny used numbers to refer to whole conversations (making no differentiation between participants). This has made it impossible for readers to sort out just which conversations were used in which study.

Although sorting conversations by study is not likely to be a task of great fascination to other investigators, it does seem appropriate to provide some clarification of the picture, a kind of audit trail of conversations. At the very least, it is of some importance to show which of our 16 strategy-research conversations were in Denny's subset.

Table 5.1 shows the numbering used for the set of relevant studies: the D&F exploratory and replication studies, the strategy-signal paper, and the present strategy studies. It may be seen which conversations were used in more than one study.

Furthermore, the numbering system used in this monograph is shown. Each participant and conversation is identified by (a) the block in which he or she participated (I through IV), (b) sex, (c) Law School (L) or SSA (S), and conversation (1 or 2). Participants conversing with each other are shown by grouping. Thus, in the first block the first two conversations were between (a) I-F-L-1 and I-F-S-1, and (b) I-M-L-1 and I-M-S-1. The figure shows that the first of these two conversations was also used in the

Table 5.1. *Participants, interactions, and their numbers used in various studies*

D&F no.	Strategy signal no.	Block	Sex	School	Conversation no.	Kanki's study no.	Denny's study
1	1M						
1	1F						
2	2Ma						
2	2Mb						
3	3Ma						
3	3Mb						
4	4Fa						
4	4Fb						
		I	F	L	1	11	
		I	F	S	1	11	
		I	M	L	1	12	Yes
		I	M	S	1	12	Yes
7	7F	I	F	L	2	13	Yes
7	7M	I	M	S	2	13	Yes
		I	M	L	2	14	
		I	F	S	2	14	
8	8F	II	M	L	1	21	Yes
8	8M	II	F	S	1	21	Yes
		II	F	L	1	22	
		II	M	S	1	22	
		II	F	L	2	23	
		II	F	S	2	23	
		II	M	L	2	24	Yes
		II	M	S	2	24	Yes
		III	M	L	1	31	
		III	M	S	1	31	
		III	F	L	1	32	Yes
		III	F	S	1	32	Yes
5	5F	III	F	L	2	33	Yes
5	5M	III	M	S	2	33	Yes
		III	M	L	2	34	
		III	F	S	2	34	
6	6F	IV	F	L	1	41	Yes
6	6M	IV	M	S	1	41	Yes
		IV	M	L	1	42	
		IV	F	S	1	42	
		IV	M	L	2	43	
		IV	M	S	2	43	
		IV	F	L	2	44	Yes
		IV	F	S	2	44	Yes

D&F "replication" study and the strategy-signal study. The second conversation was also number 12 in Denny's study.

5.2. Transcription

In an exploratory study, the purpose is to discover phenomena of interest. As described in D&F, when the exploratory study of two-person conversations was undertaken, there was no notion of what sort of phenomena might be discovered. During the transcribing phase of the study, the idea of speaking turns and their exchange had not been considered as a possible phenomenon of interest. In this situation, decisions on what actions to include in the transcription become critical. Issues of transcribing in exploratory structural research on interaction were considered in the last chapter.

Purely exploratory research may be sharply distinguished from both hypothesis-testing and hypothesis-based research. The research on interaction strategy was not designed to test the turn-system hypotheses, but it was solidly based on them. Although the strategy research was exploratory in the sense of both exploring various approaches to studying phenomena, and attempting to discover strategy phenomena themselves, it was solidly based on existing hypotheses concerning turn-system signals, rules, and the like. These hypotheses made the direct strategy work possible. For this reason, the transcribing process for the strategy research did not have the risk-taking aspect just described. Actions transcribed for studying strategy were precisely those that have been hypothesized as playing a part in the structure of conversations, in addition to certain others necessary for defining units of analysis (to be described later) and the like.

Knowing what actions and aspects of actions are necessary for the research certainly facilitates the transcribing process. For example, in the original exploratory study, arm movements and hand positions were transcribed in elaborate detail (see D&F, pp. 158-161); for the strategy study, it was necessary only to transcribe whether or not the hand and arm were engaged in a gesticulation or in a self- or object-adaptor (Ekman & Friesen, 1969).

Scheflen (1966) has stated the case dramatically. Once the stream of interaction has been organized into standard structural units (such as the turn and within-turn units we have hypothesized), he characterizes the significant actions to be *"recognizable at a glance and recordable with a stroke"* (p. 277, original emphasis). Although the individuals who transcribed the actions on this project may have felt that Scheflen has overstated the case somewhat, the point remains that the previously hypothesized structural elements dictated the actions and the various distinctions necessarily included in the transcribing process. In addition to the actions playing a part in the turn system hypothesized in D&F, other actions were transcribed that were used in the construction of units of analysis in the original structural research, or that were subsequently added to the original structural hypotheses (Brunner, 1979).

The actual transcribing process was not quite so facile as that described by Scheflen. While actions were readily recognizable, the process of accurately locating each action with respect to every other action is a demanding one, especially when done the traditional way, by hand. However, reliable information on the sequences of actions in the stream of interaction was as necessary in this study as in the preceding ones; the turn-system hypotheses were formulated in terms of action sequences involving both participants.

Actions transcribed

As indicated in the preceding discussion, great care was taken to locate all actions in the stream of interaction. The actual transcribing involved the following actions. The codes are indicated for these actions.

Words. Syllables were transcribed orthographically. Each syllable was marked as the first syllable of a word ("X-"), the last syllable, the middle syllable, or a single-syllable word. All overlaps in the participants' speech were carefully transcribed.

Word-related classes. GC marked the syllable on which a dependent or independent syntactic clause was completed, as defined in D&F. TA indicates a sociocentric sequence (Bernstein, 1962). FP indicates a filled pause, such as "uh." UFP indicates an unfilled pause. IN indicates an audible inhalation, and EX indicates an audible exhalation. CL indicates a click, and D indicates a paralinguistic drawl on a single syllable.

Intonation. Following D&F, three levels of intonation pitch were recorded, indicated by 1, 2, or 3, where 1 is the highest level, and 2, the normal or unmarked level. There was one degree of intonation stress (S); and there were three terminal junctures or contours: rising (R), falling (F), and sustained or level (L). These correspond to Trager and Smith's (1957) symbols ||, #, and |, respectively.

Body motion. Transcribed in body motion were (a) head nods and shakes (N and S), (b) head direction toward or away from the partner, (c) gesticulation, separately for each hand, and (d) smiles and laughs.

Transcribing conventions. Dashes mark the beginning (X-) or ending (-X) of an event. A plus (+) indicates a back-to-back sequence in which two events of the same class occur on the same syllable, one event ending and the other beginning. When the beginning or ending of an event, such as a gesture, occurred out of view of the camera (such as behind the body), the point of appearance or disappearance was indicated by an asterisk (*). Difficulty in transcribing the beginning or ending of an event (such as a smile) was indicated by a question mark (?). The asterisk and question mark permitted elimination of problematic events in the transcription from subsequent analyses.

Units of analysis. The stream of interaction was broken into units for the purpose of analysis, as in D&F. Briefly, a unit of analysis was defined as beginning at the onset of the first syllable following the end of a phonemic clause (indicated by an intonation terminal juncture), during or immediately after which at least one of the following actions occurred: (a) a rising or falling terminal juncture, (b) a sociocentric sequence, (c) completion of a syntactic clause, (d) paralinguistic drawl, (e) audible inhalation, (f) unfilled pause, (g) false start, (h) the ending of a gesticulation, and (i) a shift in speaker's head toward the auditor. A unit of analysis terminates when the next unit starts.

Units of analysis (SG) were indicated in the transcription, together with the following information. Does an exchange of a speaking turn follow the unit, and is that exchange a smooth one (as defined in Chapter 3), or is it marked by simultaneous claiming of the turn by both participants? Do simultaneous turns occur without an exchange of the turn? Does an instance of simultaneous turns continue from the previous unit? Is the unit the first unit of a new speaking turn?

Back channels. Three types of back channels (BC) were indicated in the transcription: (a) head nods and shakes, (b) verbal back channels, such as "yeah," and "m-hm," and (c) smiles. These were indicated for both speaker and auditor. Treatment of back channels is complicated by the fact that, within a given unit of analysis, these three types of back channels can occur in any combination and not necessarily at the same moment. In addition, more than one of the same type of back channel can occur;

examples would be "yeah, yeah," and two smiles. Second back channels of each type were indicated as such. The location of each back channel was coded as follows: (a) in the gap between the last syllable of the present unit and the first syllable of the next unit; (b) during the last syllable(s) of the present unit; (c) during the middle of a unit; (d) during the first syllable(s) of the next unit; (e) before or during a sociocentric sequence (sociocentric sequences were not treated as separate units but were included in the same unit with the syllables they followed); (f) continued from the previous unit and ending on the present unit; (g) continued from the previous unit, through the present unit, and into the following unit; and (h) before or during a filled pause. When a back channel was given by a speaker, it was additionally coded in terms of whether or not it occurred at the beginning of a turn.

5.3. Units of analysis

One final topic requires our consideration before the results are presented: definition of units of analysis. The discussion of such units does not figure prominently in the "nonverbal communication" literature, and indeed they are not necessary in "external-variable" studies. In those studies, one need only record the occurrence or duration of each action, such as gaze toward the auditor or smiling.

However, in many data analyses relevant to structural hypotheses and to consequent strategy research, it becomes necessary to know not only how many times a given action occurred but also how many times it did not occur. To count the number of times an action did not occur, we need to segment the entire stream of interaction into units of analysis; then we can observe in each unit whether or not the action occurred.

For example, many of our structural analyses are concerned with the relation between some signal by the participant and some subsequent action by the partner. In the simplest case, this relationship can be tested in a 2 × 2 table, cross-classifying the occurrence and nonoccurrence of the signal with the subsequent occurrence or nonoccurrence of the action. Obviously, one cell in the table shows counts of the number of times neither signal nor action occurred. It is to fill in this necessary cell of the table that units of analysis are required.

In exploratory research, the definition of units of analysis is a paradoxical process. One wishes the units to be as relevant as possible to the interaction phenomena to be analyzed, but these phenomena are precisely what is not known, remaining to be discovered. This is clearly a point in the exploratory-research process where the intuition, common sense – and luck – of the investigator are at a premium.

It seems unlikely that a single type of unit of analysis will suffice for all exploratory research on interaction. Different types of interaction will almost certainly require different approaches to defining units of analysis. In any event, this phase of the research demands the most careful consideration by the investigator.

The process by which units of analysis were defined in this research was described in some detail in D&F. In this section, we shall simply describe the units themselves. For our conversations, units were defined in terms of the occurrence of a variety of actions in both speech and body motion by the speaker. This approach may be contrasted with more common procedures in which units are based either on time intervals (such as a second), or on some single aspect of action (such as syntax).

In general, the boundary of a unit of analysis was located at (a) the onset of the first syllable, (b) following the end of a phonemic clause, (c) during or immediately after which there occurred at least one of the following actions.

1. *Intonation:* the presence of a phonemic clause that deviated in intonation from the 2 2 | pattern, as described in the section on intonation.
2. *Speech content:* the utterance of one of several stereotyped expressions, termed "sociocentric sequences" by Bernstein (1962). Examples of sociocentric sequences are "you know" and "or something."
3. *Syntax:* the completion of a grammatical clause, involving a subject-predicate combination.
4. *Drawl:* the utterance of a paralinguistic drawl on the final syllable or on the stressed syllable of a phonemic clause.
5. *Pitch or loudness:* a decrease of paralinguistic pitch or loudness, either across an entire phonemic clause or during its final syllable or syllables.
6. *Audible inhalation:* the occurrence of an audible inhalation by the speaker.
7. *Unfilled pause:* the occurrence of an unfilled pause (a silent pause having no phonation, such as "um" or "uh").
8. *False start:* an utterance by the speaker that is stopped and restarted for some reason.
9. *Gesticulation:* termination of any hand gesticulation or the relaxation of a tensed hand position, such that both hands are at rest (not gesticulating) and relaxed. Gesticulations are distinguished from self-adaptors (Ekman & Friesen, 1969), defined here as hand movements in which the hand comes in contact with one's own body or apparel, often with the appearance of grooming. Also excluded were object-adaptors, such as maintaining one's pipe, rubbing the arm of the chair, adjusting paper on a clipboard, and taking a tissue. Gesticulations are defined as all hand and arm movements that are not self- or object-adaptors.
10. *Head direction:* turning the head toward the partner, from a position in which the head is pointing away. This component of units of analysis was

Table 5.2. *Length (in milliseconds) of units of analysis in eight conversations*

Conversation number	N	Mean	Standard deviation	Range
12	51	890.8	667.3	196–3,580
13	31	1,190.9	700.2	395–2,845
21	31	1,363.9	720.1	507–3,170
24	33	1,064.2	728.9	160–2,963
32	44	1,182.9	701.7	161–3,321
33	32	1,155.6	598.1	547–3,095
41	37	1,021.9	678.2	243–2,920
44	38	1,071.2	710.5	232–3,595

erroneously reported in D&F as the reverse: turning of head away from the partner.

11. *Foot movement:* a relaxation of the foot or feet from a marked dorsal flexion.

Boundaries were not drawn at the onset of filled pauses or sociocentric sequences by the speaker, or at the onset of auditor back channels. A new unit of analysis was begun at the onset of each new speaking turn, regardless of the actions that preceded that new turn. Greater detail and illustrations of the procedure can be found in D&F.

Duration of units

Defined in terms of the actions of the speaker, the units did not have a uniform duration. They were designed to follow the flow of the interaction. They could be as brief as a single syllable or as long as several phonemic clauses. We were curious about the temporal length of the units because we had never measured it.

Ten percent of the units were sampled from each of the eight conversations studied by Denny, as shown in Table 5.2, and the duration (in milliseconds) of these units was measured using procedures described by Denny in Chapter 8. Results of this sampling are summarized in Table 5.2. Mean unit duration was very close to one second, with appreciable variation ranging from 160 ms to 3595 ms. All the distributions are clearly skewed. These data may be of some interest to colleagues concerned with the duration of speech events.

We are now in a position to begin looking at results.

6. Propaedeutica: structure-related research

STARKEY DUNCAN, JR., AND DONALD W. FISKE

Once the transcribing and coding processes were completed and the data were entered in the computer, we were in a position to begin data analyses. However, this did not mean proceeding to strategy analyses directly. Several preparatory tasks were necessary.

We had to show that structural hypotheses derived from studies of other interactions also applied to the interactions we had just transcribed, thereby legitimating the strategy research on these interactions. Thus, a *structure-assessment* study was necessary. We also implemented some modifications of the original structural hypotheses. These were tested in the present interactions in a *turn-system modification* study. Finally, to permit strategy analyses involving numerous partitions of the data, it was necessary to work with a simplified version of the turn system. This system was tested in a *turn-system simplification* study. In this chapter, these studies will be described before we take up the strategy research proper.

6.1. Structure-assessment study

In Chapter 2, we considered the issue of generalizing from results in studies of convention. Problems of generalizing arise because (a) members of different cultures or subcultures may use different conventions to accomplish comparable coordination problems, and (b) within a single culture or subculture and for the same coordination problem, different conventions may be used, depending on the participants' definition of the situation or context. For these reasons, a conventional regularity found to be operating in a set of observed interactions cannot be assumed to be operating in some new set of interactions; cultural or situational shifts may have occurred. It should be emphasized that we see these considerations and others mentioned in this chapter as applying to all work on convention, not just our studies of conversations.

Given these potential complexities, we could not simply plunge directly into the strategy study proper. We needed first to carry out a *structure-assessment* study designed to verify that it was reasonable to consider the structural phenomena, hypothesized on the basis of work on other conversations, to be operating also in the conversations that we would be using for the strategy research.

There were two major considerations dictating the necessity of the structure-assessment study. (a) At least at the beginning, the strategy research was to be based on previously hypothesized structural phenomena. (b) As emphasized in Chapter 2, we do not claim to know the extent to which the turn-system hypotheses can be generalized. It follows that, when strategy studies make use of new sets of conversations, investigators must check the new conversations to make sure that it is reasonable to claim that the structural elements relevant to the strategy study are actually operating in the new conversations. Obviously, it would make little sense for us to base our strategy research on the turn-system hypotheses if those hypotheses did not apply to the conversations being studied. Therefore, we began the strategy research with a structure-assessment study.

Method

Conversations. It will be recalled that one conversation in each of the four blocks has already been used in the "replication" study reported in D&F. Thus, for the structure-assessment study, we analyzed data from the remaining three conversations in each block. To permit direct comparison of structure-assessment results with results from preceding studies, we present three sets of results for most analyses: (a) exploratory study (two conversations), (b) "replication" study (six conversations, including one from each of the four blocks used for the strategy study), and (c) structure-assessment study (12 conversations, the remaining three conversations from each of the four blocks). Results from each of the blocks are shown separately for most analyses.

Analytic Procedure. In testing the new set of conversations, it was necessary, of course, to replicate as closely as possible the procedures used in the previous structural study. Actions were defined as cues and signals just as they were in D&F, and analyses strictly paralleled those in the original structure study, permitting close comparison of results. Changes and additions to the turn system noted in Chapter 3 (bracketed by pound signs) were not incorporated in these analyses. They will be treated later.

In addition to the parallel analyses, both previous and current data were analyzed using the cross-product ratio and related measures. The added analyses permit even closer comparison of results (because of their independence of N), as well as providing a more appropriate approach to analyzing these data. These points deserve brief expansion.

In D&F, data were analyzed primarily in terms of chi-square. For a "replication" study centrally concerned with comparing results across data sets, chi-square is particularly inconvenient because it is highly influenced by N, which is never constant from one set of our interactions to another. (This is because we always include in the analyses every occurrence of a given action or phenomenon, rather than sampling some fixed number. Obviously, we have no control over the number of signal displays, speaking-turn exchanges, and auditor back channels in a conversation.)

Since the publication of D&F, we have adopted log-linear analysis with its great versatility and its ability to handle complex, multidimensional cross-tabulated data. To facilitate comparison of results, we shall in the structure-assessment study retain the simple 2 × 2 table format used in D&F, even though log-linear analysis is capable of much more complex analyses. For the 2 × 2 tables we shall be using the cross-product ratio (symbolized by alpha), computed simply by dividing the product of cell 1 and cell 4 by the product of cell 2 and cell 3.

The cross-product ratio ranges from zero to infinity, reaching infinity when one cell (in a 2 × 2 table) is zero. The strength of association between the variables represented by the cross-product ratio may be evaluated by Q, computed by dividing (alpha − 1) by (alpha + 1). Q ranges from −1 to +1, "taking the value 0 when the row and column variables are independent and the value 1 or -1 when there is complete positive or negative association . . . ." (Bishop, Fienberg, & Holland, 1975, p. 379).

Q is independent of N and thus permits direct comparison across data sets. Also presented in the results will be the z score associated with the obtained Q. The z score, of course, reintroduces the effect of N, but it is included here to permit reference to more familiar statistics.

For each set of results reported in the 2 × 2 form, we shall report (a) raw numbers, (b) chi-square as presented in D&F, and (c) alpha, Q, and the associated z.

Results

Speaker turn signal. The speaker turn signal is hypothesized to account for the smooth exchange of the speaking turn in the observed conversations, and to differentiate these smooth exchanges from instances of simultaneous claiming of the turn by the two participants. Table 6.1 shows data from the comparable Table 11.5 (p. 193) in D&F, together with data from each of the four blocks in the structure assessment study. Ideal results would show zeros in cells 1 (no signal; smooth exchange) and 4 (signal present; simultaneous turns).

Results from the assessment study show a substantial percentage of smooth exchanges preceded by the turn signal. This percentage is the probability of an antecedent, discussed in the preceding chapter. Although Q varies somewhat from one set of results to another, it is generally quite high. There appears to be a consistent and strong relationship between the hypothesized turn signal and the smooth-exchange/simultaneous-turns distinction.

Relevant probabilities of a consequent may be found in Table 6.2 in the column: No gesticulation signal – Proportion turn attempts. In all of our studies, there has been a relatively low percentage of auditor attempts to take the speaking turn in response to speaker turn-signal display. These results continue to confirm our original interpretation of the turn signal as involving optional auditor response.

Speaker gesticulation signal. The gesticulation signal was hypothesized to nullify any turn signal concurrently being displayed. When the gesticulation signal was displayed during the active period of the turn signal, auditor claims of the speaking turn were strikingly reduced. The speaker gesticulation signal is hypothesized to be composed of a single cue: one or both of the speaker's hands being engaged in gesticulation or in a tensed hand position. Although data indicate that the gesticulation signal reduces

Table 6.1. *Smooth exchanges of the turn and simultaneous turns resulting from auditor's turn-taking attempts when the speaker turn signal was switched on or not switched on*

Data set	Turn signal switched on	Smooth exchange of turn	Simultaneous turns	χ^2	Proportion smooth exchanges preceded by signal	α	Q	z
Exploratory	No	0	12	52.31	1.00	∞		
	Yes	81	7					
Replication	No	3	22	56.33	.98	34.74	.94	27.08
	Yes	180	38					
Block 1	No	8	10	15.71	.92	8.48	.79	7.55
	Yes	95	14					
Block 2	No	6	8	27.32	.93	28.00	.93	18.79
	Yes	84	5					
Block 3	No	5	7	26.74	.95	24.50	.92	16.97
	Yes	105	6					
Block 4	No	6	13	19.39	.93	10.83	.83	9.44
	Yes	75	15					

Table 6.2. *Effect of gesticulation signal on auditor attempts to take the turn when the turn signal is active*

Data set	No gesticulation signal		Gesticulation signal active		χ^2	α	Q	z
	No. units	Proportion turn attempts	No. units	Proportion turn attempts				
Exploratory	416	.21	361	.01	66.31	40.92	.95	28.41
Replication	868	.24	197	.07	25.52	4.02	.60	6.53
Block 1	632	.17	139	.04	15.78	5.59	.70	5.78
Block 2	503	.17	111	.02	16.67	11.56	.84	7.93
Block 3	548	.20	202	.04	28.15	6.16	.72	7.97
Block 4	546	.17	216	.06	15.01	3.36	.54	4.80

auditor turn attempts whenever it is displayed, the hypothesized effect of the signal is related more directly to instances when it is displayed concurrently with a turn signal. For this reason, Table 6.2 shows data on auditor response to the speaker turn signal with and without a concurrent gesticulation signal. Data for the exploratory and "replication" studies were taken from Tables 11.3 and 11.4, respectively (pp. 191 & 192) in D&F.

Results from the assessment study are consistent with those from the earlier studies. Although the strength of the exploratory-study results is not matched by subsequent studies, the results of the assessment study are quite strong. Given a speaker turn signal, the presence of the gesticulation signal effected a 65%-88% reduction in speaker turn attempts. Of the 668 units in which there was both a turn signal and gesticulation signal, there were only 29 turn attempts – a rate of 4%.

Speaker-state signal. The speaker-state signal was hypothesized to differentiate two types of vocalization by the auditor: attempts to take the turn, and vocal back channels. Auditor back channels were not considered to be turns or attempts to take the turn. The speaker-state signal was hypothesized to accompany the beginnings of turn attempts, permitting the former speaker to recognize immediately that the auditor's utterance is a turn beginning, complementing and presumably facilitating the more complex judgment based on the verbal form of the utterance.

Data on the speaker-state signal were presented in Table 11.9 in D&F. These data include results on four potential speaker-state cues: (a) shift in head direction away from the partner, (b) beginning a gesticulation, (c) audible inhalation, and (d) paralinguistic overloudness. The signal itself, however, was hypothesized to involve the first two of these cues. In the structure-assessment study, the first three of these cues were also analyzed. Results were strong for both the two-cue and three-cue sets. To permit comparison of results and for the sake of brevity, Table 6.3 shows data only for the the two-cue set. The table in D&F presented results separately for the two conversations in the exploratory study; the same form is followed in Table 6.3.

Once again, the results of the assessment study conform to those of the earlier studies, with the results of the exploratory study somewhat stronger than those of the subsequent studies. The Q's for the assessment study are quite high. Few vocal auditor back channels are marked by the speaker-state signal. The proportion of turn beginnings marked by the signal in the assessment study is essentially the same as that found in the two "replication" studies. The reason why this proportion is not higher will be considered later in this chapter.

Speaker within-turn signal. Auditor back channels (either vocal or visible) were said to be preceded by the speaker within-turn signal, just as smooth exchanges of the turn were said to be preceded by the speaker turn signal. That is, the speaker within-turn signal was hypothesized to mark points in the interaction where auditors might appropriately respond with a back channel. However, like the turn signal, the within-turn signal is considered to be permissive: The auditor is not obliged to respond with a back channel upon display of the signal. Data on the within-turn signal were presented in Table 11.8 (p. 214) in D&F. Table 6.4 presents the same data, though in a slightly different form, together with the comparable data from blocks 1-4. The data shown for blocks 1-4 are different from those in D&F in one respect: they include auditor smiling as a back channel. Brunner (1979) presented evidence supporting the hypothesis that auditor smiles may be considered a form of auditor back channel. Brunner's results were replicated in blocks 1-4. Briefly, 90% of auditor smiles were preceded by the speaker within-turn signal. In Table 6.4, the new results are again consistent with the earlier ones. A high percentage of auditor back channels were preceded by the speaker within-turn signal.

Table 6.3. *Display of two-cue speaker–state signal in conjunction with turn beginnings and with vocal auditor back channels*

Data set	Turn beginnings		Vocal auditor back channels		χ^2	α	Q	z
	N	Proportion marked by signal	N	Proportion marked by signal				
Conversation 2: exploratory	20	.95	85	.14	47.09	115.58	.98	53.89
Conversation 1: initial replication	61	.62	32	.03	27.80	51.22	.96	24.38
Replication study	183	.70	179	.19	92.96	9.93	.82	19.68
Block 1	85	.66	150	.08	85.61	22.21	.91	29.31
Block 2	75	.73	48	.13	40.93	19.25	.90	18.87
Block 3	101	.71	74	.13	55.03	15.91	.88	19.57
Block 4	78	.68	125	.18	48.25	9.40	.81	13.88

Table 6.4. *Auditor back channels preceded by the speaker within-turn signal*

	No. units having display	Proportion back channels preceded by signal	χ^2	a	Q	z
Exploratory study	499	.89	39.31	5.56	.70	9.13
Replication study	718	.93	55.26	4.92	.66	10.37
Block 1	776	.85	44.50	3.85	.59	8.51
Block 2	658	.90	22.37	4.58	.64	6.39
Block 3	838	.95	22.93	6.30	.73	7.21
Block 4	713	.82	28.71	3.09	.51	6.42

Discussion

Considering the results both separately and as a whole, we conclude that the turn-system regularities observed in earlier studies are also operating in the conversations to be used in the strategy research. It therefore becomes appropriate to proceed with strategy studies on these conversations based on the hypothesized regularities.

Before moving on to the next stages of our research, we might consider for a moment what would have been the effect of a failure to obtain positive results in the structure-assessment study. To simplify the discussion, as well as to present a worst-case example, let us assume that the assessment study failed to produce positive turn-system results in most important respects, and that we were constrained to do the proposed strategy research on the set of conversations used in the assessment study, rather than the conversations previously studied.

[In this discussion, we have two sets of conversations: (a) an "old" set on which the original structural hypotheses were based, and (b) a "new" set to which these hypotheses were applied in the assessment study.]

Lack of positive results on the structure-assessment study would entail a series of events: (a) We would experience great irritation and frustration at not being able to move ahead with the planned strategy research. (b) An exploratory study would have to be undertaken to develop hypotheses concerning structural elements in the new conversations (those that did not return the expected results). (c) Assuming that this exploratory study on the new conversations produced some hypotheses concerning turn-related phenomena, the new hypotheses would be applied to the old conversations; perhaps the new hypotheses would fit those old conversations better than did the original hypotheses. (d) If the new hypotheses fit better, the old hypotheses would have been considered superseded and therefore would have been discarded. (e) If the new hypotheses did not fit well, the new conversations would be regarded as showing a different set of turn-related conventions from the old ones. At the end of this process, one would hope that there would still be some time and money left for the intended strategy research on the new conversations.

If this discussion of new and old conversations and new and old hypotheses is not too confusing, the general plan should be clear. It is necessary to establish structural hypotheses on which to base strategy research. If available hypotheses prove inadequate, then new ones must be generated.

If it proves true that the available hypotheses remain acceptable for the previously studied conversations, and that the new hypotheses fit the new conversations, then one would conclude that the two sets of conversations manifest different conventions for managing the same phenomenon (in this case, turns). The source of the shift in conventions then might itself become the object of study.

Fortunately, it turned out that all of this was unnecessary, so we can move to the next steps in the research process.

6.2. Turn-system modifications

Since the publication of D&F we have made several modifications of the turn-system hypotheses. These modifications were indicated by pound signs in Chapter 3. Some changes were suggested by further structural work done after completion of D&F; other changes resulted directly from our strategy research. Strategy research involves continued scrutiny of the structural hypotheses on which it is based. It is not surprising that improved structural hypotheses would be a by-product of strategy research.

The various modifications will be taken up in the order in which they were described in Chapter 3.

Elimination of the turn cue: decrease of paralinguistic pitch or loudness on a sociocentric sequence

This change scarcely requires discussion. The motivation for the change is entirely logical: The cue is dependent on occurrence of a sociocentric sequence. That is, the cue cannot occur alone; it can only co-occur with a sociocentric sequence. For this reason, the cue cannot contribute to the results. It cannot help to account for smooth exchanges of the speaking turn because a sociocentric sequence would always be present to accomplish that task. Similarly, it cannot help to differentiate smooth exchanges from instances of simultaneous turns. The cue was proposed in Duncan (1972), the first publication of turn-system results. However, it should never have been included in D&F.

Change of the switch-off point for termination of a hand gesticulation

In D&F, the switch-off point for this cue was the onset of the first syllable of the third unit of analysis following its display. We have changed the switch-off point to the onset of the first syllable of the next unit of analysis following its display. This change brings the switch-off point for this cue into line with all the other turn-signal cues. The change has no effect on the essential results: the percentage of smooth exchanges preceded by a turn signal, and the differentiation of smooth exchanges from instances of simultaneous turns. In fact, in the conversations used for the strategy research, the gesticulation-end cue was of only minimal importance. However, we feel that it should be retained as a component of the turn signal because it had considerable importance in other conversations we have studied. We believe that it is likely to prove useful in future studies.

Elliptical grammatical completion

This addition to the grammatical-completion cue was developed by Denny in work on half of the 16 conversations used in the strategy research. Elliptical grammatical completion was described in detail in Chapter 2. Consequently, results relevant to this change will be based on her eight conversations. These conversations are identified in Table 5.1 of Chapter 5.

Table 6.5 shows results on Denny's conversations, calculated similarly to Table 6.1. Also shown in Table 6.5 are the results on Denny's conversations when elliptical grammatical completion is added to the standard definition of grammatical completion. As a result of adding elliptical grammatical completion, eight smooth turn exchanges were shifted from

Table 6.5. *Smooth exchanges of the turn and simultaneous turns resulting from auditor's turn-taking attempts when the speaker turn signal was switched on or not switched on (gesticulation signal absent)*

Turn signal switched on	Smooth exchange of turn	Simultaneous turns	Proportion smooth exchanges preceded by signal	α	Q	z
Standard grammatical-completion definition						
No	20	28	.93	11.88	.84	16.90
Yes	263	31				
Elliptical grammatical-completion added						
No	12	28	.96	20.40	.91	25.84
Yes	271	31				

Table 6.6. *Auditor response to elliptical grammatical completion and accompanying turn cues (gesticulation signal absent)*

	Elliptical grammatical completion only	Elliptical grammatical completion plus turn cues	Total
No turn attempt	8	31	39
Smooth exchange	8	12	20
Simultaneous turns	1	0	1
Total	17	43	60

the no-turn-signal cell to the turn-signal cell. There is a moderate strengthening of associated statistical results.

Table 6.5 does not include instances in which the gesticulation signal was displayed with elliptical grammatical completion. There were only two such instances, both resulting in no auditor attempt to take the turn. In one case, elliptical grammatical completion occurred alone, and in one, it was accompanied by intonation.

Table 6.6 shows some results on auditor response to elliptical grammatical completion. As may be seen, elliptical grammatical completions typically occurred with other turn cues (43/60 = .72).Not shown in Table 6.6 is that, when elliptical grammatical completion occurred with other turn cues, the most prominent one was intonation (40/43 = .93). When elliptical grammatical completion occurred alone, there was a substantial rate of auditor attempts to take the turn (9/17 = .53). For these attempts, only one failed to result in a smooth exchange of the turn (8/9 = .89). Thus, within the limits of the small N, elliptical grammatical completion appears to function adequately as a turn cue.

We conclude that incorporation of elliptical grammatical completion into the definition of the grammatical-completion turn cue is justified. Certainly, this decision seems intuitively appropriate. It should be noted, however, that this expanded definition of grammatical completion was not used in the studies reported in Chapters 9 and 10.

Smiles as auditor back channels

Brunner (1979) described results suggesting that the occurrence and location of auditor smiling were highly similar to other auditor back channels. Based on these results, auditor smiling might be regarded as another form of auditor back channels. An alternative to this general view is provided by Mokros in Chapter 9, where a more comprehensive analysis is made of both speaker and auditor smiling. In any event, on the basis of Brunner's work it is possible to add auditor smiling to the list of back channels.

6.3. Turn-system simplification

Both the "replication" study (D&F) and the structure-assessment study (reported earlier in this chapter) showed the results of applying the original turn-system hypotheses to new data sets. In those two studies, the full turn system as originally formulated was assessed. Taken as a whole, the system appeared to operate effectively in those new data sets.

In some of the strategy studies to be described in following chapters, a change of approach is called for: It will be convenient to use an abbreviated form of the turn system. Both the complexity of the analyses performed and the need for numerous partitions of the data make it useful – and sometimes necessary – to minimize the differentiations made in the turn system.

To achieve this simplification, we propose to use a version of the turn system composed of three signals: (a) the gesticulation signal, as originally hypothesized, (b) the speaker-gaze strategy signal, as originally hypothesized, and (c) the speaker turn signal, formulated in terms of a single cue: grammatical completion.

This abbreviated version is capable of producing most of the strongest effects of the turn system. (a) The gesticulation signal powerfully suppresses auditor attempts to take the turn. (b) The speaker-gaze signal consistently increases the probability of auditor turn attempts when the turn signal is also active, and the gesticulation signal is not active. And (c) the grammatical-completion cue, considered alone, does an excellent job of differentiating smooth exchanges of the turn from instances of simultaneous turns in the conversations we used for strategy analyses.

There are several advantages to be gained from simplifying the system for strategy analyses. By simplifying the definition of the turn signal to a single cue, it is possible to decrease the number of partitions in the data resulting from displays of varying numbers of turn cues. It will be apparent in the following chapters that data partitions are a major problem in the analyses. Obviously, the number of signals included in the analyses is also reduced. This is a major help in the partitioning problem. Finally, a certain elegance in the analyses is achieved because the simplified system permits a single set of signals to account for both turn attempts and auditor back channels. Grammatical completion and speaker gaze were hypothesized as the constituent cues of the within-turn signal that systematically preceded auditor back channels.

The data relevant to the proposed simplification are shown in Table 6.7. These data, unlike those in Tables 6.1 through 6.4, are summarized over the full 16 conversations used in the strategy study. (It will be recalled that in Tables 6.1 through 6.4, four of the sixteen conversations were part of the "replication" study, and the remaining twelve were represented in blocks 1 to 4.)

Speaker gesticulation signal

In Table 6.7, when the gesticulation signal and turn signal (now defined as grammatical completion alone) are concurrently active, the proportion of auditor turn attempts is .10; when the gesticulation signal is not active but the turn signal is, the proportion is .35. These proportions are somewhat higher than in Table 6.2 because (a) some turn cues are now placed in the no-signal class, and (b) there is a higher rate of response to grammatical completion than to the other turn cues in these conversations. The cross-product ratio for the 2×2 table is comparable, however: alpha = 4.79, $Q = .65$, $z = 10.63$.

Table 6.7. *Simplified, three-signal turn system: auditor response and subsequent smooth exchange or simultaneous turns*

	Speaker gaze absent		Speaker gaze present	
	Grammatical completion absent	Grammatical completion present	Grammatical completion absent	Grammatical completion present
Gesticulation signal absent				
No auditor response	1,276	391	1,586	396
Smooth exchange	27	52	106	359
Simultaneous turns	21	4	73	17
Gesticulation signal present				
No auditor response	577	104	773	123
Smooth exchange	1	6	4	16
Simultaneous turns	5	0	24	4

Grammatical completion as speaker turn signal

In this data set, when the turn signal is defined as grammatical completion alone, 76% of all smooth exchanges are preceded by grammatical completion, as opposed to 92% for the full turn signal. In contrast, 83% of all instances of simultaneous turns are preceded by no grammatical completion, as opposed to 57% preceded by no turn signal as originally defined. Thus, the full turn signal accounts for more smooth exchanges but also precedes more instances of simultaneous turns. The statistics for the two versions of the signal are quite comparable, however. For grammatical completion alone, alpha = 15.44, $Q = .88$, $z = 32.00$. For the full turn signal, alpha = 16.12, $Q = .88$, $z = 16.12$.

Speaker gaze

Speaker gaze directed toward the auditor is hypothesized both as a cue of the within-turn signal related to auditor back channels, and, when occurring together with the turn signal, as a *strategy signal* increasing the probability of an auditor's acting to take the speaking turn. The notion of strategy signals and relevant results are presented in the next chapter.

The data in Table 6.7 indicate an effect for speaker gaze comparable to that shown in Table 7.1. When the speaker gesticulation signal is not active, the rate of auditor turn attempts in response to the speaker turn signal (defined as grammatical completion) and no speaker gaze is .125; in response to the speaker turn signal and speaker gaze, the rate is .487. The ratio of these proportions is 3.89. Comparable figures from Table 7.1 (using the full turn-signal definition) are .056, .278, and 4.93. Once again, there are higher rates of response to the simplified turn signal, but the head-direction signal has a substantial effect.

Discussion

We conclude that it is possible to carry out analyses using the simplified version of the turn system without doing violence to the data.

The proposed simplification was possible because of the effectiveness of the single cue, grammatical completion, with respect to speaking-turn exchanges. Auditors in these conversations responded to this cue at a higher rate than to any other single cue. Disregarding speaker gaze and in the absence of gesticulation, auditors responded with turn attempts to 32% of the displays of grammatical completion when it occurred alone, without other turn cues. In contrast, only 6% of single, intonation-cue displays and 15% of single, sociocentric-sequence-cue displays were so responded to. At the same time, grammatical completion, occurring either singly or in combination with other turn cues, was highly effective in differentiating smooth exchanges: 96% of all auditor turn attempts resulted in smooth exchanges when grammatical completion occurred alone, and 95%, when it occurred with other turn cues. It may be seen that grammatical completion played a central role in turn exchanges in these data.

The question naturally arises, then, whether the turn signal might be redefined to involve only grammatical completion. This question raises a number of issues that deeply involve the judgment of the investigator. We would say that, given our data, we are not inclined to change the basic definition of the turn signal.

One issue concerns the percentage of smooth exchanges of the turn that are preceded by the signal. As described above, when the signal definition is shifted from the full five cues to grammatical completion alone, the percentage of smooth exchanges accounted for drops from 92% to 83%. Evaluation of these results is complicated by the fact that of the 433 smooth exchanges preceded by grammatical completion, 352 (81%) were also preceded by other turn cues. Thus, most smooth exchanges were preceded by grammatical completion, plus at least one other turn cue. With each new data set, the investigator must decide just what percentage of smooth exchanges accounted for is adequate and must ascertain what is typically happening prior to these exchanges.

Further, it seems inevitable that there will be both variation in signal display by the speaker and variation in auditor response tendencies between individuals and between conversations. For this reason, the relative importance of various cues will not remain constant as different conversations are studied. Two simple examples illustrate this phenomenon.

First, in Table 7.1 the data show that one participant as auditor in both conversations (I-M-L-1 & I-M-L-2) never took the turn in the absence of the speaker-gaze signal. In the same interactional context, other auditors took the turn at a rate of 12% to 14%. (All auditors, of course, showed an increase in responsiveness when the gaze signal was displayed.)

The second example concerns grammatical completion itself. This cue has a potential for effectiveness as an element of the turn signal to the extent that speakers use complex grammatical constructions, so that the signal does not appear at virtually every unit boundary. This grammatical complexity was the case for our professional-school students at the University of Chicago. The grammatical-completion cue was present in only 25% of the units. This complexity has also been observed in other conversations we have studied.

However, when a participant uses simple grammatical constructions, the cue can blanket his or her units with the result that, with the cue being everywhere, it cannot effectively differentiate smooth from simultaneous exchanges of the turn. This was definitely the case in one of the conversations in the original exploratory study.

Thus, defining the turn signal in terms of grammatical completion alone would seem to be a kind of luxury that may be indulged when participants use sufficiently complex syntax, and certain other conditions obtain. It cannot be taken for granted in all conversations. And one would hesitate to define the turn signal so that it worked effectively only in relatively formal conversations between the well educated.

Drawl and gesture end. While considering cue effectiveness, it should be pointed out that two of the turn-signal cues – paralinguistic drawl and end of a gesticulation – functioned poorly as turn cues in this data set. There was only one auditor attempt to take the turn when drawl occurred alone, and that attempt resulted in simultaneous turns. Of the 29 auditor turn attempts in response to the display of gesture ending as a single cue, 18 resulted in simultaneous turns. Gesture ending, then, failed badly in differentiating smooth exchanges from simultaneous turns. These two cues would not be included in a turn signal formulated entirely on the basis of these data. Both cues functioned more effectively in other conversations we have studied, and only further research can reveal how the cues hold up in new data sets.

We are now in a position to begin presenting the various strategy studies. These studies will be described in the next four chapters.

7. Strategy signals

STARKEY DUNCAN, JR., AND DONALD W. FISKE

In many ways the first set of results to emerge from the strategy research proper was the most surprising: a set of phenomena that we termed *strategy signals*. Although the strategy research was entirely exploratory, designed to discover strategy-related phenomena, we never anticipated a need to hypothesize a new set of signals, clearly differentiated empirically and conceptually from those already posited for interaction structure. We had regarded the structure signals as entirely sufficient. The new results were unsettling because they seemed to push at the boundaries of our methodology and conceptual framework, requiring further consideration of a number of issues. Not the least of these issues is the broad differentiation of structure from strategy. Many of these issues will be taken up in the discussion section of this chapter.

The rationale for strategy signals is a somewhat complicated one. Students at Chicago are often told that the work on strategy signals bears special attention because, if they can grasp the reason why we felt compelled to hypothesize strategy signals, it is a good sign that they have a firm understanding of our approach to research as a whole. We shall consider the rationale for strategy signals before proceeding to the results.

Some of the results reported here first appeared in Duncan, Brunner, and Fiske (1979).

7.1. Rationale

Strategy signals derive from the rationale and methodology for structure signals, considered in Chapter 4. There the broad distinction between obligatory and optional signals was drawn, and criteria for hypothesizing structure signals were described. These criteria were (a) simultaneous consideration of the consequent and antecedent probabilities relevant to the signal, (b) ability of the proposed signal to differentiate various types of actions (invoked whenever possible), and (c) parsimony. All of these criteria play a major role in the decision to hypothesize strategy signals.

The three criteria relevant to structure signals are important because an action is hypothesized as a strategy signal only if it has previously been tested and rejected as a possible structure signal. There is obviously no need to posit strategy signals if structure signals suffice. This point will be elaborated later in this discussion.

Initial definition of strategy signals

A major aspect of the everyday notion of strategy, a notion that we brought to the beginning of this research, is that strategy often involves actions that influence the probability of some subsequent action by the partner. Thus, one might take a course of action that is designed to maximize the probability of a favorable response by the partner. At the most general level, we think of strategy signals as actions that have a definite effect on the probability of a specified response by the partner, but that cannot be said to be structure signals. Therefore, a critical element in the evaluation of strategy signals is the probability of a consequent. In this sense, strategy signals directly contrast with structure signals, in which the probability of an antecedent is critical. If an action does not have a distinct effect on the probability of a consequent, then the notion of strategy signal does not arise for that action.

Strategy effect of structure signals

When a distinct effect on the probability of a consequent is found for an action, it is important that the investigator test that action as a possible structure signal before hypothesizing it as a strategy signal. This is because all structure signals have a built-in strategy effect – that is, an effect on the probability of a consequent – that stems from the effect of the probability of the antecedent.

An example may clarify this confusing state of affairs. Let us say that the turn signal precedes virtually all smooth exchanges of the turn, and that there is a .25 probability of a smooth exchange after display of the signal. By token of these facts alone, the probability of a smooth exchange will be close to zero in the absence of the signal, and .25 when the signal is displayed. This contrast in the two consequent probabilities is a distinct strategy effect. But it owes its existence to the structural fact, based on the antecedent probability, that few smooth exchanges occur that are not preceded by the turn signal.

Accordingly, when an investigator discovers a striking effect attaching to the consequent probability, it becomes necessary also to examine carefully the associated antecedent probability. In addition, other criteria for a structural signal may be invoked: ability of the action to differentiate contrasting subsequent actions, and parsimony. Through this principled evaluation procedure, an appropriate description of the effect can be achieved.

Criteria for strategy signal

Based in part on the considerations just discussed, we have proposed four criteria for hypothesizing an action to be a strategy signal. (a) The potential strategy-signal action should not meet one or more of the criteria for hypothesizing it as a structure signal. That is, the proposed strategy signal should be rejected as a structure signal. (b) The action should have a distinct effect on the probability of a subsequent action. (c) This effect should be consistent across participants for which it is hypothesized. And (d) the effect should apply to action sequences involving legitimate alternatives; that is, the signal should not be invariably followed by the subsequent action in question.

Of these four criteria, the first two have already been considered. The second two, more obvious in their rationale, may be mentioned briefly. The third criterion – consistency – seems unexceptional. We view strategy signals as conventions. The requirement of consistency is included because there is always a possibility that a given convention or social practice may be confined to a single participant-partner pair or to a very small group of participants. In this case, it may occur with great regularity in their interactions but not in other observed interactions. This would be a clear-cut example of a *local convention* (D&F, p. 270), entirely accurate in describing the small set of interactions in question, but not one that is used in the larger population.

Alternatively, one participant or a small group of participants may have some characteristic of their personal interaction style that is manifested in a strategy-signal-like manner. However, this is not a component of other participants' personal style. In this case, it seems desirable to describe the effect as an element of those participants' strategy or personal style, but not as a strategy signal. These considerations lay behind the consistency criterion.

The fourth criterion disallowed obligatory effects. This criterion therefore defines all obligatory effects as part of structure. Such a definition does not seem necessary, but it does provide a clear-cut procedure for dealing with obligatory phenomena, particularly the perplexing case of negative obligatory effects, as discussed in Chapter 4. These will be further considered in the discussion section of this chapter.

Finally, it should be mentioned that in the second criterion – a distinct consequent-probability effect – the nature of the effect was not specified. It seems possible that a variety of strategy-signal effects might be possible. There seems to be no need to specify in advance exactly the sort of consequent-probability effects that should be included as potential strategy-signal phenomena.

7.2. Method

In Duncan et al. (1979), results were presented for three hypothesized strategy signals: speaker head direction, speaker smiling, and number of turn cues displayed. These results were based on data from the eight conversations used in the structural research reported in D&F. These conversations are described in detail in Chapter 9 of D&F, summarized in Table 9.1, and shown in Table 5.1 in this monograph. These included the two conversations used in the exploratory structural study, and the six in the subsequent "replication" study.

The initial three strategy-signal hypotheses were then further examined by applying them to the 12 conversations used in the structure-assessment study described in the last chapter. The results of this further application of the hypotheses – termed the *extension study* – will be presented along with the original results.

Subsequently, other strategy signals were hypothesized, at least tentatively. These, and the conversations on which they were based, will be described in due course.

Participants

It may be convenient for readers to review the composition of the eight conversations on which the original strategy-signal hypotheses were based.

Exploratory study. The first conversation was a psychotherapy intake interview. The therapist was a male about 40 years old, and the client was a female in her early twenties. They had had no contact with each other previous to this interview. The entire interview lasted about 40 minutes, of which the first 19 minutes were transcribed for the study. The second conversation was between the same therapist and another therapist, also about 40 years old. The two were good friends. This conversation was about 30 minutes long, of which the first 19 minutes were used for the study.

"Replication" study. There were six conversations in the so-called replication study (interaction numbers 3-6 in D&F). The first two were gathered on an entirely ad hoc basis. Conversation 3 was between two male college students, recruited as they emerged from participating as paid volunteers in another psychological experiment. They were unacquainted but quickly discovered that they had a number of mutual acquaintances. One was a freshman; the other, a sophomore. Their interaction was five minutes long. Each received $2.00 for participating.

Conversation 4 was between two female graduate students who worked in the same office as research assistants. They had known each other for about two years. Recruited as they were conversing in their office, they simply moved their conversation to our videotaping room and continued there. Five minutes of conversation were taped, after which they returned to their office to continue their discussion of shopping. They were not paid.

Conversations 5-8 included one each from the four blocks of conversations between Law School and Social Service Administration students, as detailed in Chapter 5.

7.3. Hypothesized signals and results

Speaker's gaze direction

Strategy-signal effect. When the speaker's gaze direction is toward the auditor, there is an increased probability of the auditor's attempting to take the speaking turn in response to a speaker turn signal (in the absence of a speaker gesticulation signal).

As described in Chapter 5 in the discussion of transcribing, head direction of the participants was transcribed instead of gaze. The resolution of some videotapes was such that actual gaze direction was not always possible to ascertain, while head direction was virtually always clear. We believe, however, that this strategy-signal effect actually has to do with speaker gaze direction. Therefore, we have chosen to use the terms "gaze" and "gaze direction" instead of "head direction." This practice will be continued in the following chapters.

Signal display and activity. The speaker's gaze was transcribed as being either directed toward the auditor or not. The signal is switched on when the gaze is toward the auditor. The active period of the signal is concurrent with its display. For the strategy-signal effect to occur, the gaze direction must be toward the auditor while the turn signal is active, and the gesticulation signal is not.

Disqualification as a structure signal. Speaker gaze direction was tested and rejected as a possible turn-signal cue for two reasons. First, inclusion of gaze direction in the turn signal would have substantially increased the number of simultaneous turns observed following the signal. In this way, the ability of the signal to differentiate smooth exchanges of the turn from instances of simultaneous turns would have been considerably impaired. It will be recalled that the turn signal was defined as the display of any single cue. In the eight conversations studied in D&F, there were 26 instances of simultaneous turns preceded by neither the turn signal nor the gesticulation signal. Nineteen of these instances (73%) were in the presence of speaker gaze direction toward the auditor. The same figure for the 16 conversations used in the strategy research was 78% (46/59). Thus, when the turn signal was not displayed, speaker gaze direction was associated with a large proportion of simultaneous turns in these data. When it occurred alone, speaker gaze direction failed to differentiate smooth exchanges from instances of simultaneous turns.

The second reason for not including gaze direction in the turn signal is that it simply was not needed. In the eight D&F conversations, virtually all smooth exchanges of the turn were preceded by at least one of the six cues hypothesized for the turn signal. Including speaker gaze direction would have substantially increased the number of turn-cue displays, while contributing negligibly to the number of smooth exchanges accounted for. Thus, parsimony was one of the factors considered.

Results. Table 7.1 shows data on auditor attempts to take the speaking turn when the speaker turn signal was displayed (a) without concurrent speaker gaze-direction signal, and (b) with concurrent speaker gaze-direction signal. These data are presented for each participant. It may be seen that the speaker's gaze being toward the auditor increases auditor response to the turn signal for each participant.

Summing across all participants, in the initial study the auditor was about 3.6 times more likely to attempt to take the turn when the speaker was gazing at the auditor. In the extension study, the comparable figure was 4.9. Considering all 38 participants in the two studies, five participants never took the turn in the absence of the speaker gaze-direction signal. In the initial study, the highest rate for taking the turn in the absence of the signal was 23.5%; in the extension study, 13.7%. For many of the participants, however, this rate was quite low.

Number of turn cues displayed

Strategy-signal effect. The number of turn cues involved in the display of the turn signal (with gesticulation absent) has a positive, linear relationship to the probability of a subsequent smooth exchange of the speaking turn. That is, the larger the number of turn cues displayed, the higher the probability of an ensuing smooth exchange.

Signal display and activity. The display and activity of each turn cue is the same as in the basic definition of the turn signal (Chapter 3). As described later in this section, initial analyses included the six-cue set reported in D&F. Subsequent analyses used the five-cue set reported in the structure assessment study (Chapter 6). This change has essentially no effect on the results.

Table 7.1. *Auditor attempts to take the turn in response to speaker turn-signal displays with and without concurrent speaker gaze*

| Participant | No gaze | | Gaze | | Ratio of proportions |
	N	Proportion of attempts	N	Proportion of attempts	
1-F-L	21	.048	53	.358	7.53
1-F-S	95	.137	57	.246	1.79
1-M-L	41	.000	58	.345	—
1-M-S	75	.027	67	.224	8.40
1-M-L	5	.000	29	.448	—
1-M-S	67	.045	65	.138	3.09
2-M-S	42	.048	60	.233	4.90
2-F-L	37	.027	40	.400	14.80
2-F-S	47	.043	65	.185	4.30
2-F-L	29	.034	33	.485	14.06
2-M-S	31	.032	70	.171	5.31
2-M-L	20	.050	29	.345	6.90
3-M-L	28	.036	52	.308	8.62
3-M-S	40	.050	63	.254	5.08
3-F-L	25	.080	40	.375	4.69
3-F-S	64	.031	82	.183	5.85
3-M-L	25	.120	45	.378	3.15
3-F-S	23	.043	61	.344	7.92
4-M-L	45	.022	45	.244	11.00
4-F-S	59	.119	21	.238	2.01
4-M-L	40	.025	58	.310	12.41
4-M-S	61	.066	38	.132	2.01
4-F-L	51	.059	62	.274	4.66
4-F-S	23	.043	43	.395	9.09
Total	994	.056	1236	.278	4.93

Disqualification as a structure signal. The speaker turn signal was defined as the display of at least one of the set of constituent turn cues. Defined in this way, the signal preceded most smooth exchanges of the turn in the conversations examined and effectively differentiated smooth exchanges from instances of simultaneous turns. The actual number of turn cues displayed at any given moment is irrelevant to the turn-signal definition and therefore to accompanying structure analyses. That is, the structure effect was shown to hold for the signal without reference to number of cues displayed.

At a very early stage in our research, however, it was noticed that there was a strong correlation between the probability of an auditor's acting to take the turn and the number of turn cues displayed. This relationship was difficult to resist in the initial work because it was a very strong one. In the earliest report of this research based on two 19-minute conversations (Duncan, 1972), the correlation between (a) number of turn cues displayed (in the absence of the gesticulation signal) and (b) percentage of auditor turn-taking attempts was .96. This correlation was interpreted in Duncan (1972) as direct structural evidence for the turn signal.

Subsequently, it was noticed that an even higher correlation could be obtained if "percentage of smooth exchanges" was substituted for "number of attempts." In this case, the correlation was .99 for the first two conversations, and .98 for the six conversations in the "replication" study.

However, in D&F (pp. 194-196), it was emphasized that reporting these correlations as direct evidence for the turn signal was an error. "It is of great importance to point out that the correlations may be properly interpreted only as indirect evidence with respect to the organization of the turn system" (p. 195).

We would now take a stronger position. The relationship between number of turn cues displayed and subsequent smooth exchanges of the turn is not a part of the structural evidence supporting the turn signal. In Duncan, Brunner, and Fiske (1979), we hypothesized number of turn cues displayed as a strategy signal, influencing as it does the probability of subsequent action by the auditor.

In this case, then, the problem is not that number of turn cues was tested and rejected as a possible turn signal. Rather, number of turn cues simply did not play a part in the basic definition of the signal and was therefore irrelevant to the hypothesis of the signal as an element of interaction structure. In any event, number of cues may be disqualified as an element

Table 7.2. *Rate of smooth turn exchanges as a function of number of active turn cues (gesticulation signal absent)*

Participant	1 or 2 active turn cues		3, 4, 5, or 6 active turn cues		Ratio of proportions
	N	Proportion smooth exchanges	N	Proportion smooth exchanges	
1F	75	.160	58	.344	2.15
1M	70	.200	27	.555	2.77
2Ma	80	.050	31	.161	3.22
2Mb	40	.075	29	.241	3.21
3Ma	46	.152	14	.285	1.87
3Mb	68	.073	15	.066	.90
4Fa	30	.100	16	.312	3.12
4Fb	27	.222	11	.272	1.22
5F	61	.163	11	.272	1.66
5M	54	.111	14	.357	3.21
6F	32	.312	20	.600	1.92
6M	77	.220	30	.200	.90
7F	99	.161	25	.200	1.24
7M	62	.225	7	.428	1.90
8F	60	.150	13	.538	3.58
8M	64	.203	9	.444	2.18
Total	945	.157	333	.318	2.02

of the turn signal because of parsimony: It is unnecessary for defining the signal.

Results. In Duncan (1972), data for the correlation between turn cues and auditor attempts were summarized over two 19-minute conversations. These data included the display of zero to six cues. In Duncan et al. (1979), data were presented on all eight conversations analyzed in D&F. Furthermore, these data were not summarized over participants or conversations but were presented for each participant in each conversation. Because it was difficult in some cases to present information for each participant on seven data points (zero to six cues) for each participant, the data were summarized in terms of (a) one or two turn cues displayed, and (b) three to six turn cues displayed.

It was expected, then, that a higher rate of smooth exchanges would follow display of three to six cues than one or two cues. These data are shown in Table 7.2. For 14 of the 16 participants, there was the expected

Table 7.3. *Correlations between number of turn cues activated by the speaker and rate of smooth turn exchanges (gesticulation signal absent)*

Participant	No. data points	r
1-F-L	4	.96
1-F-S	4	.95
1-M-L	3	.87
1-M-S	4	.94
1-F-L	3	.96
1-M-S	4	.88
1-M-L	3	.93
1-M-S	4	.96
2-F-S	3	.84
2-M-L	3	.81
2-M-S	4	.80
2-F-L	3	.88
2-F-S	4	.98
2-F-L	3	.74
2-M-S	4	.96
2-M-L	3	.92
3-M-L	4	.96
3-M-S	4	.94
3-F-L	4	.88
3-F-S	4	.95
3-F-L	3	.99
3-M-S	3	.96
3-M-L	4	.98
3-F-S	3	.96
4-F-L	4	.91
4-M-S	4	.91
4-M-L	4	−.22
4-F-S	4	.88
4-M-L	4	.95
4-M-S	4	.80
4-F-L	4	.94
4-F-S	3	.95

increase. This result is significant at the .004 level (two-tailed test). In this analysis, the presence or absence of the speaker gaze-direction signal was disregarded. When the data are analyzed only for instances in which the gaze-direction signal is present, the same results are obtained: 14 of the 16 participants showed the strategy-signal effect.

Table 7.3 shows more complete data for the 16 participants in blocks 1-4. Correlations were calculated between the number of turn cues in the display (0-5, the superfluous sixth cue being discarded) and the associated rate of smooth exchanges. Not included in the analysis were data points for which there were fewer than eight displays. This was an issue because each participant was analyzed separately. For example, if there were only six displays of five turn cues for a given participant, then the correlation would be calculated for zero to four cues. For some cases, there were not even sufficient displays to include four turn cues. The number of data points used for each participant is shown in Table 7.3. The table includes data for the four conversations also included in Table 7.2 because the calculation is somewhat different.

In 31 of the 32 cases, there was a strong linear relationship between number of cues displayed and the probability of a smooth exchange. In one case, there was a negative, zero-order correlation ($-.22$). Otherwise, the correlations ranged from .74 to .99, with 21 of the 31 correlations being greater than .90.

Number of turn cues and speaker gaze. Given that both speaker gaze direction and number of turn cues displayed have a positive effect on the auditor's acting to take the turn, it is natural to consider the relationship between these two signals. This issue is difficult to analyze satisfactorily because there are relatively few auditor attempts to take the turn in the absence of speaker gaze direction, due to the effect of that strategy signal. One can at least carry out an analysis parallel to that presented in Table 7.2, considering only units in which the speaker gaze-direction signal is present. As in Table 7.3, the full set of 32 speaker-auditor combinations used in the strategy research is considered. However, as in Table 7.2, the analysis contrasts displays of one and two turn cues with displays of three or more cues (gesticulation signal absent) because fewer data points are available. The results are essentially the same as in Table 7.2; the strategy signal holds for 31 of the 32 combinations. Thus, the results are basically unchanged when only units having speaker gaze direction present are analyzed. This outcome might be expected because the units analyzed formed the greater part of the units involved in the more inclusive analysis shown in Table 7.3. The results of this analysis parallel those reported in the preceding section for the 16 participants analyzed in D&F.

Equal weighting of turn cues. When data from the 16 conversations are pooled, it is possible to apply a more complete partitioning of the data in terms of signal displays than is possible when individual participants are studied. Mokros developed an analysis of auditor responses to the following speaker signal displays (when the gesticulation signal is not active): each turn cue alone, grammatical completion plus one or more other turn cues, two or more turn cues (not including grammatical completion), and no signal display. These data were further partitioned according to whether or not the speaker is gazing at the auditor. The data partitioned in this manner permit examination of the strategy-signal effect of each turn cue individually and of certain combinations of turn cues, but information on auditor responsiveness for individual participants is obviously lost.

In D&F, a model was proposed in which each turn cue had equal value in predicting auditor response. The predictive value of multiple displays was obtained simply by noting the number of cues in the display. Mokros's pooled data suggest that this model does not fit the 16 conversations in the present study. Auditor response to the various turn cues is not equal. Grammatical completion displayed alone clearly leads all the other single cues, both with and without gaze. There was negligible auditor response to two cues (gesture completion and drawl). Grammatical completion was involved, either alone or together with other cues, in 76% (411/544) of all smooth exchanges.

Adding one or more other cues to grammatical completion results in only a minimal increase in auditor response, when compared with grammatical completion alone. This is true both with and without gaze.

It remains true, however, that auditors responded preferentially to multiple-cue displays. These displays constituted 46% (1535/3307) of all cue displays, but they drew 71% (396/559) of all auditor turn attempts in response to turn cues.

We conclude that in these data there is a strategy-signal effect attaching to multiple-cue displays. However, this effect is not one of simply adding the value of equally weighted cues. Grammatical completion clearly is the dominant cue for these interactions, but there is also consistently greater auditor responsiveness to multiple-cue displays. The nature of this effect could be more sharply specified if there were sufficient data for full partitioning by signal display when data for individual participants are analyzed.

Speaker smiling

Strategy-signal effect. As described in Chapter 3, auditor smiling was added to the original list of back-channel actions. The evidence showed that auditor smiling was preceded by the speaker within-turn signal in essentially the same manner as were the actions included in the original set of auditor back channels. However, when speaker smiling accompanies the within-turn signal, there is an increased probability of subsequent auditor smiling. This effect does not take into consideration other auditor back channels that may co-occur with smiling. The hypothesis merely states that speaker smiling occurring jointly with the within-turn signal increases the probability that the auditor will smile in response to the within-turn signal.

Signal display and activity. The speaker was transcribed as either smiling or not. No further distinctions were made with respect to type or breadth of smile. For the strategy-signal effect to occur, the smiling must occur while the within-turn signal is active.

Disqualification as a structure signal. From a common-sense perspective, one would expect that speaker smiling would be related to subsequent auditor smiling. One might therefore consider making speaker smiling a structure signal for subsequent auditor smiling. However, data analysis showed that such a hypothesis was unnecessary. As described in Chapter 3, the speaker within-turn signal preceded 39 of the 40 auditor smiles, and a number of auditor smiles were not preceded by speaker smiling. Further, adding speaker smiling to the existing within-turn signal did not improve the statistical relationship between that signal and subsequent auditor smiling. For this reason, instead of hypothesizing a new and separate "speaker-smile signal," the existing speaker within-turn signal was pressed into service, and auditor smiles were added to the list of actions considered to be back channels. This appeared to be the most parsimonious solution.

Results. Only those conversations were analyzed that contained sufficient smiling to support analyses based on individual participants. There were data on four conversations (eight participants) presented in Duncan et al. (1979); and in the extension study, data on six participants. Table 7.4 shows results for these participants on proportion of auditor smiling in response to the speaker within-turn signal (a) without and (b) with concurrent speaker smiling. (In the table the indicated participant is the speaker.) It may be seen that the hypothesized strategy-signal effect held for all 14 of the participants: The probability of auditor smiling is increased when speaker smiling is present.

Table 7.4. *Auditor smiling in response to speaker within-turn signal displays with and without concurrent speaker smiling*

Participant	No speaker smiling		Speaker smiling		
	N	Proportion of auditor smiling	N	Proportion of auditor smiling	Ratio of proportions
4-F-L	41	.049	21	.190	3.89
4-F-S	92	.054	11	.091	1.68
4-M-L	43	.000	56	.071	—
1-F-L	43	.000	39	.154	—
3-F-L	91	.033	31	.097	2.94
3-F-S	131	.008	25	.08	10.00
Total	441	.025	183	.109	4.38

7.4. Discussion

As mentioned at the beginning of this chapter, the hypothesis of strategy signals was in some ways unsettling. We had not anticipated that such a new kind of signal would arise, and its unexpected nature caused us to reexamine the entire structure-versus-stategy distinction that lies at the heart of this research. The strategy signal was the kind of added complication that calls into question the essential features of the system. Were the conceptual distinctions unnecessary? Was there some defect in the process of marshaling evidence for these signals?

From a common-sense perspective, the strategy signal does not seem particularly exceptional. Structure signals seem to mark points in the stream of interaction at which one may, must, or must not take some action. In the research so far, strategy signals have been found to accompany optional structure signals (specifying where one may take some action). The accompanying strategy signal seems to provide at least partial information on the degree to which the signaler wishes the audience actually to take the optional action.

Getting away from turn taking for a moment, one can imagine more familiar examples of strategy signals. In a grammar-school classroom, the pupil's structure signal to indicate readiness to be called on by the teacher is raising the hand. However, the pupil can also indicate the strength of the desire to be called on. Hands can be raised so inconspicuously as to be almost undetectable, or there may be frantic and stylized waving, perhaps accompanied with anguished facial expressions and the like. From our point of view, the structural business is accomplished by the hand raise per se; the rest of it would be one or more strategy signals, potentially influencing the choice of the teacher beyond the influence exerted by the raised hand itself.

As another example, the ritual of shaking hands in greetings would seem to offer similar opportunities. Shaking hands would be the structure signal itself, while there is a variety of devices for communicating relative responsiveness to the encounter: facial expressions, firmness of grip, vigor of shaking, "doubling" the shake by taking the partner's forearm with the left hand, and the like. Depending on the shape of research results, these meaningful variations might be analyzed as strategy signals accompanying the basic structure signal, just as number of turn cues displayed and speaker gaze direction may accompany the turn signal.

It is apparent that some strategy signals may be inextricably connected to the structure signal, whereas others are not. For example, one cannot display a turn signal without concomitantly displaying some number of turn cues, just as one cannot shake hands without concomitantly exerting some firmness of grip. In contrast, speaker gaze direction may or may not accompany the turn signal, just as "doubling" the shake may or may not be a part of a greeting. This distinction, although valid, seems superficial, however. Detachable strategy signals such as speaker gaze direction are, nevertheless, appropriate potential accompaniments of their relevant structure signal (e.g., the turn signal). From this point of view, because they are potentially a part of the process, their absence is just as noticeable and significant as their presence. In this sense, they seem just as inescapable a component of the total signaling process as the physically connected signals, such as number of turn cues.

It will be apparent that we view strategy signals as being conventions in the same sense that structure signals are. Both types of signals help coordinate the actions of the participants by providing shared procedures for conducting the interaction, and by providing each partner information on the participant's internal state of affairs.

We conclude that, given the criteria established for hypothesizing structure signals, it is necessary to distinguish between strategy and structure signals. It would seem that the distinction would have to be criticized in terms of the criteria themselves. However, it seems appropriate in the case of such criticism also to suggest a viable alternative which itself is not subject to serious criticism.

The results for the hypothesized strategy signals seem quite consistent across participants and also hold up well in the extension study. In both of these senses, the strategy-signal hypotheses seem to be approximately as well supported as the structure-signal ones.

At the same time, there still remains considerable room for varying action with respect to strategy signals. Speakers vary in the extent to which a given signal is used, and auditors vary in the degree to which they respond to it, even though in virtually every case, use of the signal affected the overall probability of the auditor's response in the hypothesized direction.

For example, in the case of the speaker gaze-direction signal the data in Table 1 in Duncan et al. (1979) show that in the initial study, use of the signal varied from 48% to 92% of the turn signal displays. Similarly, the data in Table 7.1 show that the use of gaze varied from 26% to 85% in the extension study. Summing across all participants, the gaze-direction signal accompanied 67% of all turn-signal displays in the initial study, and 55% in the extension study. Across both studies, there were five auditors who never took the turn in the absence of the gaze-direction signal; otherwise, the rate of turn attempts in the absence of the signal varied from 2% to 23%. In the presence of the signal, rate of attempts ranged from 12% to 53%. All of these effects are legitimate components of a participant's strategy, or personal style, in the interactions.

Thus, it is hardly the case that strategy signals impose a lock-step of conformity on these conversations, or that display of a signal virtually compels response by the auditor. It would seem that the complexity of interactions is more than sufficient simultaneously to permit strong regularities due both to structure- and strategy-signal phenomena, and to extensive variation in the participants' strategy or personal style.

8. Pragmatically marked and unmarked forms of speaking-turn exchange

RITA DENNY

8.1. Introduction

The point of departure for the analysis presented in this chapter is the conceptualization of structure and strategy presented by D&F and Duncan, Brunner, and Fiske (1979). Within their analytic paradigm, structure refers to the organization of interaction. Structure is described by a set of signals which are conventional (D&F, p. 255) or rule governed. Thus a description of the structure of interaction is a description of the (conventional) rules within which individuals behave. In contrast, a description of strategy is in part a description of the ways individuals actually behave within the realm defined by rules:

> No convention constrains all aspects of the actions to which it applies. Interaction strategy is possible in part because of the degrees of freedom allowed by convention. Interaction strategies are describable in terms of the ways that individuals and-or groups actually use these degrees of freedom. (p. 247)

To put it succinctly, if structure constitutes rules of use, then strategy constitutes use of rules. It should be apparent, therefore, that a description of strategy is contingent on an analysis of structure. An analytic application of their conceptualization is found in the formulation of strategy signals (Duncan et al., 1979). In the present paper, the general conceptual distinction between structure and strategy is upheld though the analytic paradigm, within which rules of use are delineated, differs.

The paradigm to be used in this study is a conceptual and analytic application of the linguistic tradition of Prague structuralism, in which the indexical (as opposed to symbolic or iconic) nature of signals constitutes the focus of analysis. Specifically, it is determined whether turn exchange is a contextual feature of conversation that is indexed by linguistic and/or nonlinguistic forms, and whether other contextual parameters are simultaneously indexed at locations of turn exchange. The fundamental advantage in analyzing turn-taking as an indexical system is that the form of turn exchange is rendered compatible with other linguistic indexes and, simultaneously, the focus of sociolinguists and ethnographers of speech is expanded to include aspects of face-to-face interaction which are jointly determined actions.

Indexical forms

Within the tradition of Prague structuralism, language is viewed functionally, such that there are distinct functional styles:

> The term *functional language* pertains to the relationship between the goal of expression and the linguistic means appropriate for the attainment of this goal. In each case, a speaking individual determines the choice of a certain set of means ("a functional language") for the actual utterance. (Mukarovsky, 1940/1977, p. 82)

It can be seen that the linguistic devices, or means, constitute the functional language such that the relationship to the goal of expression is indexical.

Opposed to icons, which presuppose physical isomorphism, and symbols, which presuppose arbitrary referential meaning, indexes are signs "where the occurrence of a sign vehicle token bears a connection of understood spatio-temporal contiguity [i.e. contextual contiguity] to the occurrence of the entity signaled" (Silverstein 1976, p. 27). Indexes may be referential, as in the class of shifters, or nonreferential (pure indexes in Silverstein, 1976). In the latter case, the devices signal a value of one or more contextual variables which are independent of referential speech events.

A fundamental distinction made by these scholars was in automatized and foregrounded uses of linguistic devices or, equivalently, in pragmatically unmarked and marked devices. Briefly, an automatized device is one which is expected, given the circumstances of its occurrence, such that "the expression itself does not attract any attention" (Havranek, 1955, p. 9). Foregrounding is the use of devices which themselves attract attention and are "perceived as uncommon" (Havranek, 1955, p. 10). Of importance is that these devices are indexes. It is only by virtue of the indexical properties of a given device that the device may be automatized or foregrounded in its use.

There are a number of examples of linguistic indexes. Postvocalic (r) in New York City (Labov, 1966) is an indexical token of socioeconomic class. Use of (r) is automatized by upper socioeconomic class speakers, and the absence of (r) is automatized by lower socioeconomic class speakers. Use of (r) by lower-class speakers constitutes foregrounding. Lexical items may be indexical tokens of deference relations, as in the Javanese (Geertz, 1968), or of a specific kin relationship (e.g., "mother-in-law language," Dixon, 1972). Use of T and V pronominal forms in Russian (Friedrich, 1966), French (Brown and Gilman, 1960), and Italian (Bates and Begnini, 1975) is minimally dependent on the number of addressees and the dimensions of power and solidarity. In this case, the same indexical token has multifunctional properties: The token is both referential and a social index. The absence of speech, that is, silence itself, can assume indexical properties. Among the Western Apache, silence by one or more interlocutors in social interaction is an indexical token of an ambiguous social relationship among interlocutors (Basso, 1970).

It can be seen that in the case of indexes, the sign vehicle, i.e., observable behavioral token, is postulated to have an existential relationship to the sign (type), such that the occurrence of a given token signals the value of (or invokes the existence of) a contextual parameter. The function that describes the relationship between token and type constitutes the rule of use or, equivalently, the rule of indexicality (Silverstein, 1976). The rule of use thus describes a relationship "of mutually implied existence of sign vehicle token and certain aspects of the context of discourse" (Silverstein, 1976, p. 33). In analytic practice, it is possible (a) to observe the patterning of behavioral phenomena as a function of hypothesized contextual parameters, or (b) deductively to determine contextual parameters which account for an observed patterning. Rules of indexicality are, then, the result of analysis, being the postulated functional relationship that acts as an explanation for the observed patterning of behavior in the context of speech.

Systems of turn taking proposed by D&F and by Sacks, Schegloff, and Jefferson (1974) are indexical in that actions of the interlocutors are indexically related to the contextual parameter of turn exchange. The differences between the cited models, as well as the difference between these models and the one proposed herein, lie in the formal constitution of the indexes and/or the nature of the indexical relationship. With respect to the latter, in the models of both D&F and Sacks et al. (1974), obligatory turn exchange is not a contextual feature of conversation that is itself indexed by the action(s) of the interlocutor(s). Rather, the system of turn exchange is interpreted to be an optional system such that interlocutors' actions are indexically related to the opportunity for (smooth) exchange. While the formal construction of the indexes varies across these models, the contextual feature being indexed (opportunity for smooth turn exchange) does not.

In the model proposed by Sacks et al. (1974), speaking turns are composed of turn constructional units, and the boundaries of these units are defined as having transition relevance. Constructional units are syntactic, where the range of unit types is demarcated by grammatical categorization. The completion of any syntactic construction provides listeners with an opportunity to take the turn, but there is no obligation incurred by a structural feature of the unit to do so. These researchers proposed that a rule goes into effect at the boundaries of these salient conversational units. The rule includes the options of current speaker selects next, self-selection, and current speaker continues. If the current speaker continues, then the rule goes into effect at the next place of transition relevance.

Within this model, interlocutors uniformly orient themselves to grammatical units. It is by virtue of such units that locations for turn exchange can be anticipated and subsequently managed with a minimum of silence and overlap. Within the definition of their model, consideration of nonverbal behavior is not necessary for an adequate explication of the structure of a turn-taking system. Put otherwise, nonverbal behavior bears no indexical relationship to turn exchange. It should also be noted that the occurrence of turn exchange may be influenced by use of linguistic devices such as adjacency pairs (Schegloff and Sacks, 1973). However, in this case, turn exchange is effected by the illocutionary force of the initial utterance of the adjacency pair rather than the formal structure of the system.

In the system modeled by D&F, auditors have the option of taking the turn at terminal boundaries of phonemic clauses marked by turn-signal display. The turn signal was empirically derived from an analysis of smooth and simultaneous exchanges. It consists of those verbal and nonverbal elements, termed cues, that not only characterize smooth exchanges, but differentiate smooth from simultaneous exchanges. Nonverbal elements such as gesture and intonation were included in the analysis and found to be relevant. (Gaze was later hypothesized as a strategy signal by Duncan, Brunner, and Fiske [1979].) The turn signal, as do other structure signals (D&F, Table 11.2), embodies a rule. With respect to the turn signal, the occurrence of one or more constituent cues counts as an undifferentiated signal for the opportunity of smooth exchange. As in the Sacks model, it is possible to influence the auditor's behavior in taking the turn. Whereas in the former model the influence is derived primarily through the illocutionary force of the utterance, in Duncan's model it is primarily through the speaker's use of strategy signals or the gesticulation signal which, to date, are composed of nonverbal behavior.

In summary, a point of transition relevance or a display of the turn signal constitutes a signal for the opportunity of smooth turn exchange such that the opportunity for turn exchange is the contextual parameter being indexed. Neither is a signal (index) of obligatory turn exchange. Additionally, even for the domain of conversation in which the smooth exchange appears to be optimized, the structural elements constituting the system of turn taking or, equivalently, the formal constitution of the indexes, remains in dispute. It is not known whether the observed regularities between nonverbal behavior and turn exchange noted by D&F are redundant with respect to the syntactically motivated constructional units proposed by Sacks et al. (1974). Finally, it is also the case that the precise role of a given nonverbal action in conversation is subject to dispute. For example, Kendon (1967) claimed that speaker gaze had a "floor-apportionment" function; a modified version of this claim was supported by Duncan et al. (1979). In contrast, Beattie (1978a) and Rutter and co-workers (1978) objected to the claim on empirical grounds. The role of speaker gestural activity in turn exchange has also been argued (D&F versus Beattie, 1980), as has the role of auditor gaze (D&F versus Denny, 1982a). Although sociocultural (Philips, 1976) and situational (Beattie, 1980; D&F) differences in the display of nonverbal behavior may be expected, differences in researchers' results may well be a function of the analytic model invoked.

Sacks et al. (1974) simply assumed that nonverbal marking is redundant with grammatical marking in turn exchange. Beattie (1980) assumed that patterning of nonverbal behavior, although dependent on traditional (semantico-referential) grammar, is independent of the pragmatic meaning of utterances. Rutter et al. (1978) assumed that gaze patterns could be analyzed independently of other verbal and nonverbal actions. Duncan et al. (1979) assumed that the functional significance of gaze, while conditional on a display of the turn signal, is not conditioned by any pragmatic level of conversation. Although these assumptions may be valid, the point remains that the domains over which they may operate are not defined.

In the present study, a system of turn taking was hypothesized to be an indexical system such that the behavioral marking of smooth turn exchanges constitutes an index of this contextual parameter of conversation. Furthermore, the various patterns (forms) marking turn exchange were proposed to be indexically distinct, where each form is related to a specific set of conversational parameters, inclusive of turn exchange. Within this analytic paradigm, the structure of conversation is thus describable in terms of the range of indexical forms which are delineated as a result of analysis. Strategy, then, becomes a study of the use of indexes.

Pragmatic markedness

Once an index is delineated such that the rules of use are constituted through analysis, the use of the indexical form can be ranked along a continuum of pragmatic markedness. As noted earlier, a primary distinction is made by Havranek (1955), Mukarovsky (1940), and later by Friedrich (1966) between pragmatically unmarked and marked uses of indexes. An unmarked or automatized index is one that is usual or expected given the context of its occurrence, and by its occurrence may be said to presuppose the existence of some contextual parameter. A marked form, or one that is not usual, may be said to invoke or create some contextual parameter which would otherwise not be presupposed.

Use of silence among Western Apache (Basso, 1970) provides a good example of markedness. Silence between interlocutors who do not know each other, hence have no social relationship, is expected. In this case, silence presupposes a specific value of the social roles of interlocutors within certain contextual parameters. Silence, however, also occurs between parents and offspring, for example, when the child returns from residence at an Anglo school. In this instance, silence is marked, indexing ambiguity in a social relationship which would *otherwise be well established*. Silence thus has a performative or creative function in its marked use.

With respect to turn taking, indexes may in principle also be ranked along a continuum of pragmatic markedness. The only requirement is that more than one indexical form of turn exchange be delineated. Assuming this to be the case, the devices may be ordered by the degree to which the form is independent of the co-occurring speech events and, more broadly, the social occasion. Thus, the pragmatically unmarked index of turn exchange will be one which presupposes least about contextual parameters of the speech situation. Marked forms may also be ordered by the number of presuppositions entailed by the specific form. Thus by ranking the indexical forms of turn exchange, it is possible to observe the linkage between a system of turn exchange and the social occasion the system perpetuates.

In summary, the purpose of the analysis was to explore the indexical nature of turn taking in order to accomplish two goals. The initial goal was to establish the set of necessary and sufficient linguistic and nonlinguistic elements for effecting smooth turn exchange, and to determine whether the forms defined by these elements are indexes of turn exchange. The second goal was to determine the pragmatic markedness of indexical forms so that (a) the multifunctional indexical nature of nonverbal behavior may be systematically delineated and (b) turn exchange becomes a locus for determining a range of indexical forms that are not only present in social interaction but also, by their presence, both presuppose and create a particular form of social occasion.

8.2. Method

Data

The data consisted of eight videotaped dyadic conversations, each about seven minutes in length. The conversations were taken from the set used for the strategy study, as described in Chapter 5. The conversations used and the numbers used to refer to them are shown in Table 5.1 in that chapter. Readers will recall that the interlocutors were professional-school students attending the University of Chicago and were strangers prior to conversing. In two conversations the interlocutors were male, in two they were female, and in four conversations they were of opposite gender.

The sequential occurrence of each action and event was recorded such that the beginning and the end of any action, and the occurrence of any event, were given a sequence code. This procedure provided information about the sequential occurrence of a given action throughout the conversation and also its occurrence relative to all other actions and events.

Analytic unit

Because a silent (unfilled) pause is required, by definition, for smooth exchange of the turn, and all pauses are not followed by turn exchange, behavior occurring in conjunction with silent pauses was the focus of analysis.[1] The stream of speech was parsed into units using a criterion of a minimum duration for a silent pause. The minimum duration was a pause of 65 ms. The boundary of a unit was defined by the first sound of speech that terminated a pause, so that any given unit consisted of a verbal utterance terminated by a pause of at least 65 ms. The status of each variable (see below) was assessed at the terminal boundary of the analytic unit.

Pause-length measurement

Length of pauses was measured using DTEDIT, an interactive waveform editing program written by D. Terbeek at the University of Chicago for the PDP-11 computer. Successive samples of speech from an audiotape were passed through a low-pass filter (3500 Hz) into the computer via an A/D converter. The stored, digitalized sample was returned through the low-pass filter, and the voltage output was displayed on an oscilloscope. Sampling frequency was 10,000 Hz. In addition, the speech was simul-taneously passed through an amplifier (Realistic SA 1000) and to a speaker.

The stream of speech was thus represented on the oscilloscope as a continuous voltage output. When the output was approximately zero, indicated by a flat line on the oscilloscope, the boundaries of the flat segment were recorded in a temporary file on the PDP-11. The recorded segment was played back through the speaker so that pauses could be differentiated from other low voltage sounds such as "f," "s," and the like, and the precise location of the pauses in speech could be tracked accurately. The accuracy of measurement is 0.1 ms. Pauses were measured to the nearest 5 ms. Pauses within words were not measured. Between-word pauses of less than 65 ms were not recorded.

Variables

Many of the variables defined in this analysis were identical to those described by D&F. Nonetheless, definitions of some of the variables were modified, and other variables added. A description of each variable used in this study is given below.

Intonation (IN). Intonation was transcribed using the Trager and Smith (1957) system, in which three levels of pitch and three types of terminal juncture (rising, level, falling) are distinguished. Following D&F, the intonation element (IN) is defined by a deviation from a 2 2 | (pitch-terminal juncture) sequence.

Sociocentric sequence. This variable is identical to the one defined in Chapter 5 and in D&F (p. 171). The variable consists of stereotypic expressions, such as "you know," "but uh," etc., that are tagged on to more substantive verbalizations.

Gaze (GZ). Head direction was used as a measurement of gaze direction. The speaker gaze element (GZ) is present when gaze is directed towards the auditor's face at the terminal boundary of an analytic unit, and not present when directed elsewhere at this location.

Auditor gaze (AGZ). Auditor head direction was used as a measure of listener gaze direction. The auditor gaze element (AGZ) is present when the auditor is gazing away from the speaker at the terminal boundary of an analytic unit.

Gesture (H). Gesture was defined by the movement of one or both hands/ arms, excluding self-adapters, where movement involves self-grooming. The element is identical to the gesticulation variable described by D&F (p. 173).

Filled pauses. Filled pauses consist of vocalizations such as "uh" and "er" (Maclay and Osgood, 1959).

Grammatical completion (GC). This variable is a modification of the one defined by D&F. The modified definition matches that given in Chapter 3. Utterances designated as grammatically complete include (a) completion of any independent clause, (b) completion of any dependent clause that was linked to a preceding independent clause by a relative pronoun, (c) elliptical independent clauses which presupposed an explicit clause in the imme-diately preceding speaking turn, and (d) completion of a phrase which is part of an immediately preceding independent clause. Utterances not coded as GC were those which did not meet these criteria, such as the completion of phrases and dependent clauses which were neither coreferentially linked with, nor presupposed by, a preceding clause in the speaking turn. Grammatical classification was assessed on the last word of the utterance in a given analytic unit.

Pause length (PL). The actual duration of pauses defining boundaries of analytic units was defined as an independent variable.

Speech event. Speaking turns, or parts of turns, were categorized as one of three types of speech event: Question (Q), Answer (A), or Comment (C). Questions were identified by their formal grammatical structure (verb inversion), or by a deviation in pitch. If the speaking turn consisted of more than one pause, then at each unit boundary the appropriate speech classification was coded. Turns following Questions were defined as Answers. Speaking turns which were neither Questions nor Answers were defined as Comments. The speech event code remained constant in a speaking turn unless the turn ended with a Question, in which case the latter part of the turn (i.e., the point at which the Question began), received a "Q" code.

Turn exchange. Smooth exchange of the turn includes those instances in which the speaking turn is transferred and there is no overlap in speech ($N = 265$). Also included are those cases in which the speaking turn is transferred with no overlap, but the former speaker tags on a few words after the other interlocutor has started speaking. As a result, a short stretch of overlapping speech occurs. These cases ($N = 10$) are differentiable from (attempted) simultaneous exchange by the decreased loudness of the tagged words and by their semantico-referential relationship to the previous utterance. The focus of this chapter is on smooth exchange.

Simultaneous turns include attempted and completed turn exchange characterized by overlapping speech ($N = 69$). In some cases, the overlap occurred on a turn-initial "Well" or "Uh" ($N = 32$). In the remaining cases the overlap occurred on substantive utterance fractions.

Finally, there are instances in which turn exchange is attempted after a pause, but the interlocutors start speaking simultaneously ($N = 17$). These cases were not designated as either smooth or simultaneous. In the statistical analysis, analytic units in which these occurred were neither eliminated, nor considered smooth exchanges. These definitions differ somewhat from those used elsewhere in this monograph and those in D&F.

Back channels (BC). Auditor back channels were differentiated from speaking turns, following D&F. Although the range of back channels includes nonverbal behaviors such as head nods (D&F) and smiles (Brunner, 1979), the back-channel variable was here restricted to verbal

utterances such as "okay," "uh-huh," etc. Brief restatements and qualifying questions were included as back channels though their occurrence
was rare.

Statistical analysis

The data were analyzed using a multivariate logistic regression procedure
(SAS Institute, 1980), a log-linear method described by Hanushek and
Jackson (1977) and Bishop, Fienberg, and Holland (1975). The logistic
regression is a form of logit, or log of the odds, model in which a
dichotomous dependent variable is specified. Unlike some logit models
(see, for example, Goodman, 1978), the logistic regression procedure can
incorporate any quantitative independent variable without requiring
categorical transformation. In addition, by assuming an underlying
probabilistic function (the logistic function), the logits obtained for the
independent variables in the logistic regression procedure can be expressed
in probabilistic terms.

The logistic regression model is defined by the set of specified
independent variables. The significance of each variable specified by the
models was assessed by using a backwards stepwise procedure (unless
otherwise noted). Each parameter in the models is associated with an
estimated logit, beta. The logit represents the natural logarithm of the odds
with which the independent variable affects the occurrence of the
dependent variable.

In the following report, the beta estimates (logits) are expressed
probabilistically when the results are plotted. In each case, the probability
of the occurrence of the dependent variable is plotted as a function of pause
length. In all cases, the logistic curves are drawn through the logits
estimated in the regression procedure.

8.3. Indexes of turn exchange

If smooth exchange is a contextual parameter indexed in conversation, then
the formal elements defining the indexical form should be observable at
locations of turn exchange such that the formal distribution of verbal and
nonverbal elements has a one-to-one correspondence with turn exchange.
Furthermore, it is possible that a given element is necessary but not
sufficient for effecting smooth exchange, in which case the indexical form
would be composed of some set of elements. In order to determine the set of
necessary elements, a mathematical function that maximizes the prob-

ability of turn exchange was generated. In so doing, the probabilistic salience of a given element and co-occurrence of elements in effecting turn exchange may be obtained. The degree to which turn exchange can be predicted is, of course, also established.

Although the primary focus of analysis in this paper is on the contextual parameter of turn exchange, verbal auditor back channels were subjected to a similar analysis such that a function maximizing the probability of back channels was also generated. As is clear from the separation of analyses, back channels are posited to be functionally distinct utterances, following D&F, Kendon (1967), Yngve (1970), and Schegloff (1982). Nonetheless, a number of researchers have merged speaking turns and back channels in analyses of conversational patterns (Gerstman, Feldstein, and Jaffe, 1967; Jaffe and Feldstein, 1970; Beattie, 1978b; Cappella and Streibel, 1979) and thereby assume not only a functional equivalence of these utterances, but also that the formal distribution of back channels in conversation is equivalent to turn exchange. The purpose of the back channel analyses, then, was to assess the validity of the merging procedure.

As noted earlier, the silent pause was used as the criterion for defining analytic units, and the behavioral elements co-occurring with silent pauses constituted the set of independent variables. These variables are grammatical completion (GC), intonation (IN), speaker gaze (GZ), auditor gaze (AGZ), pause length (PL), and gesture (H).

Analytic units in which a filled pause or sociocentric sequence occurred were not included in the analysis because of the frequency distributions of these two variables. Rather than include them and introduce noise in the results, these analytic units were excluded from statistical analysis.

The initial results are generated from grouped data. The adequacy of these models in describing individual conversations is subsequently determined. In the eight conversations, there were 1594 analytic units, 226 smooth exchanges, and 181 verbal auditor back channels.

Results

Grouped data. The rate of smooth exchange, transition, is given for a variety of behavioral contexts in Tables 8.1-8.3. The cells in each table represent mutually exclusive contexts in conversation. In Table 8.1, the rate of transition is given as a function of the grammatical completion (GC), speaker-gaze (GZ), and intonation (IN) elements. The context GCGZ refers to the co-occurrence of the first two of these elements. The data in

Table 8.1. *Rate of transition as a function of grammatical completion, intonation, speaker gaze*

| | Intonation element (IN) | |
	Absent	Present
GC	.074	.088
GZ	.029	.063
GCGZ	.346	.341

Table 8.2. *Rate of transition as a function of grammatical completion, speaker and auditor gaze elements*

| | Auditor gaze element (AGZ) | |
	Absent	Present
No GC, GZ, or GCGZ	.003	.091
GC	.032	.353
GZ	.027	.182
GCGZ	.197	.753

Table 8.1 indicate that the presence of IN with GC, GZ, or GCGZ has no effect on the rate of transition. In contrast, the auditor gaze element (AGZ) consistently increases the rate of transition (Table 8.2). These results are formalized as logit estimates in Equation (1).

$$\Pr(Tr = 1) = -5.7 + [2.01 \text{ GC} + 1.69 \text{ GZ} + 3.87 \text{ GCGZ}]$$
$$+ 2.37 \text{ AGZ} + .81 \text{ PL} \qquad (1)$$

It should be noted that the GC, GZ, and GCGZ logits are mutually exclusive because they represent levels of a single polytomous variable. Estimates of a polytomous variable are enclosed by brackets. Consistent with the data in Tables 8.1 and 8.2, the intonation element is not a significant parameter, though the auditor gaze element is. Additionally, pause length is a significant parameter, where increased length of pause increases the probability of turn exchange.

The logit estimates in Equation 1 are used to plot simulated probability distributions of each element and combination of elements in relation to turn exchange (Figure 8.1). The simulated functions assume an underlying logistic function: $\Pr(Tr = 1) = 1/(1 + \exp^{-X\beta})$, where β = pause length

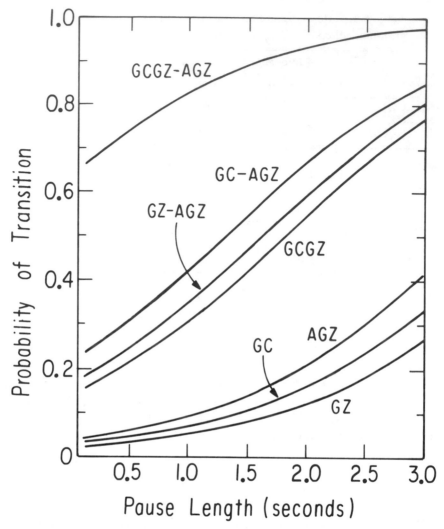

Figure 8.1. Probability of transition as a function of pause length and speaker and auditor actions.

and X = a given behavioral element or combination of elements. It can be seen from Figure 8.1 that the most salient context for turn exchange is the co-occurrence of the GC, GZ, AGZ, and PL elements (GCGZ-AGZ in Figure 8.1). Thus turn exchange can be virtually ensured by a combination of speaker and auditor elements.

In a comparable analysis of back channel responses, it was found that

Table 8.3. *Salience of GC, GZ, GCGZ as a function of AGZ, H, and speech event (rate of transition)*

	AGZ element absent		AGZ element present	
	Gesture	No gesture	Gesture	No gesture
Questions				
No GC, GZ, or GCGZ	(N = 7)	.000	(N = 1)	(N = 3)
GC	(N = 0)	(N = 6)	(N = 0)	(N = 2)
GZ	.000	.143	(N = 6)	(N = 3)
GCGZ	.308	.523	(N = 2)	.918
Answers				
No GC, GZ, or GCGZ	.000	.000	(N = 6)	(N = 8)
GC	.000	.012	(N = 3)	.231
GZ	.000	.022	(N = 1)	.111
GCGZ	.000	.158	(N = 3)	.657
Comments				
No GC, GZ, or GCGZ	.000	.008	(N = 4)	.182
GC	.000	.077	(N = 4)	.583
GZ	.000	.029	(N = 2)	.250
GCGZ	.000	.242	(N = 4)	.647

Note: N is entered in parentheses when it is too small (<10) to calculate a rate.

grammatical completion, speaker gaze, intonation, and pause length were salient elements. The logit estimates are given in Equation (1a).

$$\Pr(BC = 1) = -3.86 + [2.12\ GC + 1.35\ GZ + 2.1\ GCGZ]$$
$$+ .69\ IN + -.54\ PL \tag{1a}$$

In contrast to turn exchange, the probability of back channel is equivalent in the contexts of GC and GCGZ, and auditor gaze is not probabilistically related to back channel response. Perhaps most interesting is the observation that the probability of an auditor back channel decreases as a function of pause length.

The speech event and gesture variables are considered next. By including the speech-event parameter, it is possible to determine whether (a) a pragmatic level of conversation is itself a salient parameter in effecting turn exchange, and (b) the probabilistic salience of elements in Equation (1) is dependent on the speech event within which the elements are embedded.

In Table 8.3, rates of transition are given as a function of the GC, GZ, AGZ, and gesture elements within each type of speech event.

Gestural activity has a clear effect on the rate of transition. When the auditor gaze element is not present, gesture obviates the salience of the GC, GZ, and GCGZ contexts regardless of speech event. The only exception is the probabilistic salience of GCGZ embedded within Questions which, though reduced, is not negated. This effect of gesture is expected from the results reported by D&F. Also note that the auditor gaze (AGZ) and gesture elements rarely co-occur (column 3 in Table 8.3).

Due to the frequency distribution of the gesture variable, the logistic regression included only units in which there is no gestural activity. Since the speech event variable is polytomous, one level of the variable is stipulated as a baseline against which the other levels are compared. Answers were designated as the baseline. The tested model included the GC, GZ, GCGZ, AGZ, PL, Q, and C elements, as well as interactions of the C and Q parameters with GC, GZ, and GCGZ. Note that the Q-GC term could not be included because of sample size ($N = 8$, Table 8.3). A stepwise procedure that eliminated insignificant components produced the estimates in Equation (2).

$$\begin{aligned}
\Pr(\mathrm{Tr} = 1) = {} & -5.91 + [1.89\ \mathrm{GC} + 1.42\ \mathrm{GZ} + 3.46\ \mathrm{GCGZ}] \\
& + 2.19\ \mathrm{AGZ} + 1.07\ \mathrm{PL} + .78\ \mathrm{C} \\
& + [2.25\ \mathrm{Q{-}GZ} + 2.14\ \mathrm{Q{-}GCGZ}]
\end{aligned} \tag{2}$$

It can be seen from Equation (2) that the main effect of Questions (Q) was eliminated from the model. In doing so, the interaction parameters, including a Q term, are biased. Thus Equation (3) represents a model in which all terms in Equation (2) plus the main effect of Q were stipulated.

$$\begin{aligned}
\Pr(\mathrm{Tr} = 1) = {} & -5.88 + [1.88\ \mathrm{GC} + 1.4\ \mathrm{GZ} + 3.44\ \mathrm{GCGZ}] \\
& + 2.2\ \mathrm{AGZ} + 1.07\ \mathrm{PL} + .77\ \mathrm{C} \\
& + [-.27\ \mathrm{Q} + 2.52\ \mathrm{Q{-}GZ} \\
& + 2.4\ \mathrm{Q{-}GCGZ}]
\end{aligned} \tag{3}$$

The main effect of Q is not significant, but its inclusion gives unbiased estimates of other (significant) parameters.

When speech event and gesture are considered in back-channel models, it is found that gesture bears no relationship to back-channel response though the speech-event designation does. Briefly stated, back channels occur rarely in the context of Questions, as is reflected in the logit estimates of Equation (2a)[2]. The probability estimates of back channel within Answer and Comment speech events are equivalent.

$$\begin{aligned}
\Pr(\mathrm{BC}) = {} & -3.88 + [2.1\ \mathrm{GC} + 1.39\ \mathrm{GZ} + 2.35\ \mathrm{GCGZ}] + .76\ \mathrm{IN} \\
& + -.53\ \mathrm{PL} + [-.38\ \mathrm{Q} + -1.58\ \mathrm{Q{-}GCGZ}]
\end{aligned} \tag{2a}$$

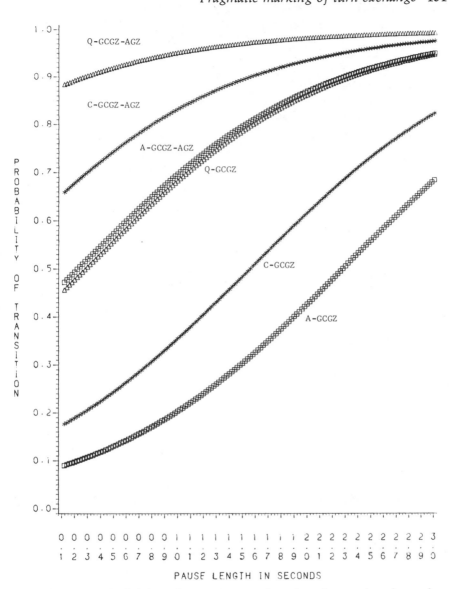

Figure 8.2. Probability of transition as a function of pause length, speaker and auditor actions, and speech event.

Probability distributions of elements and combinations thereof in effecting turn exchange and back channel are plotted in Figures 8.2 and 8.3. The curves are simulated using the estimates in Equations 2a and 3. In Figure 8.2, the probability distributions of GCGZ-AGZ and GCGZ within

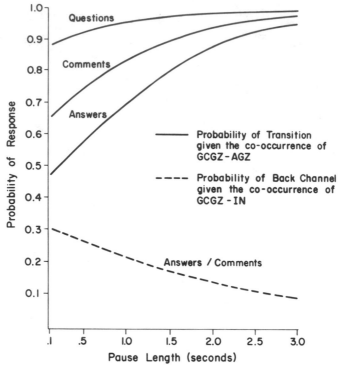

Figure 8.3. Probability of auditor response as a function of pause length and speech events.

Questions, Answers, and Comments, respectively, in relation to turn exchange are plotted as a function of pause length. In Figure 8.3, the probability distributions of GCGZ-AGZ within Questions, Answers, and Comments, respectively, in relation to turn exchange, and GCGZ-IN in relation to back channel are plotted as a function of pause length. The differential relationship of pause length to turn exchange and back channel is clearly illustrated in Figure 8.3.

Turn exchange versus back channels. The data in Table 8.3 and their formalization in Equation (3) indicate that the significance of grammatical completion, speaker- and auditor-gaze, and pause-length elements is independent of the type of speech event, as none of these elements co-varies exclusively with a type of speech event. Nonetheless, knowledge of the speech event is a significant component with respect to both turn exchange and back channel. Questions provide a more salient context for embedded elements, such as GZ and GCGZ, than do Answers and Comments in relation to turn exchange (cf. Figure 8.2), but not in relation to back channels. It is also the case, however, that the salience of Questions cannot be perceived independently of co-occurring (embedded) elements, as there was no significant main effect of Questions in Equations (2a) and (3). The lack of main effect is due to the rare occurrence of pauses unmarked by grammatical completion and speaker and auditor gaze elements (Table 8.3). Thus the Question speech event is in part definable by a formal distribution of verbal and nonverbal elements.

It may be concluded that though knowledge of the speech event has an effect on the probabilistic salience of embedded elements, the elements themselves are necessary parameters in a function maximizing the probability of turn exchange or back channel.

Furthermore, knowledge of the speech event is not necessary for maximal prediction of turn exchange. The estimates in Figure 8.2 indicate that the co-occurrence of grammatical completion, speaker and auditor gaze elements, and extended pause length (GCGZ-AGZ in Figure 8.2) constitutes the set of elements that is both necessary and sufficient for ensuring exchange of the speaking turn. By affecting the salience of embedded elements, knowledge of the speech event has its most marked effect on the parameter of pause length, that is, on the length of silence beyond which turn exchange is virtually ensured (cf. Figure 8.2).

In contrast to turn exchange, back channels cannot be predicted with an accuracy approaching 1.0. Instead, the maximum probability is .3 (Figure 8.3). Thus, though several elements are probabilistically related to verbal back channels, no element or co-occurrence thereof bears a one-to-one correspondence with this form of speech utterance. By this contrast alone, it is clear that the contextual distribution of back channels in conversation differs from that of turn exchange.

Furthermore, the occurrence of back channels in relation to silence differs markedly from the occurrence of turn exchange in relation to silence. While the probability of back channel decreases as a function of pause length, the probability of turn exchange increases. Thus research focusing on patterns of talk and silence that does not differentiate these utterances (most notably Jaffe and Feldstein, 1970; Cappella and Streibel, 1979) may well yield confounded results on temporal properties of conversation.

Adequacy of the turn-exchange models. Thus far, the analysis of verbal and nonverbal elements in relation to turn exchange has shown that elements are differentially distributed in their probabilistic salience, as are combinations of elements. Furthermore, turn exchange can be predicted with a probability approaching 1.0 by a specific set of elements that is independent of the speech event (as defined). The purpose of the following analysis is to determine the validity of these results within each conversation.

The rates of transition as a function of the GC, GZ, GCGZ, AGZ, and gesture contexts are given for each conversation in Table 8.4. In each conversation, of speaker behaviors, the co-occurrence of GC and GZ (GCGZ) provides the most salient context for turn exchange. The presence of the auditor gaze element (AGZ) increases the rate of transition across conversations, so that for each conversation GCGZ-AGZ provides the most salient context for turn exchange. The presence of gesture neutralizes the probabilistic salience of other behavioral elements in all conversations, and, as seen previously, rarely occurs in conjunction with AGZ.

The salience of the GC and GZ contexts is not consistent across conversations. In five conversations (12, 13, 24, 33, 44), turn exchange never occurs in conjunction with GC. In four of these (12, 24, 33, 44), the AGZ element occurs rarely ($N = 4$ at most) or not at all with GC, such that the context of GC-AGZ is rare. In three conversations (32, 33, 44), turn exchange never occurs in conjunction with GZ and, as with GC, co-occurrence with AGZ is rare. Thus, though the co-occurrence of grammatical completion and speaker gaze, GCGZ, provides a salient context for turn exchange in each conversation, as does GCGZ-AGZ, the salience of GC, GZ, GC-AGZ, and GZ-AGZ contexts is not consistent.

Inclusion of the speech-event variable has demonstrated that the probabilistic salience of embedded elements could be affected. Because none of the behavioral contexts co-varied exclusively with a type of speech event, it could be concluded that behavioral context is not redundant with illocutionary force of the utterance with respect to turn exchange. These results are reflected in each conversation (Table 8.5). (Units in which gesture occurred are not included in this table.)

In each conversation, the context GCGZ derives increased salience when embedded within Questions opposed to Answers or Comments. Thus the Q-GCGZ interaction observed in Equation (3) appears to be consistent across conversations. The Q-GZ interaction (Equation 3) is found in three conversations (12, 21, 24), although because of the low frequency of GZ and GZ-AGZ in the other conversations, the consistency of this effect is unknown.

Table 8.4. *Salience of GC, GZ, GCGZ, AGZ, gesture in each conversation (rate of transition)*

	AGZ absent		AGZ present	
	Gesture	No gesture	Gesture	No gesture
Conversation 12				
No GC, GZ, or GCGZ	.000 (20)	.000 (41)	(1)	(0)
GC	(2)	.000 (25)	(0)	(4)
GZ	.000 (18)	.083 (36)	(1)	(0)
GCGZ	.000 (11)	.170 (47)	(2)	.867 (15)
Conversation 13				
No GC, GZ, or GCGZ	(6)	.000 (39)	(0)	(8)
GC	(4)	.000 (27)	(1)	.286 (14)
GZ	.000 (10)	.067 (15)	(0)	(3)
GCGZ	(7)	.308 (26)	(1)	.773 (22)
Conversation 21				
No GC, GZ, or GCGZ	.000 (13)	.000 (22)	(0)	(1)
GC	(2)	.214 (14)	(0)	(0)
GZ	(8)	.058 (52)	(1)	(3)
GCGZ	(2)	.298 (57)	(0)	.941 (17)
Conversation 24				
No GC, GZ, or GCGZ	.000 (24)	.000 (25)	(4)	(2)
GC	(3)	.000 (15)	(0)	(1)
GZ	.000 (15)	.111 (18)	(4)	(0)
GCGZ	.000 (13)	.192 (26)	(1)	.813 (16)
Conversation 32				
No GC, GZ, or GCGZ	.000 (17)	.000 (35)	(1)	(2)
GC	(2)	.059 (17)	(0)	(3)
GZ	.000 (29)	.000 (34)	(1)	(6)
GCGZ	.053 (19)	.324 (34)	(1)	.778 (9)
Conversation 33				
No GC, GZ, or GCGZ	(8)	.022 (46)	(0)	(0)
GC	(1)	.000 (14)	(0)	(0)
GZ	(6)	.000 (44)	(0)	(2)
GCGZ	(5)	.185 (54)	(0)	.636 (11)
Conversation 41				
No GC, GZ, or GCGZ	.000 (40)	.000 (19)	(5)	(6)
GC	.000 (13)	.111 (18)	(6)	(3)
GZ	.000 (27)	.068 (15)	(2)	(5)
GCGZ	.056 (19)	.313 (16)	(3)	.688 (32)
Conversation 44				
No GC, GZ, or GCGZ	.000 (9)	.000 (33)	(0)	(3)
GC	(3)	.000 (26)	(0)	(2)
GZ	.000 (17)	.000 (25)	(0)	(5)
GCGZ	(7)	.188 (48)	(1)	.700 (20)

Table 8.5. *Frequencies of GC, GZ, GCGZ by speech event and conversation and associated frequencies of transition* (N)

	Questions		Answers		Comments	
	AGZ absent	AGZ present	AGZ absent	AGZ present	AGZ absent	AGZ present
Conversation 12						
No GC, GZ, or GCGZ	1(0)		11(0)		29(0)	
GC			12(0)	1(0)	13(0)	3(1)
GZ	4(1)		15(1)		17(1)	
GCGZ	8(4)	4(4)	10(0)	5(4)	29(4)	6(5)
Conversation 13						
No GC, GZ, or GCGZ	1(0)	2(0)	17(0)	1(0)	21(0)	5(2)
GC	1(0)	2(0)	14(0)	7(2)	12(0)	5(2)
GZ	1(0)		6(0)		8(1)	3(1)
GCGZ	3(2)	8(7)	12(2)	4(3)	11(4)	10(7)
Conversation 21						
No GC, GZ, or GCGZ	1(0)		15(0)	1(0)	6(0)	
GC	1(0)		9(1)		4(2)	
GZ	11(2)	1(1)	34(1)	1(0)	7(0)	1(1)
GCGZ	5(4)	12(12)	48(10)	5(4)	4(3)	
Conversation 24						
No GC, GZ, or GCGZ	4(0)	1(1)	12(0)	1(0)	9(0)	
GC	2(0)		8(0)	1(0)		
GZ	5(2)		12(0)		5(0)	
GCGZ	4(1)	8(5)	15(3)	7(7)	7(1)	1(1)
Conversation 32						
No GC, GZ, or GCGZ			15(0)	1(0)	19(0)	1(0)
GC			6(0)	1(0)	11(1)	2(2)
GZ	5(0)		18(0)	2(0)	11(0)	4(0)
GCGZ	6(4)	3(3)	13(2)	3(3)	15(5)	3(1)
Conversation 33						
No GC, GZ, or GCGZ	2(0)		18(0)		26(1)	
GC			5(0)		9(0)	
GZ	5(0)		22(0)		17(0)	2(1)
GCGZ	6(2)	3(3)	23(3)	3(2)	25(5)	5(2)

Table 8.5. *(continued)*

	Questions		Answers		Comments	
	AGZ absent	AGZ present	AGZ absent	AGZ present	AGZ absent	AGZ present
Conversation 41						
No GC, GZ, or GCGZ	1(0)		9(0)	1(0)	9(0)	5(0)
GC	1(0)		7(0)	2(0)	10(2)	1(1)
GZ	1(0)		7(1)	3(0)	7(0)	2(0)
GCGZ	3(2)	13(13)	6(2)	11(4)	7(1)	8(5)
Conversation 44						
No GC, GZ, or GCGZ			32(0)	3(0)	1(0)	
GC	2(0)		23(0)	1(1)	1(0)	1(1)
GZ	4(0)	2(1)	20(0)	3(1)	1(0)	
GCGZ	9(4)	10(9)	38(4)	9(4)	1(1)	1(1)

Note: The values in parentheses are frequencies of transition.

Table 8.6. *Estimated logits within conversations*

	Logits[a]		
Conversation	GCGZ	AGZ	PL
12	3.4	2.8	1.4
13	3.0	2.6	.5
21	3.2	3.3	− .9
24	3.3	2.8	1.9
32	4.1	1.9	1.9
33	3.0	2.3	1.7
41	3.2	1.5	.4
44	2.5	2.9	− .2

[a]Speech-event parameters were not stipulated in the models generating these estimates.

The only remaining result to be evaluated within each conversation is the effect of pause length. Logistic regression models were generated for each conversation. Due to frequency distributions, the speech event parameter could not be stipulated. The GCGZ, AGZ, and pause-length logits for each conversation are given in Table 8.6. Clearly, the salience of pause length is highly variable across conversations, and only in four conversations (12, 24, 32, 33) is it reflective of the results in Equation 3.

In order to determine whether speech event has an effect on pause length, the conversations were divided into two groups based on these results: Group 1 includes conversations 12, 24, 32, 33; Group 2 includes 13, 21, 41, 44, for purposes of statistical analysis. Two models were tested in each group. The first model used only Questions and stipulated the GCGZ, AGZ, and PL parameters. The estimates for Group 1 are given in Equation (4).

$$Pr(Tr = 1) = -2.27 + 1.95 \, GCGZ + 2.19 \, AGZ + .43 \, PL \tag{4}$$

The estimates for Group 2 are given in Equation (5).

$$Pr(Tr = 1) = -3.07 + 3.45 \, GCGZ + 2.01 \, AGZ + .6 \, PL \tag{5}$$

The second model used only Answer/Comment units and stipulated the GC, GZ, GCGZ, AGZ, and PL parameters. The estimates for Group 1 are given in Equation (6).

$$Pr(Tr = 1) = -7.02 + [2.14 \, GC + 1.93 \, GZ + 4.37 \, GCGZ] \\ + 2.51 \, AGZ + 2.05 \, PL \tag{6}$$

The estimates for Group 2 are given in Equation (7).

$$Pr(Tr = 1) = -4.78 + [2.14 \, GC + 1.42 \, GZ + 3.24 \, GCGZ] \\ + 1.95 \, AGZ + .2 \, PL \tag{7}$$

These results are plotted in Figure 8.4.

In both groups, pause length is not a significant parameter in the context of Questions (illustrated in Figure 8.4). The difference between the groups is found in the context of Answer/Comment speech event, where pause length is of major importance in Group 1 and irrelevant in Group 2 (see Figure 8.4). Logit estimates of pause length were then obtained for each conversation for the speech event context of Answer/Comment. (The two were merged due to sample size.) The results are reported in Table 8.7. In five of eight conversations, pause length is a necessary component in maximizing the probability of turn exchange when exchange occurs in a context other than Questions. In three conversations, it has little relation to turn exchange.

Analysis of residuals

The purpose of the analysis just presented was to determine whether turn exchange, specifically the smooth or nonoverlapping exchange, is a feature

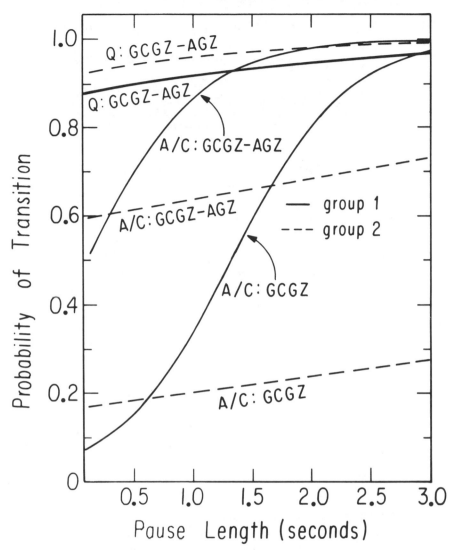

Figure 8.4. Probability of transition as a function of pause length, speaker and auditor actions, and speech event. Conversations are grouped in terms of salience of pause length.

of conversation indexed by interlocutors. Analytically, it was proposed that if some set of elements exhibited a one-to-one correspondence with turn exchange, then it could be concluded that the set constituted an index. Furthermore, the analytic contrast was not between smooth and simul-

Table 8.7. *Estimated logits for pause length (PL) in the context of Answer/Comment*

	Conversation							
	12	13	21	24	32	33	41	44
PL logit	2.4	1.2	−.5	1.8	2.2	2.2	.3	.2

taneous turn exchanges, but between smooth turn exchange and no exchange (at locations of silent pauses).

The results indicate that a number of elements are probabilistically related to turn exchange, as would be expected given the results of D&F, Duncan et al. (1979), and Sacks et al. (1974). Co-occurrences of elements also provide salient contexts for turn exchange, where the specific sets of co-occurring features are probabilistically differentiated. Given the empirical fact that turn exchange can be maximally predicted ($p \approx 1.0$) by the co-occurrence of GCGZ-AGZ-PL elements, then it may be concluded that the set of elements indexes this contextual feature of conversation. That is, the form GCGZ-AGZ-PL is a signal of, or index of, turn exchange.

It is also the case, however, that turn exchange occurs in other contexts or, equivalently, in conjunction with other forms. These contexts or forms are defined by elements which constitute subsets of the maximally salient GCGZ-AGZ-PL form, such as GCGZ, GC-AGZ, GCGZ-PL, and the like. As none of these contexts has a one-to-one correspondence to turn exchange, they cannot be considered indexes of turn exchange. Given the analytic definition of index used thus far, it would have to be concluded that, though turn exchange is a contextual parameter of conversation that may be indexed by interlocutors, it is not always so indexed. This conclusion, however, does little to explain the sources of variation observed in the results, specifically, the differential distribution of behavioral contexts within and across conversations. In an attempt to explain this variation, a further analysis of indexical properties was undertaken.

It is proposed that each context which is probabilistically but not indexically related to turn exchange is also an index, but of other aspects of conversation. This would mean that when turn exchange per se is not indexed, the form marking turn exchange has other indexical functions, such that turn exchange becomes a locus for observing a range of signals used by interlocutors in a particular social occasion. In order to support this interpretation, it is minimally necessary to demonstrate that each form consituting a subset of GCGZ-AGZ-PL elements is related to some aspect of conversation. To determine whether contexts probabilistically related to turn exchange are indexes, an analysis of residuals was undertaken in which speaking turns marked by forms lacking a common element were analyzed as a residual group.

The AGZ element. All speaking turns following a form that lacked the AGZ element were analyzed as the first residual group. Because these results have been reported elsewhere (Denny, 1982b), they will be described here only briefly. On analysis, it was documented that speaking turns following turn exchange marked by a form lacking AGZ were short. The definition of a short utterance was empirically derived as containing just one grammatical clause terminated by a pause of at least 65 ms. Such speaking turns do not correspond to a specific form of speech event, and thus may be Questions, Answers, or Comments. For these data, then, absence of the AGZ element in any context of turn exchange indicates the length of the subsequent speaking turn.

Exceptions to the short-turn rule occur. These are speaking turns which consist of both an Answer and a Question (A-Q) as in (1) and (2) below:

    Q: Where are you at?
(1) A-Q: I'm at the law school here. (595 ms, BC) You're a graduate student?

    Q: And you're from (205 ms) social services?
(2) A-Q: Right (185 ms, BC) right (295 ms, BC) what year are you in?
    A-Q: Second year (1500 ms) and what (105 ms) are you a graduate student?

Note that in the A-Q exceptions, the short turn is still preserved. That is, the Answer meets the criterion of a short turn, but the speaking turn itself is extended, in some cases by repetition of the Answer, and always by the subsequent Question. The occurrence of auditor back channel (BC) during pauses embedded in A-Q constructions suggests that these speaking turns are interactively achieved by the interlocutors such that the back channel replaces turn exchange and thereby extends the current speaking turn. Such back channels are termed "continuers" by Schegloff (1982). It is proposed that these exceptions index a feature of the social event itself, namely the reciprocity which is expected in casual conversation between interlocutors of equal status.

The PL element. It was seen in Equations (5) and (7) that pause length is not a significant parameter in modeling the occurrence of turn exchange when the exchange marks the completion of a Question. It was also documented that elements embedded within questions derive increased probabilistic salience, such that turn exchange is maximally predicted ($p = .9$) by the form GCGZ-AGZ. It would seem then, that the illocutionary force of the question renders pause length redundant with respect to turn exchange. Thus the form GCGZ-AGZ (absence of PL) entails that the current turn is a Question, or more generally, the absence of PL indexes the type of speech event. In a form such as GCGZ, in which both the AGZ and PL elements are absent, the form is an index of both type of speech event and length of subsequent turn.

It was also the case, however, that pause length was not consistently significant in the contexts of Answers and Comments. In three conversations, constituting the second residual group, PL is unrelated to turn exchange. It is in this residual group of conversations that the exceptions to the short-turn rule were observed. It may be suggested that pause length is neutralized by virtue of the (A-Q) construction, in which completion of an Answer is no longer predictive of turn exchange. Rather, it becomes predictive of a Question posed by the same speaker. In the construction of this sequence of speech events, a form of reciprocity is instantiated, though the salience of a specific element in relation to turn exchange has been overridden. Thus a tradeoff is observed between indexing turn exchange per se, and using the construction of speaking turns to index a feature of the social occasion itself.

The GZ element. There are 16 speaking turns constituting the residual group lacking GZ. Of the 16, eight deviate from GCGZ or GCGZ-AGZ only by virtue of the coding system. That is, speaker gaze co-occurs with grammatical completion but switches off prior to turn exchange. Of the remaining cases, six share a common characteristic – speaker gaze is not present during the turn, and the turns themselves are short. Of these turns, three are greetings, for example: "I'm Sandra Day." The other three are Comments which, in each case, are followed by a Question as in (3).

(3)C: That's a big place.

Q: Oh, are you from Iowa?

Although these short comments may be an indirect means of shifting the focus of conversation by eliciting the initiation of a Question-Answer sequence, the small number of cases precludes any statement about the functional significance of the absence of the GZ element.

The GC element. There are 16 speaking turns constituting the residual group lacking GC, six of which are not analyzable because of technical problems. In the remaining cases, the absence of the GC element is not due to grammatical incompleteness per se, but is reflective of the criteria used for defining a grammatically complete utterance. It should be remembered that a designation of clausal completion was contingent on fully explicit independent clauses, or on dependent clauses or phrases that were extensions of immediately preceding independent clauses. The major exceptions to the "fully explicit" criterion were those utterances which were complete by virtue of a specific form of ellipsis: The deleted components of the clause were present in the immediately preceding speaking turn.

The speaking turns constituting the residual group did not meet the criterion of complete clause by ellipsis, though they were elliptical utterances. In two cases, the deleted components were present in the immediately preceding back channel rather than speaking turn. In one case, the Answer to a preceding Question was entirely nonverbal. In three cases, the utterance presupposed an elliptical clause in the preceding speaking turn. In three cases, the clause presupposed knowledge about the experimental situation, or topic of conversation. In one case, the utterance presupposed an explicit clause occurring several turns previously.

What is of interest, then, is not grammatical completeness per se, but the formal structure used by these interlocutors to instantiate completeness. In the majority of cases, fully explicit clauses were used. Such utterances presuppose least about shared knowledge. When ellipsis is used, the utterance in most cases makes presuppositions only about the immediately adjacent turn. In only 10 cases, across eight conversations, did elliptical utterances make greater presuppositions.

Indexical forms

Turn exchange. In the system of turn taking modeled by Sacks et al. (1974), completion of any grammatical unit constitutes a salient conversational unit with respect to the exchange of the speaking turn. In order to explain the frequency of exchanges which were characterized by both nonoverlapping speech and a minimal silence, rules about the transfer of speakership were invoked. Grammatical structure constitutes the only metric necessary for the description of the observed interactional organization. If a grammatical juncture was observed and an exchange did not occur, the absence of exchange is interpreted as a particular option available to, and exercised by, the hearer.

In the system modeled by D&F, completion of a phonemic clause marked by at least one turn cue constituted a relevant location for turn exchange. Similar to Sacks et al. (1974), if an exchange did not take place, then an option allowed by the rule regulating turn exchange was exercised. The system is thus interpreted to be organized to mark or index opportunities for smooth turn exchange, so that the absence of exchange at relevant places is perceived as the exercise of an option.

The results presented in this chapter indicate that the form GCGZ-AGZ-PL unambiguously marks a turn boundary prior to the onset of the next turn, such that it is functionally specific as a *signal of* – that is, index of – turn exchange. Note that this signal is a product of an interactive negotiation prior to what is usually recognized as the interactional event – namely, speaker display of a functional *signal for* turn exchange and subsequent turn exchange or lack thereof. Since all other forms were not distributed uniquely with respect to turn exchange, it may be concluded that the actual occurrence of turn exchange is not a function of specification by these signals. That is, they are not signals of turn exchange. To the extent that turn exchange is not indexed by interlocutors, the results support Duncan and Fiske's (1977) and Sacks and associate's (1974) claim that only the opportunity for turn exchange is indexed by structural elements.

Based on the analysis of residuals, however, it can be seen that the presence or absence of elements in forms probabilistically related to turn exchange corresponds to specifiable contextual features of conversation. Thus the absence of the AGZ element corresponds to a feature of turn length; the absence of the PL element corresponds to a feature describing the type of speech event; absence of GC corresponds to forms of elliptical utterances or, more generally, cohesive devices. In all cases, it is proposed that the relationship of correspondence constitutes an indexical relationship, such that each of the forms marking turn exchange is an index, though not necessarily of the contextual parameter of turn exchange. It is argued, therefore, that the location of turn exchange has become a locus for the instantiation of indexical signals.

The issue then arises as to why turn exchange is not always indexed. One possibility is that the location for turn exchange has been made unambiguous by other means, specifically, by the illocutionary force of the speech event. For example, completion of a question can be unambiguously anticipated by the auditor as a result of the formal characteristics of the question speech event. In this case, the auditor's marking of the utterance with the AGZ element (or the mutual marking of PL) is redundant. The AGZ element, under these conditions, is free to acquire an indexical function. Speaking turns which were marked to be short (i.e. having followed exchanges lacking AGZ) are themselves subject to specific expectations by the current auditor – namely, that the turn will be short. Thus a series of short speaking turns can be generated, all of which are characterized by the absence of AGZ at locations of turn exchange.

That the illocutionary force of the speech event is a source of explanation for the occurrence of turn exchange not only is seen in the data presented herein, but also is consistent with more general claims about speech acts in conversation (Franck, 1979; Good, 1979; Keller, 1979). Adjacency pairs (Schegloff & Sacks, 1973) are, after all, two consecutive speech acts, where the second is logically dependent on, and conventionally entailed by, the first. Completion of a first utterance of a given adjacency pair would thus render the location of turn exchange unambiguous.

Neither D&F's model nor Sacks and colleagues' (1974) model precludes higher-order effects such as illocutionary force; the latter model, in fact, depends upon them. But implied by both models is that such linguistic or nonlinguistic devices are superimposed on a structural system of turn taking. Thus in each of the models the metric constituting structure is unchanging. In Sacks and associates' (1974) model, each point of transition relevance (closure of a grammatical unit) is functionally equivalent to any other with respect to turn exchange. In D&F's model, each display of one or more turn cues is functionally equivalent to any other with respect to turn exchange (if strategy signals are discounted). In contrast, it is argued herein that a given instance of closure of a grammatical clause, for example, may not be related to turn exchange. Depending on the specification of co-occurring elements, it may have an indexical relationship to turn exchange. Depending on the speech event within which the element is embedded, turn exchange may not be indexed at all. Rather, the location of turn exchange becomes an interactively achieved phenomenon where other indexical signals may be observed. Thus higher-order effects such as illocutionary force are not superimposed on a system of turn taking but constitute an alternative to indexing turn exchange. Illocutionary force renders the index redundant, such that the location of turn exchange becomes a rich source for marking other aspects of conversation.

A salient feature generally ascribed to turn-taking systems (Levinson, 1983) and present in the models of both D&F and Sacks et al. (1974) is the permissiveness characterizing a system of turn exchange. That is, exchange of the turn is an option that may or may not be exercised by a given hearer. The results reported herein do not affect this feature of a system of turn exchange, though the behavioral actions constituting optional or permissive behavior do differ. In the case of the form GCGZ-AGZ-PL, it is argued that the occurrence of turn exchange is not an option that may or may not be exercised. As noted above, use of this form entails turn exchange. The occurrence of this index, however, is interactively achieved, and thus its construction is optional. Both speaker and auditor gaze elements can and often do precede verbal completion of the utterance. If the auditor marks a particular utterance with the AGZ element, a speaker has the option of exhibiting the other formal elements defining the index, and vice versa. The occurrence of turn exchange at a particular location is, therefore, negotiable because the construction of the index of turn exchange is a product of both speaker and hearer actions.

Back channels. In contrast to the parameter of turn exchange, back-channel response is not indexed (as defined) by actions of interlocutors. [This claim is based on the results presented in Equation (2a) and illustrated in Figure 8.3.] Instead, verbal and nonverbal elements are probabilistically related to verbal back channels. Consistent with D&F, it may be concluded that the opportunity for back channel response is being indexed by interlocutors. Other explanations are also possible. First, it may be the case that the set of elements indexically related to back channels was simply not defined by the models presented above. Second, it may be the case that verbal back channels are functionally differentiated within conversation such that they cannot be analyzed as a homogeneous set of utterances. Instead, depending on their placement in conversation, they assume distinct conversational functions, as Schegloff (1982) has argued. In any case, however, it is clear that speaking turns can be formally differentiated from back channels.

The analysis and discussion thus far have been concerned with indexical properties of verbal and nonverbal elements in relation to turn exchange or verbal back-channel response. It is concluded that though turn exchange itself is indexed, back-channel response is not. Furthermore, delineation of indexes relating to turn exchange was argued to constitute a structural or rule-governed description of turn taking. In contrast, and following D&F, strategy is a description of actual behavior within the realm defined by rules. Given the conceptualization of structure here, strategy becomes a description of the use of indexes. The particular axis invoked to describe the use of indexes is the axis or continuum of pragmatic markedness.

8.4. Pragmatic marking of turn exchanges

The focus of this paper has been on turn taking, and more specifically, on the indexical properties of verbal and nonverbal elements in relation to turn exchange. As a result of analysis, several indexical signs were delineated. These signs, occurring in the context of turn exchange, index turn exchange itself or some other feature of conversation. Because of the temporal contiguity between a given index and turn exchange, forms of turn exchange may be said to be defined by the indexes marking them. Assessing the pragmatic markedness of these indexes is simultaneously an assessment of pragmatically marked and unmarked forms of turn exchange.

As noted earlier, an unmarked or automatized use of an index is a use that is expected under certain conditions, whereas a marked or fore-grounded use is one that is unexpected. Whereas the unmarked index presupposes some contextual feature and conditions, the marked use is creative, as it invokes the existence of a contextual feature that would otherwise not be presupposed. Obviously, the same indexical form may be unmarked or marked depending on the context in which it occurs, and the definition of expected or unexpected is dependent on the metric used to calibrate expectation.

With respect to turn taking, an expected sign is defined as one that is functionally specific to turn exchange. A pragmatically marked sign is one that presupposes other aspects of conversation. Such signs are said to be creative in that they index features of conversation that would otherwise not be presupposed *by a system of turn taking*. Marking turn exchanges in this fashion is, then, a creative use of turn-taking machinery. Given the data reported in this chapter, the pragmatically unmarked form is the index GCGZ-AGZ-PL, and all other indexes are pragmatically marked.

Unmarked forms

In Table 8.8, GCGZ-AGZ-PL is designated as P_0, and constitutes the unmarked form of turn exchange. The absence of both a filled pause and speaker gestural activity is simultaneously presupposed. As emphasized earlier, this form is a product of both interlocutors' actions. Whereas the presence of speaker gaze invariably precedes verbal completion, the

Table 8.8. *Pragmatic marking of turn exchange*

Unmarked	P_0 Index of turn exchange
	GCGZ-AGZ-PL
	Presupposes no gesture or filled pause

Marked P_1 Index of discourse-related feature
(1) GCGZ-PL (absence of AGZ)
 Entails: Current turn is an Answer or Comment, [GCGZ-PL](A)(C); subsequent turn is short; index of turn length.
(2) GCGZ-AGZ (absence of PL)
 Entails: Current turn is a Question, [GCGZ-AGZ]Q; index of speech event.
(3) GZ-AGZ-PL (absence of GC)
 Entails: Current turn is elliptical; index of cohesive devices.
(4) GCGZ (absence of AGZ and PL)
 Entails: Current turn is a Question, [GCGZ]Q, subsequent turn is short; index of turn length and speech event.
(5) GZ-AGZ (absence of GC and PL)
 Entails: Current turn is elliptical Question; index of speech event and cohesion.

P_2 Index of social event, presupposing P_1
(1) [GCGZ]Q
 Entails: Subsequent turn is [Short Answer − Q] such that all forms marking turn exchange lack PL to produce:
(2) [GCGZ](A)(C)
(3) [GCGZ-AGZ](A)(C), etc.

location at which the auditor gaze element occurs is more variable. It may or may not precede verbal completion. The point to be made is that the construction of this index occurs over time and is negotiable.

The unmarked form is composed of elements which are pervasive components of face-to-face interaction, rather than specific to the social occasion of casual conversation. Nor do the components co-vary with a form of speech event (as defined). Though the salience of clausal completion (GC) may, in fact, be specific to the social roles instantiated by the interlocutors, it is suggested that the salience of grammatical construction is not. Thus the instantiation of grammatical completeness will vary; the relevance of this category or element will be constant.

It can be seen, then, that the unmarked form of turn exchange for these interlocutors is one that has been negotiated. The turn exchange neither indexes other pervasive features of conversation, nor does it index features which are specific to the social occasion at hand. Thus the exchange places no constraints on the subsequent speaking turn(s).

Marked forms

Indexes other than GCGZ-AGZ-PL are designated as pragmatically marked forms in Table 8.8. Two levels of pragmatic markedness are differentiated, P_1 and P_2. Differentiation of pragmatic marking is based on the degree of presupposition entailed by the indexical signal. The pragmatically marked level, P_1, indexes or presupposes discourse-related features such as turn length, type of speech event, or devices of cohesion (see Halliday and Hasan, 1976). The pragmatically marked level, P_2, indexes both features of discourse, that is, P_1 and features of the social occasion itself.

Forms subsumed by P_1 are formal deviations from the P_0 form. That is, each form is composed of some set of elements which defines the unmarked device. In P_1 (1) of Table 8.8, the AGZ element is absent in the form GCGZ-PL. Use of this form in conjunction with turn exchange results in a short subsequent turn, such that the form is an index of turn length. In P_1 (2), the PL element is absent in the form GCGZ-AGZ. Use of this form entails that the current turn be a Question, such that the form is an index of the current speech event. In P_3 (3), the GC element is not present in the form GZ-AGZ-PL. Such a form indexes an elliptical utterance that presupposes more than an explicit clause in the immediately preceding speaking turn. It may presuppose an explicit clause occurring several turns earlier or an elliptical clause which, in turn, presupposes a previous explicit clause. In either case, the linear sequence of talk is being hierarchically organized by use of these cohesive devices.

In P_1 (4-5), more than one element is absent. In P_1 (4), both the AGZ and PL elements are absent in the GCGZ form. In this case, both length and type of speech event are indexed, such that the turn following an exchange marked by GCGZ will be a Short Answer. In P_1 (5), the PL and GC elements are absent in the GZ-AGZ form. In this case, the current turn is a Question and also elliptical. Note the additive relationship among indexical properties which is observed when more than one element is absent. In principle, each form uniquely identifies a set of discourse-related features. In actuality, there is some redundancy because the function of the GZ element could not be derived from the data.

Forms subsumed by P_2 are not formal deviations from P_1 as much as exceptions to the P_1 forms. Examples of P_2 forms include GCGZ-AGZ and

GCGZ embedded within Answers and Comments, which are observed in three conversations (best represented by Group 2 in Figure 8.4). Pause length has ceased to be a salient element in a system of turn exchange in these conversations. Consequently, there are no unmarked forms of turn exchange in these conversations.[3] P_2 (1) is defined by GCGZ in the context of Questions (designated [GCGZ]Q), in which the Short Answer-Question (A-Q) is observed rather than the expected Short Answer. It is suggested that the significance of pause length has been neutralized in all speech event contexts by virtue of this construction. Thus other P_2 forms are causally related to (i.e., a product of) the construction of this form. It is also suggested that the indexical function of each element remains intact. Thus, the absence of AGZ still indexes turn length. Nonetheless, a particular sequence of utterances has become the expected form of response to Questions, a sequence which reciprocates prior queries posed by the other interlocutor. Such reciprocity, it is argued, is expected in a social occasion where interlocutors have equal status. The difference between these conversations and the others is that the construction of speaking turns themselves is being used to instantiate reciprocity.

It can be seen that use of the unmarked form of turn exchange is most powerful by permitting maximal flexibility in what is said or how an idea is expressed. Use of the maximally presupposing form, subsumed by P_2, results in a highly restricted of stylized form of speech event: the short answer and question. Similarly, forms which index turn length, type of speech event, or cohesion place greater restrictions of the subsequent speech utterance than does the unmarked form.

At the same time that pragmatically marked exchanges restrict the subsequent speaking turn in some way, they help to organize the unfolding linear sequence of talk. One finds that the Question-Answer adjacency pair is a focal construction for indexical elaboration. Question-(long)Answer, Question-Short Answer, and Question-[Short Answer-Question] sequences are formally differentiated within these conversations, and all are foregrounded sequences of turns. Use of ellipsis where the elliptical construction presupposes an explicit clause occurring several turns previously is a formal device linking the current and subsequent turns to some block of preceding turns. A speaking turn using this form of cohesion is also foregrounded.

I suggest that the forms of foregrounding noted above are expected given the particular form of social event at hand. One expects and finds in "getting acquainted" interaction that the conversation focuses on aspects of the interlocutors' backgrounds which may account for their being in the same city, university, and behavioral science "experiment." Questions thus become a much used vehicle for information, and the extensive occurrence of the speech event, itself, indexes the lack of mutually shared knowledge. Because social status of the interlocutors is equal, it is also expected that the knowledge learned about the respective interlocutors is roughly equivalent. Achievement of such equivalence can be accomplished through reciprocating questions or the volunteering of comparable information. Use of an elliptical question or statement that achieves reciprocity either locally (preceding question) or nonlocally (across several turns) foregrounds blocks of speaking turns having relevance to the social roles being instantiated.

As a result of analysis, it can be seen that the segmentation of utterances need not be based solely on traditional grammatical form, designated as grammar (G) by Silverstein (1976): "a finite, recursive set of rules which relate semantico-referential representations to utterance types" (p. 45). By viewing speech behavior as a composition of functional styles and by delineating the pragmatic markedness of turn exchange, segmentation of utterances based on pragmatic properties becomes possible. The analysis, then, makes a contribution to a grammar (G') of speech acts: "a set of rules which relate pragmatic meanings . . . to the 'surface form' of utterances" (Silverstein, 1976, p. 45). Documentation of this pragmatic relationship has clearly been a focus of ethnographers of speech (see Bauman and Sherzer, 1973; and more recently, Sankoff, 1980; Sansom, 1980; Eads, 1982; McDowell, 1983). The analysis reported here differs from this previous work in that the identification of pragmatically marked and unmarked utterance fractions was derived from an analysis of turn taking which, in turn, was contingent on an analysis of the patterning of verbal *and* nonverbal actions in conversation.

The research presented herein provides further evidence that nonverbal behaviors have assumed distinct indexical functions in conversation and, in conjunction with verbal actions, their patterning is a source for determining pragmatic organization. It would seem, then, that nonverbal patterning is not only a result of an interactive process, as Duncan and his colleagues have emphasized (Duncan and Fiske, 1977; Duncan et al., 1979; Duncan et al., 1984; Mokros, 1983), but directly linked, through an indexical relationship, to pragmatic aspects of speech behavior. A given display of nonverbal behavior is dependent not only on other actions in conversation, but also on the co-occurring speech event. Moreover, the functional significance of a given display is largely dependent on co-occurring indexical tokens and the illocutionary force of the utterance. It is suggested, therefore, that pragmatic components of speech behavior be considered in any functional analysis of nonverbal behavior.

When the social roles being instantiated by interlocutors differ, one surely expects different conversational features to be indexed. Both pragmatic marking and the formal constitution of the indexical signals may also differ. Finally, it must be noted that turn taking is but a single dimension by which to gauge pragmatic markedness of speech utterances: "For any given utterance fraction, there may be many speech acts which motivate its presence in a speech event, that is, any utterance fraction may be a constituent of pragmatic structure in several modes" (Silverstein, 1976, p. 46). The point remains that the construction of a grammar G' rests, fundamentally, on the identification of indexical signs, such that our understanding of the relationships between pragmatic meaning and surface utterances may be maximized. This analysis has shown that the behavioral marking of surface forms (in the form of indexes) is not only pervasive, but the formal constitution of such marking is not solely linguistic. It is suggested, therefore, that nonverbal behavior represents a focal aspect of conversation whose analysis is relevant for ethnographers of speech. Though behavior exhibited by individuals in social interaction is multi-dimensional, the actions are not stratified but linked to the common core of the surface form. The researcher's task, it would seem, is to decipher the surface form as a hierarchy of signs.

8.5. Summary

The initial purpose of this chapter was to determine whether smooth turn exchange and verbal back channels were contextual parameters of conversation that are indexed by actions of the interlocutors. An indexical relationship was understood if the actions exhibited a one-to-one corre-spondence with the designated contextual parameter. On this criterion, it was concluded that verbal back channels were not indexed. It was suggested that this group of utterances is functionally differentiated within conversation and thus cannot be analyzed as a single group. In contrast to back channels, it was concluded that smooth turn exchange is indexed by actions of the interlocutors. On this basis alone, it is clear that speaking turns and back channels are structurally distinct utterance fractions.

Though turn exchange is indexed in these conversations by the co-occurrence of the grammatical structure element, speaker and auditor gaze elements, and pause length element, it is not always indexed. Thus, in many cases, turn exchange occurs in the absence of the complete "GC-GZ-

AGZ-PL" form. In such cases, however, some subset of the cited form is present. Furthermore, on analysis it was documented that the *absence* of a given element corresponds to a specifiable contextual parameter of conversation. For example, the absence of the auditor gaze element corresponds to (i.e., is a signal or index of) turn length. It was thus concluded that turn exchange has become a locus for the instantiation of indexical signals. Specifically, it was suggested that the illocutionary force of the speech event often renders the index of turn exchange redundant, allowing the location of turn exchange to become a source for marking other aspects of conversation. Finally, indexes associated with turn exchange were ranked according to pragmatic markedness, where the unmarked form is defined as the index functionally specific to turn exchange, and marked forms are those that presuppose other aspects of conversation.

Of fundamental significance is that the precise co-occurrence of verbal and nonverbal actions in conversation is critically relevant to both a system of turn taking and the analysis of conversational structure. The indexical nature of a given nonverbal or verbal event is proposed to be dependent on co-occurring events, such that analysis of the precise patterning is a means for determining pragmatic organization.

Acknowledgments

An abbreviated version of this paper was presented to the Max Planck Institut für Psycholinguistik. I am grateful for the comments received on that occasion. I am also grateful to Russell Tuttle, Starkey Duncan, Jr., and Michael Silverstein for their support of the research presented herein.

Endnotes

1 A recurrent argument implied or explicitly invoked by researchers who exclude non-linguistic markers is as follows: If visual markers were necessary (opposed to redundant) in face-to-face interaction, then their role should become apparent when telephone conversation is used as the point of comparison. For example, in discussing the role of speaker gaze, Levinson (1983) argues: "It seems roughly true, for example, that a speaker will break mutual gaze while speaking, returning gaze to the addressee upon turn completion . . . . The problem here is that if such signals formed the basis of our turn-taking ability, there would be a clear prediction that in the absence of visual cues there would either be much more gap and overlap or that the absence would require compensation by special audible cues. But work on telephone conversation shows that neither seems to be true." (p. 302)

This argument assumes that there is a single elementary system of turn taking operating in conversation such that necessary parameters of a turn-taking system are those which are common to the generic entity "conversation." According to this argument, the physical situation within which talk takes place is a peripheral feature rather than a defining or formal characteristic of the conversation itself. In contrast, the organization of conversation presented in this paper is fluid, such that the construction of indexes and the entities being indexed shift according to the social business at hand. Although comparison of telephone and face-to-face interaction may be fruitful, identifying salient elements as those which are common to both social situations seems an unnecessary form of reductionism, one that does little justice to the richness of human communication.

2 As in the model of turn exchange expressed in Equation (3), the "Q" term in Equation (2a) is not significant. It was stipulated in order to obtain unbiased estimates of parameters including a Q term.

3 Forms of turn exchange may have been unmarked in the early parts of any of these conversations. However, once an expected P_2 form of turn exchange is created, thereby neutralizing pause length, unmarked forms of turn exchange are precluded.

9. Patterns of persistence and change in action sequences

HARTMUT B. MOKROS

9.1. Introduction

The thesis of this chapter is that the shape or pattern of a person's actions in face-to-face interactions is notably affected by both interactive processes and noninteractive, presumably automatic processes. This thesis has been developed as an interpretation of regularities that emerged during the course of exploratory investigations of the 16 conversations described in Chapter 5. The data and analyses reported below should therefore not be viewed as representing a formal test of the thesis, but as steps toward the development and refinement of an interpretation.

Thus, whereas the focus of most of this monograph concerns the relation of interactional processes to the actions of individuals, the primary concern of this chapter is with an interpretation of observed patterns of action as noninteractively determined; as products of elementary information processes (Simon, 1979; Posner & McLeod, 1982). These patterns will be described as production regularities or action structure. The goal of this chapter is to convince the reader that transcriptions of nonmanipulated interaction can produce data whose patterns could be interpreted as reflecting elementary information processes. In order to achieve this goal, it is necessary to establish criteria and also to develop variables that make it possible to distinguish empirically between patterns of action stemming from interactive processes and those stemming from noninteractive processes.

The criterion for establishing that observed patterns of action represent production regularities is that the patterns remain constant across individuals and interactions. If homogeneity in the pattern of an action is observed across interactional settings, then there must be some source of regularity aside from interactional processes. Thus, the assumption made here is that elementary information processes *constrain* the production of actions comparably across individuals and to some extent across actions. That is, although the extent of use of an action may certainly be assumed to differ over time and over individuals, the production of that action involves common processes. Just as interactional structure may be identified and accounted for through hypothesized interactional rules, so also may action structure be identified and accounted for through hypothesized rules of production. And whereas interactional rules are assumed to derive from social convention, rules of production are assumed to reflect limitations or constraints on the process of enactment.

Empirical evidence for production regularities is presumably most likely to be located in the durational or persistence properties of actions and in patterns of change among actions. This presumption is based on observation of the success that research on the encoding, storage, and retrieval of information has had using chronometric measures (Posner, 1978). In this line of research, the study of duration and change is viewed as indirect evidence for elementary mental operations. The concern with elementary information processes is not founded on the quest for the understanding of social meaning or intentions behind actions. Instead, the concerns of research into information processing have been with identifying capacity and retention limitations along with constraints on the ordering of symbols in the handling of information. For describing processes of this type, measures of persistence and change would appear most appropriate. Two types of variables that represent measures of the durations of actions and change among actions, run-sequences and events, respectively, will be discussed in this chapter. These variables, it will be seen, represent simple extensions of D&F's action-sequence variables.

Three studies are presented in this chapter to provide some basis for the basic thesis. The actions analyzed in the first two studies have been hypothesized to function as interactional signals by D&F. All of these actions are speaker actions, and include speaker gaze, speaker gestures, and grammaticalness of speaker utterances. Whereas the first two studies focus on the structure of speaker actions, the third study focuses on the simultaneous smiling activity of interactants. Each study may also be thought of as a first trial of the effectiveness of run-sequence and events variables for representing and analyzing action patterns in interactions.

Before describing in more detail the methods and result of the three studies, this research will first be placed within the context of our explorations of interaction strategy, the context in which the variables discussed in this chapter were developed. It was as a result of looking at actions in the form of run-sequences (i.e., in the form of behavioral durations) that the possibility of analyzing interactional behavior in terms of information processing regularities was first considered.

What is strategy?

In our studies of two-person, face-to-face interactions, we have taken the position that the study of strategy, or more appropriately, interaction strategy involves analysis of the patterns of action or behavior of individuals within interactive contexts. This conceptualization of strategy was introduced by D&F to characterize what they viewed to be a major source of regularity observable in human interactions, namely "patterns of action resulting from a participant's exercising choice and initiative with respect to options provided by convention" (D&F, p. 288). Strategy represents one element of interactional behavior hypothesized within a methodological framework developed by D&F for the study of human interaction. This framework emphasizes the interrelationship between the social shaping of interaction (i.e., interactions as rule governed), referred to as interaction structure and the behavioral expressions of individuals during interactions (i.e., interaction strategy) within specific social-psychological-temporal-spatial contexts, referred to as situation.

Working within this framework, the investigation of strategy involves the description of on-line, sequential behavior. Empirically, research on strategy may therefore be conceptualized as the study of consequent probabilities. That is, if we hold that the study of strategy involves the analysis of patterns of action produced by interactants, then the identification of such patterns must be expressed in linear terms, as forward-moving probability statements. The study of strategy would thus involve the collection of data that enable us to answer questions about sequential dependencies. For example, given some behavior x at time t, what are the empirical rates or the associations of x with various possible behaviors at time $t + 1$?

Two main points made thus far should be emphasized: We have suggested (a) that strategy phenomena are to be identified by studying the exercise of options provided by convention, and (b) that empirically, strategy phenomena are to be represented in the form of forward moving sequential dependencies. The first point suggests that the patterns of display of actions or signals previously shown to be associated with social conventions provide the best candidates for strategy research. The second point suggests that probabilistic statements would best describe those patterns, once options are defined and signals identified. Given the extent of research on turn-taking in conversation, actions or signals associated with turn taking behavior would appear to be logical choices for strategy research.

Speaking-turn exchange represents an interactive phenomenon that has been hypothesized to be governed by social convention. It has often been observed that the modal pattern for the alternation of speaking turns in conversations is smooth turn exchange – that is, exchange without overlap in speech. For the 16 conversations discussed in this monograph, 82% of turn exchanges were smooth exchanges. Obviously, interactants must cooperate if their actions are to exhibit such coordination. How this coordination is accomplished has been of particular interest for researchers of interaction (e.g., Sacks, Schegloff, and Jefferson, 1974; D&F; Denny, Chapter 8 in this volume).

In investigating this issue, Duncan (1972) identified a set of six speaker actions (discussed in Chapter 3 of this monograph), referred to collectively as the speaker turn signal, that regularly preceded smooth turn exchanges. Moreover, Duncan found that, where the speech of the interactants overlapped, the speaker turn signal was negatively associated with claims to the speaking turn. This led Duncan to hypothesize that the coordination problem confronted by interactants is eased in the case of turn exchange by the conventional identification of certain actions as turn signals that serve as markers of points during interaction at which speakers are willing to relinquish the speaking turn. Duncan did not say that the speaker turn signal was invariably followed by smooth exchange. Instead, his data indicated that speaker turn signals distinguished turn exchanges that involved overlap in speech from those that involved no overlap.

By focusing on the relationship of antecedent display (turn signal versus no turn signal) to turn exchange (no overlap in speech versus overlap), Duncan was able to document statistically the apparent interactional function of the turn signal. Furthermore, within the model of turn-taking behavior proposed by D&F, based on the analysis of antecedent probabilities, the behavior of both the speaker and auditor was described in terms of options, in permissive terms rather than coercive terms. That is, speakers were not obliged to display turn signals, and auditors were not obliged to claim the speaker role when a turn signal was displayed. Instead, what Duncan had shown was that when smooth turn exchanges were observed, turn signals preceded them and when exchanges were not smooth, no turn signals were observed. This method of analysis, emphasizing antecedent probabilities, provides an elegant approach for identifying and describing interactional cooperation that by hypothesis must be based on shared understanding, on convention.

Recall that earlier we defined strategy as *patterns of action that result from choice among options made possible by convention*. Hence, prior to the investigation of strategy, conventions had to be identified. However, our knowledge of conventions is based on the analysis of actions and hence is in some sense inseparable from, and only apparent because of, manifestations of strategy, because of actions produced.

Furthermore, to say that strategy appears as the patterns of action produced by an interactant within a system of rules – that is, conventions – is to say that conventions define, or more appropriately *constrain* or pattern actions. This is not intended to suggest that the constraints imposed by convention are coercive. To the contrary, this notion of constraint defines the limitations established by available options, by the degrees of freedom available for actions.

However, if sources of influence other than convention constrain the very actions or signals identified through research on convention as candidates worthy of strategy research, relying on convention exclusively will leave our interpretations of empirically defined patterns of such actions incomplete and presumably prone to error. A worthwhile complement of strategy research would therefore be a general concern with the identification of possible sources and types of constraints on patterns of actions, along with an empirical commitment to the investigation of these constraints.

Types of constraints on actions

Three major sources of constraint on behavior or action seem theoretically most obvious. The first of these are *environmental constraints*. Constraints of this type may be thought of as products of either the physical environment or of the social environment. Whorf's (1956) cultural relativity hypothesis represesents a strong claim that physical surroundings delimit the way individuals living within those surroundings will think about and symbolize the world. Whorf's hypothesis has been questioned by psychologists and anthropologists alike (Rosch [1977] on basic categories; Berlin and Kay [1969] on basic color terms) because of the extreme behavioristic implications of the hypothesis. Nevertheless, the physical environment cannot be dismissed as an insignificant influence on patterns of action and interaction prior to systematic research.

For example, a recent study (Rosenthal et al., 1984) identified a possible treatment for a group of individuals who suffer from recurrent depressions that appear at the same time each year. Referred to as seasonal affective disorder (SAD), this syndrome, according to Rosenthal et al. (1984) responds to change in climate and latitude. Additionally, exposing the SAD sufferer to extended periods under bright artificial lights appears to have an antidepressant effect.

The social facet of environmental constraint, studied by Barker (1963) and his associates, has become known as ecological psychology. It studies variation in the frequency and the types of interactions that occur across social settings. Consider, for example, the difference in frequency as well as form that courting behavior takes in a church, at a grade school, at a party of peers, or at a football game. D&F refer to such constraints in terms of situation. In their metatheory, the notion of constraints imposed by the social environment implies that the likelihood of actions as well as certain forms of actions may be observed to vary because of social rules or conventions that are identified with social settings.

The second type of constraint on action, which we shall refer to as *interactional constraints*, differs from constraints of the environment in that these constraints are on-line and specifically social. They result from the process of interacting with others. Interactional constraint may also be thought of as consisting of two general types: constraints that result from *rules of use* or *conventions*, such as those hypothesized by D&F for turn-taking behavior, and interactive constraints of *simultaneous activity* (e.g., social facilitation effects, reinforcment contingencies). That is, the behavior of an individual is shaped in part by the presence or absence of feedback from social others as well as from self.

The moves of a game of chess provide an analogy for both types of interactional constraint: those imposed by convention and those resulting from simultaneous activity. In no sense, however, is this analogy intended to reflect a model or perception that holds in human interactions. At the beginning of the game, all 16 of White's pieces are arranged in a prescribed order on two rows of the chessboard, with the pawns in front of the other pieces. Black's pieces are similarly placed. With any other arrangement of the pieces on the board, the game is no longer chess. White moves first. That move is constrained: Only a pawn or a knight may be advanced. The conventions of the game give White the option of advancing a pawn either one or two rows. Thus, White has 8 × 2 or 16 possible pawn options available. In addition, White may also move either knight, each to two unique positions, thus giving White four possible knight options. Any other than one of these 20 moves would indicate either White's ignorance of the rules of chess or a mocking of the conventions. Once White has moved, Black has available the option among the same 20 moves. However, Black's move, assuming familiarity with the game of chess, will be responsive to, hence be constrained by, White's move.

The familiarity that White and Black have with the game of chess will further influence, that is, constrain the choice of moves they make, particularly on the first turn. This is, of course, because the aim of a game of chess is to checkmate one's opponent. To achieve checkmate is to eliminate the options available to one's opponent. Each move, including the first, may be thought of as introducing a constraint on the options available to one's opponent. That some moves like P-K4 are extremely common first moves, while others like P-KR3 are extremely rare indicates that, based on experience, the constraints introduced by certain moves are preferable to others relative to the goal of checkmate.

Finally, the third type of constraint includes those at a noninteractive level, that reflect limits of the processes of perception, storage, and production of information, namely, *information-processing constraints.* That is, our ability to perceive, remember, and produce actions may be thought of as limited by the design and availability of hardware and software that have evolved for the purpose of handling information. For example, thresholds that stimuli must attain in order to be noticeable along with limits on the learning, recall, and recognition of information have been of traditional interest to psychologists since these phenomena are at the interface of mental and physical description. Discussions of the processes entailed in the production of action have, likewise, emphasized that these processes be thought as constrained and describable in terms of the degrees of freedom available for that production (Bernstein, 1967; Greene, 1972; Turvey, 1977). However, psychologists have shown less concern with the production and organization of action than with processes of perception and memory.

What is meant by information-processing constraints on the production of an action? As an example, consider a driver approaching a "Stop" sign. Proceeding along a street, the driver glances at the street and at the sides. Perceiving an octagonal red sign and reading it, the driver shifts a foot from the accelerator to the brake. The stimulus initiates a psychophysiological process culminating in an action. Note that the driver will not execute that action if the sign is not perceived and if the foot is already on the brake pedal. If the driver is already slowing down because the car ahead is decelerating, the action is merely continued, not initiated. Similarly, a speaker who is gazing at the auditor can continue the gaze or terminate it, but cannot initiate such a gaze.

Certainly, the types of constraint on action presented here are not intended to be viewed as an exhaustive set. Additionally, the boundaries between the types of constraint are far from clearly delineated. This discussion of types of constraints on action has tried to indicate the potential complexity involved in strategy research and has established a framework for the interpretation of the studies to be reported. As stated at the outset, this chapter is concerned with the possibilities that data from transcriptions of interactional behavior offer for the understanding of elementary information processes through identifying constraints on patterns of actions. The examination of two action-sequence variables will introduce that concern.

9.2. Analysis of sequences

In recent years, a sizable literature has addressed issues relevant to the analysis of interactional sequences (e.g., Castellan, 1979; Gottman and Bakeman, 1979; Allison and Liker, 1982; Wampold and Margolin, 1982). For the most part, this literature consists of methodological distinctions or statistical techniques deemed necessary or useful for the analysis of interactional data in the form of sequences. Although the development of interest in these issues is encouraging, there still are few examples of research programs committed to the systematic analysis of sequential data transcribed from naturalistic, nonmanipulated interactions (cf. discussion of this point by Collett & Lamb, 1982). D&F advocate this type of interactional description, through the analysis of action sequences.

Action-sequence data

As defined by D&F, action-sequence variables retain information on the sequential organization of actions of both participants in dyadic conversation. As such, they preserve information about the temporal structure of interaction, an aspect of behavior that Fiske (1977, 1978) notes psychologists studying persons have been particularly prone to ignore.

As stated earlier, persistence and change represent likely dimensions of actions that may enable us to distinguish between interactional and noninteractional patterns. These two dimensions of actions may be straightforwardly measured by expanding action-sequence variables. The following sections introduces some formal extentions of action-sequence variables. Specifically, two variables, run-sequences and events, will be considered.

Run-sequences. Analyses of action-sequence data in our laboratory have typically focused on the relation of pairs of actions, such as the association between turn signals and turn exchange. A dimension of actions largely ignored in these analyses is information on the duration or persistence of antecedent and consequent actions. That is, by focusing on the immediate interactional event, like turn exchange, we lose information about the number of successive units during which a turn signal was displayed as well as of the number of successive units that the speaker held the turn following exchange. Durational information of this type has been largely neglected in interactional research.

The inclusion of durational information on actions greatly expands the possible interactional hypotheses that may be tested. For example, we might ask whether the lack of display of a turn signal over a stretch of units increases the probability of turn exchange once a signal is displayed. For present purposes, precise durational information is essential in order to disentangle patterns of action that result from convention or interactional process, as opposed to noninteractional process.

Consistent with the emphasis on sequences of actions in this laboratory, run sequences will use behavioral time, not chronological time, as the measure of the persistence of actions. Measures of run sequences reported in this chapter consist of counts of successive units of analysis, as defined by D&F, that an action was displayed (or not displayed) from the onset of that action to its termination. Table 5.2 suggests that we can think of units as lasting approximately one second on the average.

Everyday life is full of examples of run-sequence data. For example, descriptions of weather conditions often report the persistence of a given type of condition. For example, "Today represents the 14th consecutive day of below zero temperature in Chicago." The world of sport is particularly noteworthy for interest in run-sequence variables, known colloquially as "streaks" or "strings." The feats of individual players, of specific teams, and of a sport over an entire season have all been talked about in run-sequence terms. For example, during 1983-1984, Wayne Gretsky, the hockey player, set a record by scoring points in more than 50 consecutive NHL games. Run sequences make unique happenings stand out. They quite nicely separate the extraordinary from the ordinary.

For studies of interactions, run sequences intuitively appear to represent a powerful tool for describing and comparing many sorts of patterns of actions. For example, we can talk about a continuous behavior, such as a smile, as a run sequence of specific duration. Here we are measuring the behavior or action of smiling. We could also just as well talk about the run of units of analysis during which no smile beginning was observed, no back channel, no turn signal, and the like. Using the notion of run sequences, we can create variables that preserve an important property of actions: the duration of those actions within the context of interaction.

Additionally, run sequences may be qualified by, that is, be conditional on other run sequences or contextual variables. For example, we could study the tendency for run sequences of smiles by auditors to overlap with smiles by speakers. Two of the studies that will be reported in this chapter analyze speaker signals. The speaking turn as a run sequence represents an obvious conditional variable for the analysis of speaker signals. The speaking turn consists of a string of units during which one person was the speaker and the other the auditor. If we cross-classify run sequences of speaker actions by speaker turns in which these actions occurred, then we can determine whether the duration of speaker actions within speaking turns varies according to the length of the speaking turn. Likewise, we could ask whether the length of speaking turns relates to the position of actions or the duration of actions within turns. That is, are run sequences for speaker gaze a function of speaking turn duration, or are speaking turn-durations a function of positioning or duration of the display of some action within them? At the very least, we can use positions within speaking turns as anchoring points from which we measure the durations of actions.

Events. In this chapter, the term event will be used in a restricted sense, referring simply to two adjacent units of analysis. Such a sequential pair may be identical – no change in the actions examined – or may include a change in at least one action. The term "event" will be further restricted to pairs of units described solely in terms of actions of one person, the speaker. Descriptions of the partner's actions will be introduced in the formation of subgroupings of these events. We are now in a position to introduce the three studies that provide examples of analyses of run-sequence and event variables.

Things to come

Three studies are reported in this chapter. Each study presents a unique analytic problem, both in terms of the action variable(s) studied and in terms of specifications that are made for counting these action variables.

In the first study, patterns of speaker gaze behavior are presented as runs over units of analysis. Run-sequence data of increasingly complex form are presented. The first run-sequence analysis presents durations of speaker gaze that are unqualified by any other variable. The second analysis cross-classifies durations of speaker gaze by the length of the speaking turn in which they occurred. The third set of analyses cross-classifies speaker gaze durations according to the position of onsets of runs within speaking turns (initial position or later, internal position) and according to the auditor's actions (takes the turn or does not take the turn). In this way, the consistency of durational patterns of speaker gaze is assessed across a variety of settings within the interactions studied.

The second study examines the interrelationship of three speaker actions: speaker gaze, speaker gesture, and the grammaticalness of speaker utterances over successive units of analysis. This study analyzes the patterns of association and of change that occur among these three speaker actions over time. This study is referred to as the study of speaker-signal sequences.

Finally, the third study assesses the patterns of interactional smiling. Unlike the first two studies which measure the behavior of speakers, the smiling study explicitly examines the moment-to-moment smiling activity of both interactants. The focus of this study is on the durations of smiles. Hence, the data collected for this study are in the form of run sequences. But in addition, contextual variables are incorporated to qualify the smile run sequences. This study includes the most complex specifications as to how the actions of interest are to be counted.

9.3. Statistical methods: log-linear analysis

Because the data in this study consist of counts of the occurrence and nonoccurrence of actions in units of analysis, cross-classified by other actions or contextual variables, multivariate techniques appropriate for the analysis of categorical data were used in the analysis. These techniques are known as log-linear methods (see Goodman, 1970, 1971, 1972a,b; Knoke & Burke, 1980). Applications of these methods to interactional data have been considered by Castellan (1979) and Allison and Liker (1982). In this chapter, the ECTA and CTAB computer programs were used to generate the results reported below.

The aim of a log-linear analysis is to account for nonrandom variation in cell frequencies within multidimensional contingency tables. In order to accomplish this aim, log-linear methods provide the researcher with two types of statistical procedures: model fitting and the determination of specific sources of association.

Model fitting attempts to identify the most parsimonious set of sources of association that will estimate cell frequencies, such that residuals from a comparison of these estimated data with the observed frequencies are minimized while degrees of freedom are maximized. Models are identified by the fitted marginals they include. In other words, the marginal distributions of variables and cross-classification of variables based on the observed data specified in a model are used as estimators of cell frequencies.

At the core of log-linear analysis is the saturated model. This model, which includes all possible effect parameters, reexpresses the observed cell frequencies in either a multiplicative or additive equation. Nonsaturated and, hence, testable models are formed by hypothesizing that one or more specified parameters have no effect and can be omitted from the model. On the basis of the estimated cell frequencies generated by a specified model, that model may be assessed for its ability to "fit" the observed data by calculating either the Pearson or the likelihood-ratio chi-square statistic. The statistical result of such a test refers to variation unaccounted for by the model specified. A statistically significant result indicates the presence of such variance. If the estimates do not significantly differ (e.g., $p < .10$) from the observed frequencies, then the researcher may conclude that only the effect parameters specified in the model appear to be of significance for the description of the observed data.

Additionally, any two unsaturated models may be compared in order to determine the variation accounted for by the specific effect parameters included in one model but not in the other. This may be done by comparing the chi-square statistics and the degrees of freedom for these two models. The use of the likelihood-ratio chi-square is preferred since it may be partitioned uniquely, thus enabling the researcher to test specific hypotheses of conditional independence. All results reported in this chapter will be expressed in terms of the likelihood-ratio chi-square statistic (G^2).

9.4. Study 1: speaker gaze run sequences

It is widely assumed that, of the actions by which interactants communicate in face-to-face encounters, social looking (gaze direction) is second only to speech in terms of the social impact it creates. Within the domain of the nonverbal-communication literature, gaze represents one of the behaviors most often studied. By and large, investigators have been interested in gaze behavior as a behavioral marker of psychological state, attitude, or reactance (cf. Argyle & Cook, 1976). The communicative role of gaze in the process of interaction has been studied less often. Relatively few studies have reported data on such phenomena as gaze patterns in interaction or the relation of gaze to other actions.

In general, studies that have specifically focused on the patterning of gaze behavior have been carried out within two domains: (a) by researchers interested in principles of interactional organization, and (b) by researchers interested in psycholinguistic and cognitive processes.

Research within the interactional framework stems from two distinct concerns: (a) fundamental developmental concerns studied in the context of mother-infant interaction, wherein the aim guiding the research has been to describe the emergence of communicative competence (e.g., Stern, 1974; Kaye, 1982); and (b) principles of interactional coordination at turn exchange (e.g., Kendon, 1967; Beattie, 1978a; Duncan, Brunner, & Fiske, 1979) and within speaking turns (D&F). In both types of studies, gaze is treated as a communicative channel.

Within the psycholinguistic and cognitive literature, noninteractional patterns of gaze direction and, more extensively, eye movements are studied as patterned manifestations of specific cognitive processing strategies involved in the retrieval and encoding of information (e.g., Kinsbourne, 1972; Russo & Rosen, 1975; Just & Carpenter, 1976).

Some recent studies have investigated patterns of speaker gaze as a measure of the on-line relationship between cognitive and interactive processes (e.g., Beattie, 1978b, 1979, 1980, 1981; Butterworth & Goldman-Eisler, 1979), an hypothesis that Kendon's (1967) seminal paper first discussed. These studies examine the hypothesis that speakers divert gaze away from auditors at times of speech planning. According to the hypothesis, speakers do this in order to minimize the interference that

Table 9.1. *Speaker signals hypothesized by D&F that include speaker gaze direction*

Direction of speaker gaze	Hypothesized signal	Subsequent event to which signal is related
Toward auditor	Gaze strategy signal	Increased probability of turn attempts when concurrent with speaker turn signal
Toward auditor	Within-turn signal	Auditor back channels
Away from auditor	Speaker-state signal	Claim to speaking turn
Away from auditor	Speaker continuation signal	Maintain the speaking turn

visual input has on cognitive processing (i.e., speech planning processes). Interesting criticisms of this view of speaker gaze patterning, from two quite distinct perspectives, have recently been articulated by Ehrlichman (1981), Ehrlichman and Barrett (1983), and Goodwin (1981).

The present study augments research of this type by providing a systematic analysis of constraints on the durations of speaker gaze. Specifically, speaker gaze behavior will be analyzed using run-sequence variables. A series of analyses of increasing specificity will be presented. Run sequences of gaze behavior will first be presented without qualification, that is, without any stipulation of contexts in which runs were observed. Runs will then be cross-classified, first by turn length, then by interactional position and interactional move. This series of analyses will indicate how interactional constraints may be identified in patterns of speaker gaze and differentiated from patterns of speaker gazing that are proposed to be a reflection of noninteractional processes.

The rationale for examining run sequences of gaze produced just by speakers is based on the assumption that speakers do more with gaze than do auditors. A consistent observation reported in the literature is that auditors have a pronounced tendency to look at the partner during much of the time that they are auditors. The notable exception to this observation is the turning of gaze away by auditors that occurs prior to the beginning of speaking turns (Denny, Chapter 8; Duncan & Niederehe, 1974; Kendon, 1967). Speakers, to the contrary, have been consistently described in the literature as shifting their gaze toward and away from their interlocutors (e.g., Cook, 1979; Kendon, 1967).

Within D&F's turn system, the direction of speaker gaze is included as a component of a number of signals. Speaker gaze therefore represents an obvious choice for strategy research. Table 9.1 identifies those signals, along with their hypothesized function, that involve speaker gaze direction in D&F's model.

Summary statistics of speaker gaze for 16 conversations

For the 16 conversations analyzed, speakers gazed at auditors during 59% of all units of analysis. The percentage of speaker gazing for the 32 individual speakers ranged from 34% to 90%. The ratio of gaze onsets to speaker units for all 16 conversations was .24, indicating that a new gaze onset occurred on the average at approximately every fourth speaker unit. Across 32 individual speaker performances, this ratio ranged from .12 to .34, indicating that the likelihood of a new gaze onset varied from one in every 8 speaker units to one in every 3 speaker units. The mean duration of a gaze run was 2.51 units. Across 32 individual speaker performances, the range in the mean duration of a gaze runs was from 1.68 to 4.24 units.

These statistics are presented as a reference for comparison with the run-sequence data reported below. It appears that speaker gaze durations by and large are quite brief. However, the range in speaker gazing as a function of speaking time is considerable. This would indicate that it is difficult to interpret the meaning of a statement like "Speakers gaze at their partner 60% of the time that they are speaking." Similarly, the range of ratios for speaker gaze onsets to speaker units is sufficiently large, as is the range of mean gaze durations, as to indicate that general statements about speaker gaze ignore a sizable variance in performance.

Unqualified speaker gaze run sequences

As a first step in analyzing the persistence characteristics of speaker gaze, counts were made of the consecutive units of analysis during which the speaker's gaze was directed at the auditor. That is, the duration of each speaker gaze was measured in units of analysis. Tallies of these counts were then made according to the lengths of gaze runs observed, summing over all participants. The proportions of each run-length observed are reported in Table 9.2.

These runs are "unqualified" in the sense that no specification or additional criteria were set for how runs of gaze were counted. Thus, for each participant was tabulated, across all of his or her speaking turns, the number of runs of 1 unit, of 2 units, of 3 units, etc. Gaze runs ranged from less than 1 unit of analysis in duration to 17 units in duration. There were eight runs longer than 10 units. By far the majority of observed runs (69%)

Table 9.2. *Proportions of run lengths of speaker gaze in units of analysis*

<1	1	2	3	4	5	6	≥7
.083	.306	.239	.148	.080	.058	.028	.063

were between 1 and 3 units in duration. Very brief durations of gaze, less than 1 unit in length, were unlikely to occur, as were runs of 4 units and longer.

Examination of the distributions of gaze runs by individuals indicates that for 21 of the 32 speaker performances the modal run length was one unit, whereas for an additional nine individuals the modal run length was two units. The remaining two speakers had modal runs of five and six units. These data suggest considerable consistency in the run lengths of gaze across individuals, much more so than we would suspect from the rates of gazing over speaker units reported earlier.

These data, however, may indicate the pattern of speaker gaze, but also the correlation of gaze with other variables. Specifically, to identify patterning of speaker gaze, the extent of that patterning resulting from covariation with turn length must be determined. Turn length, after all, represents a logical constraint on speaker gaze since, by definition, a speaker gaze cannot be longer than the speaking turn.

Speaker gaze runs by speaking turn duration

In order to determine if gaze run length covaried with the length of the speaking turn, we cross-classified run lengths of speaker gaze runs by the lengths of the turns in which they occurred. Turns ranged in length from 1 to 54 units, with a mean length of 8.4 units.

Table 9.3 reports summary data derived from the cross-classification of speaker gaze runs by turn length (i.e., runs of speaker units). The three rates reported in this table are

1. The *rate of gaze onset*, computed by dividing the number of gaze onsets by the number of speaker units (N gaze onsets/N speaker units). This rate reflects the frequency of onsets of new gaze runs in terms of speaker units.
2. The *mean gaze run-length*, computed by dividing the number of gaze units by the number of gaze runs (N gaze units/N gaze runs).
3. The *proportion of speaker gazing*, computed by dividing the number of gaze units by the number of speaker units (N gaze units/N speaker units).

Table 9.3. *Summary data for the cross-classification of speaker gaze runs by turn length*

Turn length	N	Rate of gaze onset	Mean gaze run-length	Proportion of speaker gazing
1	122	.87	.97	.87
2	104	.46	1.70	.78
3–7	207	.26	2.75	.72
8–12	113	.21	2.96	.62
13–17	47	.22	2.57	.56
18–22	35	.18	2.92	.54
23–27	26	.20	2.50	.49
28–32	17	.19	2.86	.54
33–37	4	.19	1.93	.37
38–42	14	.20	2.39	.48
43–54	5	.19	2.85	.55

These rates are reported for turns of various length. To minimize small N's, turn lengths greater than three units are grouped by fives (with the exception of the last group, turns over 43 units in length).

The most intriguing aspect of these results is the stability of the rate of gaze onset and of the mean length of a gaze run across speaking turns of varying length. Although the duration of a speaking turn logically constrains the duration of a gaze run, the pattern of speaker gaze runs as reflected in these two rates, appears comparable across long turns and short turns (except for turns one and two units in length). Onsets of new gaze runs occur approximately every fifth unit for turns eight units and longer. Runs of gaze units following these onsets are most likely to be from one to three units in length.

For turns shorter than eight units, particularly for the one- and two-unit turns, both of these statistics are misleading. This is because many of these short turns have speaker gaze directed toward the auditor at the onset of the speaking turn and have no shifting away of gaze prior to exchange. Thus, for the rates of gaze, the first two or three groupings deeply reflect turn length rather than gaze patterns per se, since for these cases gaze runs covary with turn length. The pronounced tendency of short turns is to be "saturated" by gaze directed toward the auditor, a finding that will be considered in the following section.

Two additional points are of interest with regard to the data in Table 9.3. First, it should be noted that the distribution of speaking-turn lengths is skewed such that turns seven units or less in length account for 62.4% of all turns, with 32.6% of all turns only one or two units in length. For these short turns, the proportion of gaze units to speaker units is higher than for longer turns. Second, although there is a decrease in the proportion of gaze units to speaker units as turns become longer, indicating an increased tendency for the speaker to gaze away from the auditor during the course of these turns, this decrease appears to level off. Thus, although turn length appears to represent an important qualifying variable to be considered when representing an individual or interaction in terms of the proportion of gaze while speaking, turn length does not aid in understanding the shape of the distribution of speaker gaze runs presented in Table 9.2.

Speaker gaze direction as states: single-state and multiple-state turns

Based on the results reported in the previous section, it appears that the unqualified distribution of speaker gaze fairly represents the pattern of gaze runs across speaking turns. Gaze directed toward the auditor was most often brief in duration regardless of the length of the speaking turn. Moreover, onsets of gaze runs occurred quite regularly, indirectly suggesting that speakers directed their gaze away from the auditor in runs that were of similar brevity to gaze toward the auditor. In addition, the proportion of the time that gaze was directed away from the auditor was considerably larger for longer turns than for short turns. Since these data appear to indicate comparable regularity for gaze toward the auditor and gaze away from the auditor for the longer turns, a thorough analysis of the patterns of speaker gaze requires data on both run sequences of gaze directed away from the auditor as well as toward the auditor. This and the following section will report direct results of the run-sequence characteristics of both speaker gaze directed toward the auditor and away from the auditor. For convenience, these complementary *gaze states* will be referred to as "gaze runs" and "no-gaze runs," or simply as gaze/no-gaze.

The previous section noted that many of the short turns were "saturated" by gaze (toward the auditor). That is, the speaker was gazing at the auditor throughout the turn. The longest gaze-saturated turn was ten units in length (N = 2). An additional representation of the relationship between speaker gazing and turn length is suggested by this observation. Thus, it

Table 9.4. *Comparison of summary statistics for single gaze-stage and multiple gaze-state turns*

	Single gaze-state turns	Multiple gaze-state turns
Percent of all turns	46%	54%
Mean length	2.52	13.30
Gaze state at onset:		
Toward auditor	85%	26%
Away from auditor	15%	74%
Gaze state at turn exchange:		
Toward auditor	(85%)[a]	84%
Away from auditor	(15%)[a]	16%

[a]This pair of values is by definition identical with the pair above.

might be of interest to compare summary statistics for speaking turns consisting of a single gaze-state (either gaze or no gaze) with multiple gaze-state turns.

Table 9.4 shows some descriptive statistics for single gaze-state and multiple gaze-state speaking turns. Single gaze-state turns account for 46% of all turns. The mean duration is 2.5 units. Of these turns, 85% start and end with gaze, while 15% start and end with no-gaze.

Multiple gaze-state turns make up 54% of all turns. The mean duration is 13.3 units. Unlike single-state speaking turns, multiple-state speaking turns can begin with one gaze-state and end with the other. In our data, 74% began with no-gaze and 26% began with gaze. This contrasts sharply with the beginnings of single-state turns. However, 84% of the multiple-state turns ended with speaker gaze directed at the auditor, and 16% with gaze directed away. These proportions are essentially identical to those for single gaze-state turns.

Thus, the sharp distinction between single- and multiple-state turns (other than length) is in the way they begin. Most single-state turns start with gaze, and most multiple-state turns begin with no-gaze. Closely related is the fact that turns beginning with speaker gazing at the auditor tend (73%) to become single-state turns. That is, the auditor takes the turn before the speaker gazes away. This obviously makes for short turns since gaze durations tend to be short. Conversely, turns beginning with the speaker gazing away from the auditor tend (86%) to become multiple-state turns.

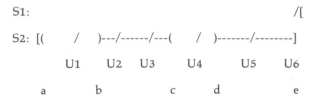

Figure 9.1. Gaze runs produced by hypothetical speaker S2 during one speaking turn divided into units of analysis. [= speaking turn onset;] = speaking turn ending; ---- = gaze; ( ) = no gaze; / = unit of analysis boundary.

Speaker gaze/no-gaze runs by interactional position and by interactional moves

Thus far, data on the distribution of speaker gaze runs have been presented without explicitly qualifying these distributions. The results displayed in Table 9.4 did, however, suggest additional ways in which gaze/no-gaze runs may fruitfully be classified: their location within a speaking turn and the way the gaze state ends. With these classifications, we may begin to examine the extent to which elements of the interactional environment contribute to the variation observed in distributions of gaze runs.

Each run-sequence onset was therefore coded according to one of two interactional locations or positions (P): (a) turn initial (initial), or (b) turn internal (internal). Turn-initial runs were the first run of the turn, whereas turn-internal runs were not the first run of the turn.

Each run-sequence ending was coded according to one of two inter-actional moves (M): (a) speaker ended, or (b) auditor ended. Speaker-ended runs were those in which the speaker switches to the complementary gaze state, that is, from gaze to no-gaze or from no-gaze to gaze, with no associated turn exchange. Auditor-ended runs were those in which a turn exchange occurred during the run.

Figure 9.1 illustrates how various gaze state runs were classified. This figure represents the gazing activity of hypothetical speaker S2 during a speaking turn which was six units in length. The following gaze state runs are codable from Figure 9.1:

1. A 1-unit, initial, no-gaze, speaker-ended run (a to b)
2. A 2-unit, internal, gaze, speaker-ended run (b to c)
3. A 1-unit, internal, no-gaze, speaker-ended run (c to d)
4. A 2-unit, internal, gaze, auditor-ended run (d to e)

Not all of the eight possible classifications of a gaze run are illustrated in this figure. Table 9.5 lists all possible classifications.

Table 9.5. *Eight classifications of gaze-state runs*

Interactional position (P)	Interactional move (M)	Gaze state (G)
Initial	Speaker ended	Gaze
Internal	Speaker ended	Gaze
Initial	Auditor ended	Gaze
Internal	Auditor ended	Gaze
Initial	Speaker ended	No gaze
Internal	Speaker ended	No gaze
Initial	Auditor ended	No gaze
Internal	Auditor ended	No gaze

Table 9.6. *Three-way cross-classification of observed frequencies of gaze states*

Interactional position (P)	Interactional move (M)	Gaze state Gaze	No gaze
Initial	Speaker ended	98	279
Internal	Speaker ended	477	513
Initial	Auditor ended	271	46
Internal	Auditor ended	315	61

Log-linear analysis of gaze/no gaze by position and by move

Before examining the eight distributions of run sequences generated according to the classifications in Table 9.5, let us first consider a log-linear analysis of gaze states, interactional position, and interactional move. These data represent the marginal distributions, that is, the total runs for each of the eight run-sequence distributions. These data are shown in Table 9.6. (Runs that were less than one unit in length were dropped from the analysis for this and all subsequent discussions of speaker gaze run-sequences.)

Tendencies in these data, such as for gaze to be auditor ended and for no-gaze to be speaker ended, have already been pointed out. Table 9.7 presents a series of log-linear models that formally analyze these associational tendencies.

Model M1 tests the hypothesis that there was no three-way interaction among the variables – that is, that the three-way interaction PMG

Table 9.7. *Chi-square values for some log-linear models pertaining to the three-way cross-classification in Table 9.6*

Model	Fitted marginals	df	Likelihood-ratio chi-square (G^2)[a]
M1	(PM)(PG)(MG)	1	19.74
M2	(PM)(PG)	2	418.90
M3	(PM)(MG)	2	57.69
M4	(PG)(MG)	2	120.06
M5	(PM)(G)	3	423.22
M6	(PG)(M)	3	485.59
M7	(MG)(P)	3	124.37
M8	(P)(M)(G)	4	489.91

[a]All values for $p < .001$.

(position–move–gaze state) was not significant. The G^2 value for the test of model M1 is 19.74, which with one degree of freedom is significant at the .0001 level. This result indicates that there is "complete" interaction among the variables. In other words, any inferences about speaker gaze based on these data must be in the form of conditional statements that simultaneously consider the state of gaze (i.e., gaze or no-gaze), the position of that state within the speaking turn, as well as the interactional move that ends the gaze state.

We may compare other models to establish the measure of association for each of the three other possible effects of interest. For this purpose, model M8, a model that assumes "complete" independence, hence no association among the variables, was chosen as the baseline model against which other models are compared. The G^2 difference between M8 and M7 is a test of significance of the MG interaction, with one degree of freedom. The resulting G^2 difference is 365.54, which with one degree of freedom is significant at the .0001 level. Substantively, this result tells us that there is significant association between interactional moves and gaze state. That is, gaze was associated with auditor ending. Thus, as was indicated in Table 9.4, and as has been reported elsewhere (e.g., Kendon, 1967; Duncan et al., 1979), auditors predominantly claimed the speaking turn during speaker gaze runs, and speakers retained their turns during no-gaze runs.

We could also express the association between moves and gaze state in terms of the variation accounted for in the "complete" independence model by the MG effect. Following methods introduced by Goodman (1970, 1971), an index for categorical data similar to the correlation coefficient can be calculated by comparing a model of interest with a baseline model like the model of complete independence. Goodman refers to this index as the coefficient of multiple determination or R^2. R^2 may be interpreted in terms of the proportional decrease of the unexplained variation provided by the alternative model relative to the baseline model, or correlatively, as a measure of how well a model fits the data. The computation of R^2 involves solving the following formula: $R^2 = [(G^2$ value for the baseline model) $- (G^2$ value for the alternative model)$]/(G^2$ value for the baseline model). For the MG interaction just discussed, this result is $R^2 = (489.91 - 124.37)/489.91 = .75$. This means that the association between interactional move and gaze state (i.e., if gaze, then auditor takes turn; if no-gaze, then speaker continues with the turn) accounts for the major portion (75%) of the variation left unexplained by the independence model.

Analyzing the other effects similarly, the comparison of M8 and M5 identifies the association accounted for by the (PM) effect relative to the assumption of "complete" independence; $G^2 = 66.69$, $df = 1$, $p < .0001$, $R^2 = .14$. Comparing M8 and M6 identifies the association accounted for by (PG); $G^2 = 4.32$, $df = 1$, $p < .05$, $R^2 = .009$.

Four conclusions can be based on these analyses: (a) The strongest source of association is between interactional moves and gaze state. It is quite apparent in these analyses that the direction of gaze is strongly associated with interactional outcomes. Although durations of individual gaze runs were shown not to vary across turn length, the extent to which a person does gaze certainly has consequences for the amount of time they spend talking. (b) Additionally, there is significant association between position and interactional move. (There are significantly more internal states than initial states. This merely says that there is a tendency for turns to be more than one state in duration.) (c) The association between gaze state and interactional position (GP), although significant, explains less than 1% of the variation unexplained by the assumption of complete independence. (d) However, in any case, the interpretation of the above results must take into account that the three-way interaction of gaze state, interactional position, and interactional move (PMG) was significant. Turn-initial auditor-ended gazes form one level of a three-way association, with turn-internal, speaker-ended, no-gazes the other. It would therefore seem that discussions of speaker gaze must minimally stipulate the relations between interactional position and move when making inferences about persons based on their gaze behavior.

Analysis of run-lengths

The previous section analyzed the relationships among position, move, and gaze state. Systematic variation was identified in the association between gaze states and the two interactional variables used to contextualize each observed occurrence of gaze and no gaze.

In this section, the distributions of run lengths for each of the eight types of run-sequence variables defined in this study are compared. The key question for analysis is whether these distributions differ significantly from one another, and if so, how. That is to say, the purpose is to determine whether, when, and which interactional variables influence the duration of gaze runs. To accomplish this, a series of logit models are presented (log-linear models that distinguish between dependent and independent variables). Run length is treated as the dependent variable, whereas position, move, and gaze state are the independent variables in these models.

For the eight run-sequence types, row proportions of each run length are presented in Table 9.8. The mean run length for each distribution is noted under the row totals as an aid for visually comparing these distributions.

Of the eight types, the most atypical distribution is for runs of internal, auditor-ended gaze (row 4). These runs tend to be longer. They have distinctly fewer runs of one unit and distinctly more runs of seven and more units than any other distribution. In contrast, both the initial and internal, auditor-ended, no-gaze runs (rows 7 and 8) have more one-unit runs than the other distributions. These two run types also have by far the fewest total number of runs of any of the eight distributions (see Table 9.6). Hence, conclusions about these two run distributions are more prone to sampling bias. The remaining five run distributions appear quite comparable in terms of the run-distributions.

Logit analysis of Table 9.8. Table 9.9 presents a series of logit models based on the data reported in Table 9.8. These models always include the (PMG) term on the left-hand side of the model's fitted marginals. This is because the (PMG) term represents the effects associated with the independent variables, analyzed above, which in logit analysis are not interesting in and of themselves. Effects among these variables are held constant in the analysis. Effects of variables P, M, and G are of interest only insofar as they interact with the dependent variable R, run length. Thus, on the right-hand side of every model is included the R term: the dependent variable.

Table 9.8. *Four-way cross-classification of gaze states expressed as row proportions of cases for each run length*

		Run type	1	2	3	4	5	6	≥7
				Run length in units					
1.	(P) (M) (G)	Initial Speaker Gaze	.378	.173	.194	.082	.061	.020	.092

Mean run length = 2.85 units

2.	(P) (M) (G)	Internal Speaker Gaze	.346	.354	.164	.103	.044	.034	.057

Mean run length = 2.66 units

3.	(P) (M) (G)	Initial Auditor Gaze	.376	.266	.159	.081	.037	.030	.052

Mean run length = 2.49 units

4.	(P) (M) (G)	Internal Auditor Gaze	.232	.203	.133	.108	.114	.038	.171

Mean run length = 3.80 units

5.	(P) (M) (G)	Initial Speaker No gaze	.362	.194	.140	.133	.079	.043	.050

Mean run length = 2.80 units

6.	(P) (M) (G)	Internal Speaker No gaze	.335	.287	.150	.103	.053	.027	.045

Mean run length = 2.62 units

7.	(P) (M) (G)	Initial Auditor No gaze	.435	.261	.109	.087	.022	.022	.065

Mean run length = 2.67 units

8.	(P) (M) (G)	Internal Auditor No gaze	.590	.164	.115	.033	.016	.016	.066

Mean run length = 2.07 units

Table 9.9. *Chi-square values for some log-linear models pertaining to the four-way cross-classification in Table 9.8*

Model	Fitted marginals	df	Likelihood-ratio chi-square $(G^2)^a$
M9	(PMG)(R)	42	119.60
M10	(PMG)(PR)	36	111.71
M11	(PMG)(MR)	36	96.74
M12	(PMG)(GR)	36	103.18
M13	(PMG)(PR)(MR)	30	84.59
M14	(PMG)(PR)(GR)	30	95.97
M15	(PMG)(MR)(GR)	30	89.04
M16	(PMG)(PR)(MR)(GR)	24	78.16
M17	(PMG)(PMR)	24	46.37
M18	(PMG)(PMR)(GR)	18	37.27
M19	(PMG)(PMR)(PGR)	12	32.74
M20	(PMG)(PMR)(MGR)	12	14.86^b
M21	(PMG)(PGR)	24	78.66
M22	(PMG)(PGR)(MR)	18	57.81
M23	(PMG)(PGR)(MGR)	12	29.08
M24	(PMG)(MGR)	24	67.45
M25	(PMG)(MGR)(PR)	18	54.66
M26	(PMG)(PMR)(PGR)(MGR)	6	7.89^c

^{a}For all except those marked, $p < .005$.
$^b p = .249$.
$^c p = .246$.

Model M9 generates estimates of the data in Table 9.8 under the assumption that all eight run-length distributions are comparable, that is, they do not significantly differ. Thus the (R) parameter is the only term specified on the right-hand side of the model. (The assumption tested by M9 is that none of the three independent variables influences run length.) Another way of describing this model is that it represents a test of independence of run length from the influence of variables P, M, and G. The G^2 value for M9 is 119.60, ($df = 42$, $p < .001$) indicating that this assumption does not result in a "good fit" of the observed data.

Each of the other models in Table 9.9 represents a different assumption about the relationship between the independent variables P, M, and G and the dependent variable R, run length. For example, Model M16 tests the assumption that the inclusion of the three main effects in the model on R (i.e., the three interactions with R) generates estimates that do not differ significantly from the observed data. Again, this hypothesis results in an inadequate fit of the data; $G^2 = 78.16$, $df = 24$, $p < .001$. This indicates that at least one interaction effect must be specified in order to fit the observed data of Table 9.8.

Models M20 and M26 both fit the data such that the estimates they generate do not significantly deviate from the observed frequencies. G^2 p values indicate that these two models fit the observed data comparably. However, the test of M26 required six additional degress of freedom in estimating the data as compared with M20. M20 and M26 differ in that M18 includes the PGR effect, whereas M20 does not. Comparison of the G^2 values of M26 and M20 results in a difference G^2 of 6.97, $df = 6$, $p > .25$. This comparison indicates that the addition of PGR to the specifications of model M20 does not significantly improve the model's fit of the data.

A basic purpose of scientific explanation and also of the log-linear approach is the identification of parsimonious models that fit the data. Thus, the best-fitting model for the observed data in Table 9.8 is M20. M20 indicates that run length is influenced by the interaction of gaze state and interactional move MGR and the interaction of position and interactional move PMR. This model excludes two effects in the estimation of the data: (a) the three-way interaction of gaze state, position, and move with run-length, and (b) the two-way interaction of gaze state and position with run length.

In order to fit the observed data, the MGR interaction was included in M20 because of the strong run-length distinction between internal, auditor-ended, gaze runs and internal, auditor-ended, no-gaze runs (See Table 9.8). Internal, auditor-ended gaze runs include the largest relative proportion of long runs, whereas internal, auditor-ended, no-gaze runs include the largest relative proportion of short runs. However, by itself the MGR effect provided an inadequate fit of the data, as is indicated by model M24. This is because the ratio of gaze to no-gaze, internal, auditor-ended runs $(315/61 = 5.16)$ showed a major disproportion. For this reason, the PMR interaction, which does not distinguish between gaze states (i.e., collapses over gaze state) was included in M20. Internal, auditor-ended runs were distinct from all other run distributions when gaze state was not considered. However, as with the MGR effect, by itself the PMR effect provided an inadequate fit of the data, as is indicated by model M17. Thus, it was necessary to include both effects in order to fit the data. The important point to note from model M20 is that interactional move (M) is specified in both effects. Interactional move, that is, speaker ending or auditor ending, appears to be the most important variable for under-standing run lengths of speaker gaze in these data. Analyses in the next section show this in a more straightforward manner.

Log-linear comparisons of speaker-ended and auditor-ended run lengths

The logit models in Table 9.9 provide quantitative descriptions of the data in Table 9.8. The aim in these analyses was to distinguish between run sequences that were interactively patterned from those that were not interactively patterned in terms of the variables included in this study. However, making this distinction based on the models in Table 9.9 is cumbersome, in part because of the hierarchical nature of log-linear models. Therefore the speaker-ended and auditor-ended run distributions were analyzed separately, in essence partitioning the interactional move variable (M).

Separate analysis of speaker-ended run-sequence distributions indicate that run length was independent of gaze state (G) and position (P). This conclusion is based on the test of the model (PG)(R) for the four speaker-ended, gaze, run-length distributions. The G^2 value for this test was 22.40, $df = 18$, $p = .215$. This indicates that the four speaker-ended distributions in Table 9.8 do not vary significantly across classifications by gaze state (G) and position (P). Run lengths ended by speakers are comparable for gaze and no-gaze states and for turn-initial and turn-internal positions. The homogeneity of these four distributions appears to provide evidence for a noninteractive constraint on patterns of speaker gaze: Runs of both gaze and no gaze are comparably brief.

The comparable analysis for the four auditor-ended run lengths tested again with model (PG)(R) results in $G^2 = 74.33$, $df = 18$, $p < .0001$. This result indicates that within the context of auditor turn taking there is association between run length (R) and either position (PR) or gaze state (GR), or both independently (PR)(GR) or in interaction (PGR). Durations of speaker gaze vary systematically only in auditor-ended situations. In these situations, gaze runs tend to be of longer duration and no-gaze runs of shorter duration. Obviously, the longer durations of gaze must be attributable to the speaker. That is, a speaker tended to gaze toward the auditor for longer stretches immediately prior to auditor turn claims than when auditors did not claim the turn. Given that gaze is strongly associated with turn exchange and gaze durations vary in length most notably prior to turn exchange, it would seem that gaze direction and duration both represent interactional signals associated with turn exchange. If this is the case, then the shorter durations for no-gaze runs that were auditor ended may merely include late responses by the auditor to the gaze signal that preceded these no gaze runs (where the median length is one unit).

Finally, if we sum the G^2 values for the models just reported, this value is equivalent to the G^2 value for model M11 in Table 9.9. The two (PG)(R) models thus represent a partitioning of the model M11 in Table 9.9 by levels of variable (M).

Conclusions

Based on the results reported in this study, speaker gaze (present or absent) must be characterized as strongly patterned or constrained by both interactive and noninteractive processes. Three major points are offered as support of this conclusion:

1. The state of speaker gaze was strongly associated with subsequent interactional moves; gaze was much more likely to be auditor ended than was no-gaze.
2. The state of gaze in the initial position was strongly related to the subsequent interactional move. If the speaker gazed toward the auditor at the turn-initial position, rapid turn exchange was very likely. If the speaker gazed away from the auditor at the turn-initial position, the speaker was likely to produce a longer speaking turn, in part because the auditor delayed claiming the speaking turn.
3. The typical duration of gaze and no-gaze runs was very brief. When they were not, the likelihood was that they were auditor ended. A long run of speaker-ended gaze was a highly unlikely occurrence. It was much more likely that a long run of gaze was ended by the auditor.

These conclusions, and especially the first, can be seen as extensions and refinements of the identification of speaker gaze as a strategy signal. Gazes present in the first unit of a turn and gazes that have continued beyond just one unit are more likely to lead to termination by the auditor taking the turn.

The only run distribution that was truly anomalous relative to any of the other seven was the distribution of internal, auditor-ended gaze. This result can only have been a function of speakers displaying gaze differently (more persistently) in situations prior to turn exchange. It cannot be determined through these analyses whether this indicates that the speaker signaled the auditor in this fashion, or that the auditor perceived this pattern as unusual and, therefore, responded. Possibly the perseveration of gaze by the speaker created a monotonic effect such that auditor took the speaking turn so as to be able to look away (reduce arousal); perhaps the speaker here was straightforwardly signaling; perhaps the speaker was already assuming the role of the auditor. Whatever interpretation one chooses, the fact of the matter is that durational pattern of speaker gaze was strongly associated with the interactional context of auditor claims to the speaking turn.

Thus, speaker gaze is constrained in several fashions. There are specific options that may be characterized in the gaze of the speaker, but to say that they are easily interpretable would be most misleading. As indicated elsewhere in this monograph (Chapter 1), such strategies are created through the joint action of speaker and auditor.

Of greatest interest for the thesis of this chapter was the brevity of most speaker gaze as well as no-gaze runs. Whatever the mechanism that causes a turning of the head back and forth by the speaker, this mechanism creates patterns of gaze that have upper limits on duration, such that the most deviant cases are responded to distinctively within the interactional environment. Indeed, an interesting hypothesis would be that the development of the apparent durational signaling property of gaze has been shaped by constraints observable in behavior – that is to say, shaped by the idiosyncracies of the production system.

9.5. Study 2: speaker-signal sequences

In Study 1, patterns of persistence in speaker gaze behavior were described through analysis of run sequences. Persistence represents one of the two properties of actions that were measured in this research. The second is change. In this study, events are analyzed in order to describe the types of changes occurring in sequences for three speaker actions examined together.

Specifically, the aim of the analyses is to determine if there is constraint in the sequencing of onsets and terminations for speaker gaze, speaker gestures, and the grammatical completeness of speaker utterances when these three actions are considered simultaneously. These actions are elements of six speaker signals in D&F's turn system. Therefore, the analyses describe the sequencing of signals produced by speakers. This type of information is of interest for strategy research because it describes individuals in terms of patterns of action that are important for understanding interactional organization. The critical question, in terms of the thesis of this chapter, is the extent to which these patterns of actions may further be described in terms of the speaker exercising choice in the production of these patterns.

The relation of gaze and gesture to speech production has been an area of growing interest in psycholinguistic research. Recent studies indicate that gaze directed away from the auditor is associated with hesitant phases of speech whereas gaze directed toward the auditor is associated with fluent phases of speech (e.g., Beattie, 1980). According to Butterworth and Goldman-Eisler (1979), hesitant speech reflects cognitive planning whereas fluent speech reflects the execution of that planning. From this perspective, gaze is diverted from the auditor in order to minimize interference with planning, and presumably gaze is directed at the auditor during execution in order to monitor the auditor's response to what was said.

Dittmann (1972) proposes a similar notion of the relationship between body movements in general, including hand gestures, and speech. He argues that increased bodily activity during hestitant phases of speech relates to speech encoding processes. However, research that has specifically analyzed the relation between gestural and speech production indicates that gestures do not merely reflect motoric leakage resulting from cognitive processing demands. Indeed, contrary to the expectations of this perspective, Beattie (1980) reports that gestures are much more likely to occur during fluent phases of speech than hesitant phases. Moreover, a prominent current point of view (e.g., McNeill, 1979) is that the timing of gestures with speech, as well as the relation of the shape of gestures to concurrent speech, is so finely synchronized that gesture and speech must represent parallel manifestations of the same thought process.

Thus, aside from the evidence for the interactional importance of the three actions analyzed in this study, there is also considerable evidence that suggests these three actions are coordinated through common information-processing mechanisms. Yet, there has apparently been no study investigating the interrelation of these actions through time. This study seeks to fill this void.

As was stated at the beginning of this chapter, a point of change in action, where one activity ends and another begins, is referred to as an *event*. This idea of event is comparable to that of von Wright (1963) and more recently of McNeill (1979). To say that an event occurred is to say that a change from one state of affairs to another state of affairs was observed. Events may therefore be identified and coded in terms of two-place sequences: an antecedent state and a consequent state. Thus, rather than focusing on occurrences of actions, the analyses that follow examine the temporal relationship among actions.

Coding of variables and data collection

For the purpose of this study, activity of the three behaviors studied was coded – categorically, as present or absent – for each unit of analysis as follows. For gaze, the orientation of the speaker's gaze was coded as either directed toward the partner or away from the partner. For gesture, the code assigned each unit indicated either that speaker gestural activity was observed or that gestural activity was not observed. For grammatical completeness, the coding was based on whether either the formal completion of a subject-predicate construction or noncompletion of a subject-predicate construction had occurred during the unit of analysis.

Each unit of analysis was thereby identified according to one of eight possible combinations of the three actions included in the study. Labels for each of these combinations are presented in Table 9.10.

Counts were then made for sequences of adjacent units according to these combinations (e.g., HGQ → HGQ; HGQ → HQ). This resulted in a transition matrix of 64 such two-place sequences, with each sequence defined in terms of one of eight antecedent states, and one of eight consequent states. Each sequence identifies a class of events.

Analysis of the 8 × 8 table

Counts for the 64 two-state sequences of speaker signals are presented in Table 9.11. The row headings of this square, 8 × 8, contingency table identify the behavioral states at time T, and the column headings identify the behavioral states at time $T + 1$. The test of the independence model, no association between states at T and $T + 1$, resulted in a G^2 value of 2804.18 with 49 degrees of freedom (df), which is significant at the .0001 level. This result indicates the presence of considerable association between states at time T and $T + 1$. Actions observed in consequent units were systematically related to actions observed in the antecedent unit.

Table 9.11 also shows for each cell standardized residuals that result from comparison of the observed frequencies with expected frequencies generated by a test of independence between states at time T and $T + 1$ [residual = (expected − observed)/expected$^{1/2}$]. These residuals represent the variability that remains unexplained by the model tested. Residuals are approximately normally distributed with mean zero and unit variance of less than one (Haberman, 1973). Residuals may, therefore, be compared, and thereby the "strength" of association between states at T and $T + 1$ approximated.

Table 9.10. *Labels for eight combinations of speaker signals*

Labels for states (antecedent or consequent)	Actions included in state
HGQ	Active gesture (H) Gaze toward the auditor (G) Grammatical completion (Q)
GQ	No gesture Gaze toward the auditor (G) Grammatical completion (Q)
HQ	Active gesture (H) Gaze away from the auditor Grammatical completion (Q)
Q	No gesture Gaze away from the auditor Grammatical completion (Q)
HG	Active gesture (H) Gaze toward the auditor (G) No grammatical completion
G	No gesture Gaze toward the auditor (G) No grammatical completion
H	Active gesture (H) Gaze away from the auditor No grammatical completion
Z	No gesture Gaze away from the auditor No grammatical completion

Examination of the cell residuals indicates that for each of the eight behavioral states at T, there were both strongly positive and strongly negative associations with states at $T + 1$. For example, an HGQ was most strongly and positively associated with a subsequent HG (residual = 10.73). Of 125 total HGQ states, 64 or 51% were followed by HG. Since HGQ states were quite uncommon, accounting for only 2.4% of states at T, and since HG represents 14.6% of the possible states at $T + 1$, it should be apparent that this sequential relation is not due to chance. Similarly, each state at T was strongly and positively associated with at least one state at $T + 1$. GQ is most strongly and positively associated with a subsequent G;

Table 9.11. *Observed frequencies (data) and standardized residuals resulting from the test of quasi-independence for the 8 × 8 cross-classification of sequential speaker signals*

Time (T)	Time (T + 1)							
	HGQ	GQ	HQ	Q	HG	G	H	Z
HGQ								
Data	5	3	6	6	64	21	9	11
Residual	0.98	−3.32	2.18	−1.06	10.73	−2.61	−1.06	−2.88
GQ								
Data	2	56	5	15	37	175	20	77
Residual	−2.53	0.68	−1.00	−2.54	−2.54	5.69	−3.12	−0.26
HQ								
Data	2	1	4	4	19	7	50	15
Residual	−0.39	−3.39	1.35	−1.28	1.07	−4.20	12.23	−1.29
Q								
Data	3	9	5	41	19	64	34	201
Residual	−2.15	−5.77	−0.93	2.50	−4.83	−4.45	−0.73	14.11
HG								
Data	78	66	17	27	331	164	54	29
Residual	13.07	−3.49	0.39	−3.93	20.78	−4.11	−2.76	−10.21
G								
Data	25	431	12	114	83	721	41	131
Residual	−2.41	15.70	−3.46	−0.10	−9.55	12.19	−9.39	−10.54
H								
Data	9	18	39	21	138	46	207	93
Residual	−1.50	−6.61	8.09	−3.26	6.01	−9.43	19.40	−2.22
Z								
Data	8	90	15	149	52	307	108	489
Residual	−4.18	−5.58	−1.93	6.22	−9.41	−2.75	−1.50	15.14

HQ with a subsequent H; Q with a subsequent Z; HG with a subsequent HG and HGQ; and G with a subsequent G and GQ; H with a subsequent H, HQ, and HG; and Z with a subsequent Z and Q. Clearly, sequences of speaker signals were not randomly paired within speaking turns.

Analysis of quasi-independence

Several of the largest cell residuals in Table 9.11 were associated with cells that identify sequences with the same states at T and $T + 1$ (e.g., for the

HG → HG sequence, the residual is 20.78). These cells identify persistence of the same state for all three actions. Because the notion of an event in this study is of change in state, sequences characterized by no change are of interest only insofar as they represent a principal source of variation in Table 9.11 unaccounted for by the model of independence. However, as Goodman (1968) demonstrated for social mobility data, retaining events in the analysis that are not characterized by change impedes understanding the nature of change within the data set. For these reasons, counts in cells identified by the same state at T and $T + 1$ (the main diagonal cells) are treated as structural zeros (Bishop, Fienberg & Holland, 1975: pp. 296-299). Assuming that a large source of deviation from independence was attributable to the main diagonal cells, the data were re-analyzed as an "incomplete" table by applying methods developed by Goodman (1968) for such tables. The test of "quasi-independence" resulted in a G^2 value of 1613.30 with 41 degrees of freedom, which is significant at the the .0001 level. This result indicates that significant association exists in the off-diagonal cells; that is, change in actions between states from time T to $T + 1$ was not random.

The cell residuals that result from the test of quasi-independence are shown in Table 9.12. Again, positive residual values represent likely sequences, while negative residuals represent unlikely sequences. As with the pattern of residuals for the complete table, there is a distinct tendency for each behavioral state at T to be strongly and positively associated with a specific state at $T + 1$.

Three major points are apparent from these results: (a) The lack of independence in the complete table (Table 9.11) was not exclusively a function of the persistence of actions in the same state between T and $T + 1$. (b) Changes in speaker actions that occur between sequential units are not random. And finally, (c) the pattern of change for speaker actions between sequential units appears orderly and describable.

Computing the contribution of the main diagonal to the lack of independence

Comparing the G^2 values and the degrees of freedom between the test of independence for the complete 8×8 table reported earlier, and the incomplete table may be thought of as an analysis of the contribution of the main diagonal cells to the lack of independence in the 8×8 table. The G^2 value associated with the main diagonal cells is 1190.88 with 8 degrees of freedom (i.e., G^2 2804.18 − G^2 1613.30 = G^2 1190.88; df 49 − df 41 = df 8). This indicates the presence of significant association between same

Table 9.12. *Observed frequencies (data) and standardized residuals resulting from the test of quasi-independence for the 8 × 8 cross-classification of sequential speaker signals*

Time (T)	Time ($T + 1$)							
	HGQ	GQ	HQ	Q	HG	G	H	Z
HGQ								
Data		3	6	6	64	21	9	11
Residual		−4.00	1.56	−1.65	12.77	−2.36	−0.61	−2.44
GQ								
Data	2		5	15	37	175	20	77
Residual	−3.10		−1.65	−3.69	−1.56	5.82	−2.63	0.45
HQ								
Data	2	1		4	19	7	50	15
Residual	−0.73	−3.94		−1.77	2.01	−4.01	13.70	−0.78
Q								
Data	3	9	5		19	64	34	201
Residual	−2.64	−6.90	−1.46		−3.78	−3.94	0.18	16.26
HG								
Data	78	66	17	27		164	54	29
Residual	15.20	−2.16	1.20	−2.84		2.09	1.50	−6.43
G								
Data	25	431	12	114	83		41	131
Residual	−2.20	15.98	−3.28	0.42	−4.75		−6.16	−5.59
H								
Data	9	18	39	21	138	46		93
Residual	−1.17	−6.18	8.95	−2.69	13.07	−6.28		2.35
Z								
Data	8	90	15	149	52	307	108	
Residual	−3.97	−5.24	−1.66	7.12	−5.27	3.50	3.20	

states at T and $T + 1$. This G^2 difference can be viewed as the proportion of the unexplained variation in Table 9.11 accounted for by the no-change cells (i.e., $R^2 = [2804.18 − 1613.30]/2804.18 = .42$).

Patterns of change across events

Earlier, the main-diagonal cells were called no-change cells. This suggests an interesting possibility for representing the pattern of residuals. For

Table 9.13. *Absolute number of changes for each event along with residuals reported previously in Table 9.12*

Time (T)	Time (T + 1)							
	HGQ	GQ	HG	Q	HG	G	H	Z
HGQ								
Changes		ONE	ONE	TWO	ONE	TWO	TWO	THREE
Residual		−4.00	1.56	−1.65	12.77	−2.36	−0.61	−2.44
GQ								
Changes	ONE		TWO	ONE	TWO	ONE	THREE	TWO
Residual	−3.10		−1.65	−3.69	−1.56	5.82	−2.63	0.45
HQ								
Changes	ONE	TWO		ONE	TWO	THREE	ONE	TWO
Residual	−0.73	−3.94		−1.77	2.01	−4.01	13.70	−0.78
Q								
Changes	TWO	ONE	ONE		THREE	TWO	TWO	ONE
Residual	−2.64	−6.90	−1.46		−3.78	−3.94	0.18	16.26
HG								
Changes	ONE	TWO	TWO	THREE		ONE	ONE	TWO
Residual	15.20	−2.16	1.20	−2.84		2.09	1.50	−6.43
G								
Changes	TWO	ONE	THREE	TWO	ONE		TWO	ONE
Residual	−2.20	15.98	−3.28	0.42	−4.75		−6.16	−5.59
H								
Changes	TWO	THREE	ONE	TWO	ONE	TWO		ONE
Residual	−1.17	−6.18	8.95	−2.69	13.07	−6.28		2.35
Z								
Changes	THREE	TWO	TWO	ONE	TWO	ONE	ONE	
Residual	−3.97	−5.24	−1.66	7.12	−5.27	3.50	3.20	

example, the sequence H → HG identifies one change (the onset of G) between T and T + 1. By the same logic, the sequence GQ → H identifies three changes: the termination of G and Q and the onset of H. Using this idea, i.e., the "number of changes" in behaviors between states at T and T + 1, the pattern of cell residuals may be examined. This is done in Table 9.13. Each cell in this table is identified in terms of the absolute number of changes between T and T + 1 with the cell residuals that resulted from the test of quasi-independence reported below.

Examination of Table 9.13 indicates that the number of changes characterizing an event is systematically related to the value and sign of the residual associated with that event. That is, a change of one behavior between states identifies those events most likely to occur; an event characterized by change in all three behaviors was rare and in all cases occurred significantly less often than would be expected by chance. The range of residuals for changes of one was from −6.90 to 16.26 with a median residual of 2.22. The range of residuals for changes of two was −6.43 to 2.01, with a median residual of −1.91. The range in residuals for changes of three was from −6.18 to −2.44, with a median residual of −3.53.

Differences between the three distributions of residual become even more apparent if events that have a Q in both the antecedent and the consequent unit (e.g., HGQ → GQ, GQ → Q) are ignored. These events were extremely rare in these data, accounting for 2% of all change events. All but one of these events have an associated negative residual. As a result, the differences in distributions of residuals just noted are conservative. If these events are ignored, the median residual for changes of one jumps to 6.47, whereas the medians for changes of two and changes of three remain unchanged.

A corollary of the rarity of events with Q in both units is the observation that the most frequent events are those with a Q in the first state but no Q in the second state, or the reverse. These patterns involving Q and its absence stem from the nature of Q: A grammatical completion requires a subject-predicate construction, and such constructions typically extend over more than one unit of analysis.

Patterns of change for individuals

For 32 individual speaker performances, proportions of *all* events characterized by changes of one (24 types of events), two (24 types of events), and three (8 types of events) were calculated. The range in proportions for changes of one was from .59 to .86, with a mean proportion of .72 (SD = .07); the range in proportions for changes of two was from .11 to .38, with a mean proportion of .24 (SD = .07); and the range in proportions for changes of three was from .00 to .11, with a mean proportion of .04 (SD = .03).

Based on these data, the patterns observed for the aggregate data hold generally for individuals. There was a clear tendency for the individuals studied in this research to minimize change between successive units. Change among the three actions studied was typically held to one change at a time over two successive units of analysis.

Turn-taking and speaking events

As pointed out at the beginning of this study, the three speaker actions analyzed here represent signal or constituent elements of signals hypothesized to function in the coordination of turn exchange and turn maintenance in conversation. Given that the patterning of these signals is not randomly distributed over time, an obvious question is whether specific patterns of change have distinctive signaling properties. That is, does the type of sequence (e.g., G → GQ) or the extremity of change (e.g., H → GQ) influence the probability of auditor responsiveness? A number of hypotheses concerning the nature of association between specific sequences (i.e., between specific changes, *not* single antecedent states) and subsequent auditor turn attempts were tested. None of these tests revealed the presence of any notable association between auditor claims to the turn and speaker behavioral displays at time T or the extremity of change between T and $T + 1$.

Conclusions

The results of this study indicate that changes in actions between successive units of analysis, differing by at least one action, were not randomly distributed. Instead, the pattern of change in states is highly ordered as a function of (a) the state displayed at time T, and (b) the extent of the change that could have occurred. This patterning of change does not, however, appear to be associated with turn-taking conventions. These findings are interpreted as providing evidence that production regularities constrain the onsets and terminations of actions. Such regularities could stem from underlying cognitive or control processes. That both the form and extent of change characterize the regularity of these sequences implies the involvement of a common central processing mechanism in the production of actions for three distinct behavioral modalities. One of the characteristics of this mechanism appears to be a constraint on the complexity of change that can be processed at any given time.

The perspective taken here is that a key problem continually confronted by the interactive organism is that of coordinating several potentially communicative modalities simultaneously. This problem is present at two levels of analysis: (a) at the level of the message (or signal) and (b) at the level of production. At the message level, the coordination problem involves integrating a set of instructions that will create a behavioral expression isomorphic with the intended message. This, of course, assumes that a conventional interpretation exists for the articulated behavior. At the production level, the coordination problem is defined by possibilities and constraints that result from the structural-functional characteristics of the organism's central and peripheral processors. Here, limits on short-term memory, on dividing, focusing, and sustaining attention while simultaneously monitoring the environment and confronting the press of both internal and external arousers are obvious considerations for getting a sense of what the coordination problem entails.

9.6. Study 3: interactional smiling

Studies 1 and 2 focused on patterns of persistence and change for three speaker actions. The simultaneous patterns of auditor actions, other than turn-taking moves, were not considered in those studies. In this study of the process of interactional smiling, the analyses are not restricted to speaker actions. Instead, the moment-to-moment smiling patterns of both individuals are studied as overlapping run-sequences. The purpose of this study is twofold: first, it will show that patterns of occurrence and persistence for smiles may be differentiated according to influences of individual difference, interactional process, and noninteractional process; second, it will show the effectiveness of run-sequence data for studying simultaneous activity.

Prior research has characterized smiling behavior as a product of both individual differences and of interactive processes. For example, studies have indicated that females smile more frequently and more of the time than do males (e.g., Mackey, 1976). In terms of interactive process, reciprocation of smiles has been claimed to be the normative pattern in social encounters (e.g., Rosenfeld, 1972). However, the relative contribution of individual differences as opposed to interactive factors in accounting for observed patterns of smiling has not been considered.

Additionally, most previous discussions of smiling behavior have ignored information on sequences in which smiling occurs (e.g., D&F: Part II; Rosenfeld, 1966, 1967, 1972). Motivated from an ethological perspective, Van Hoof's (1972) discussion of smile behavior is an exception, as are some infant-caretaker studies (e.g., Kaye, 1982). For casual adult conversation, Brunner (1979) and Duncan, Brunner, and Fiske (1979) analyzed smile sequences, although both of these studies focused primarily on auditor smiling in response to speaker-initiated smiling.

The first part of this study describes a method for representing data on smiling that simultaneously incorporates sequential, contextual, and durational information. A series of log-linear analyses is then reported that

Participant 1: [----------] [------]   [----]

          A   C D G   I   J

Participant 2:   [------------] [-----]
             B   E F H

Figure 9.2. Hypothetical smile spans.

assesses the contributions of individual differences (e.g., sex differences) and interactive processes in accounting for the observed patterns of smiling.

Classification of smiles

Before the results of analyses of interactional smiling are examined, the methods used for analyzing simultaneous run sequences must be given since they represent conceptually and logistically a different type of problem for data collection compared with Studies 1 and 2.

Smile spans. In order to make the analysis of the data a more manageable task, the on-line smiling activity of both individuals (smile spans) was classified as being of one of two general types: reciprocated or nonreciprocated smiles. Reciprocated smile spans refers to participants' smiles which overlap to some degree. Specifically, they consist of smiling by a participant, during some part of which the partner also smiles. A reciprocated smile span was considered terminated when neither participant was observed smiling.

Figure 9.2 should aid in clarifying what is meant by a reciprocated and a nonreciprocated smile span. The brackets indicate the onset or termination of a smile and the dashes between brackets indicate the continuation of that smile. The reciprocated smile span in Figure 9.2 extends from point A to H. Prior to point A, neither participant was observed smiling. Between A and H, at least some mutual smiling (overlap of smiling of the participants) was observable. These stretches of mutual or overlap smiling are B to C, D to E, and F to G. Throughout A to H, smiling is observed continuously, although it is not displayed continuously by both participants. The necessary criterion for the identification of a reciprocated smile span was that there must be some overlap in smiling within a stretch of smiling bordered by no smiling by either participant.

The other type of smile span, nonreciprocated smiles, was the product of only one participant's smiling. Thus, no overlap was observed in a nonreciprocated smile span. In Figure 9.2, I to J constitutes an example of a nonreciprocated smile span.

Smile initiations. The present study focuses on a subset of smiles within smile spans. Specifically, the focus will be on the initiation of smile spans and on the duration of just these initiated smiles. For nonreciprocated smile spans, the duration of the initiation smile is equivalent to the observed nonreciprocated smile span (e.g., I to J in Figure 9.2). For reciprocated smile spans, the duration of the initiation smile may, but need not, be equal to the length of the entire smile span. The duration of the initiation smile is equivalent to the duration of the first smile in the reciprocation smile span. In Figure 9.2, only the duration A to C is considered a reciprocated smile initiation. Other stretches of smiling within the reciprocated smile span, such as D to G, B to E, and F to H, in Figure 9.2, as well as the organization of the reciprocated smile span as a whole, will not be considered here.

Conceptually, the motivation for considering only A to C and I to J smiles as initiations is that these smiles can be directly compared. Both begin after some period of nonsmiling by both participants in the conversation. The first, the reciprocated initiation, is marked by the onset of smiling by the partner before the offset of the smile by the "initiator," whereas the second, nonreciprocated initiation, lacks overlap with a smile by the partner. Thus, these two types of smile differ only in the partner's response.

Smile reciprocation latency. Also included in the subsequent analyses is an examination of smile reciprocation latency: that portion of the initiation smile, within the reciprocated smile span, that precedes the onset of the partner's smile. In Figure 9.2, this duration is a measure of A to B. By comparing smile-reciprocation latencies with the duration of nonreciprocated smile initiations, the effect of smile duration on the likelihood of reciprocation can be assessed. With this latency measure, comparisons can be made of the durations of nonoverlapping stretches of initiation smiles that were either (a) reciprocated, or (b) not reciprocated.

Contextual variables

The potential association of a number of contextual variables with patterns of smiling was also explored. The variables considered in analyzing smile initiations were sex of the initiator, the sex of the partner, and the conversational state of the initiator (i.e., speaker or auditor) in the conversation.

Cases excluded

Aside from the stretches of smiles embedded within multistage reciprocated smile spans, some additional cases were not included in the analysis. These were smiles that were present at the beginning of the videotapes ($N = 12$) and smiles that were present at the end of the videotapes ($N = 3$), for which it was impossible to determine the point of initiation and termination, respectively. In addition, two cases where the raters could not distinguish which person smiled first were also excluded.

Measuring smile duration and reciprocation latency

As with speaker gaze, smiles were measured in units of analysis. Smile duration was determined by the number of final boundaries of units of analysis spanned by a smile. Given the set of U sequential units {U: U_1, U_2, U_3, . . . , U_n}, a smile that began in U_1 and then was terminated in U_2 is one unit in length. Smiles observed within only a single unit were also included in the analysis. Reciprocation latency was measured as the duration of the smile before it was reciprocated.

Distribution of runs for three types of smiles

Figure 9.3 graphs the relative frequencies of runs for the three measures of smiles analyzed in this study: (a) reciprocated smile initiations, (b) nonreciprocated smile initiations, and (c) smile reciprocation latencies. The durations for reciprocated smiles ranged from less than one unit to 38 units, whereas the durations for nonreciprocated smiles ranged from less than one unit to 9 units. The pronounced tendency was for smiles to be brief if not reciprocated, and longer if reciprocated. The majority (54%) of nonreciprocated smiles were less than two units long; in contrast, the majority (56%) of reciprocated smiles were six or more units long. Clearly, the distributions of runs for the two types of smile initiations differ dramatically. Whereas the durations of initiation smiles obviously differ, the durations of reciprocation latencies appear comparable to the durations of nonreciprocated smiles. Additionally, the odds that a smile initiation was reciprocated or nonreciprocated were essentially equal. Of 328 smile initiations, 48% were reciprocated whereas 52% were not reciprocated.

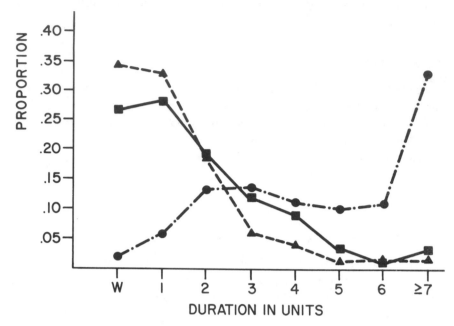

Figure 9.3. Distributions of three measures of smile duration: ●--●--●--● = reciprocated smile initiations (N = 159); (■————■ = nonreciprocated smile initations (N = 169); △----△ = reciprocation latencies (N = 159).

These data suggest that the duration of smile initiations in these data was interactively constrained. Once one participant began smiling, he or she very rapidly stopped smiling unless the partner also began smiling. Interestingly, the time it took for the partner to begin smiling in the presence of an ongoing smile appears comparable to the time that an individual smiled in situations where their partner did not begin smiling. In the following sections, a series of log-linear analyses of smiles are presented. Again, as in the prior studies, the aim of these analyses is to differentiate patterns of smiling that are a product of individual difference or interactional process from patterns that may reflect processing regularities.

Log-linear analyses of smile initiations

Initiation smiles (N = 328) were cross-classified by three contextual variables: the sex of initiator (I), the sex of partner (P), and conversation state of initiator (C). This three-way cross classification is shown in Table 9.14. Several log-linear tests of these data were performed. These models are reported in Table 9.15.

Table 9.14. *Three-way cross-classification of 328 smile initiations*

Sex of initiator	Sex of partner	Conversation state of initiator	Observed frequencies
Male	Male	Speaker	43
Female	Male	Speaker	53
Male	Female	Speaker	30
Female	Female	Speaker	71
Male	Male	Auditor	25
Female	Male	Auditor	41
Male	Female	Auditor	27
Female	Female	Auditor	38

Table 9.15. *Chi-square values for some log-linear models pertaining to the three-way cross-classification in Table 9.14*

Model	Fitted marginals	df	Likelihood-ratio chi-square (G^2)	p
M27	(I)(P)(C)	4	5.32	.255
M28	(I)	6	18.74	.005
M29	(P)	6	37.42	.000
M30	(C)	6	24.10	.001
M31	N	7	37.47	.000

In log-linear analysis, the simplest testable model is the equiprobability model (M31). This model fits no marginals, only the observed N, and assumes, therefore, that the frequency of each variable at each level in the cross-classification was equally probable. As may be expected from perusal of the data in Table 9.14, the equiprobability model provides a poor fit of the data ($G^2 = 37.47$, $df = 7$, $p < .001$). This model was calculated as a baseline model for computing "main effects" (Goodman, 1978) for each variable. Comparison of models M28 through M30 with M31 may be viewed as tests of the equiprobability between the two levels of a variable (i.e., for variables I and P, the levels are male and female; for variable C, the levels are speaker and auditor).

Comparing M30 and M31 tests the null hypothesis that there were as many initiations of smiles by males as there were by females ($G^2 = 18.37$, $df = 1$, $p < .001$). Females initiated significantly more smiles ($N = 203$) than did males ($N = 125$).

Table 9.16. *Four-way cross-classification of 328 smile initiations*

Sex of initiator	Sex of partner	Conversation state of initiator	Action of partner: reciprocation	
			Yes	No
Male	Male	Speaker	18	25
Female	Male	Speaker	19	34
Male	Female	Speaker	22	8
Female	Female	Speaker	41	30
Male	Male	Auditor	13	12
Female	Male	Auditor	12	29
Male	Female	Auditor	13	14
Female	Female	Auditor	21	17

In addition, there was also a main effect for the conversation state of the initiator variable. This is shown by comparing M30 and M31. The difference in G^2 between these two models is a test of the null hypothesis that initiations of smiles by speakers are equiprobable to those initiated by auditors ($G^2 = 13.37$, $df = 1$, $p < .001$). Speakers initiated more smiles than did auditors ($N = 197$ and $N = 131$, respectively).

There was no significant difference in the initiation of smiles as a function of the sex of the partner (G^2 M31 $- G^2$ M29 $= .05$, $df = 1$, $p > .50$). There were 166 initiations observed in the presence of female partners and 162 initiations observed in the presence of male partners.

Model M27, the model of independence, which tests for association among the (contextual) variables in Table 9.14, was not significant. This result indicates that none of the four possible interaction effects or associations (e.g., sex of initiator conditional on sex of partner, or on conversation state, etc.) was significant.

Logit analysis of contextual variables on smile reciprocation

In the previous section, reciprocated smiles were not differentiated from nonreciprocated smiles. Whether a smile was reciprocated or not reciprocated must certainly be a function of the action of the partner of the smile initiator. That is, either the partner also smiled or did not smile. However, it probably was also the case that contextual variables influenced whether a person reciprocated a smile or not. This section considers this issue through a logit analysis of the influence on the action of the partner (A) of the three contextual variables included in this study. Table 9.16 shows the frequen-

Table 9.17. *Chi-square values for some logit models pertaining to the four-way cross-classification in Table 9.16*

Model	Fitted marginals	df	Likelihood-ratio chi-square (G^2)	p
M32	(IPC)(IA)	6	19.90	.003
M33	(IPC)(PA)	6	7.98	.240
M34	(IPC)(CA)	6	20.38	.003
M35	(IPC)(A)	7	21.41	.003

Table 9.18. *2 × 2 cross-classification for 328 smile initiations describing the relation between sex of partner (P) and action of partner (A)*

Action of partner	Sex of partner		Total
	Male	Female	
Reciprocation	62	97	159
No reciprocation	100	69	169
Total	162	166	328

cies of reciprocated and nonreciprocated smiles cross-classified by the three centextual variables.

Table 9.17 reports four logit models for the data in Table 9.16. In these models, action of partner (A) was treated as the dependent variable and the contextual variables were treated as the independent variables (I is sex of initiator, P is sex of partner, and C is conversation state of initiator).

Model M35 tests the hypothesis that none of the three contextual variables has an effect on the action of the partner. The test of this model was significant, indicating the presence of at least one significant effect.

Models M32, M33, and M34 each test the fit of the data when one main effect (on the dependent variable: action of partner) is specified. These three models were compared with Model M35 in order to determine the significance of each of the three possible main effects on the action of the partner (i.e., sex of initiator [I] on [A], sex of the partner [P] on [A], and conversation state of initiator [C] on [A]).

Comparing M33 and M35 revealed a significant sex of partner effect ($G^2 = 13.44$, $df = 1$, $p < .001$). The 2 × 2 marginal table, Table 9.18, cross-classifying sex of partner by action of partner, pinpoints this effect. Males reciprocated 38% of their partner's smile initiations, whereas females reciprocated 58% of their partner's smile initiations.

However, there was no statistically significant influence on the action of the partner as a function of the sex of the initiator or the conversation state of the initiator. This may be seen by comparing models M32 and M34 with model M35 ($G^2 = 1.51$, $df = 1$, $p > .10$ and $G^2 = 1.03$, $df = 1$, $p > .25$). Thus, even though females and speakers initiated significantly more smiles (as indicated in the log-linear results of the previous section), this did not relate to the pattern of reciprocation by the partner.

Finally, model M33, which specifies only the main effect of sex of partner (PA) in the terms of the model, generates estimates that do not vary significantly from the observed frequencies in Table 9.16. Model M33 represents the best-fitting model for these data.

Logit analysis of smile runs

In the two previous sections, the relationship of three contextual variables to smile initiation and to smile reciprocation was analyzed. In this section, the run lengths of smiles are analyzed as a function of four variables: the three contextual variables along with the action of the partner. For the sake of analysis, run sequences of smiles were redefined dichotomously as either "short" ($\leq$ 2 units; $N = 156$) or "long" ($\geq$ 3 units; $N = 172$). Runs were reclassified in this manner in order to avoid the difficulties for the analysis posed by having zeroes and small frequencies in many of the cells. Obtaining an even split of the data was the sole criterion in dividing the distribution of smiles into short and long runs. The data that resulted from this reclassification are shown in Table 9.19.

Logit models that were fit to the data in Table 9.19 are reported in Table 9.20. Model M40 tests the hypothesis that run length (R) was not influenced by the three contextual variables and the action of the partner. That is, this model assumes that there were no main or interaction effects on run length. The G^2 value for this model (98.34, $df = 15$) is significant. This indicates that at least one of the 15 main or interaction effects not included in model M40 was significant. Models M36, M37, and M38 do not significantly improve the fit of the data provided by model M40. Substantively, these models differ from model M40 in that each specifies the main effect of one of the three contextual variables. None of these variables by themselves account for much of the unexplained variation in run length noted in model M40.

However, comparing M39 and M40 revealed a significant action of partner main effect ($G^2 = 93.65$, $df = 1$, $p < .001$). Specifying the main

Table 9.19. *Five-way cross-classification of 328 smile initiations*

Sex of initiator	Sex of partner	Conversation state of initiator	Action of partner: reciprocation (Yes or No)	Run length of smile	
				≤ 2	≥ 3
Male	Male	Speaker	Yes	4	14
Female	Male	Speaker	Yes	3	16
Male	Female	Speaker	Yes	5	17
Female	Female	Speaker	Yes	7	34
Male	Male	Auditor	Yes	2	11
Female	Male	Auditor	Yes	2	10
Male	Female	Auditor	Yes	4	9
Female	Female	Auditor	Yes	6	15
Male	Male	Speaker	No	17	8
Female	Male	Speaker	No	24	10
Male	Female	Speaker	No	7	1
Female	Female	Speaker	No	23	7
Male	Male	Auditor	No	9	3
Female	Male	Auditor	No	20	9
Male	Female	Auditor	No	11	3
Female	Female	Auditor	No	12	5

Table 9.20. *Chi-square values for some logit models pertaining to the five-way cross-classification in Table 9.19*

Model	Fitted marginals	df	Likelihood-ratio chi-square (G^2)	p
M36	(IPCA)(IR)	14	98.33	.000
M37	(IPCA)(PR)	14	97.58	.000
M38	(IPCA)(CR)	14	97.65	.000
M39	(IPCA)(AR)	14	4.69	>.500
M40	(IPCA)(R)	15	98.34	.000

effect of action of partner reduces the unexplained variation in model M40 by 95% (i.e., $R^2 = [98.34 - 4.69]/98.34 = .95$). This effect is shown in the 2 × 2 marginal table, Table 9.21, which cross-classifies action of partner by duration of smile.

Additionally, model M39, which specifies only the main effect of action of partner (AR) among the terms of the model, generates estimates that do not vary significantly from the observed frequencies in Table 9.19. Model M39 represents the best-fitting model for these data. The 14 degrees of

Table 9.21. *2 × 2 Cross-classification for 328 smile initiations describing the relation between action of partner (A) and duration of smile (R)*

Action of partner	Duration of smile		
	≤ 2	≥ 3	Total
Reciprocation	33	126	159
No reciprocation	123	46	169
Total	156	172	328

freedom associated with the test of this model refer to the 14 possible main and interaction effects excluded from M39 (i.e., 14 effects were not used in generating cell estimates).

None of the other variables significantly improve the fit of the data. Of particular interest is the lack of effects for sex of initiator and sex of partner. Although these variables were significantly associated with the tendency for a person to initiate a smile and to reciprocate a smile, respectively, they were not associated with the length of smiles. That the durational pattern of smiling does not vary across persons who differ quite dramatically in their tendencies to start smiling or join in on smiling, indicates the presence of a constraint on smile duration. Whether this constraint reflects convention or noninteractive processes is not at all clear.

Analysis of smile reciprocation latency

It might be argued that the action of partner effect on smile run length may reflect a confounding of the specific duration that a smile was displayed by the initiator with the type of partner action observed. Possibly partners, because of constraints posed by perceptual thresholds, cannot consistently reciprocate with a smile before some identifiable response latency. It might, therefore, be the case that the reason two distinct distributions of smile durations were observed for initiators is not a function of reciprocation, but rather the fact that initiators maintained smiles longer at some times than at others. That is, the length of an initiation smile was a function of the initiator and not the action of the partner. Hypothetically then, in some cases initiators smiled for extended periods, and in other cases they smiled briefly. And when they smiled briefly, their smiles were not reciprocated with a smile by the partner, but when they smiled for extended periods, they were reciprocated by the smiles of the partner. It is because of this ambiguity in interpreting the results that reciprocation latency was measured and analyzed.

If it were the case that the action of the partner is restricted by the length of time that the initiator's smile has been displayed, then partner smiles should follow some characteristic latency period. In addition, most nonreciprocated smiles should be consistently shorter than this latency period if partner response is to the perseveration of smiling by the initiator. In order to determine if the latency of the partner's response is a function of the extent of initiator display, the distributions of nonreciprocated smiles and reciprocation latencies graphed in Figure 9.3 were compared. A test of the heterogeneity of these run-length distributions was not significant ($G^2 = 10.44$, $df = 7$, $p > .10$). Reciprocation latencies were neither constrained by the extent of time that a smile was displayed, nor do they appear to be randomly distributed. The conclusion that may be drawn is that the duration of any given smile is substantially patterned by the action of the partner. However, this patterning was consistent across interactional contexts, individuals, and interactions analyzed in this study.

Conclusions

Given that the major purpose of this chapter is to explicate constraints on the optional expression of behavior through the analysis of expanded action-sequences, the principal results of the analysis of smiling are twofold. First, in the conversations studied, smiles initiated within the context of nonsmiling were durationally constrained by the partner. That is, the smile of a person initiating a smile was predictably brief unless the other person also smiled. Of smiles that were three units in length or longer, 73% were reciprocated, and of smiles that were seven units in length or longer, 92% were reciprocated. Simultaneous activity, rather than taking turns, appeared to be the preferred mode for smiling by the interactants studied. (Refer to discussion of this point in the context of research on mother-infant interaction by Kaye [1982].) In contrast, the occurrence and specific patterns of gaze, grammatical completion, and gesture considered earlier in this chapter were assumed to be closely linked to speaking turns, and hence represent interactionally asynchronous activities.

The second main result was that the distribution of durations of nonreciprocated smiles was comparable to the distribution of durations of smile-reciprocation latencies. The durational characterisitics of nonreciprocated smiles and smile reciprocation latencies were remarkably uniform and similarly skewed. Thus, the probability of a smile being ended by the initiator at any given point was comparable to the probability of the partner's reciprocating. Either smile initiations resulted in mutual smiling or they were terminated within approximately the same durational frame. Although it might be argued that the brevity of this durational frame reflects conventional preference for mutuality in visual display, the evidence may also reflect parameters of perception of an action's occurrence for both participants. From this perspective, one may ask whether conventional preference is intimately related to perceptual processes.

9.7. Discussion

The purpose of this essay is to support the thesis that noninteractive processes constrain the patterns of a person's actions in interactional settings. Most readers would find no particular problem with the thesis as originally stated. And likewise most readers would acknowledge that very regular patterns are apparent in the actions analyzed in the three studies presented in defense of the thesis. However, there are two key questions that must be answered about the findings reported: (a) Do the patterns of actions that were identified reflect noninteractive process, and (b) if they do, how useful are such data for our understanding of such processes? The brevity of runs of gaze/no-gaze across various contexts along with the strong tendency for speaker actions to change systematically but minimally between units represent those patterns that seem most likely to be of interest in answering these questions. Before addressing these questions directly, it is first necessary to point out some obvious limitations of this research as well as to review why the thesis is of interest, that is, why it is not trivial.

Limitations

Measurments of durations. Throughout this chapter the notion of persistence has been of central importance. Indeed, we measured the duration of actions in order to provide evidence for patterns in actions and compared the distributions of durations of actions to gauge when and how patterns differed. However, all of the measurements of duration were in units of analysis, not in chronological time. Although they averaged a little more than one second long, the temporal durations of units of analysis varied considerably. Units were defined in terms of speaker actions. Thus, differences in durations that are apparent between specific actions when measured in terms of run sequences, might not be noticeable, or might even be reversed when measured in chronological time.

Obviously, this means that the measurements of patterns that are offered as evidence for elementary information processes are extremely crude relative to orthodox experimental approaches. Central to the information-processing approach has been the view that mental operations take time. The assumption of the approach is that it is possible to break down or partition measurements of the time it takes an individual to perform a speeded task, with the various partitions inferred to reflect underlying processes involved in the performance of the task. In contrast, this research measured time through the occurrence and nonoccurrence of actions. That such measures provide data on elementary mental operations has not at all been substantiated by this research. Instead, the research has intended to raise the possibility that such data might be useful for understanding mental processes. Additionally, although it seems intuitively appealing to measure behavior in terms of actions, it is always possible that an important behavior has not been included in the criteria for establishing a unit of analysis, and that if it were, the units would tend to be shorter.

Ignoring the auditor. In the first two studies concerned with speaker gaze patterns and changes among speaker actions, the simultaneous activity of the auditor was largely ignored. This of course creates a difficulty because these studies did not test the fundamental claim of this chapter, that there are consistent, noninteractive patterns displayed by speakers in these interactions. For example, in the gaze study, the activities of the auditor were limited to turn claiming. Therefore, the obvious potential influence of auditor gaze patterns and back channels on the pattern of speaker gaze was ignored. D&F have noted that speaker gaze is associated with auditor within-turn activity (i.e., the within-turn signal and the continuation signal are associated with back-channel signals). It would seem that consideration of the auditor in future analyses would be essential in order to determine if there is systematic variation in speaker gaze behavior associated with preceding or concurrent actions of the auditor.

Criteria for production regularities. Inferences about elementary information processes were to be based on observed patterns of actions referred to as production regularities. The criteria for determining that a pattern of action represented a regularity of the participant's production rather than a regularity that resulted from interaction was (a) that the pattern would not vary as a function of person, interaction, or interactional context, and (b) by definition, that the pattern not be associated with known interactional phenomena. Although such patterns were defined, particularly in the first two studies, it is questionable whether one can infer that these production regularities provide evidence for elementary mental processes. What is particularly problematic is what "not vary" in this criterion means. Implicitly, the considerable variation present within patterns was treated as measurement error. But as Cronbach (1957) noted, one researcher's error term is another's individual differences.

Strategy research

The thesis of this chapter – that actions observable in interaction reflect patterns of noninteractive processes – evolved within the context of research on interaction strategy. The initial aim of the strategy project was to describe what people do in interactions with options that are available to them. In the research, options that were considered available to interactants were empirically defined in terms of a system of rules and signals governed by convention. This approach is intuitively appealing, as Fiske (1978) emphasizes, because of the reliability and exactness of the types of statements that may be made about persons.

The approach is straightforward. However, in assuming that the relationship or pattern between signals and responses is largely a function of convention, the influence of other sources in shaping or constraining the patterns of signal display and the patterns of response was left unconsidered. Thus, the conceptualization of strategy research, as well as the empirical approach suggested for the study of strategy phenomena, was problematic. Left unstudied in the structural research were patterns of those actions that either constituted signals or were constituents of signals. Consideration of other patterns for an action than those that may be phrased in terms of convention represents an obvious area of interest for the interpretation of strategy findings, as well as for the understanding of interactional phenomena in general. Thus, one empirical aim of the research described in this chapter was to determine the extent to which actions that had been hypothesized to function as interactional signals could be described as also patterned in terms other than convention. In an effort to reach this aim, three methodological issues were pivotal for this research. It is to these we shall now briefly turn.

Methodological issues

Variables. The development of variables for describing patterns of actions in sequence represented a principal goal of the strategy research in general. This chapter explicitly examined the effectiveness of two variables, *run sequences* and *events* for describing interactional behavior. Both variables seemed intuitively appealing for interaction research since they preserve information on two important characteristics of interaction and of actions: persistence and change. Because these variables are amenable to qualification by other variables, their potential for research on interaction appears sizable.

Besides their descriptive potential, there are two aspects of run-sequence and event variables that offer particular rewards. First, certain patterns of persistence and change may be considered as signals. For example, speaker gaze prior to auditor turn claims was systematically longer in duration than in any other context. This seems to suggest that speakers on occasion use persistence to signal their readiness to relinquish the turn. Additionally, persistence and change are aspects of actions that no doubt are of psychological importance. That is, organisms respond to changes and contrasts in stimuli differently from the way they respond to persistence of stimuli. Changes in stimuli tend to arouse, to orient the organism, whereas the persistence of a stimulus tends to passify and habituate the organism to that stimuli's presence. Thus, not only do these variables retain potentially important aspects of interactional behavior, but they also preserve aspects of psychological arousal-function character that are missed in studies that code only whether or not an action occurred.

Studying individuals through action sequences. In Study 2 and largely in Study 1, only the actions of the speaker were analyzed. Prior research using action-sequence variables has always been carried out on the actions of two participants. The action-sequence approach was explicitly developed for the purpose of studying interaction. The results of Study 2, in particular, should indicate that action-sequence data have merits for the analysis of patterns of actions within individuals as well.

Data analysis. All of the studies in this project were exploratory. The application of log-linear methods is ideally suited for the purposes of exploratory data analysis because the log-linear approach assumes that a data set has a structure that can be identified and quantified. Each analysis or test of a model may be viewed as a naturalistic experiment. For example, the analyses of speaker gaze examined the distribution of durations that had been observed within different interactional contexts. In this way, it was possible to test the relation of those contexts to the distributions of gaze runs.

Elementary information processes

Along with higher cognitive processes and neural processes, the identification and modeling of elementary information processes represents one of three levels of empirical and theoretical concern for researchers of human cognition (Simon, 1979). Elementary information processes refer to an assumed small number of mental operations that are usually defined through two types of examples: of function (e.g., searching semantic memory and mental rotation [Chase, 1978]), and of constraints on operation (e.g., capacity limitations of the "common processor" and competition with other operations for common resources [cf. Simon, 1979]).

Elementary mental processes are proposed to represent an enduring and stable set of operations that have evolved as an interface with neural subsystems and higher cognitive processes for the purposes of handling information. Similar to 19th-century theories that assumed that mind could be defined in terms of a mental chemistry, researchers of elementary information processes view such processes as the building blocks for the performance of specific and adaptive tasks. Posner and McLeod, in their (1982) review article, state this view explicitly: "Elementary mental operations may be assembled into sequences and combinations that represent the strategy developed for a particular task" (p. 480). Moreover, Posner and McLeod (1982) believe that "detailed studies of particular task configurations will lead to the identification of fundamental operations that can be used to characterize the human mind" (p. 478); (cf. Simon, 1979).

In this chapter, the interest in elementary information processes is motivated by two complementary concerns. First, the notion of elementary processes is of interest as a possible explanatory concept for regularities in patterns of actions described in this study that were not obviously associated with or shaped by interactional phenomena. Second, detailed studies of everyday interactions may provide evidence of constraints on actions that may have interesting parallels to findings from highly structured experimental studies of elementary mental processes.

The tendency of durational patterns of speaker gaze to be brief along with the pattern of change in speaker signals is interpreted here as reflecting noninteractive processes because all efforts to identify individual difference and interactive influence on these patterns were unsuccessful. In what sense, then, may these patterns be described as elementary information processes?

The back-and-forth pattern of speaker gaze suggests an elementary orienting process whose function is to seek information from the environment and orient the individual within the environment. But why is it that speakers display this pattern?

As discussed earlier, others have also noted this pattern in speaker gaze and have discussed it in terms of cognitive regularities (e.g., Beattie, 1980), specifically in relation to speech encoding processes. The predominant interpretation has been that looking at one's partner while speaking interferes with speech encoding. Thus, looking away represents a strategy to avoid this interference. However, as Ehrlichman (1981) has shown, speakers shift their gaze back and forth when facing extremely neutral stimuli as well as when in complete darkness (Ehrlichman & Barrett, 1983). This would tend to indicate that the back-and-forth pattern of speaker gaze behavior is automatic and not so much a reflection of a cognitive strategy but a reflection of the interface between cognition and underlying neural systems.

There are two possible explanations for why speakers and not auditors are characterized by an on-off pattern of gaze. First, there is some evidence to suggest that patterns of head movements and eye movements iconically reflect patterns of neuronal activation (e.g., Kinsbourne, 1972). The second explanation follows from a key concept of the information-processing literature, namely that elementary processes compete for limited processing capacity. Given the heavy processing demands that the production of speech places on a limited capacity processing system, it would seem that fairly automatic elementary processes would go unchecked. This proposal would suggest that it takes processing capacity to keep gaze directed or focused, as in the activity of the auditor. When demands on processing capacity become too great, as when a speech plan is being organized, the control of gaze is relaxed, and the tendency is to turn gaze away.

Study 2 provided evidence that the changes occurring over successive units of analysis among three speaker actions were systematic. There was a pronounced tendency for minimal change to occur. McNeill (1979) suggests that gesture and speech are intimately related such that they represent parallel output of a common thought unit, which he terms a *syntagma*. The pattern of gaze relative to speech may be associated with retrieval processes or generally with the amount of processing time available for constraining the elementary pattern of gaze. Based on the data reported in Study 2, it would appear that speech, gesture, and gaze are commonly constrained. This suggests that these actions are organized through a common processor before output. It is assumed in most information-processing models that prior to the articulation of an action or response, the component features of the action are passed from short-term memory to some sort of response organizer or assembler. Possibly, the pattern of changes among speaker actions indicates the involvement of and constraints of such a processor.

To be sure, the data and the reasoning presented here are sketchy. The intention has not been to argue that the patterns that emerged from the analyses represent manifestations of elementary process, but only that their interpretation could be approached from this perspective. The ultimate usefulness of data of this types for understanding elementary information processes cannot presently be known. Minimally, I would hope that data of this type may suggest the wide range of constraints that operate on everyday behavior.

10. Participant differences and interactive strategies

BARBARA G. KANKI

10.1. Introduction

The following study is an attempt to tackle the problem of individual differences in interaction research. We share with many other studies of human behavior focusing on variability within samples, a basic goal of generating descriptions of persons that differentiate the actions of some individuals from those of others. A second goal often sought in such research is the demonstration that the descriptions represent relatively stable or enduring qualities belonging to the individuals so categorized.

A description satisfying both objectives also presupposes that its constituent parameters or "measures" are unilaterally determined; that is, each description is purely the product of one individual. In many domains, the assumption is warranted; for example, when measuring physical attributes such as the height, visual acuity, or manual dexterity of an individual. Similarly, measurements of skilled performances such as GRE scores, typing speed, or writing style are also presumed to embody individual achievements. The research presented here is concerned with behaviors which are inherently interactive in nature; that is to say, an individual's behavior at any given moment is always in some way affected by the interpersonal context within which it occurs. Since the data consist of dyadic conversations, there are always two participants to consider with respect to any interactive events chosen for examination. Thus, the measurement of any single person's behavior is automatically confounded by the behavioral context of the other participant.

Controlling the interactive context

In this particular research domain, the assumption of unilaterality is quickly disconfirmed. Thus, the underlying problem becomes that of designing variables or measurements which not only will provide differentiated characterizations of individuals but at the same time will account for their interactive context. Only when this problem is solved can we return to the original consideration of individual differences.

Using confederates. This is not a new problem in interaction research where there have been various attempts to solve it. One such attempt (which has been discussed at length in Chapter 1) has involved the use of confederates wherein each "subject" interacted with a person who was instructed to act in a preestablished way. It was assumed that such a planned performance by a confederate could effectively control the interactive context for all subjects. What escaped attention was the fact that confederates are interactants themselves and their behaviors take on meaning within the behavioral context of the subjects (who are, presumably, not performing according to a predetermined plan). Thus, it is not clear that a confederate's performance is even definable, not to mention executable. Nevertheless, this approach does reflect an awareness of the problem of interpersonal effects and constitutes a conscientious, though dubious way of dealing with it.

Averaging over samples. A second response to the problem of interactive contexts is one which is more of a side step than a true attempt to confront the issue. This approach assumes that by gathering enough samples of a person's behavior, one can then devise or calculate an average or rate which characterizes the individual. It is based on the premise that interactive contexts are random variations; thus, a large enough sampling will cancel out any such unique effects on the subject's behavior. Although the logic is reasonable, it has no bearing on the problem of interactive contexts. The weakness lies in the faulty assumption that random variation is equivalent to the interactive effect of partners on each other. Whether sampling is performed across different partners (for a given subject), or across trials for the same interactive partner, it can only offset residual variation after a systematic interactive effect is accounted for.

Accounting for the interactive context

Because the use of confederates proves highly problematic in controlling interactive effects, and because we cannot automatically assume a null effect, the remaining alternative is to try to account for it. Such an account would demand some kind of concomitant examination of subject and partner, specifically, the investigation of behavioral regularities produced by the partner which relate to the subject behavior in question. Until this is accomplished, there is no way to distinguish whether subjects' behaviors are solely attributable to self or whether they are partially a function of the partner. Although the adequacy of sampling technique remains critical with respect to issues of generalizability and validity, no amount of careful sampling can warrant the a priori assumption of zero interactive effects between participants.

Action-sequence variables. This study attempts to follow the approach that takes interpersonal context into account. Instead of trying to control or suppress these effects, they are treated as conditional factors which can be built into the definitions of the variables. As such, any given variable represents actions of the partner as well as actions of the subject. Following the terminology of D&F, variables of this type will be called action-sequence variables (cf. pp. 314-321 in D&F and Chapter 1 for description and examples). This approach is costly in terms of careful, preliminary groundwork since the examination of behavioral sequences involving both participants is required in order to construct such variables. However, as discussed in Chapters 6 & 7, a number of previously constructed action-sequence variables were already available for the present study.

Action-sequence variables represent patterns of behavior which partly derive their meaning from hypothesized conventions. As such, they not only provide a viable means of accounting for interactive effects, but they also benefit from an existing interpretive basis. The remaining problem is the means by which we can return to the original focus on individual differences or what shall be termed *participant differences* since the descriptions to be generated differ so radically from the typical indices in individual-differences research. The exploratory goal is to determine whether action-sequence variables (which simultaneously characterize both participants) can serve as a vehicle for developing differentiated descriptions of each individual participant.

Interpretation considerations

Because action-sequence variables incorporate information about pairs of participants, descriptions generated from them characterize conversations rather than individuals. Similarly, patterns of variation among such descriptions constitute conversation differences as opposed to participant differences. Since there are no a priori categories hypothesized with respect to potential conversation differences, the overall analysis is highly exploratory and data driven. Thus, much attention will be given to the interpretation of the emergent conversation groupings.

Structural constraints. Although these interpretations are necessarily post hoc, they are inherently constrained by the existing structural values of the variables themselves. For instance, each action-sequence variable used in this study consists of a response made by one participant which is preceded by some configuration of behaviors (signal) of the other participant. By hypothesized convention, particular action sequences already entail expected signal-response relationships. (In addition, various configurations of behaviors can suppress or enhance the signal effectiveness in the above example.)

Although the structural values of action-sequence variables guide interpretation, they are part of a convention system which retains a certain degree of optionality. Thus, variation among participant performances can also legitimately exist. If particular variations can be shown to characterize some conversations and not others, a basis for conversation differences can be established.

Speaker vs. auditor behaviors. Since conversations in this data normally proceed in a turn by turn fashion, with relatively little speech overlap, participants can be classified in either the speaker state or auditor state at any given moment. Thus, there exist two basic categories of behaviors: those which occur while a participant is in the speaker state, and those which occur while in the auditor state.

Action-sequence variables can be described as expressing speaker/auditor relationships, where signals are speaker behaviors and responses are auditor behaviors. Since both participants (P1 and P2) take turns as speaker and auditor, there are two versions of every action-sequence variable in each conversation: one where P1 is the speaker displaying signal configurations, and P2 makes auditor responses; and the reverse.

Both versions of an action-sequence variable within a conversation are potential sources of variability, and the characterization of a conversation must include both. Although this makes the interpretation of conversation differences more complicated, the differentiation of the two versions is critically important. First, we want to create conversation descriptions that maintain the integrity of each individual participant (i.e., which do not average over participants). Second, the availability of each participant's version of a particular behavior makes it possible to consider the relative value of each performance given the other's (i.e., the interactive context is taken into account).

The patterns of P1:P2 relationships (P1, speaker, and P2, auditor):(P2, speaker, and P1, auditor) indicate that participants in the same conversation are either similar or dissimilar with respect to particular behavior performances. Since this study focuses on aspects of auditor behavior primarily, patterns of response behaviors exhibited by each pair of participants will be closely examined and contrasted in order to describe the type of relationship that holds between them. Conversation descriptions are then directly built upon distinguishable variations in these P1:P2 relationships.

Finally, since each participant can be identified with one of the two halves of the relationship describing the conversation, he or she, as an individual, can be described to some extent. For instance, when the P1:P2 relationships are dissimilar in a conversation, the relative positions of P1 and P2 as individuals can be evaluated.

Overall research strategy

The overall strategy for this analysis begins by exploring the use of particular action-sequence variables (signal-response) for both participants in each conversation. The relationship of one participant to the other with respect to various response patterns constitutes a description of the conversation as a whole. Assuming that these conversation descriptions (or P1:P2 relationships) show some variation, the next step is to find the source and delineate its various forms. The conversations may then be grouped according to these forms and tested for homogeneity.

On the one hand, we can be reasonably confident that the distributions will not be totally random (which would prevent our finding any groupings) because it is already known that the participants in these conversations adhere to particular structurally defined conventions. On the other hand, it is an empirical question whether participants exercise their options within these limits in a systematic (hence distinguishable) way. If patterns at the conversation level do emerge, individual performances can also be considered. At this point, we reach the end of the basic procedure, and the primary goal of differentiating conversations (and to some extent, individuals) is attained.

However, a very major part of this analysis just begins. Given the exploratory nature of this study, a fully developed interpretive framework could not be preestablished. Thus, the construction of a system for describing and explaining the obtained differences comprises a large and important part of this study. Nevertheless, a scheme for interpreting cannot be totally ad hoc. For instance, the definitions of variables themselves include built-in information concerning their interactive value. In particular, several signal-response relationships have been empirically established by prior research.

The underlying motives and justifications for interpreting will be more comprehensible after the methods and basic results have been presented. For instance, we shall see that one of the four conversation groupings which emerges is based on P1 and P2 behavior patterns which essentially match each other. In the other three groupings, the P1:P2 relationship is marked by imbalances with respect to their response patterns, their preferences to respond to particular signal types, or both. Thus, an interpretive scheme will largely focus on what it means when participants match each other as opposed to what it means when they produce differentiated, contrasting performances.

However, the first step will be to give an account of how the basic variables are derived. In addition to the action-sequence variable, signal-response, participants (of which there are two per conversation), and conversations ($N = 16$) complete the design. The source of the data in this study is the set of 16 two-person conversations that is fully described in Chapter 5.

10.2. Method

Definition of variables

The full design for this analysis consists of the complex-variable signal-response cross-classified by participant (two per conversation) and conversation (total set of 16). In order to examine the signal-response

Signals

Responses	HM/-GZ	GZ + ZQ	GZ + GC
SM	1	2	3
SI/EBC	4	5	6
BC	7	8	9

Figure 10.1. Final categories of the signal-response variable, where HM/ −GZ = gesticulation signal (hands in motion) *or* no speaker gaze; GZ + ZQ = speaker gaze, no grammatical completion and no gesticulation signal; GZ + GC = speaker gaze and grammatical completion, no gesticulation signal; and SM = smooth turn exchange; SI/EBC = simultaneous turns *or* early back channel; BC = back channel (other than early).

variable more closely, however, we can consider it separately as the two-way table shown in Figure 10.1. In the full analysis, 32 such tables are constructed, one for each participant in every conversation.

Figure 10.1 depicts the final categories of the signal-response variable for this analysis. Note that the response categories include auditor behaviors which represent turn phenomena (smooth exchanges and simultaneous turns), as well as within-turn activity (back channels and "early" back channels). The signal-variable categories are three configurations of speaker behaviors, including gesticulation signal, gaze, and grammatical completion. Similar to the response variable, the signal displays incorporate behaviors which are relevant to both turns and back channels.

Since each response is cross-classified by each signal display, the nine cells of the final table represent the full set of action sequences available for study in this analysis. For instance, cell 3 in Figure 10.1 represents the following action sequence: the auditor makes a turn attempt, which results in a smooth turn exchange in the presence of a speaker signal display, which consists of gaze and grammatical completion, no gesticulation signal.

In order to obtain both meaningful and statistically analyzable action sequences, the construction of both signal and response variables was guided by theoretical concerns but complicated by methodological constraints. A description of this process follows.

Selection of response categories. Responses of interest were selected from previously examined auditor behaviors in the turn system (cf. Chapter 3). These include two contrasting types of auditor turn attempts, one which results in a smooth transition from auditor state to speaker state with no overlapping speech (SM), and one which results in simultaneous speech (SI).

Two more types of responses involve back channels: (a) speech overlap or sociocentric-sequence back channels (termed "early," EBC), which begin mid-unit or prior to the end, and (b) pause and postboundary back channels (BC) which are located, respectively, in the pause between units and just slightly after the pause. All back channels, including smiles and head nods, are analyzed.

Selection of signal categories. The above four responses provide natural contrasts for each other with respect to the particular speaker signal displays which precede them. In these data, the single most powerful cue in these conversations is grammatical completion when performed in the absence of the gesticulation signal (the inhibitor of any auditor turn attempts). Thus, both grammatical completion and gesture are included in the signal variable. To complete this simplified signal set, gaze, a strategy signal in the turn system, is a third factor in differentiating signal display types in the present analysis.

With respect to BCs, the entire within-turn signal consists of two cues: (a) gaze and (b) grammatical completion. When both structure and strategy signals are considered, the signal set overlaps with that for turns except for the fact that the gesticulation signal does not play an inhibitory role for BCs. Such overlap is nonconflicting, however, given the degree of optionality characterizing the turn system. For instance, for the speaker, there is always a choice of cues which can act as signal. Furthermore, a signal display itself is only permissive in nature; that is, the auditor has the option of not responding. Thus, speaker behaviors never have a deterministic effect on auditor responses.

Constructing the signal-response variable. In defining the signal-response variable, the aim was to construct a set of speaker signal behaviors which

Signals

Responses	HM	ZQ	GC	GZ + HM	GZ + ZQ	GZ + GC
SM	1	2	3	4	5	6
SI	7	8	9	10	11	12
EBC	13	14	15	16	17	18
BC	19	20	21	22	23	24

Original 24-cell table ➔ *Final 9-cell table*

Signals	HM or ZQ or GC or GZ + HM	=	HM/-GZ
Responses	SI or EBC	=	SI/EBC
Cells	1 + 2 + 3 + 4	=	1
	5	=	2
	6	=	3
	7 + 8 + 9 + 10 + 13 + 14 + 15 + 16	=	4
	11 + 17	=	5
	12 + 18	=	6
	19 + 20 + 21 + 22	=	7
	23	=	8
	24	=	9

Figure 10.2. Original signal-response cross-classification.

have shared relevance for contrasting auditor responses in spite of the fact that two different types of responses are represented (turn attempts and BCs). Again, the full definition of the response variable is the following: turn attempts resulting in smooth transitions (SM), turn attempts resulting in simultaneous turns (SI), back channels (BC), and "early" back channels (EBC).

The speaker signal variable initially consisted of three categories of display: gesticulation signal (HM, for hands in motion), no grammatical completion and no gesticulation signal (ZQ, for zero turn cues), and grammatical completion and no gesticulation signal (GC). When cross-classified with the dichotomous variable, gaze (GZ), the signal variable expands to six categories (HM, ZQ, GC, GZ+HM, GZ+ZQ, GZ+GC), and the total signal-response complex defines a 4 × 6 cross-classification (24 cells) or 24 different action sequences (cf. Figure 10.2).

Unfortunately, the data become hopelessly overpartitioned when a 4 × 6 table is generated for every conversation. In fact, over half the cells in each table have an average frequency of 2 or less. Such a proportion of low-frequency cells per table is too high by typical statistical guidelines. Therefore, this original signal-response variable was restructured in order to reduce the number of cells, thereby increasing cell frequencies.

Final cross-classification. Redefining the signal-response variable was guided by both methodological and substantive objectives: (a) Extremely low frequency categories should be eliminated. (b) A badly skewed frequency distribution should be avoided. (c) The resulting categories should be interpretable with respect to signal-response relationships delineated in the turn system or back-channel system noted earlier. (d) The number of classifications should be sufficiently reduced to permit the analysis of each conversation separately.

The first alteration was the reduction of the four response categories to three by combining turn attempts ending in simultaneous turns (SI turn attempts) with early back channels (EBC). Although they represent different types of actions (turns attempts vs. back channels), they are very similar in two ways. First, they primarily occur midunit as opposed to between units. This is true for early back channels, by definition, and SI turn attempts, in practice. Second, their nonassociation with particular signal displays is strikingly similar; for example, neither is typically preceded by grammatical completions, and neither is inhibited by gesticulation signals.

The signal variable was then drastically reduced from six to three types of displays. The obvious mainstay in this variable is the GZ+GC configuration (gaze and grammatical completion, no gesticulation signal), which is highly associated with both turn attempts and BCs. In fact, it precedes a full 34% of all responses pooled. Less obvious, but almost equally prevalent (at 31%), is the GZ+ZQ configuration (gaze, no

grammatical completion, no gesticulation signal), which is again structurally relevant to both turns and BCs. Whereas the four remaining
categories (HM, ZQ, GC, and GZ+HM) separately precede the pooled
responses a mere 6 to 11.5%, their combination accounts for the final third
(34%) of all responses. A seemingly diverse set of signal types, the four
categories are actually easily represented as a simple disjunction, HM or
−GZ (HM/−GZ). A summary of these reclassifications in Figure 10.2,
depict which of the original 24 cells were combined to create the final 9-cell
table.

Thus redefined, the signal-response variable results in the 3 × 3 cross-
classification already shown in Figure 10.1, with nine categories of action
sequences. When we also consider each participant (P) separately within
each of 16 conversations (C), the full design for this analysis is the four-
way table: signal (S) × response (R) × participant (P) × conversation (C),
or the 3 × 3 × 2 × 16 (288) cells depicted in Figure 10.3.

Although each participant is observed in two conversations, the
assignment of the labels P1 and P2 is arbitrary with respect to individuals;
a person labeled P1 in Conversation 1 may or may not be labeled P1 in
Conversation 2. In fact, P1 and P2 labels are assigned so that they reflect
particular P1:P2 relationships. For example, in Conversation 1, we may
find a P1:P2 ratio of 75:25, where person A is P1 and person C is P2 (75:25
corresponds to A:C). In Conversation 2, the ratio 25:75 is obtained
corresponding to the B:C relationship. Rather than asssign person C the P2
label in both conversations, we let the P1:P2 labels correspond to the 75:25
pattern. Thus person C is P2 in Conversation 1 and P1 in Conversation
2.

Conversations are also assigned labels: C11-C14, C21-C24, C31-
C34, and C41-C44. The four sets of four conversations each are labeled
in this way because each set is composed of four participants who are
paired in one way for Conversation 1 and another way for Conversation 2.
Thus, no individual has a conversation partner from outside their set.
In addition to set number (I, II, III, and IV) corresponding to the
conversation labels above, each individual is identified as male or female
(F or M) and by school affiliation, Social Service Administration or Law
School (S or L). Although specific hypotheses are not being generated
from these descriptors for this analysis, they serve to identify individuals
uniquely. In combination with the P1 and P2 labels, the behavioral
performances observed in this study can always be linked with a particular
individual.

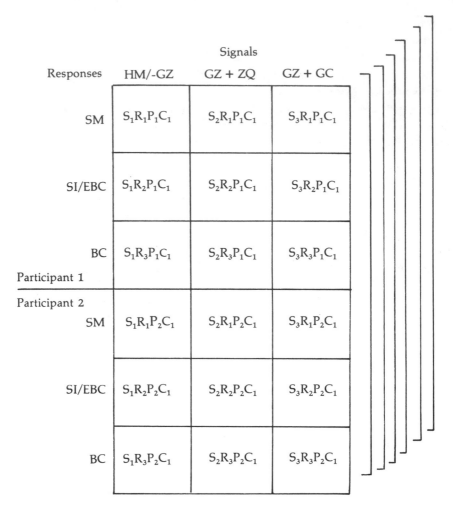

Figure 10.3. The four-way cross-classification (S × R × P × C). Conversation 1 (C1) (18 cells) is shown on top. C2 through C16 (18 × 15 or 270 cells) follow.

Cell frequencies

After establishing the set of variables which defines the full cross-classification for this analysis, there is the separate problem of defining the means by which the cell frequencies are obtained. Unlike the other studies presented in this book, the counts for this analysis are obtained on the basis of *responses* rather than units of analysis. Thus, instead of an N which represents the total number of units per conversation (average $N = 370$), the N of this analysis represents the total number of responses per conversation (average $N = 114$).

The decision to use this type of frequency count was motivated by a primary interest in response behavior. Therefore, it was desirable to maximize responses without promoting a highly skewed frequency distribution. The elimination of units of analysis in which there were no auditor responses greatly improves the symmetry of the distribution since over 72% of all units fall into this single category (the remaining 28% to be split among the four types of responses). Furthermore, by changing the count basis from units of analysis in which there were responses to auditor responses themselves, full advantage could be taken of those units in which multiple responses occurred (where auditor responses included both a turn attempt and back channel or back channels of different types).

In these data, multiple responses occur frequently enough to warrant their inclusion yet not frequently enough to support the creation of complex response categories (e.g., SM transition *and* BCs). When counting on a unit basis, the only alternative is to classify units by one response alone, thereby losing any other response within the same unit. Strictly speaking then, this analysis is conditional on response; that is, given a response, we then cross-classify according to the other variables: (a) the preceding signal display, (b) the participant who gave the response, and (c) the conversation in which the response occurred.

The basic procedure

Since we are dealing with discrete, multivariate data, a log-linear approach may be taken; in particular, we may take advantage of a useful set of model-fitting techniques. In the first application of these techniques, the entire four-way contingency table is examined in order to determine an indication of overall variability. Specifically, we are interested in which of the signal, response, and participant main effects (or their interactions) vary across the whole set of 16 conversations. If there are no terms which interact with conversation (i.e., conversation is independent of all other parameters), we can then consider the set of 16 conversations as one homogeneous group and discontinue the search for conversation differences.

Assuming, however, that variation does exist across conversations (some parameter interacts with conversation), we then apply model-fitting techniques to each conversation separately in order to begin characterizing distinct forms of variability. This is accomplished by generating model descriptions of each conversation with respect to the signal, response, and participant parameters. On the basis of these descriptions, conversations can be initially grouped according to similarity.

Once tentative groupings have been formed, the homogeneity of each can then be assessed by testing an appropriate model. If homogeneity is not achieved, alternative groupings can be considered. When necessary, other measures related to model fitting such as standardized residuals and post hoc contrasts can be used in refining the model descriptions. The final conversation groupings will constitute the categories of variation across conversations and will be described in detail in the early part of Section 10.3, Results and discussion. Their interpretation and implications with respect to both conversation and participant differences will be addressed in the latter part of the same section.

Log-linear techniques. However, a short digression will be made in order to provide some background on the statistical techniques employed. In taking a log-linear approach, the four-way cross classification presented earlier is reexpressed as a specification of parameters. For the signal × response × participant × conversation table, the full set of parameters consists of the following: the grand mean; the single parameters signal, response, participant, and conversation (S, R, P, and C); the two-way interactions SR, SP, SC, RP, RC, and PC; the three-way interactions SRP, SRC, SPC, and RPC; and the four-way interaction SRPC.

In the major part of this analysis, however, conversations are examined individually, thus splitting the single four-way classification into 16 three-way tables (signal × response × participant). For each of these tables, the full set of parameters reduces to the following eight parameters: the grand mean, the single parameters (S, R, and P); the two-way interactions SR, SP, RP; and the three-way interaction SRP.

Model fitting. A basic feature of log-linear techniques is model fitting, a procedure aimed toward identifying the underlying structure of cross-classified data. When the model consists of the full set of parameters, as stated above, it is called the saturated model and is necessarily untestable because the expected frequencies generated will be exactly the same as the observed frequencies.

Although the saturated model for the three-way table consists of eight parameters,[1] as shown in Table 10.1, it is simply specified as the (SRP) model because the typical application of log-linear techniques assumes that models are hierarchically constrained. That is, models which contain

Table 10.1. *All possible models for three-way cross-classification (signal ✕ response ✕ participant)*

Saturated model	(SRP)
Parameters	(SRP)(SR)(SP)(RP)(S)(R)(P)

Subsets of models	
M1	(S)
M2	(R)
M3	(P)
M4	(S)(R)
M5	(S)(P)
M6	(R)(P)
M7	(S)(R)(P)
M8	(SR)
M9	(SP)
M10	(RP)
M11	(SR)(P)
M12	(SP)(R)
M13	(RP)(S)
M14	(SR)(SP)
M15	(SR)(RP)
M16	(SP)(RP)
M17	(SR)(SP)(RP)

parameters of a higher-order relationship (e.g., interaction of variables) implicitly include the lower-order effects of those variables. For instance, model (SR) implies the inclusion of single parameters S and R in addition to the SR interaction. To set a convention in this chapter, models will be distinguished from specific parameters by being enclosed in parentheses (e.g., model (SR) as opposed to the SR interaction or SR parameter).

Models: subsets of parameters. Models consisting of fewer parameters than the saturated model can be evaluated in terms of how well that particular subset of parameters explains the variation generated by the table frequencies. For instance, for each of the 16 three-way tables, there exist 17 possible models which can be tested because there are 17 different subsets of the full set of parameters (as hierarchically constrained). These are listed in Table 10.1 along with the full specification of the saturated model.

With respect to this data set, however, the range of meaningful alternatives reduces to the following four models (in Table 10.1): (M11), the (SR)(P) model (independence of P and interaction SR); (M14), the

(SR)(SP) model; (M15), the (SR)(RP) model; and (M17), the (SR)(SP)(RP) model. This simplification is possible partly because the SR interaction term cannot be eliminated for any of the 16 conversations. A full explanation will follow when the results are presented.

Model of "best" fit. The best-fitting model for each conversation consists of the subset of parameters which both adequately and parsimoniously accounts for the variation generated by the particular contingency table. Very generally, each conversation will be described in terms of a best-fitting mode. These models will, in turn, provide criteria for determining similarity among conversations.

Testing various models for best fit typically proceeds in a stepwise addition or elimination of parameters until a model is located which sufficiently explains the variation in cell probabilities. The likelihood-ratio chi-square statistic (G^2) is a measure of how well a model fits and, because it partitions uniquely, it is generally preferred over the goodness-of-fit chi-square (χ^2).[2]

Since the object is to accept a model, the criteria for acceptability are reversed from those used in hypothesis testing. Specifically, the lower the G^2 value relative to degrees of freedom, the smaller the difference between the model's prediction and the observed data. A $p > .10$ is a generally acceptable indicator that a model "fits." Of the models that fit, the one consisting of the fewest parameters (most parsimonious) would be considered the best fit.

Single parameter effects. Log-linear techniques also provide several additional means of fine-tuning the model-fitting procedures. For instance, in addition to testing a set of models which consist of hierarchically constrained subsets of parameters, it is also possible to ascertain the amount of variance attributable to specific parameters (analogous to ANOVA which partitions the variance for continuous data). This is accomplished by taking the G^2 differences between two models which differ only by the single parameter of interest.

Standardized residuals. Another useful technique is that of computing standardized residuals for any particular model. For instance, if a model fails to fit, the standardized residuals computed for each cell of the table provide a measure which expresses both degree and direction of its deviation from the expected values generated by that model. This information is descriptively useful in itself, and it also provides guidance for further model fitting.

In the case where a single parameter is omitted from a model, the residuals are a clear expression of that one parameter. For example, if the omitted term represents a significant 2 × 3 interaction, the residuals will indicate which of the six cells should be high and low relative to each other. (This is only approximately true when more than one parameter is omitted from a model.)

Post hoc contrasts. A third supplementary technique to model fitting is that of performing within-variable contrasts. In essence, a contrast partitions the G^2 value for a single parameter or model by considering partial effects of the variable (analogous to testing pairs of means in ANOVA). These partial effects are structured as specific comparisons among levels of the variable, some of which are orthogonal and others not. In any case, a set of contrasts can be chosen to reflect the most meaningful distinctions within the variable.

Summary. Given the introduction to log-linear terminology and techniques presented above, the basic procedure outlined in greater detail follows:

1. For the four-way table (S × R × P × C):
   a. Begin model fitting with the model consisting of all three-term interactions: (SPC)(SRP)(SRC)(RPC). Eliminate one term at a time; assess the fit of each resulting model.
   b. Determine each of the single-parameter effects particularly with respect to interactions with conversation (e.g., SPC, SRC, and RPC).
   c. Continue model-fitting procedure until the best-fit model is found.
   d. If no interaction exists between any parameter and conversation, the exploration for conversation differences ends at this point.
2. For each of the 16 three-way tables (S × R × P) (one for each conversation):
   a. Begin model fitting with the model consisting of all two-term interactions (SR)(SP)(RP). Eliminate one term at a time; assess the fit of the resulting models.
   b. Determine the single-parameter effect of each two-term interaction in order to evaluate its respective contribution to the total variance within the table (i.e., within each conversation).
   c. Continue eliminating nonsignificant terms until the model of best fit is located.
3. Grouping conversations
   a. Determine the range of models which have been identified as best fit.
   b. Group together those conversations which are described by the same best-fit model. Each grouping now consists of a four-way table (S × R × P × C), where the levels of the conversation variable are determined by the number of conversations in the grouping.

Table 10.2. *Model fitting all conversations as one group*

Model: single-parameter effect	df	G^2	p
a. (SPC)(SRP)(SRC)(RPC)	60	63.09	.3678
difference due to SRPC	60	63.09	.3678
b. (SRP)(SRC)(RPC)	90	164.40	<.0001
difference due to SPC	30	101.32	<.0001
c. (SPC)(SRC)(RPC)	64	66.90	.3778
difference due to SRP	4	3.81	.4318
d. (SPC)(SRP)(RPC)	120	118.73	.5156
difference due to SRC	60	55.65	.6353
e. (SPC)(SRP)(SRC)	90	112.34	.0555
difference due to RPC	30	49.26	.0148
f. (SPC)(RPC)(SR)	124	124.03	.4823
g. (RPC)(SR)(SP)(SC)	154	224.83	.0002
h. (SPC)(SR)(RP)(RC)	154	172.67	.1442

4. Testing groups for homogeneity
   a. In order to test for homogeneity, the best-fit model corresponding to each grouping is modified as follows: The conversation parameter is added in such a way that it does not interact with the original best-fit model. For example, the (SR)(P) model becomes the (SR)(SC)(RC)(PC) model. Conversation is allowed to interact with each single parameter but remains independent of the model description.
   b. If the models testing for homogeneity do not provide an adequate fit, alternative groupings may be a consideration, and more refined model descriptions may be necessary.

10.3. Results and discussion

Model fitting

Fitting a model for all conversations as one group. We can determine the level of overall variation across all conversations by finding the best-fitting model for the entire four-way contingency table (S × R × P × C). This stepwise procedure begins by (a) testing the model which includes all three-way interactions and (b) eliminating each three-way interaction one at a time in order to assess its relative contribution to the total variance generated. In lines *a-e* of Table 10.2, the top line evaluates the fit of the model, and the second line gives the difference or amount of variance attributable to the eliminated parameter.

Line *a* shows that a model consisting of all three-way interactions is more than adequate for these data; that is, the model includes more parameters than are necessary. The G^2 value of this model is equivalent to the value of the SRPC interaction since this is the only parameter which has been excluded. As such, SRPC is clearly a nonsignificant interaction term. From lines *b-e*, we see that the single-parameter effects of SRP and SRC are also nonsignificant and their associated models fit the data more than adequately. Therefore, the next model (line *f*) excludes both of those parameters. Note that in excluding those particular three-way interactions, the SR parameter must be added into the remaining models as it is no longer hierarchically implied by the remaining two parameters, SPC and RPC.

Although both the SPC and RPC interactions attain significance as single parameters, we consider the fit of the models which eliminate one or the other in lines *g* and *h*. When SPC is eliminated, we are left with model (RPC)(SR)(RP(RC), in line *g*, which is clearly a bad fit of the data. On the other hand, when (RPC) is omitted, in line *h*, the remaining model (SPC)(SR)(RP)(RC) fits the data adequately. Since this is also the simplest model, it could be considered the best fitting. However, in this case, the single-parameter effect of RPC is significant, both statistically and in terms of the variability across conversations that we are seeking. Therefore, the model to be designated best fitting for this analysis is (SPC)(RPC)(SR) in line *f*.

In applying this model-fitting procedure to the conversations as one homogeneous group, a number of "parameter-related" conclusions that broadly apply across the entire set can be made. As the principal outcome, the (SPC)(RPC)(SR) model is found to be the best description of its observed frequency distribution. Reexpressing this model, including the parameters that are hierarchically implied, yields the following:

(SPC)(RPC)(SR)|(SP)(SC)(RP)(RC)(PC)(S)(R)(P)(C)

Note that all of the terms to the right of the bar are implied by the higher level interactions to the left of the bar. In addition to the simple main effects (S, R, P, and C), we can see that signal, response, and participant each interact with conversation (SC, RC, PC); that is, signal, response and participant ratios vary across conversations.

Second, signals and responses interact with participant (SP, RP), thus allowing signals and responses to vary across participants. Third, the SR interaction (i.e., signals varying across responses) is a direct expression of the structural relationships implied by the turn system.

Finally, when considering the set of all 16 conversations as one group, the three-way interactions SPC and RPC are necessary parameters in the best-fitting model. This indicates not only that the signals and response vary across participants, but, also that these relationships vary across conversations.

Of the parameters omitted from the best-fitting model, two terms are notable: the SRP and SRC interactions. These omissions mean that the signal-response relationship is independent of both participants and conversations; that is, essentially the same SR relationship holds over all participants and conversations. Since the SR term represents the signal-response action sequences, these results can be interpreted as supporting turn-system hypotheses. We shall consider the implications of these results later.

Fitting a model for each conversation separately. Let us now consider the effect of model fitting for each conversation separately. Although each conversation consists of a three-way contingency table (S × R × P), as depicted in Figure 10.3, testing for the best-fitting models (one for each conversation) may follow a procedure similar to the one described above. Beginning with a model consisting of all two-way interactions (SR)(SP)(RP), we can then eliminate each two-way term, one at a time, in order to (a) test the adequacy of the model made up of the remaining terms, and (b) assess the relative significance of each omitted term.

Tables 10.3a-c show that model (SR)(SP)(RP) fits most of the 16 conversations very well, and only C32, C34, and C41 are somewhat marginal (.10 > p > .05). (Conversations in Tables 10.3a-c are listed in an order which roughly groups conversations according to their respective best-fitting models.) Since the G^2 value of this model is equivalent to the value of the SRP interaction, this implies that the SRP term may probably be omitted from the model for all conversations. However, at the next level of model fitting, we eliminate each of the two-way interaction terms one at a time, and the homogeneity we have seen so far begins to break down.

Grouping conversations

Variation in best-fitting models. Thus, we may begin to consider the primary objective of delineating variation among conversations. In assessing the various models (and associated single parameter effects) in lines *b-d* of Tables 10.3a-c, the first model (SP)(RP) in line *b* provides a

Table 10.3a. *Model fitting each conversation separately*

Models: single-parameter effect	df	Conversation 12 G^2	p	Conversation 13 G^2	p	Conversation 24 G^2	p	Conversation 31 G^2	p
a. (SR)(SP)(RP)	4	3.56	.469	5.18	.269	2.23	.694	3.40	.493
b. (SP)(RP)	8	40.25	<.001	25.55	.001	11.21	.190	16.81	.032
difference due to SR	4	36.69	<.001	20.37	<.001	8.98	.061	13.41	.009
c. (SR)(RP)	6	6.54	.366	8.16	.227	10.44	.107	7.73	.259
difference due to SP	2	2.98	.235	2.98	.226	8.21	.017	4.33	.115
d. (SR)(SP)	6	4.70	.583	6.27	.393	2.37	.883	7.73	.258
difference due to RP	2	1.14	.566	1.09	.580	0.14	.934	4.34	.114
e. (SR)(P)	8	7.87[a]	.446	9.15[a]	.329	10.50[a]	.232	10.40[a]	.238
f. (S)(R)(P)	12	44.76	<.001	29.43	.003	19.40	.079	22.16	.036

Models:	df	Conversation 32 G^2	p	Conversation 33 G^2	p	Conversation 42 G^2	p	Conversation 44 G^2	p
a. (SR)(SP)(RP)	4	8.61	.072	2.73	.604	0.45	.978	0.68	.954
b. (SP)(RP)	8	40.03	<.001	18.13	.020	10.19	.252	23.07	.003
difference due to SR	4	31.41	<.001	15.40	.004	9.74	.045	22.39	<.001
c. (SR)(RP)	6	8.91[a]	.179	4.92	.554	11.13	.085	4.16	.655
difference due to SP	2	0.30	.860	2.19	.335	10.68	.005	3.48	.175
d. (SR)(SP)	6	14.29	.027	4.04	.672	1.33	.970	3.44	.753
difference due to RP	2	5.68	.058	1.31	.520	0.88	.644	2.75	.252
e. (SR)(P)	8	14.63	.067	5.61[a]	.691	11.62[a]	.169	8.82[a]	.358
f. (S)(R)(P)	12	46.09	<.001	20.40	.060	20.96	.051	33.11	.001

[a]Signifies best-fit model.

Table 10.3b. Model fitting each conversation separately

Models: single-parameter effect	df	Conversation 22 G^2	p	Conversation 43 G^2	p	Conversation 21 G^2	p	Conversation 34 G^2	p	Conversation 41 G^2	p
a. (SR)(SP)(RP)	4	1.84	.766	6.09	.192	1.85	.764	9.28	.055	8.00	.092
b. (SP)(RP)	8	19.68	.012	27.61	.001	26.14	.001	40.42	<.001	42.01	<.001
difference due to SR	4	17.85	.001	21.52	<.001	24.29	<.001	31.14	<.001	34.01	<.001
c. (SR)(RP)	6	7.20	.303	16.97	.009	13.21	.040	28.35	<.001	13.81	.032
difference due to SP	2	5.36	.069	10.88	.004	11.36	.003	19.07	<.001	5.81	.055
d. (SR)(SP)	6	3.49[a]	.746	6.74[a]	.345	1.91[a]	.928	10.28[a]	.113	8.89[a]	.180
difference due to RP	2	1.65	.438	0.65	.722	0.06	.970	1.00	.607	0.89	.641
e. (SR)(P)	8	14.33	.074	18.95	.015	14.26	.075	30.46	<.001	14.59	.068
f. (S)(R)(P)	12	37.65	<.001	41.80	<.001	39.54	<.001	62.71	<.001	48.49	<.001

[a]Signifies best-fit model.

Table 10.3c. *Model fitting each conversation separately*

Models single-parameter effect	df	Conversation 11		Conversation 14		Conversation 23	
		G^2	p	G^2	p	G^2	p
a. (SR)(SP)(RP)	4	1.46[a]	.834	6.16[a]	.187	5.39[a]	.249
b. (SP)(RP)	8	26.38	.001	18.70	.017	37.47	<.001
difference due to SR	4	24.92	<.001	12.54	.014	32.08	<.001
c. (SR)(RP)	6	13.87	.031	10.82	.094	17.33	.008
difference due to SP	2	12.41	.002	4.67	.107	11.94	.003
d. (SR)(SP)	6	16.74	.010	16.13	.013	17.32	.008
difference due to RP	2	15.28	.001	9.97	.007	11.93	.003
e. (SR)(P)	8	28.84	<.001	21.65	.017	24.90	.002
f. (S)(R)(P)	12	53.44	<.001	35.05	.001	52.62	<.001

[a]Signifies best-fit model.

highly inadequate fit for nearly all conversations (C24 and C42 excepted). In conjunction with this model, the SR interaction is found to be significant at the .05 level for all but C24 (at .061). Because the SR term embodies the structural relationship between signals and responses, it is not surprising that this parameter should show consistently strong effects. It is not so obvious however, that the SR interaction should take essentially the same form for each conversation (i.e., a nonsignificant SRC interaction). This aspect will be discussed later.

Having dismissed model (SP)(RP) from serious consideration across the board, we turn to model (SR)(RP), line *c*, which excludes the SP interaction. These results show considerably more variation: C12, C13, C22, C24, C31, C32, C33, and C44 are all fit quite adequately by the (SR)(RP) model. In addition, C14 and C42 are marginally well fit. This implies that for at about half of the conversations, the single parameter SP is not a critical parameter. On the other hand, we see that the difference due to SP is significant for C11, C21, C23, C24, C34, C42 and C43 (and marginally significant for C14, C22, and C41. We may tentatively conclude that most of these 10 conversations must minimally include both the SR and SP terms.

This conclusion is directly tested in line *d*, which is the (SR)(SP) model that excludes the RP term. Of those 10 above, only three (C11, C14, and C23) are not adequately fit. Not surprisingly, those three are also the conversations which show a significant RP interaction (although C10 also shows a marginally significant RP interaction).

By the end of the model fitting in lines *b-d*, it is clear that most of the conversations can omit at least one of the two-way interaction terms (SP or RP). The next step is to test whether both may be omitted. Since we already know that some conversations have nonsignificant SP and RP terms, these, of course, will be our best bets for fitting the (SR)(P) model in line *e*. As expected, C12, C13, C24, C31, C33, C42, and C44 are well described by the simple SR interaction (independent of P), although several other conversations, namely C21, C22, C32, and C41, also show a marginally good fit.

Finally, to round out the picture, the most unlikely model (S)(R)(P) is tested with fairly consistently bad-fitting results. This model, which asserts the independence of all three parameters, is unlikely because of its omission of the SR term. In three cases (C24, C33, and C42), a marginal fit is obtained; these are conversations whose two-way interactions generate less variation than most. (Compare the G^2 values for single parameters.) For instance, the G^2 values for the SR term range from 36.69 to 8.98, and the SR values for C24, C33, and C42 all fall in the low end of the range: 8.98, 15.4 and 9.74, respectively.

In terms of best-fitting models, a marginal fit may or may not be acceptable depending on the researcher's purpose and level of parsimony desired. Since the model-fitting procedure in the present analysis is subservient to a higher goal – that of grouping conversations – best-fitting models will not be considered to be rigid categorizations of conversations. Rather, they constitute our guidelines for constructing grouping alternatives.

Tentative groupings. Conversations can be tentatively grouped according to their model descriptions. Those which are best fitting by the (SR)(P) model, for example, will be characterized by frequency distributions which are similar in very basic respects, particularly with respect to which parameters are nonsignificant.

The existence of models which are only marginally well fit gives us flexibility in grouping choices, and the ambiguity is easily resolved since each grouping can be tested for homogeneity. If a conversation can potentially fit in more than one grouping, the amount of variation it contributes to each (G^2 values) can be assessed and compared to the amount of variation present when the conversation is excluded from the grouping. Essentially, we want to retain the conversation in the group in which it creates the least variance, thereby choosing the most homogeneous grouping.

Table 10.4. *Conversation groupings*

Group	Conversations	Model/parameters	G^2	df	p
1	C12,C13,C24, C31,C32,C33, C42,C44	1 (SC)(PC)(RC)|(SR)	107.03	92	.1353
2	C22,C43	2 (SC)(PC)(RC)|(SR)(SP)	14.74	18	.6796
3	C21,C34,C41	2 (SC)(PC)(RC)|(SR)(SP)	37.52	30	.1626
4	C11,C14,C23	3 (SC)(PC)(RC)|(SR)(SP)(RP)	49.84	28	.0067
	(C14,C23)	(SC)(PC)(RC)|(SR)(SP)(RP)	22.99	16	.1139

Final groupings. Table 10.4 lists the conversations in their final grouped order and gives the G^2 value of the model which best describes each grouping as a whole. For instance, the conversations in Group 1 are individually best described by the (SR)(P) model (see Table 10.3a). The comparable model which both retains the (SR)(P) relationship and adds conversation as a fourth variable is the (SC)(RC)(PC) | (SR) model. While this model allows the main effects signal, response, and participant to vary across conversations (SC, RC, and PC), it preserves the independence of the SR interaction from the conversation variable (as well as from the participant variable).

Groups 2 and 3 are both characterized by model (SC)(RC)(PC) | (SR)(SP), which is derived from the best-fitting model (SR)(SP) when each conversation is considered separately (see Table 10.3b). Although both groups are described by the same model, there is variation within the SP interaction, which necessitates the formation of two separate groups as shown in Table 10.4 (to be described in detail later). Finally, Group 4 is characterized by model (SC)(RC)(PC)| (SR)(SP)(RP) which is derived from best-fitting model (SR)(SP)(RP) for each conversation separately (Table 10.3c). C11 is separated from the rest of the group (in Table 10.4), again due to within-parameter variation (SP and RP); yet it is best described by the same model as describes the others in Group 4.

Thus each grouping retains the basic description derived from the individual model-fitting procedure (as applied to each conversation) which will be called the *key description*: (a) SR alone, (b) SR and SP, or (c) SR, SP, and RP. In order to test the homogeneity of each grouping, the conversation variable is added into the model specifications in such a way that it does not interact with the key parameters SR, SP or RP. Specifically, the SC, RC, and PC interaction terms are added, but SRC, SPC, and RPC are not. In keeping the conversation variable independent of the two-way interactions, we are constructing models which disallow conversation differences with respect to the key parameters. Therefore, if the model fits the data adequately, we can assume that the conversations are homogeneous, thus justifying the particular grouping.

Aspects of homogeneity over all conversations

Before discussing each grouping, the results of fitting models to all 16 conversations as one group will be considered. We originally examined the four-way contingency table (S × R × P × C) in order to get an overview of the total variability among the the whole set of conversations. But the same results, slightly reexpressed, also constitute a statement of homogeneity among conversations.

If we again consider all three-way interaction terms (SPC, SRP, SRC, RPC), three of the four are directly involved with the conversation variable. SPC, as we saw in Table 10.2, was highly significant as a single parameter. Thus, conversations are not homogeneous with respect to the SP parameter. It would also appear that conversations are not homogeneous with respect to the RP parameter; RPC is also significant as a single parameter. Note, however, that its G^2 value (51.46) is only half that of SP (103.88) with the same degrees of freedom. Furthermore, its omission from the model does not result in a "bad" fit. Thus, conversations are not totally homogeneous with respect to the RP parameter, but the amount of variation is much less than that generated by the SP parameter. This is consistent with our groupings since there are seven conversations requiring the SP term in their model description and only three conversations requiring the RP term.

The SR parameter, on the other hand, is clearly independent of conversation variation (i.e., the SRC parameter is nonsignificant); it is, therefore, a solid index of homogeneity. When we consider that the SRP parameter is also nonsignificant, the homogeneity of the SR parameter is extended to every participant in every conversation as well.

Such a display of homogeneity is an impressive finding because the SR interaction is a necessary parameter in the key descriptions of every grouping. Recall that the SR term itself consists of a 3 × 3 cross-classification. A significant interaction, therefore, can take any number of different configurations among the nine cells. The fact that the SR parameter is significant for many conversations in no way guarantees that the form of the interaction would be the same in each.

Form of the SR interaction. Nevertheless, such homogeneity is obtained, and its overall pattern is summarized in Figure 10.4a, which gives the cell frequencies and row percentages for the signal × response table, collapsing over conversations and participants. When the SR interaction term is examined for each participant within each conversation (32 separate tables), the source of the interaction appears to be generated by only three or four of the total nine cells. Figure 10.4b indicates the cells in which standardized residuals reach significance when the independence model (S)(R) is tested. The +'s and −'s indicate the direction of significant deviation from the expected values, and entry number refers to the number of tables (participants, in this case) which show a significant residual in the particular cell. (Note that a significant interaction is not always accompanied by significantly deviant residuals because the imbalances may be distributed over several cells.)

Strictly speaking, some variation can be expected because participants differ in their degree of deviance from the (S)(R) model. However, it is always the case that when significant deviations are obtained, the same pattern emerges. There is not a single case of a significant cell residual which reverses its direction from that of the other participants.

The basic SR pattern shown in these data is the following: (a) GZ+GC most frequently precedes the SM response, the other two signal categories appearing less often; (b) GZ+GC least frequently precedes SI/EBC responses, the other categories being more frequent; and (c) all three signal categories precede BC responses about equally often.

Structural considerations. The above results are consistent with the turn-system hypotheses since the GZ+GC category would be most favored for smooth transitions and the combined GZ+ZQ and GZ+GC category more favored than HM/-GZ for BCs. In terms of the combined early responses (SI/EBC), a lower GZ+GC signal frequency should be obtained because early responses occur before the end of a unit whereas grammatical completions (GC) occur at ends of units, by definition.

Thus the SR relationship shown in this analysis strongly reflects the original structural research, though in a single, condensed analysis. It is a necessary parameter in every group's key description and takes essentially the same form in each. If we had limited our exploration of variation to the SR relationship alone, we would be left with practically null results. Fortunately, other parameters have been identified by the model-fitting procedure which provide expressions of conversation differences.

Frequency (row %'s)	Signals		
	HM/-GZ	GZ + ZQ	GZ + GC	
Responses				
SM	107 (18.9)	104 (18.4)	355 (62.7)	566
SI/EBC	228 (45.4)	222 (44.2)	52 (10.4)	502
BC	285 (37.8)	250 (33.2)	218 (29.0)	753
	620 (34.1)	576 (31.5)	625 (34.3)	1821

Figure 10.4a. Signal × response cross-classification pooled over participants and conversations.

Responses	Signals		
	HM/-GZ	GZ + ZQ	GZ + GC
SM	1) − (6)	2) − (1)	3) + (15)
SI/EBC	4) + (2)	5)	6) − (7)
BC	7)	8)	9)

Figure 10.4b. Summary of significant residuals from model (S) (R) for each participant (32 contingency tables), where "−" and "+" = direction of significant residual and entry (no.) = number of tables showing significant residual.

Effect of the SR interaction on additional parameters. Although parameters SP and RP will be discussed in detail as they become relevant to particular group descriptions, one general point can be made in advance: A significant SP or RP parameter is always accompanied by the SR parameter in these data. This is not to suggest that these parameters are in any way caused by or dependent on the SR relationship, but the co-presence of the SR parameter in every model description has an effect on the interpretation of the other parameters.

To take a simplified example, the interpretation of the SP relationship in model (SP)(R) is quite different from its interpretation in model (SP)(SR). In the (SP)(R) model, the SP interaction (which consists of the S × P marginal cells, collapsing over R) is completely independent of the main effect of R; that is, the SP relationship is the same within each level of R. In the (SP)(SR) model, the SP interaction is represented by the very same S × P cells, but this time we cannot say that the relationship holds over every level of R. We must instead acknowledge a coexisting interactive relationship between S and R. That is, on the one hand, the distribution of signal varies with participant independent of the response distribution; on the other hand, in the (SP)(SR) model, the distribution of response also varies with the signal.

SR constraints. Consider again the basic form of the SR relationship in Figures 10.4a,b. The distribution of frequencies over the nine cells is largely regulated by a strong positive association of SM response with signal GZ+GC (cell 3) and a strong negative association of SI/EBC response with signal GZ+GC (cell 6). In addition, cells 1 and 2 are negatively associated with HM/−GZ and GZ+ZQ as a consequence of the dominating effect of cell 3. That is, relatively little opportunity for variation remains for cells 1 and 2 because most of the SM responses are absorbed by cell 3 (assuming that each signal cell per response type can be allocated 33% of the particular response frequency by equiprobability). Conversely, the strong negative association in cell 6 supports the opportunity for variation in cells 4 and 5 simply by the fact that a larger proportion of early responses (90% as opposed to 67% by equiprobability) remain available.

Thus, among the nine (S × R) cells (which represent nine action sequences), we can conclude that the use of action sequences represented by cells 1, 2, 3, and 6 are constrained by the SR relationship and therefore, less likely to be the source of variation across participants or conversations.

In contrast, the distribution of frequencies across cells 4, 5, 7, 8, and 9 is relatively unconstrained, thereby permitting more options to be exercised with respect to this set of action sequences. This is not to imply that variation must occur in a particular way or that particular distributions must be obtained. The SR relationship simply makes the opportunity for variation more restricted for some action sequences than others.

Since this relationship coexists with any other key parameters that might be obtained (SP and RP), two general conditions may be assumed at the very least: (a) that an SP interaction will not hold equally over all levels of the response variable and (b) that an RP interaction will not hold equally over all levels of the signal variable. Rather, the SP and RP relationships observed will be consistent with the constraints imposed by the SR interaction.

For instance, although an SP interaction is based on frequencies pooled over responses, most variability among signal ratios across participants will probably least involve the actions sequences constrained by the SR relationship. In short, most differences in signal ratios will emanate from the early and back channel response categories (specifically, the unconstrained cells 4, 5, 7, 8, and 9).

Similarly, the RP interaction is based on frequencies pooled over signal. Since this is a response-based analysis, however, constraints on overall response ratios take on a different perspective. On the one hand, we cannot assess the effect of particular signal displays on response giving because we have no measure of signals without response (i.e., "zero" responses are not considered here). On the other hand, the response variable is internally constrained across participants by the nature of its own SM category. SM responses include nearly all turn transitions and are therefore very close to equal for both participants (since turns alternate). Thus, an interpretation of RP variation must be attributable to differences in early and back channel ratios: (a) The average rate of early and back channel response per turn must be varying across participants, or (b) the ratio of early response to back channels must be varying across participants.

Although the SP interaction is constrained by the SR relationship, the RP interaction is not; nor does the RP interaction override the SR relationship in any way. The SR patterns simply coexist with the RP interaction; they are observed regardless of the overall response ratios across participants (similar or dissimilar). To reiterate, we can expect that differences in response ratios will be consistent with the SR constraints.

Aspects of variability

Of all the key parameters, it should be clear that the SR interaction represents the common denominator for all conversations. As the primary source of homogeneity, it sets definite limits on possible variations. We will see in the sections to follow that in fact, many of the conversations show no further deviation from a basic model which features the SR parameter alone. In these conversations (Group 1), the relationship of P1 to P2 is highly symmetrical; although the response patterns and signal preferences observed may vary from conversation to conversation, each pair of participants within these conversations match each other.

Groups 2 and 3, however, consist of conversations in which significant variation exists outside the SR interaction. Specifically, this variation is attributable to the SP interaction; that is, each pair of participants in these two groups show contrasting signal preferences. Because the SP interaction pattern takes two distinguishable forms, two conversation groups are distinguished as well.

Group 4 conversations show the greatest amount of variation outside the SR interaction. Within each of these conversations, the pairs of participants show contrasting response patterns, though again, the form of the RP interaction may vary. In addition, some of these conversations show diverse signal preferences, a factor which also contributes to their total variance. A more detailed discussion of each grouping follows.

Group 1 description

The Group 1 key description consists exclusively of the SR parameter. Insofar as all other groups require its inclusion as well, it is not a distinctive feature. What is distinctive is the fact that the SR parameter is sufficient; no other key parameters are needed. It can be seen in Table 10.4 that Group 1 is fit very well by the (SC)(RC)(PC)|(SR) model despite its relatively large group membership and relatively simple description. In fact, C32 is the only conversation in this set for which the (SR)(P) model is only marginally fit (line *e* in Table 10.3a).

Absence of parameters. The omission of the key parameters SP and RP is the distinctive feature of Group 1. Thus, to a large extent, the description of Group 1 focuses on the significance of these absences. In general, the absence of the RP interaction is a statement about response ratios (pooled over signal contexts), comparing P1 to P2 in each conversation. When the ratios among response levels (SM vs. SI/EBC vs. BC) are relatively the same, the response proportions of the two participants can be said to *match*; no RP interaction is produced.

Similarly, the absence of an SP interaction indicates that the two participants match each other in their proportional responses to the signal categories (HM/−GZ vs. GZ+ZQ vs. GZ+GC). Recall, however, that the signal categories are conditional on the occurrence of *some* response since frequencies of the signal variable in the absence of response are excluded from this analysis.

Thus, although signals are performed by the speaker, they are reflecting aspects of the auditor's response behavior; that is, responses are being made in the presence of particular signal configurations. The absence of SP interaction implies that both participants are making responses to signal displays that are proportionately similar to each other.

Matched ratios. The absence of the RP or SP interaction term has been described as the situation in which participants match each other. However, such matching does not imply that the proportions be the same; it only requires that the direction of ratios be similar. For example, a proportion of 10:90 may be matched by 30:70 since the direction of the ratio is preserved, even though the percentages themselves are not the same.

Furthermore, a matched conversation requires its two participants to match each other and not match only all participants in all conversations of Group 1. (Homogeneity at that level would require the omission of the SC and RC parameters as well.) Thus, a second conversation may reverse the proportions in the above example: 90:10 for P1 and 70:30 for P2. Yet, the two conversations would be grouped together since the matching of their respective participants would result in the same model description. In short, the pairs of participants of Group 1 can be matching in very different ways.

Group 1 interpretation

Certain general principles will be observed in attempting to construct an interpretation of these results (as well as in those to follow). First, it is presumptuous to assert that participant matches or nonmatches are consciously intended or planned (though they might be). Along the same lines, it is premature to assert that participant matches or nonmatches accomplish particular interactive or communicative goals (though they undoubtedly serve functions of this general type). Nevertheless, particular outcomes (in this case, matched performances) co-produced by the participants have been achieved, and we can attempt to assess their significance.

Group 1 is somewhat unusual because we are trying to account for absences rather than presences. Although it is a legitimate and meaningful endeavor, methodological limitations are imposed because of the fact that these are essentially nonsignificant results. When we obtain significant interactions (i.e., key parameters required for a model), there are numerous techniques for examining these relations in greater detail. On the other hand, we cannot further examine what is not there. Nevertheless, the row percentages of the signal and response marginals for each participant in these matching conversations can give us a general idea of what constitutes a statistical "match" (i.e., no statistical interaction across participants).

Signal and response percentages. In Table 10.5, the signal row percentages are based on signal marginals collapsed over response type, and the response row percentages are marginals collapsed over signal types. Perhaps the most striking aspect of this table is the amount of variability tolerated across both signal and response categories. Taking the signal categories first, we see that HM/-GZ ranges from 7% to 73%; GZ+ZQ, from 8% to 51%; and GZ+GC, from 15% to 58%. Clearly the participants are matching each other in very different ways. Ranges of response category percentages are consistently smaller (but still substantial), probably due to the constraint of equal turn number. For SM, SI/EBC, and BC, the ranges are 20% to 50%, 8% to 46%, and 24% to 57%, respectively.

There also appear to be substantial differences within several conversations. For instance, both C24 and C42 not only exhibit large percentage differences but large reversals of differences between P1 and P2 as well. These observations are substantiated by the fact that the single-parameter effect of SP is significant in both cases (cf. line *c* in Table 10.3a). However, both conversations are easily fit by the (SR)(P) model in line *e*. This can be due to several factors. For instance, a smaller N (as in C24) can produce percentages which look extreme but are actually based on small frequencies which are subsequently taken into account in model testing. Another factor may be small overall variance; that is, there is so little variability to account for over the whole table that the SR parameter can be easily substituted for SP in its model description. Note that both C24 and C42 are nearly fit by

Table 10.5. *Signal and response percentages in matched conversations (Group 1)*

Conversation	P1/P2	Signals			P1/P2	Responses			Total responses
		HM/–GZ	GZ+ZQ	GZ+GC		SM	SI/EBC	BC	
C12	P1	32.5	39.8	27.7	P1	20.5	32.5	47.0	N = 83
	P2	20.0	51.4	28.6	P2	25.7	24.3	50.0	N = 70
C13	P1	42.9	24.3	32.9	P1	35.7	22.9	41.4	N = 70
	P2	28.6	24.5	46.9	P2	38.8	28.6	32.7	N = 49
C24	P1	34.6	7.7	57.7	P1	50.0	7.7	42.3	N = 26
	P2	6.9	34.5	58.6	P2	48.3	10.3	41.4	N = 29
C31	P1	15.0	28.3	56.7	P1	30.0	28.3	41.7	N = 60
	P2	7.3	43.9	48.8	P2	46.3	24.4	29.3	N = 41
C32	P1	40.8	35.2	23.9	P1	25.4	29.6	45.1	N = 71
	P2	44.0	30.0	26.0	P2	30.0	46.0	24.0	N = 50
C33	P1	17.0	40.4	42.6	P1	29.8	29.8	40.4	N = 47
	P2	7.5	40.0	52.5	P2	30.0	37.5	32.5	N = 40
C42	P1	73.1	11.5	15.4	P1	28.8	34.6	36.5	N = 52
	P2	39.0	24.4	36.6	P2	26.8	29.3	43.9	N = 41
C44	P1	36.1	31.9	31.9	P1	22.2	30.6	47.2	N = 72
	P2	19.1	33.8	47.1	P2	27.9	14.7	57.4	N = 68

independence model (S)(R)(P) in line f, thus discrediting the significance of the SR parameter as well.

With respect to the response row percentages in Table 10.5, there is only one case (C32) in which the response differences across participants seem to reverse themselves substantially. Unlike the cases above, this seems to be a simple case of borderline results, therefore, a matter of judging in which grouping C32 is most homogeneous.

Summary. The first point to be made about Group 1 conversations is that there are eight of them, or half of the conversations studied. It may be unwarranted to suggest that the "matching" conversations are the default or prototype for this kind of social interaction, but we can certainly say that they are not unusual or outliers in any sense.

The second point is to disclaim that matching is occurring by chance. If it were the case that all participants in this Group were showing similar ratios of signals and responses, one might surmise that the ratios represented some kind of external effect and that the act of matching was either an artifact of that effect or a chance phenomenon. However, it is not the case that matching occurs in one way alone; rather, it is characterized by great variability (differences in signal preferences even more than in response differences). Thus, the argument for random occurrence becomes very unlikely.

What seems more reasonable is that the matching phenomenon is requiring a real effort on the part of one or both participants. Furthermore, it must be an on-going process since one cannot expect to "even things up" in a few seconds (particularly if the overall rate of responding is high). Although it would be overly deterministic to suggest a "cognitive calculus," it nevertheless appears that a certain amount of interactive monitoring must be occurring at some level. Finally, a matched conversation represents a special kind of interactive outcome – specifically, one which avoids or cancels out the kinds of differences represented in Groups 2, 3, and 4.

Groups 2 and 3 description

Groups 2 and 3 are characterized by the same model, both featuring the key parameters SP and SR. Since virtually all conversations conform to the SR pattern (as already discussed), we turn directly to a description of the SP term. Within the limits of the SR constraints, the SP interaction implies

Table 10.6. *Groups 2 & 3 – Helmert contrasts – SP interaction*

Conversation/ participant		Signal variable (row percents)			Contrasts (a or b)	G^2	df	Significance
		HM/-GZ	GZ+ZQ	GZ+GC				
		1	2	3				
Group 2								
C22	P1 (a)	.213	.468	.319	(a) 2 vs 3	5.34	1	—[a]
	P2	.125	.125	.750				
		1	(2+3)/2					
	P1 (b)	.213	.326	—	(b) 1 vs $\dfrac{2+3}{2}$	.02	1	ns
	P2	.125	.425	—				
		1	2	3				
C43	P1 (a)	.548	.323	.129	(a) 2 vs 3	4.45	1	—[a]
	P2	.294	.294	.412				
		1	(2+3)/2					
	P1 (b)	.548	.283	—	(b) 1 vs $\dfrac{2+3}{2}$	6.43	1	—[a]
	P2	.294	.353	—				

Group 3

			1	2	3				
C21	(a)	P1	.309	.273	.418	(a) 2 vs 3	1.72	1	ns
		P2	.057	.509	.434				
			1	(2+3)/2					
	(b)	P1	.309	.355	—	(b) 1 vs $\dfrac{2+3}{2}$	9.64	1	—[b]
		P2	.057	.359	—				
C34	(a)	P1	.582	.127	.291	(a) 2 vs 3	.27	1	ns
		P2	.164	.327	.509				
			1	(2+3)/2					
	(b)	P1	.582	.323	—	(b) 1 vs $\dfrac{2+3}{2}$	18.80	1	—[b]
		P2	.164	.377	—				
C41	(a)	P1	.648	.085	.268	(a) 2 vs 3	2.00	1	ns
		P2	.500	.222	.278				
			1	(2+3)/2					
	(b)	P1	.648	.318	—	(b) 1 vs $\dfrac{2+3}{2}$	3.82	1	—[a]
		P2	.500	.320	—				

[a] Significance $p < .05$ (1 df).
[b] Significance $p < .01$ (1 df).

that the participants fail to match each other with respect to their signal display preferences when response types are pooled.

Unlike the SR interaction, which takes one basic form, the SP interaction shows some variation. When we examine the row percentages for the signal variable (in line *a*, Table 10.6) for the five pairs of participants, we can see that proportional differences can highlight different categories of the variable.

For instance, in C22, P1 responds proportionally more to the HM/-GZ signal category than P2 (.213:.125). The same holds for GZ+ZQ (.468: .125). The direction reverses for GZ+GC; P2 responds to GZ+GC signals proportionately more than P1. Thus, the reversal takes place between the categories in columns (*1 or 2*) and *3*.

In C41, P1 again starts out with a higher proportion of responses to HM/-GZ than P2 (.648:500), but the proportions reverse and P1 responses involve proportionately less GZ+ZQ and GZ+GC signals. Thus, the reversal occurs between columns *1* and (*2 or 3*). A large enough reversal of proportions across participants will produce a significant SP interaction, but as pointed out above, the reversal can be located in different places.

Consider again the row percents in line *a* for each conversation in Table 10.6. Group 2 conversations C22 and C43 show an interaction pattern which can be distinguished from C21, C34, and C41. Specifically, the signal ratios of P1 and P2 reverse themselves when only GZ+ZQ and GZ+GC categories are considered. In Group 3 conversations, P2 has a greater proportion of frequencies than P1 in both GZ+ZQ and GZ+GC. However, these conversations – C21, C34, and C41 – are distinguished by a reversal of the ratios when HM/-GZ signals are compared to the average of GZ+ZQ + GZ+GC (the combined GZ category). These row percents are shown in line *b* for each conversation in Table 10.6.

Contrasts. These various ratios within the signal X participant interaction can be tested by performing Helmert contrasts. [Discussion as well as examples of using these and other contrasts appear in Bock (1975; in press); specific computer programming information appears in Bock & Yates (1973).] For example, in Table 10.6, we can contrast column 2 (GZ+ZQ) with column 3 (GZ+GC) across participants and then contrast the average of columns (*2 + 3*) with column *1* (HM/-GZ). Although many other contrasts are possible, these capture an obvious difference within this set of conversations and remain orthogonal as well. As a counterexample, we would not contrast column *1* with column 2 *and* column 2 with column 3 because these would not be independent tests.

Thus, C22 and C43 feature significant interactions for contrast *a*, GZ+ZQ vs. GZ+GC, whereas C21, C34, and C41 do not. The latter are further characterized by their significant interactions in contrast *b*, HM/-GZ vs. GZ. Performing contrasts (in conjunction with model fitting) can thereby provide an additional guideline for grouping conversations. In Table 10.4, it can be seen that the two subgroups as distinguished by these contrasts are each well fit by the (SC)(RC)(PC)|(SR)(SP) model.

Groups 2 and 3 interpretation

Interpreting the SP parameter is more complicated than the SR parameter for two reasons: (a) the SP interaction takes more than one form, and (b) the interaction of signals by participants cannot be interpreted as a direct expression of speaker behavior. Rather, as mentioned earlier, they must be considered expressions of a type of auditor preference in responding to particular signal displays, since this analysis only includes signals to which a response is made.

Let us first consider how such a preference for signals may be interpreted. Within response types, it is easy to determine which signal displays should be favored and which are not (given the SR relationship). The SP parameter, however, is based on marginal frequencies which collapse over response types. Thus, the SR relationship is not sufficient to account for differences in signal display ratios.

On the other hand, a slightly more general characterization of signal displays can provide some explanatory constructs. Consider again the effect of the SR relationship on the categories of signal display. Earlier, in discussing the effects of SR constraints on the SP interaction, we concluded that differences in signal ratios would more likely be found in the unconstrained cells 4, 5, 7, 8 and 9 (in Figure 10.4b). Thus, we can characterize both HM/-GZ and GZ+ZQ categories (which are linked only to the single response SM) as being less constrained by response relations than GZ+GC, which is linked both positively to SM responses and negatively to early responses. This characterization of signals as high or low with respect to constraint by response type is summarized in Figure 10.5.

A second aspect of the signal display categories is the diversity or specificity of forms that each category represents. In the process of restructuring the original signal variable (shown in Figure 10.2), the HM/-GZ category was created from four distinct signal forms (HM, ZQ, GC, and HM+GZ). In contrast, GZ+ZQ and GZ+GC each retained their

Signals

Responses	HM/-GZ	GZ + ZQ	GZ + GC
SM	1) (−) SR constraint 4 Sig forms	2) (−) SR constraint 1 Sig form	3) (+) SR constraint 1 Sig form
SI/EBC	4) 4 Sig forms	5) 1 Sig form	6) (−) SR constraint 1 Sig form
BC	7) 4 Sig forms	8) 1 Sig form	9) 1 Sig form
	LC + LS	LC + HS	HC + HS

HM/-GZ   GZ + ZQ   GZ + GC

$\longleftrightarrow$

Low predictability   High predictability
(Undifferentiated)   (Specific)

LC + LS   HC + HS

Predictability continuum

Figure 10.5. Characterizing signal categories, where LC = low SR constraint: constrained by SM response only; HC = high SR constraint: constrained by SM and SI/EBC responses; LS = low specificity of form: 4 undifferentiated signals (HM, ZQ, GC, or HM + GZ); HS = high specificity of form: 1 signal form only.

original form as unique configurations. Thus, we may consider the HM/-GZ signal as exhibiting low form specificity while both GZ+ZQ and GZ+GC exhibit high form specificity.

When we consider the two descriptions conjointly, also in Figure 10.5, a single continuum may be constructed. Labeling the opposite ends of this continuum "undifferentiated" and "specific," the HM/-GZ category falls at the undifferentiated end, first, in terms of being less tied to response categories (low response constraint) and, second, in terms of consisting of diverse signal configurations (low form specificity). At the "specific" end,

GZ+GC is most strongly tied to response types (high response constraint) and consists of a unique signal display (high form specificity). Obviously, the GZ+ZQ category falls somewhat between the two ends since it is described by relatively low response constraints but high form specificity.

Because the SP interaction refers to differences in auditor response preferences, the values of the continuum can be useful in contrasting and interpreting auditor differences. For instance, when one participant tends, more than the other participant, to make responses to signal displays which are more specific (less undifferentiated), he or she is responding in a way which exhibits a more easily discernible pattern (i.e., given a response, it is easier to anticipate the signal displays that can be associated with it). This is because the number of options (signal-response action sequences) at this end of the continuum is fewer because of high response constraints and high form specificity. Conversely, at the "undifferentiated" end of the continuum, the number of action-sequence options is far greater because (a) there is greater diversity of signal displays represented (low form specificity) and (b) response relations to particular signals are less constrained (low response constraint).

In a general way, we may think of the entire continuum as representing *predictability*. That is, given a participant's preference to respond in the presence of signals which fall at the more "specific" end of the continuum, the more easily his or her signal-response pattern can be predicted. When the participant prefers to respond to signals more at the "undifferentiated" end of the continuum, a signal-response pattern is harder to discern. The results of performing Contrasts *a* and *b* allow us to state this relation more concretely.

Contrast a. We saw that C22 and C43 could be differentiated from C21, C34 and C41 (creating Groups 2 and 3) on the basis of differing contrasts within the SP interaction. The imbalance of ratios which distinguishes Group 2 is best described by Contrast *a*, GZ+ZQ vs. GZ+GC. In terms of preferences for signals, P1 is responding more often to a GZ+ZQ signal display, and P2, more often to a GZ+GC signal display. Note again that these preferences are relative. We are not concerned with individual rates that differ, but rather with the direction of differing ratios when the two participants are compared.

In Contrast *a*, GZ+ZQ represents the less specific, more undifferentiated signal. Thus, it is P1 who is less predictable with respect to signal-response patterns. Outside of SM responses, which are constrained by the SR relationship for all participants, let us consider the options available to each participant given his or her respective response preferences. The

Given preference:

GZ + ZQ > GZ + GC   GZ + ZQ < GZ + GC

Responses

Signals				Signals		
	HM/-GZ	GZ + ZQ	GZ + GC	HM/-GZ	GZ + ZQ	GZ + GC
SM	1) X	2) X	3) X	1) X	2) X	3) X
SI/EBC	4) 4	5) 1	6) X	4) 4	5) P	6) X
BC	7) 4	8) 1	9) P	7) 4	8) P	9) 1

Total action-sequence options = 10   Total = 9

Figure 10.6a. Action-sequence options, given SR constraints and constraints due to preference: Contrast *a* (GZ + ZQ vs GZ + GC), where X = constrained by SR relationship and P = constrained by preference.

Given preference:

HM/-GZ > GZ   HM/-GZ < GZ

Responses

Signals				Signals		
	HM/-GZ	GZ + ZQ	GZ + GC	HM/-GZ	GZ + ZQ	GZ + GC
SM	1) X	2) X	3) X	1) X	2) X	3) X
SI/EBC	4) 4	5) P	6) X	4) P	5) 1	6) X
BC	7) 4	8) P	9) P	7) P	8) 1	9) 1

Total action-sequence options = 8   Total = 3

Figure 10.6b. Action-sequence options, given SR constraints and constraints due to preference: Contrast *b* (HM/−GZ vs GZ), where X = constrained by SR relationship and P = constrained by preference.

participant who prefers GZ+ZQ to GZ+GC (P1, in this case) is represented by the left-hand table in Figure 10.6a. If an early response is made, GZ+GC is the disfavored signal because of both SR constraints and preference, thus leaving GZ+ZQ and HM/-GZ unconstrained. (HM/-GZ is included by default because it is not evaluated in this contrast.) The number in each unconstrained cell indicates the number of different signal forms included in that category. When a BC response is made, all three signals are unconstrained with respect to the SR relationship, but the GZ+GC signal is constrained because of the GZ+ZQ preference.

The right-hand table in Figure 10.6a represents the options available to the participant with the GZ+GC preference (P2, in this case). In this table, responses are just slightly easier to associate with particular signals. For instance, given an early response, the GZ+GC signal is constrained because of SR associations, and GZ+ZQ is constrained by preference, leaving only the HM/-GZ. Given a BC response, only the GZ+ZQ signal is constrained by preference.

The participant with the GZ+ZQ preference is left with four totally unconstrained cells. Since HM/-GZ includes four signal types, this is equivalent to having 10 different action-sequence options free to vary with respect to the partner's signal ratios. Following the form, signal — response, they are the following:

1. HM — SI/EBC
2. ZQ — SI/EBC
3. GC — SI/EBC
4. GZ+HM — SI/EBC
5. GZ+ZQ — SI/EBC
6. HM — BC
7. ZQ — BC
8. GC — BC
9. GZ+HM — BC
10. GZ+ZQ — BC

Action sequences 1-4 come from cell 4 in Figure 10.6a, action sequence 5 comes from cell 5, action sequences 6-9 come from cell 7, and action sequence 10 comes from cell 8. Cells 4 and 7 contribute four action sequences each because four signal types make up the HM/-GZ category. The participant with the GZ+GC preference is only slightly easier to predict since there are only three unconstrained cells or nine action-sequence options to account for the variance in the partner's signal ratio.

Group 3 conversations (C21, C34, and C41) all produce Contrast *a* results that are nonsignificant. In other words, given an auditor response, Group 3 participants are responding similarly to each other with respect to the signal displays GZ+ZQ and GZ+GC.

Contrast b. Whereas Contrast *a* distinguishes the Group 2 conversations, Contrast *b*, HM/-GZ vs. GZ (the average of GZ+ZQ + GZ+GC), best characterizes the conversations in Group 3. The difference between these two signal categories is much more striking with respect to the predictability continuum than the subtle contrast between GZ+ZQ and GZ+GC. Considering the options in Contrast *b*, shown in Figure 10.6b, we see that a preference to respond to the most undifferentiated, least specific signal, HM/-GZ, results in seven constrained cells (four due to the SR relationship and three by preference). A preference for the combined GZ category, however, results in six constrained cells (the same four due to SR constraint and two by preference). Therefore, whereas there are eight action sequences free to vary for the participant who prefers HM/-GZ, there are only three for the participant who prefers the GZ class because the two cells constrained by preference are the most highly undifferentiated. Thus, the participant preferring the GZ categories is clearly the more predictable.

In Group 2, C22 shows nonsignificant results for Contrast *b* whereas the result of testing this contrast for C43 is both significant and consistent with Contrast *a*. In Contrast *a*, P2 (with the GZ+GC preference) was considered more predictable than P1 (with the GZ+ZQ preference). Contrast *b* indicates that P1 also shows a bias for HM/-GZ with respect to the combined GZ category, thus further establishing him or her as the less predictable. P2, on the other hand, can be characterized as more predictable by preferring GZ+GC in Contrast *a* and the GZ category when HM/-GZ is considered.

Group 3 conversations show their homogeneity both by their significant Contrast *b* results and their nonsignificant Contrast *a* results. In other words, these participants are not responding differently within the GZ class (i.e., the participant with the greater proportion of responses to the GZ+ZQ signal also responds more to signal GZ+GC). However, a signal preference is shown with respect to the HM/-GZ vs. the combined GZ class. P2 makes a greater proportion of responses to the more differentiated, more specific GZ categories, thereby severely decreasing his or her number of unconstrained action sequences. Because P1 shows a relative preference for the undifferentiated, less specific signal category, he or she leaves open a greater diversity of action sequences, thus favoring behavior patterns which are potentially harder to predict.

Summary. The feature common to both Groups 2 and 3 is the mismatch between participants with respect to signal display preferences. One participant appears to respond to signals which are more undifferentiated relative to his or her partner's preference of signals. The partner thus tends to respond to the more specific signal categories. With respect to degrees of predictability, the contrast in Group 2 is subtle (GZ+ZQ vs. GZ+GC), whereas the contrast in Group 3 (HM/-GZ vs. GZ) is dramatic.

Group 4 description

Although the key parameters for Group 4 include SR and SP, we shall focus on the RP interaction term because it is the distinguishing addition. The RP interaction is fairly easy to describe because (a) it pertains directly to response behaviors, and (b) the smooth response category provides an internal constraint on possible variation. Because participants have basically the same number of speaking turns in a conversation, differences in SM responses are necessarily constrained. This may account for the fact that the RP interaction is less frequently a significant parameter in model descriptions.

Group 4 interpretation

Similar to the SP parameter, the RP interaction may take different forms (i.e., find its source in different locations). One source of variance across participants which results in a significant RP interaction is a reversal in the direction of the ratios between the early response and BC categories (Contrast *a*). Since early responses are largely early BCs (71%), this contrast represents a difference in how actively participants use one type of back channel versus the other.

Another source of the RP interaction is the significant contrast between the SM response class and the average of the SI/EBC and BC response classes (Contrast *b*). For the most part, Contrast *b* reflects the situation in which one participant is producing relatively more back channels of both types (including early BCs) than the other, in general displaying a higher degree of auditor responsiveness. This combined BC + SI/EBC class will be labeled within-turn responses. (Turn attempts which result in simultaneous turns rather than a turn exchange are also included in this class, but their relative contribution is small.)

RP interaction – Contrast a. Considering first the contrast between the early responses and BCs, we see in Table 10.7a that C11 alone shows a significant difference. This contrast, which may be considered almost purely stylistic, deals entirely with auditor responses that occur within a speaker turn and not at turn junctures; that is, turn exchanges are not addressed by this contrast. Differences with respect to responses within turns tell us not so much about general auditor responsiveness but about the form of response that participants prefer to give.

In C11, P1 seems to give proportionately more BCs, whereas P2 gives more early responses. Insofar as early responses may be considered more anticipatory than (regular) BCs, we might consider this preference as an index of transition readiness (as discussed in D&F, p. 239). In this case, readiness would be for the transition to the next within-turn unit.

RP interaction – Contrast b. The contrast between the smooth-response category and the average of the two within-turn response categories, BCs and early responses (also in Table 10.7a), gives us a clearer index of general auditor responsiveness. However, the constraint due to equal numbers of turn exchanges places the source of variability on the combined within-turn response category. All three conversations in Group 4 have a significant Contrast *b* (though C11 is more strongly characterized by its Contrast *a*). In each, one participant is giving proportionately more within-turn responses (displaying greater auditor responsiveness), thereby causing the other participant to have a higher ratio of SM responses.

SP interaction. Although differences in response ratios across participants are sometimes accompanied by differences in signal ratios, a necessary connection is not implied. Furthermore, when a significant SP interaction does accompany an RP interaction, we cannot predict its form; the two parameters are independent, conceptually as well as statistically. In fact, among these three conversations, the SP interaction shows a variety of forms. Thus, they contribute less toward determining the conversation groupings since they do not generate stable patterns of ratios.

In C11 (Table 10.7b), P1, who is attributed with greater auditor responsiveness (by the RP parameter), is also found to have a preference for the undifferentiated signal display, HM/-GZ (Contrast *b*). In other words, P1 is responding relatively more but is responding in a way which would be hard to predict. In contrast, P2 is less responsive as auditor but responds in a more predictable way (given the preference for signal GZ).

C23 shows the subtler form of the SP interaction, though again P1 shows more responsiveness as auditor. P1 also shows a relative preference for the GZ+GC signal category, when contrasted with GZ+ZQ (Contrast *a*).

Table 10.7a. *Helmert contrasts within the RP interaction (Group 4)*

Conversation/ participant		Response variable (row percents)			RP interaction: Contrasts (a or b)	G^2	df	Significance
		SM	SI/EBC	BC				
C11 P1 (a)		*1*	*2*	*3*	(a) 2 vs 3	10.08	1	—[b]
		.255	.274	.472				
P2		.465	.395	.140				
P1 (b)		*1*	(2+3)/2		(b) *1* vs $\dfrac{2+3}{2}$	5.20	1	—[a]
		.255	.373	—				
P2		.465	.268	—				
C14 P1 (a)		*1*	*2*	*3*	(a) 2 vs 3	.51	1	ns
		.116	.244	.640				
P2		.394	.212	.394				
P1 (b)		*1*	(2+3)/2		(b) *1* vs $\dfrac{2+3}{2}$	9.46	1	—[a]
		.116	.442	—				
P2		.394	.303	—				
C23 P1 (a)		*1*	*2*	*3*	(a) 2 vs 3	2.86	1	ns
		.197	.268	.535				
P2		.320	.400	.280				
P1 (b)		*1*	(2+3)/2		(b) *1* vs $\dfrac{2+3}{2}$	9.07	1	—[b]
		.197	.401	—				
P2		.320	.340	—				

[a]Significance $p < .05$ (1 df).
[b]Significance $p < .01$ (1 df).

Table 10.7b. *Helmert contrasts within the SP interaction (Group 4)*

Conversation/ participant		Signal variable (row percents)			SP interaction: Contrasts (a or b)	G^2	df	Significance
		HM/-GZ	GZ+ZQ	GZ+GC				
		1	*2*	*3*				
C11	(a) P1	.519	.264	.217	(a) 2 vs 3	.20	1	ns
	P2	.209	.419	.372				
		1	(2+3)/2					
	(b) P1	.519	.241	—	(b) 1 vs $\frac{2+3}{2}$	12.21	1	—[b]
	P2	.209	.343	—				
		1	*2*	*3*				
C14	(a) P1	.291	.512	.198	(a) 2 vs 3	1.17	1	ns
	P2	.424	.273	.303				
		1	(2+3)/2					
	(b) P1	.291	.300	—	(b) 1 vs $\frac{2+3}{2}$	3.49	1	ns
	P2	.424	.326	—				
		1	*2*	*3*				
C23	(a) P1	.282	.296	.423	(a) 2 vs 3	8.97	1	—[b]
	P2	.400	.420	.180				
		1	(2+3)/2					
	(b) P1	.282	.356	—	(b) 1 vs $\frac{2+3}{2}$	2.97	1	ns
	P2	.400	.295	—				

[a]Significance $p < .05$ (1 df).
[b]Significance $p < .01$ (1 df).

Thus, P1, the more responsive auditor, tends to give his or her responses in a relatively predictable way. P2, although less responsive, tends to give responses in a more unpredictable way though the differences here are slight.

Finally, C14, which is most similar to C23 in terms of the RP interaction, shows virtually no significant SP contrasts, and the total SP interaction is only marginally significant. Thus, C14 is the simplest member of this grouping, whose description is most clearly contained in the RP interaction alone.

Summary. In considering Group 4 as a whole, we can characterize each of the P1 participants as being the more responsive auditor (more within-turn responses), though stylistic differences in terms of preferred types of auditor response-giving (early vs. BC responses) are also observed (C11). Accompanying SP interactions take variable forms, showing different contrasts or none at all. Thus we may consider that conversations in Group 4 are essentially characterized by specific RP contrasts; an accompanying SP interaction is an optional feature.

In terms of testing the homogeneity of Group 4, we can see in Table 10.4 that the test of the model is not fit well for all three conversations. This may be due to the fact that these conversations require three key parameters, and the addition of each increases the opportunity for variation. Specifically, each parameter may take a variety of interaction forms. However, the patterns of the RP interaction contrasts in Table 10.7a suggest that C14 and C23 are most similar. Although all three conversations have a significant Contrast *b*, only C11 also shows a strongly significant Contrast *a*. When we consider C11 as a separate variety of Group 4, the remaining two – C14 and C23 – fit the criterion of homogeneity.

Conversation descriptions

The conversation groupings differentiated in this analysis are based on differences in the distribution of signal × response frequencies across participants. By means of an assortment of exploratory log-linear techniques (viz., model fitting, standardized residuals, and within-parameter contrasts), we were able to distinguish four conversation groupings, each homogeneous by statistical criteria.

Each grouping is intended to represent a distinct conversation type, as interactively defined and jointly produced. A grouping is not a simple combination of independent, unilateral descriptions of their participants.

Thus, a conversation description is considered an interactive outcome based on relative values, that is, each participant's performance is evaluated in terms of the other.

As such, the features distinguishing one group from another are not differences in counts, rates, or averages of participants. Rather, they reflect particular relationships which hold between participants with respect to the responses they give and the signals to which they respond, making the patterns of the conversations distinctive. These relationships are embodied in the key parameters SP and RP. The presence of any given parameter in a best-fit model generally implies that the parameter accounts for a significant amount of the variance shown in the observed frequency distribution.[3]

Since the key parameters SP and RP are both two-way terms, they represent significant interactive effects; that is, within each conversation fitted by a model with such a parameter, the main effects of signal and response vary across participants. By the same token, the omission of one of these key parameters implies that the main effects of signal or response do not vary across participants, that P1 and P2 have frequencies which are proportionately similar.

Insofar as the SR parameter is required for all groupings, it drops out as a differentiating feature. Nevertheless, it is vital to this analysis because it accounts for the variance due to the structural relationship between signals and responses. As such, it is essentially controlling for SR variance so that we can explore variance across participants (SP and RP) without confounding the results. As we have also seen, its co-presence greatly influences the interpretation of the other parameters.

Model descriptions. If we consider the three different model descriptions generated in this analysis as three basic conversational outcomes, the groupings are somewhat simplified. This is not to deny the existence of variations, distinguished by within-parameter contrasts included in these basic types (e.g., Grous 2 vs. Group 3, and Group 4 vs. C11). We can summarize the model differences by the degree to which participants create a matched conversation as opposed to one in which their respective response patterns are unmatched.

In particular, there are two distinctive features. The first, represented by the SP interaction (in both of the contrasts between signals), involves the auditor preference to respond to signals which differ along a continuum of predictability. This continuum is based on the degree of SR constraint and degree of form specificity embodied in each signal-response action sequence. Thus, participants can differ in their preference to respond to signals which are relatively more undifferentiated, thus less predictable, as opposed to signals which are relatively more specific, hence more predictable.

The second distinctive feature is the relative difference in overall auditor responsiveness represented by the RP interaction, specifically, Contrast *b*. Contrast *a* drops out as a primary difference because it is significant in only one conversation, C11. On the other hand, all three conversations described by key parameters SR, SP, and RP show a significant Contrast *b*.

How might these differences be interpreted? In terms of signal preferences, there are various and sometimes conflicting ways of interpreting the predictability continuum. For instance, we can think of the participant who responds in the more predictable way as acting in a more formal, polite, conservative, reserved, or guarded manner. A less predictable participant might be considered as being casual, familiar, lively, impulsive, or spontaneous. We might suggest that these attributes represent speaking styles which index the participant's interpretation of the social context (e.g., formal vs. informal, or polite vs. familiar), but a second possibility is that they represent personal traits providing a general description of the person. Without any additional information, either interpretation is reasonable: We cannot presume that matching in terms of signal preferences can be specifically attached to any one of the above possibilities more than any other.

A similar problem arises when we consider differences in general responsiveness; that is, it is not difficult to imagine a fairly substantial list of personal attributes that could correspond to this concept. For instance, a more responsive auditor may be considered more interested, friendly, alert, and the like. A less responsive auditor may be considered more disinterested, unfriendly, and dull or slow. However, it is dangerous to apply these terms too quickly since it is just as reasonable to label the responsive auditor aggressive, impatient, or perfunctory, and the less responsive auditor as relaxed, patient, or thoughtful.

Thus, matching on responsiveness cannot be tied unequivocally to one of the attributes mentioned above. In fact, it is questionable that the interpretation of a match (on either response or signal variables) can be meaningfully extended from an interpretation based on differences at all. The problem stems from the fact that the relational aspect of these attributes is central to their basic value: e.g., P1 is more X than P2. Thus, the attribute has a meaning relative to its value for the other participant, not an independent, absolute meaning.

In contrast, we can recast these relative differences in responsiveness or predictability as outcomes which serve less as a description in themselves, and more as a mechanism by which such descriptions are built – specifically, a general means of differentiating P1 from P2. Differentiation may be desirable for any number of reasons, for instance, creating impressions of personal traits (e.g., P1 is more friendly than P2). Alternatively, a differentiation may index or create differences in inter- active or social roles (e.g., P1 is assuming a role of more control or authority than P2). While differentiations are sometimes slight, as expressed by the SP interaction (Contrast *a*), they are sometimes sizable, as expressed by the Contrast *b* interactions for SP and RP. In either case, we can assume that a cooperative effort is being made; both participants to some extent buy into the differentiation they have created.

The three models to be described are simply: Model 1, the absence of SP and RP interactions (identical to Group 1); Model 2, the presence of SP interaction (including Groups 2, 3, and two conversations of Group 4); and Model 3, the presence of RP interaction (exclusively Group 4).

Model 1. Since Model 1 (Group 1), is distinguished by its absence of SP and RP interactions, the participants in these conversations are matching each other in terms of the signals to which they make responses and also in terms of general auditor responsiveness. But what does it mean to create a conversation whose outcomes are matched in these ways? First, we know that simple rates of response are irrelevant because each participant is matching the partner and not a "prescribed" or "chance" level. This is supported by the fact that the range of matching across conversations is great.

When matching is achieved, the differentiation of participants is suppressed. If we take the unmatched case to mean that two participants are creating a differentiation between each other, the matched case would signify an index of nondifferentiation or simply equality. Again, we can suggest numerous and varied reasons why this state might be desirable. These would include a broad spectrum of motives ranging from a genuine show of unity on behalf of both participants, to the strategy in which one participant discloses nothing by closely following the partner's lead in patterns of responding.

However, a single interpretation would require the acceptance of a forced choice when richer explanations are possible. For example, if the signifi- cance of "uniforms" in the military were the topic, one might hypothesize that the wearing of a uniform promotes solidarity as opposed to anonymity (or vice versa). Given a broader perspective, however, one could entertain both possibilities by framing the question at a slightly higher level (e.g., homogeneity vs. individuality). Given a bias for this latter approach (at the expense of simplicity), matched conversations are interpreted somewhat abstractly, as an end state in which participants have failed or refused to differentiate themselves with respect to their interactive response patterns. An outcome has been created which indexes some kind of equality or consensus between participants.

Model 2. The Model 2 conversations produce outcomes that differentiate participants on the dimension of predictability; that is, participants are shown to differ in their response patterns in terms of the signals to which they respond. Their respective signal preferences determine their degree of predictability. Although highly specific interpretive solutions have been rejected, we can still make several general observations about this particular strategy that creates differentiations between participants.

First, differences in signal preferences are the most common pattern of differences, occurring in 7 of the 16 conversations (though admittedly C22 and C23 show only the subtle variety, Contrast *a*). Second, as the five Group 2 and 3 conversations show, these differences need not be accompanied by overall differences in auditor responsiveness. In other words, it does not matter what level of responsiveness is attained by either participant, nor does it matter whether participants attain the same or different levels.

Finally, we can consider the issue of control, that is, whether one participant can effectively instigate this imbalance or whether equal participation is necessary. An interesting aspect of the signal continuum of predictability is that, although it is theoretically unbounded, it is actually somewhat constrained by the signal categories themselves. For example, if P1 shows a strong preference for signals at the specific end (GZ+GC), P2 cannot always choose to be relatively *more* specific. Sometimes, the best he or she can do is match P1, especially when we consider that the SR relationship is being maintained concurrently. In other words, because the signal classification is not open ended, a participant who holds extreme preferences (at either end), may not permit the partner to surpass him or her in the same direction. Thus, we can conclude that at least within the limits of this signal set, one or the other participant with extreme preferences can potentially reduce the partner's options. Even in this case, however, P2 can match or not match; only the direction of a nonmatch is constrained.

Thus, Model 2 conversations are characterized by an outcome in which participants have differentiated themselves in terms of their response patterns; specifically the imbalance between participants has been created by a relative diference in the type of signals to which they respond.

Model 3. The Model 3 (Group 4) description represents a second strategy which participants can use to differentiate themselves. Although considerable variation exists across the three conversations falling under this model description, there is one common outcome: The presence of the RP parameter indicates that a conversation is produced in which one participant is clearly the more active respondent within turns.

Unlike the signal variable, whose categories can be placed on a single continuum, the response categories fall into two discrete classes. SM responses, which are approximately equal for both participants, represent turn exchanges, a class in itself. The early and BC categories, on the other hand, are basically two types of within-turn responses. The response variable is also different from signal variable because there is really no upper limit to the number of within-turn responses that can be produced, hence, no constraints of the sort that extreme signal preferences impose. A participant can always (within time constraints) match and even surpass the partner's response rate. Nevertheless, there is one way in which a participant can somewhat perpetuate a response imbalance. Since responses are cumulative, one can never subtract or withdraw responses which have been made. Therefore, if P1 maintains a very low rate of within-turn responses, P2 may never be able to slow down enough to achieve a match or become the less responsive.

Thus, the Model 3 conversations are distinctive because the participants have created an imbalance which is based on relative differences in degree of within-turn responsiveness. Such a differentiation may be further characterized by differences in signal preferences, but these are not necessarily implied.

Sex and school differences

A natural question to consider is whether the basic model distinctions correspond to particular external factors that are known in these data. For instance, sex of participants and School of participants are two such factors, and are coded in the participant labels as "F" vs. "M," and "L" vs. "S" (Law vs. Social Service). Thus, we can precisely identify unique individuals (including their sex and school identification) with the P1 and

P2 of each conversation (see Table 10.8). For example, in conversation C11, participant P2 is I-F-L, a Law student who is female. She is P1 in conversation C13.

Considering matched conversations first (C12, C13, C24, C31, C32, C33, C42, and C44), we see that there are five same-sex conversations and three mixed-sex conversations represented. Since participants were never paired with a partner from the same school, matching always occurs across schools. With respect to first and second conversations, there is an even split: four of each type. Thus, it is clear that these external factors have little if any connection with the matched conversations.

Let us now consider nonmatched conversations C11, C14, C21, C22, C23, C34, C41, and C43. Since we started out with an equal number of same- and mixed-sex conversations, the ratio of same:mixed reverses from the 5:3 for matched conversation to 3:5 for nonmatches. Similarly, half are first conversations and half are second.

Of more interest is whether sex of participant or sex of partner corresponds to particular sides of the imbalances (i.e., more or less responsive and more or less predictable). For instance, the three more-responsive participants are all in Social Service (and all are female), and the three less-responsive participants are from Law School (two female and 1 male). However, we cannot conclude much from only 3 conversations, particularly since one individual (I-F-S) is represented twice. In terms of predictability, the more predictable include four females and three males: three from Social Service and four from Law School. The breakdown is similar for sex of partner. The less predictable include four females and three males, and the ratio of Social Service:Law is simply reversed from the previous example since the same schools are never paired together. In short, it is probably safe to say that these external variables are not showing much correspondence to the differences indicated in the nonmatched conversations. In fact, the external factors seem to be distributed quite evenly over the main groupings in spite of the small sample sizes.

Individual descriptions

Let us again turn to Table 10.8 and consider the participants of each conversation as individuals with distinct identities. Since individuals participated twice (Conversation 1 and Conversation 2), we can observe each in two interactive settings. We may also compare the outcomes of the two conversations and determine how the participants contributed to those outcomes; that is, what sort of auditor performance was given relative to

Table 10.8. *Individual descriptions*

	Conversation 1			Conversation 2	
Participant	RP parameter: responsiveness	SP parameter: predictability	Participant	RP parameter: responsiveness	SP parameter: predictability
C111 (I-F-S)	High	Low	C131 (I-M-S)	Match	Match
C112 (I-F-L)	Low	High	C132 (I-F-L)		
C121 (I-M-L)	Match	Match	C141 (I-F-S)	High	Match
C122 (I-M-S)			C142 (I-M-L)	Low	
C211 (II-F-S)	Match	Low	C231 (II-F-S)	High	High
C212 (II-M-L)		High	C232 (II-F-L)	Low	Low
C221 (II-F-L)	Match	Low	C241 (II-M-L)	Match	Match
C222 (II-M-S)		High	C242 (II-M-S)		
C311 (III-M-S)	Match	Match	C331 (III-M-S)	Match	Match
C312 (III-M-L)			C332 (III-F-L)		
C321 (III-F-S)	Match	Match	C341 (III-M-L)	Match	Low
C322 (III-F-L)			C342 (III-F-S)		High
C411 (IV-M-S)	Match	Low	C431 (IV-M-S)	Match	Low
C412 (IV-F-L)		High	C432 (IV-M-L)		High
C421 (IV-F-S)	Match	Match	C441 (IV-F-L)	Match	Match
C422 (IV-M-L)			C442 (IV-F-S)		

his or her partner. Since partners differ from one conversation to the next, however, it should be obvious that every individual's performances must be understood relative to the partner's performance.

Individual patterns. Although the external variables were not productive, we can still look for consistencies within individuals from Conversation 1 to Conversation 2. Considering matched conversations first, we observe that of the total 16 individuals, 12, participate at least once in a matched conversation. Of these 12 however, only four individuals appear in two matched conversations. These four are I-M-S, III-M-S, III-F-L, and IV-F-S. Since participants are never paired more than once with a particular partner, each or these four is matching two different individuals. Although it might be reasonable to suggest that these four are somehow more responsible for matches (since they consistently appear in them), strong supporting evidence is unobtainable because matches are defined as nonsignificant interactions.

However, we can examine the individuals involved in nonmatched conversations more closely. Again, there are 12 individuals who participate in nonmatched conversations and four of these appear in nonmatched conversations exclusively; that is, in both Conversation 1 and Conversation 2. These four are I-F-S, II-F-S, II-F-L, and IV–M-S. Interestingly, three of the four retain the same role in the imbalance from Conversation 1 to 2. I-F-S is the more responsive in both (RP interaction, Contrast *b*); II-F-L has the less predictable signal preference in both (SP interaction, Contrast *a*); and IV-M-S also has the less predictable signal preference in both (SP interaction, Contrast *b*).

II-F-S differs from Conversation 1 to Conversation 2, but is also found in a unique position. In Conversation 1, she was characterized by a less predictable signal preference. Conceivably, she would have retained that preference in Conversation 2, except that she was paired with II-F-L who showed the same signal preference in Conversation 1. If both individuals had been consistent with their Conversation 1 strategy, they might have ended up matching each other, thereby creating a nondifferentiated conversation outcome. This however, does not occur in conversation 2. Instead, a nonmatched outcome is produced by means of two different strategies: One is the same strategy used by both participants in Conversation 1, and the other is the addition of an imbalance in responsiveness. Specifically, II-F-L, who yielded her signal preference, has now become more responsive, an alternative strategy for differentiation.

Again, it is tempting to equate consistency across conversations with control, but these results do not support such an assertion. For instance, a participant showing consistency in these nonmatched conversations is either more responsive or less predictable in signal preference. As mentioned earlier, it is really only the very low responders who can somewhat force a nonmatch. A participant's extreme signal preferences can possibly prevent the partner from surpassing him or her in the same direction but can in no way enforce a nonmatch. Thus, we would have to assume that the partners of these consistent individuals are significantly contributing to these conversational outcomes. To some extent, both participants must endorse a differentiated outcome since each always has the power to effectuate a match.

It would appear that these consistencies within individuals (for non-matches) could easily reflect various types of personal attributes, but only because they are recognized or ratified by their partners. It is difficult to generalize about the consistencies shown by those participants who appear only in matched conversations because there are fewer concrete details available to examine. It can be suggested that they are doing the matching because it is easily in their power to do so, but matching can also be simply due to the particular individuals involved in these pairings.

With respect to the eight individuals who are involved in both matched and nonmatched conversations, we can suggest only that the very nature of each pairing changes the relative value of their behavior patterns. For example, A may appear responsive compared to B but much less responsive compared to C. And when A and D are paired, the situation may look neutral, that is, if they look the same with respect to responsiveness, then degree of responsiveness cannot be evaluated.

10.4. Summary

This study was undertaken with the primary goal of developing a procedure for exploring participant differences where interactive behaviors were concerned. It was apparent from the onset that many of the traditional concepts and established methods typically associated with individual-differences research would have to be abandoned, for many of the same reasons that action-sequence variables were developed in earlier research. For instance, one such reason was based on the premise that unilateral descriptions are simply inadequate to account for behaviors which take place in an interactive context.

This study is built on a conceptual foundation that presumes that action sequences provide a viable solution to the above problem. It is, likewise, vitally concerned with discovering behavior patterns which retain their interactive quality. In addition, however, this study is an exploration of behavioral patterns which can be characterized by distinctive features, thereby differentiating some patterns from others.

The first departure from typical studies of individual differences was made when action sequences were adopted as the basic variables of interest. Since these variables represent both interactants simultaneously, the study of individual participants shifted its focus to become a study of conversation differences. Behavior patterns to be explored involved relationships between participants, thus describing conversations and not individuals per se. This is not to imply that the integrity of individual descriptions is lost; on the contrary, conversation differences are completely dependent on differentiated participant performances. We cannot, however, make the assumption that these descriptions of participants represent independent and enduring personality traits. Instead, the relationship between the two participant performances is the basis upon which a description of the conversation as a whole is built. In short, individuals are described on the basis of the part they play in the total performance.

In these data, each individual participated in two conversations, one immediately following the other. Thus, it was possible to observe each person under essentially constant conditions with only the partner being different. Although there was some consistency in the type of strategy used by individuals who appeared in two conversations producing similar outcomes, this is not the kind of consistency typically associated with classical trait theorists. The results are slightly more supportive of those who take the position that the person-situation interaction is the critical factor for understanding personality phenomena, but only if "situation" is defined in such a way that specifically includes the interactive context of the partner. Action patterns in these conversations were highly specific to the particular constellation of components embodied in the situation, and especially to the particular partner.

The shift in perspective from individuals to conversations was accompanied by a serious absence of both methodological and interpretive guidelines. Consequently, one major part of this study is the development of concrete, analytic procedures that can generate stable differences within this set of conversations. Since the data were categorical and it was essential to the analysis to deal with more than two variables at a time, the procedure was firmly based on log-linear techniques which specifically apply to multivariate cross-classifications of discrete data.

The second major part of this study is devoted to constructing an interpretive framework for the complex, relational descriptions implied by the distinctive features of each conversation type (and to some extent, individual performances). The viewpoint taken in this study has emphasized inherent values of the variable categories as well as basic action-sequence relationships demonstrated in prior research and reaffirmed here. Speculation was held to a minimum with respect to exact meanings of the conversation outcomes to the participants themselves, or to specific ties with personal attributes. Instead, a somewhat more abstract interpretation was adopted, partly because specific, concrete solutions were often problematic or inconsistent. Furthermore, strategies serving relatively general functions may be useful in giving participants greater opportunity for creating more distinctive outcomes. (Participants may, of course, choose to present an ambiguous outcome.)

This extended study, has taken a somewhat circuitous route, but only because its specific destination could not have been anticipated. As an exploratory enterprise, it has taken certain liberties in devising procedural strategies and capitalizing on sometimes unfamiliar statistical techniques. Nevertheless, three goals were attained: A procedure for analyzing interactional variation was developed, some basic conversation patterns emerged, and the construction of an interpretive scheme was initiated. The accomplishment of each of these goals contributes to formulating a solution to the problem of individual differences in interactive research. Perhaps more important, they contribute to a solution that is committed to the principle that the interactive quality of the phenomenon should not be jeopardized.

Endnotes

[1] Strictly speaking, the term "parameter" is reserved for the terms of the log-linear equation used in calculating expected frequencies for each cell. For example:

$$F_{ijk} = n\tau_i^S \tau_j^R \tau_k^P \tau_{ij}^{SR} \tau_{ik}^{SP} \tau_{jk}^{RP} \tau_{ijk}^{SRP}$$

where F = expected cell frequencies

Alternatively, the expected frequencies may be expressed in terms of the natural logs of each term:

$$G_{ijk} = 0 + \lambda_i^S + \lambda_j^R + \lambda_k^P + \lambda_{ij}^{SR} + \lambda_{ik}^{SP} + \lambda_{jk}^{RP} + \lambda_{ijk}^{SRP}$$

where $G_{ijk} = Ln(F_{ijk})$.

The equation is thus transformed into "log-linear" form. In order to simplify the exposition of results in this study, models are described simply by the main effects and interactions which correspond to the parameters in either equation. For example, the terms listed in parentheses for the saturated model in Table 10.1 are, more precisely, the main effects and interactions that are described by the parameters (τ or λ) shown above.

Another convention (as used in Chap. 9 but not in this study), specifies a model by labeling its "fitted marginals." Again, these describe the main effects and interactions included in the model and correspond to the parameters in the log-linear equation.

[2] Because this study is exploratory, it is particularly convenient to use a statistic that partitions uniquely. One reason stems from the fact that the research goals cannot be stated in a limited number of specific hypotheses. Instead, the strategy is to adopt a scanning technique, that is, to explore a variety of possible relationships in order to isolate distinctive patterns for further analysis. A general approach which adopts the multiple-comparison ideas developed for ANOVA can be applied to qualitative variables and includes numerous log-linear techniques such as the ones used in this study. To use Goodman's term (1969), we can thoroughly "ransack" the cross-classification table.

Many times when multiple-test procedures are invoked, a G^2 value representing the amount of variation attributable to a particular model or single parameter requires further analysis. For instance, within a model, it may be desirable to specify how total variation is distributed over its single parameters. Only when the statistic partitions uniquely, as G^2 does, is it possible to take the difference between models differing by one parameter, as an exact calculation of the variation attributable to that parameter.

Similarly, a G^2 value of a specific parameter may be partitioned into components that represent particular contrasts within the parameter. For instance, if the variable A has three categories (A_1, A_2, and A_3), the G^2 value of the main effect, A, may be broken down into components: the contrast A_1 vs. A_2, and the contrast between the average of ($A_1 + A_2$) and A_3. When the contrasts are independent, the sum of the G^2 values of the two contrasts will equal the G^2 value of the total main effect.

Finally, it is possible to partition a model into subsets of models which, again, add up perfectly in terms of their G^2 values. For instance, the model (AB)(AC) generates a particular G^2 value for a set of data. This model can be restated as model (B)(C), given each level of A. If variable A is composed of three categories as in the example above, this would result in a subset of three models: (B)(C) for A_1, (B)(C) for A_2, and (B)(C) for A_3. The sum of the G^2 values for these three models will be equal to the G^2 value of model (AB)(AC).

[3] In some cases, however, a parameter is in a model not because it accounts for a significant amount of variation by itself, but because the model containing it fits better than a model lacking it when all other parameters are the same.

11. Structure, strategy, and research

STARKEY DUNCAN, JR., AND DONALD W. FISKE

Three major considerations led us to undertake a major project on interaction strategy. On the positive side, as psychologists we were and remain convinced of the value of individual-differences research in general, and we were interested in pursuing individual-differences studies in interaction in particular.

A negative experience giving impetus to the project was the failure of our earlier search for individual differences reported in D&F (Part II), a failure we interpreted in terms of the inability of simple-rate variables to support inferences to interaction process. Investigators have, however, largely ignored our modest proposal that such variables be abandoned altogether in interaction studies: Studies using simple-rate variables have continued apace.

Finally and once again positively, we were convinced that the analysis of sequential data and the study of strategy based on the notion of structure provide a productive general approach to individual differences in interaction. Further, the problems with simple-rate variables seemed solvable through the use of variables like the sequence variables described in D&F and used in the structure research reported there.

We began our strategy research as an exploratory study. Our goals were to develop methods for studying strategy, and to discover strategy phenomena. Although we recognized that there was much to be learned, we did not begin to appreciate how thoroughly exploratory the work would prove to be. After all, the strategy research was to be based on the preceding structural studies; these would provide a solid and well-situated base camp for our explorations of strategy. Relevant structural hypotheses were in place; the transcribing process would be highly streamlined, focusing on turn-system actions; and we had in mind some plausible candidates for strategy phenomena. Although these perceptions may have been appropriate, our initial data analyses shocked us when we realized how thoroughly at sea we were. To place the problems we encountered in a broader perspective, it is useful to review some major themes that have successively emerged in studies of face-to-face interaction.

11.1 The message-centered theme

The notion of communication in face-to-face interaction has evolved significantly over the past several decades. One early influence was the work of Shannon and Weaver (1949) on the flow of information. For some investigators, Shannon and Weaver's elegant and practical work in the field of telecommunication suggested a metaphor or perspective for understanding interaction. To simplify the metaphor a bit, it is as if participants were taking turns handing each other slips of paper, each slip containing a message. Communication would be optimized if the writing were clear, spelling and syntax were error free, the slips were not crumpled or torn, and the like.

The effect of this metaphor was to focus research attention on the message of a participant, an emphasis already firmly entrenched in the tradition of linguistics. We shall term this the *message-centered* theme or perspective. In this view, what transpires between participants in interaction is the exchange of messages. It is important that these messages be clear and consistent, minimizing error, ambiguity, and conflicting elements within the message.

Some of the external-variable research on individual differences examined in Chaper 1 (including parts of the individual-differences study described in Part II of D&F) seems congruent with this metaphor. In this kind of external-variable research, variables summarize the properties (usually of "nonverbal" elements) of a participant's message over some stretch of interaction. These variables are then related to such things as personality characteristics, status, and sex of the participant. The focus remains squarely on the individual and the individual's messages.

11.2 The interpersonal-influence theme

Although message or information is certainly a valid and important element of interaction, most current investigators look beyond the exchange of discrete messages. The properties of interaction require expanding the message-centered perspective. An initial step in this expansion would be to examine the relation between successive messages or actions. (This is something that many external-variable investigators do.) In interaction, a participant's message appropriately takes into account at least the partner's preceding message and probably earlier elements of the interaction. Thus, a participant's action at each point in an interaction potentially influences the partner's subsequent action. This eminently reasonable observation gives rise to the *interpersonal-influence* theme.

The interpersonal-influence theme has provided the rationale for many studies examining the probability of a consequent: the extent to which some action by a participant affects the probability of the partner's ensuing action. Certainly the issue of influence was one of the central concerns of the strategy-signal study in Chapter 7 and of Denny's analyses in Chapter 8. For example, in our conversations the speaker's display of a greater number of turn cues increased the probability of the auditor's taking the turn, and the speaker's use of the gesticulation signal decreased it.

(Unfortunately, evidence on consequent probabilities, considered alone, is sometimes interpreted as direct evidence for interaction structure. In Chapter 4, we described why we take an alternative approach.)

From the interpersonal-influence perspective, the sequential process of interaction is seen as the exchange between participants A and B of an ordered sequence of messages: A1, B1, A2, B2. . . . In this case, B1 appropriately takes into account what occurred in A1; A2 appropriately takes into account at least B1; and the meaning or interpretation of each successive action is influenced by the string of preceding actions. Simple examples of this sort of process would be any sort of board game, such as chess or tic-tac-toe. Each move constitutes a "message." The move is in some sense contingent on and interpreted in terms of what has occurred before it, and it also exerts its own influence on what follows.

The effect of a given action on succeeding actions is often measured by investigators in terms of the probability of a consequent: for example, the degree to which knowing A1 permits prediction of B1. To the extent that this sort of prediction is successful, the results are typically interpreted as the flow of influence from A to B.

In interaction, the influence process is complicated by the fact that it is mutual and concurrent. Each participant is influencing the other as the interaction proceeds. The recognition of possible mutual influence undoubtedly lies behind the attempts of some investigators to control the actions of one participant by using confederates in experimental studies of interaction, a practice we criticized in Chapter 1.

11.3 The structural theme

There is the question, of course, of what mediates the influence process in interaction. What, exactly, is the connection between A1 and B1? Why, for example, should there be any relation between number of turn cues and auditor response? Why should the speaker's gesticulating suppress the auditor's attempts to take the turn? Our response to such questions involves a further shift in perspective. We have described in Chapter 2 our view of the deep relation between influence and convention-based action. Thus, the operation of convention not only provides a structure within which it is possible to carry out an interaction, but also inevitably creates several types of sequential effects, all broadly interpretable as influence. When we began this strategy research, our notion of strategy was essentially defined in terms of patterns of interpersonal influence mediated through convention. Our experience with this project has forced us to broaden this perspective.

Kendon (1974) expresses a basic element of convention with great clarity, contrasting it with the message-centered perspective:

> The word "communication" comes from the Latin communis which means "common." In its modern and most frequent meaning, according to the Oxford English Dictionary, it refers to "the imparting, conveying or exchange of ideas, knowledge, etc." However, it has also been used to mean "common participation." It can thus mean the transmission of information from a source that possesses it to a receiver that does not, or it can mean the common participation of individuals in something. It may thus be used to refer to the processes by which people are sustained as members of a commonality.
>
> If we study how behavior functions in communication, the questions of interest will be different, according to which sense of the

term "communication" we follow. If we follow the first sense, our orientation will be to the individual person as an entity who has some news to transmit. We shall study his behavior in order to find out what that news might be. On the other hand, if we follow the second of the two senses distinguished, the orientation is not to individuals and their news, but to patterns of behavior and the way in which these function in sustaining individuals in interrelationship with one another. "Communication" in this sense is not a matter of messages but a matter of systems of behavioral relationship that can be observed between individuals. The task of a study of communicative behavior with this orientation becomes the systematic description of behavior patterns and an analysis of how these function in systems of behavioral interrelation. (p. 526)

The notion of behavioral interrelations defined by convention is shared by all investigators of interaction structure. Convention provides the structured, or rule-governed, aspect of interaction. Following Lewis (1969) and others, we view a convention as a solution to a coordination problem requiring the collaborative effort of two or more individuals (cf. Chapter 2). This might be termed the *convention-based*, or *structural*, perspective. It is apparent that this perspective includes but significantly expands upon those limited to the notions of messages and sequentially influenced actions. It is not just that earlier actions influence later ones, but that participants' actions are guided by commonly held rules concerning how the interaction is to be conducted. These rules define meaningful relationships between actions, providing a framework for the operation of influence.

Further, the relation between convention and situation (Chapter 2) is central to the investigation of individual differences. Here the questions involve the connection between a participant's actions and various attributes of that participant. For example, why should female subjects in many studies tend to look at their partners more than male subjects? Simply appealing to the greater "affiliativeness" of female subjects does not answer the question but only labels it. The question then becomes, why should there be a specific connection between affiliativeness and gazing, as opposed to any other action? For us, the indexical relationship between convention and situation provides the connection between, say, "affiliation" and gaze direction. That is, within some conventions, increased gazing at the partner assigns a higher value to the social category of "affiliation." But studies of situation (such as those cited in Chapter 2) also strongly suggest that the operation of situation in interaction is vastly more complex than a unitary relationship between a single action and a single attribute.

Certainly, considerations such as the relative status and personality characteristics of participants may be major factors affecting the actual parameters of the influence. Many of these factors have been carefully examined by investigators. But the actual sequences of actions by which the flow of influence is manifested, not to mention the notions of status and personality characteristic themselves, are defined by convention. We have argued vigorously that, in view of the operation of convention, it is potentially fruitless—and definitely highly inefficient—to attempt to examine the influence process directly, bypassing the central role of convention. The definition of what constitutes influence in a specific interaction—and thus the key to observing it—is provided by convention. Thus, the structural theme significantly expands on, and provides a rationale for, the interpersonal theme.

11.4 The common-participation theme

Although we have long held to the convention-based perspective on interaction, it contains an implication for at least some forms of interaction that we did not realize when we began the strategy research. And, as fate would have it, this implication was deeply relevant to the particular interactions we were studying and thus not to be avoided in our strategy research.

It is not enough to say that participants in interaction are engaged in a common, convention-based enterprise that involves definite expectations regarding their respective actions. That notion is one of joint action based on shared rules for conduct. It is critically important to add that in some interactions what A is doing at the moment is affected by what B is doing (or not doing) at the same moment. That is, the actual unfolding of a participant's message—the carrying out of a given action or complex of actions—can be directly affected by the partner's actions.

It is possible for each participant to influence or affect the character of the other's action on a continuous basis. This is *in addition to* the influence manifested in sequential actions (A1, B1, etc.) described above. Each participant may directly affect, through both action and inaction, the partner's message as it evolves. That is, B has a distinct role in the message that A is sending to B. This is the sense, we think, that Kendon had in mind in the preceding passage. We shall use, then, his apt term, *common*

participation, in referring to this perspective. Although common participation appears to be a corollary of the structural perspective, we feel
that it is useful to highlight the additional implications that common
participation carries.

Direct participation in the partner's action occurs in a variety of ways,
most of which doubtless remain to be discovered. But simple examples
have already been mentioned. The length of a speaker's gaze cannot be five
units long if the author takes the turn after two units. The auditor cannot
return the speaker's gaze after three seconds if the gaze lasts only two. The
speaker cannot yield the speaking turn if the auditor simply refuses to take
it. A participant's smile will tend to be relatively brief if the partner fails to
smile in return (cf. Chapter 9).

We do not view common participation as simply a spin-off of the
mutual-influence theme in which influence is operating between successive
messages. Common participation involves the partner's direct effect on the
participant's current message.

It is the presence of common participation that limits the investigator's
ability to regard a participant's action as exclusively his or her own, giving
rise to the discussion of pseudounilaterality in Chapter 1. Despite the
somewhat tongue-in-cheek, hyperjargonish character of that term and its
unaesthetic acronym, it has a serious purpose: to refer to the error of failing
to take common participation into account when variables are formulated,
data are analyzed, and results are interpreted. This, then, seems to be the
source of the problem with simple-rate variables, explored in Chapter 1.
They do not allow for the possibility of each participant's contributing to
the parameters of the partner's action. We regard this error as a potentially
major factor impeding the continued development of individual-differences research on interaction.

This examination of common participation brings out the fact that
interaction and the influence of each participant on the other are occurring
simultaneously at each and every level of analysis. Each message is
influenced by the preceding one and, to a lesser degree, by all of the earlier
ones. Within a message unit or speaking turn, each action by one
participant is influenced by preceding actions of the other, and perhaps to
some small degree by all preceding actions of both participants. Furthermore, the carrying out of each action seems affected by what the other
person is doing or not doing at the moment.

The implications of such simultaneous and continuing influence of one
participant on the other are fundamental to our understanding of
interaction. At each level of analysis, we can detect sizable influences from

immediately preceding units but probably cannot hope to assess the smaller effects from still earlier ones. And at each level, the broader unit is affected not only by coordinate units but also by smaller ones: for example, the production of the message by the carrying out of actions during it. Yet throughout this enormous complexity, the particular observed units are generated not only by effects from the other participant but also by attributes of the individual participant. Each participant is contributing. While A is influenced by B in one interaction and by C in another interaction, A is also influencing B and C and, hence, contributing to what happens in both the A-B and the A-C interactions. The challenge to the investigator is to see whether there is something in common between A's contributions to interactions with different partners, whether there are some kind of individual differences in the broad classical sense. At the least, we find continuing regularities in A's interaction with B, and similarly during A's interaction with C.

The challenge to interaction research is to devise methods for dealing with this ongoing effect of each participant upon the other. To an essayist or interaction theorist, the process of common participation (not to mention continual mutual influence) might appear as a fascinating theme to be developed and elaborated in all its variety and complexity. However, to a researcher, that fascinating process might be seen as more of an infernal, convoluted tangle of simultaneous effects. The research task becomes an exercise in a delicate and complex disentangling of these effects.

Whatever one's attitude might be, the common-participation phenomenon, although elusive in character, seems to have the potential for contributing substantial effects to interaction process. What presently exists as noise and error in results can instead become the source of stronger and more interpretable effects. Common participation poses a major issue as investigators continue to explore the nature of interaction process and individual strategies within that process.

On first glance, the common-participation theme, taken to its logical conclusion, might seem to imply that it is meaningless to study individual differences in interaction. From this view, if common participation is an element of an interaction, the notion of analytically separable individual action in interaction appears undermined. Each participant's action is an amalgam or product of the action of both participant and partner. Perhaps because we were trained as psychologists, we are reluctant to take this view. For us, the question of individual differences in interaction remains a valid one.

Rather than seeing the participants as merging or becoming indistinguishable, we regard the phenomenon of common participation as significantly complicating but not eliminating the study of individual differences. It does seem appropriate, however, to reformulate what the study of individual differences involves. We shall return to this problem in the discussion of Kanki's study reported in Chapter 10.

11.5 Principal arguments regarding individual differences

One of the main concerns in D&F and this monograph has been the methodological and conceptual issues in doing research in face-to-face interaction. These were discussed in some detail in Chapters 1–6, preceding the reports on strategy research. The primary focus has been on issues related to doing individual-differences research on interaction, but also considered have been matters relating more basically to interaction itself, as well as a number of issues presupposed by individual-differences research.

At the risk of gross oversimplification and serious omission, we shall briefly list some of the major themes in the discussion, along with the chapter in which each was first taken up. We shall not be enumerating either the turn-system hypotheses described in Chapter 3 or the set of substantive results reported in Chapters 6–10. The reader should keep in mind that all of these points are made strictly in relation to research on face-to-face interaction. To avoid redundancy, we shall omit repeated qualifications, such as "in interaction" and the like.

Chapter 1

1. The use of confederates as an element of experimental control is fraught with seemingly insurmountable practical difficulties. Further, this practice appears paradoxically to require control of the subject as well.
2. Simple-rate variables (i.e., those that do not contain information on interaction sequences) cannot support inferences regarding interaction process.
3. In research on individual differences, it appears to be an error to regard a participant s action as determined uniquely by that participant, thus reflecting solely his or her characteristics. We termed this the error of pseudo-unilaterality.
4. The analysis of sequences of action is essential. Such analysis can be accomplished in several different ways. The run-sequence variable carries more information than any other we have been able to devise.

Chapter 2

5. All our research is based on the view of interaction as a structured (i.e., rule-governed) activity.
6. The notion of structure necessarily entails the notion of strategy, and, we believe, provides the most effective framework for individual-differences research.
7. The third essential element of interaction is situation or context, which is not directly investigated in this monograph.

Chapter 3

8. We make no specific claims concerning the generality of the turn-system hypotheses. As conventions, the turn system, as described in Chapter 3, is presumably used in some conversations and not others, depending on the situation in which the conversation occurs. We regard turn-system generality as strictly an empirical issue.

Chapter 4

9. We do not consider it unreasonable to expect investigators to present evidence (beyond that of examples) in support of their structural hypotheses.
10. We have used three primary criteria in evaluating results relevant to structural hypotheses: (a) antecedent and consequent probabilities, jointly considered, (b) effectiveness in differentiating contrasting kinds of action, and (c) parsimony.
11. The distinction between optional and obligatory action is central to our hypotheses of structure.

These points, considered in some detail in the chapters indicated, also recur repeatedly in subsequent sections. With these broad points in mind, we may proceed to discussion of the strategy-research chapters.

11.6 Strategy signals

The first product of this project was in some ways the most surprising and perplexing. When we analyzed some data relating to patterns of inter-personal influence, the results seemed to call for a whole new class of signal, entirely unanticipated in our previous studies or in the "metatheoretical" discussions in D&F. This development caused us to question the adequacy of our definition of structure signals and our criteria for hypothesizing structure signals. Was there a flaw in our original formulations that required us to add on such an ad hoc notion as strategy signal?

Strategy signals as conventions

Strategy signals are considered to be conventions, just as are structure signals. Strategy signals are defined in terms of both negative and positive criteria. On the negative side, they must have failed one or more of the criteria posited for structure signals and therefore be rejected as structure signals. Positively, their use by a participant must have the effect of changing the probability of some response by the partner and must not be limited to the response characteristics of some single participant. (See Chapter 7 for a more detailed description of strategy-signal criteria.)

In these characteristics, strategy signals seem to fit squarely within the general structural theme elaborated earlier in this chapter. They seem to be part of the set of conventions shared by the participants in our conversations. Strategy signals are defined in terms of regularities in sequences of actions between participants. Issues of common participation do not appear to play a major role in the evaluation of strategy signals.

Consequentiality of alternatives. Because strategy signals seem to be part of our participants' repertoire of conventions, nonuse of a strategy signal is as consequential as its use. The notion of consequentiality of conventional alternatives is usefully elaborated by Schegloff and Sacks (1973). If a signal might have been used but was not, that omission is as meaningful as the actual use of a signal. If speaker gaze may be used with a turn signal to facilitate auditor response, speaker activation of the turn signal without gaze takes on significance beyond the turn-signal display itself. This situation, applicable throughout the turn system and characteristic of convention-based action, clearly applies to responses as well as to signal displays. When the possibility for response exists at a specified point in the stream of interaction, both its occurrence and nonoccurrence become meaningful events.

Criteria for structure signals

Although strategy signals do not seem particularly exceptional as turn-system phenomena, they may also raise questions regarding the criteria posited for structure signals. As discussed in Chapters 4 and 7, these criteria were (a) simultaneous consideration of consequent and antecedent probabilities applying to signal display and auditor response, (b) ability of the proposed signal to differentiate various types of actions (invoked whenever a suitable contrast in actions can be formulated), and (c) parsimony. Because strategy signals must be rejected as structure signals in terms of these criteria, consideration of strategy signals will necessarily include these structure-signal criteria.

Strategy signals were hypothesized because we found strong sequential regularities associated with actions that had been tested but rejected as structure signals. Two examples may help illustrate the issues that arise.

Speaker gaze. The rejection of speaker gaze as a structure signal may seem counterintuitive to some readers. Gaze being so closely connected with turn taking, many investigators have assumed that it must be a turn signal. Yet with respect to the data, gaze appears to be the most unambiguous case of a structure-signal failure.

In terms of consequent and antecedent probabilities, speaker gaze fares well. Turn exchanges are often preceded by speaker gaze. Although it raises the probability of a consequent turn exchange, it clearly does not compel such an exchange, so it would be considered a signal providing for optional action just like a turn cue. In terms of this first criterion, speaker gaze is entirely acceptable as an element of the turn signal.

However, when occuring alone (i.e., without other turn cues), speaker gaze fails to differentiate smooth exchanges of the turn from instances of simultaneous turns—a requirement of all turn cues. This requirement in itself seems reasonable because such differentiation would seem to be a prime function of a turn signal in the sorts of conversations we have studied. Further, other turn cues seem quite capable of meeting this criterion, although the occurrence of single turn cues is not frequent in our data. As indicated in Chapter 7, speaker gaze conspicuously fails this criterion. The single greatest source of simultaneous turns in our data is auditor attempts to take the speaking turn in response to speaker gaze alone.

Although the failure to meet the second criterion renders evaluation of the third criterion—parsimony—irrelevant, it remains true that speaker gaze fares poorly in that respect also. Smooth exchanges of the turn are well accounted for in our data without recourse to speaker gaze.

These considerations led us to reject speaker gaze as a turn cue early in the structural research, and we have not had reason to change this judgment since.

Speaker smiling. More problematic as a strategy signal is speaker smiling, which is perhaps the most intuitively acceptable candidate. Speaker smiling, when occurring in conjunction with the speaker within-turn signal, was hypothesized as a strategy signal, increasing the probability of an auditor smile in response. (In a previous study, auditor smiling had been classified as one form of auditor back channel.) Speaker smiling was rejected as a structure signal primarily on the grounds of parsimony.

In the conversations initially analyzed for strategy signals, it was found that the speaker within-turn signal preceded most auditor smiles, and a number of auditor smiles were not preceded by speaker smiling, so that speaker smiling simply was not needed to account for auditor smiling. In this sense, speaker smiling failed the parsimony criterion and was rejected as a structure signal. However, when speaker smiling accompanied the speaker within-turn signal, the probability of auditor smiling as part of an ensuing back-channel response was increased. Therefore, speaker smiling was hypothesized as a strategy signal.

The whole issue of invoking parsimony in interaction research appears to be a knotty one, however. An action yielding only marginal results in one set of interactions may play a more prominent role in other interactions merely as a function of shifts in participants' response tendencies. This has occurred in our data. As discussed in Chapter 6, turn cues critically important in the first conversations we studied were overshadowed by the grammatical-completion cue in the strategy-study conversations. But the importance of grammatical completion would be expected to fade in other conversations in which participants used a less complex grammatical structure than did our professional-school participants.

All of this suggests that investigators should not be too hasty in discarding actions yielding marginal results or apparently playing a superfluous role in a given data set. Those same actions may be more centrally used or responded to in other interactions. Caution would appear to be the motto when parsimony is invoked in interaction research. This criterion is desirable because it contributes to conceptual simplicity and to ease in understanding a hypothesized system. It is not necessarily a major concern in some absolute sense. This issue is further considered in Chapter 6 with respect to the various turn cues.

Conclusion. Having considered these various complications of the structure criteria, as well as possible alternatives, we have concluded that the original structure criteria, though not without complications, continue to appear appropriate, reasonable, and workable, at least for the interactions we have studied. Possible alternatives we have examined have had serious weaknesses of one sort or another. We are inclined, therefore, to accept the strategy-signal hypothesis as another facet of the rich and complex interaction process.

Strategy signals as analogic modifiers

Recall that within the turn system, structure signals are considered discrete. They either occur or do not occur, generally indicating points in the stream of interaction where it is appropriate for the partner to do something or not to do something. In this sense, the structure signals we have hypothesized occur in a fairly yes/no manner.

It seems that, within this context, strategy signals function to add analogic information to the digital structure signals. That is, a strategy signal permits the signaler to give more or less emphasis to the structure signal that it accompanies. For example, there is a much lower probability of an auditor's attempting to take the turn in response to a turn signal consisting of a single turn cue unaccompanied by gaze, than to five turn cues with gaze. Thus, by manipulating the components of signal display, the speaker can produce turn signals of appreciably different effectiveness in eliciting auditor responses.

More familiar examples of this analogic modification were given in Chapter 7. A handshake may be given more or less firmly. A smile may be displayed more or less broadly. Here the shake itself would be the structural action; firmness of grip would be the analogic modifier; and similarly for the smile. In this sense, strategy signals may naturally accompany many structure signals, providing valuable supplementary information.

Strategy signals as indexes

The hypothesized signals and other elements of convention-based interaction cannot occur in a vacuum. As we pointed out in D&F, signals occurring in the course of interaction are presumably about something.

Beyond their function as conventions facilitating the accomplishment of the interaction, we take them as serving an indexical function, that is, as giving information on values a participant assigns to various elements of the situation. For example, the particular conventions used by participants may carry information of several kinds: for example, characteristics of the participant, of the partner, and of the relationship between them; the nature of their interaction; and momentary reactions, perceptions, emotions, and other inner states of each participant. (Indexicality and situation were touched on in Chapter 2.) We regard both the structure signals and the strategy signals as carrying this sort of indexical information, particularly information on transitory inner states of the signaler.

This general idea was behind the notion of *transition readiness* described in D&F (pp. 196–198; 238–239). This notion was intended to represent an inner state of the speaker, reflecting the extent to which the speaker desired an exchange of the speaking turn or a retention of the present speaker—auditor status quo. A participant's transition readiness was considered to be subject to rapid fluctuations during the course of the interaction. Degree of transition readiness could be indicated by the speaker through turn-system signals. The discussion in D&F involved only turn cues and the gesticulation signal. We would now add speaker gaze as a signal contributing to information on transition readiness.

Displaying the gesticulation signal was said to represent a negative transition-readiness value. Displaying no turn signal and no gesticulation signal would indicate a zero transition-readiness value. And displaying the turn signal with, say, four turn cues (and no gesticulation signal) would be a positive transition-readiness value of four. In this manner, a speaker's transition readiness could be represented to the auditor on an ordinal scale running from some negative value, through zero and ending at six. Results on speaker gaze suggest that gaze increases the probability of an auditor's turn-taking response to a given turn-cue display by a factor of four or five, thereby considerably increasing the range of values that can be communicated regarding transition readiness.

There was more to transition readiness than signal display, but we need not be concerned with that. The important point here concerns not transition readiness per se but the indexicality of convention-based action, including strategy signals. Structural research leads inevitably to the hypothesis of social categories of one sort or another. Many psychologists concerned with individual differences may be particularly interested in more stable categories such as affiliation or dominance, or more transient categories such as emotions. As we have repeatedly stated, these interests seem to us entirely legitimate.

Problems arise, not in studying individual differences through inter-action, but in using standard psychological techniques to accomplish that purpose. No one would deny that individuals differ, but how are such differences to be construed most fruitfully? How should we go from observed differences in action sequences to any more general statements categorizing such differences? As we see it, the most effective approach to the study of the various characteristics and states associated with individual-differences research is through structural research, although such a route may initially seem circuitous. Convention provides the critical link relating action, such as a form of address or a turn signal, to more transient inner states, such as transition readiness, or to more stable interactional characteristics, such as relative status. If there is, indeed, some connection between gaze and affiliativeness (at least in those participants involved in existing studies) as many investigators have asserted, that connection is provided through the indexical aspect of one or more conventions. In the case of gaze, these conventions have not been specified.

Finally, we believe that exploratory research designed to discover conventions operating in interaction is an excellent vehicle for generating hypotheses of novel inner states and the like, thereby expanding our current set of constructs relating to individual differences.

Strategy signals as a source of regularity in interaction

Our research has impressed on us the variety of sources of regularity that may be found in interaction. Each set of results reported in this monograph is based on a different sort of interactional regularity, and we are sure that many others remain undiscovered.

In this sense, strategy signals provide a specific kind of interactional regularity: They increase the probability of a partner's response over some baseline rate. The strategy-signal hypothesis specifies neither the level of response to be expected nor the amount of increase over the baseline. Clearly, there are individual differences both in the baseline itself and in the size of the strategy-signal effect.

We describe strategy signals as increasing the probability of the partner's response. If there are strategy signals that decrease that probability, we have not found them yet. It is easier to think about such signals in terms of positive actions and positive effects. But just as the absence of a structure signal conveys information, so the absence of a strategy signal has a negative effect. Strategy signals should be construed as present or absent: Their presence increases a probability; their absence decreases it.

Certainly strategy signals as we have defined them do not require response from the partner. That is, strategy signals do not operate in an obligatory manner. Through use of strategy signals, a participant may influence the probability of a partner's response but not control it. The course of interaction remains a dynamic process created through the joint action of both participants. In none of the interactions we have studied does one participant call all the shots.

In short, strategy signals are an identifiable source of regularity in interaction, but they leave plenty of room for the many complex effects that seem to be in play continuously in interaction.

11.7 Pragmatic marking and speaking-turn exchange

In Chaper 8, Denny reports a series of results that significantly expands our view of the turn-taking process. These results carry both substantive and methodological implications for research on face-to-face interaction.

Before considering the more substantive aspects of Denny's work, it is of great importance to point out that the primary goal of her analyses is significantly different from that of the structural analyses reported in Chapter 6. That is, the questions she asks of the data are not those described in earlier chapters.

At least initially, she does not seek to discover and document structural phenomena per se (as defined in D&F and this volume), although she does make extensive use of earlier results on structural and strategy signals. Rather, her analyses explore the predictive power of various actions: primarily, the power of one participant's actions to predict the ensuing action of the partner. This goal motivates her reliance on logistic regression as her basic analytic technique. As her investigation developed, many analyses focused on the power of the speaker's and the auditor's actions to predict the occurrence of turn exchanges or "transitions."

(As indicated in the discussion of "turn exchange" in Chapter 3, Denny's term "transition" and her use of the term "smooth exchange" differ from the definition of smooth exchange given in Chapter 3, but the differences need not affect the discussion at this point.)

Thus, she does not consider the antecedent probability of actions, and in her analyses of turn exchanges she does not examine the power of the actions to differentiate smooth exchanges of the turn from instances of simultaneous turns. Both of these considerations were, of course, essential criteria evaluating the turn signal as an element of structure. In this way, Denny is clearly asking different questions of the data, questions oriented toward strategy issues. This does not mean, however, that the phenomena she examines are irrelevant to structural hypotheses, as we shall see.

Very broadly speaking, Denny's results point to (a) the importance of grammatical completion (GC as defined in Chapters 3 and 8), of speaker gaze toward the auditor (GZ), and of the auditor's gazing away (AGZ) in the process of speaking-turn exchange in our data; (b) sharply constrasting effects of different combinations of these and other behavioral elements on the probability of turn exchange; (c) contrast in the way pause length (PL) operates in auditor back channels, as opposed to turn exchange; (d) the relevance of *speech event*, broadly construed as question, answer, or comment, for both turn exchange and auditor back channels; (e) the relation of auditor gaze at the beginning of a turn to the length of that turn; and (f) the role of ellipsis as an element of the grammatical-completion turn cue.

These results carry important implications for various aspects of research practice, and also expand the framework within which interaction research is pursued. At the same time, Denny's interpretations of her results differ at some points from those of Duncan and Fiske. All of these points deserve careful consideration.

First of all, it will be obvious to readers of Chapter 8 that many of Denny's results have already been incorporated into the turn-system hypotheses and the way in which this research has been carried out. Denny's suggestions were the source of the more elaborated definition of the grammatical-completion turn cue and the inclusion of ellipsis within that definition. In addition, she was a contributor to early analyses that led to the reduced signal set used in the strategy analyses. Results relevant to these issues were presented in Chapter 6 within the analytical framework used for the structural analyses.

Pause length

We regard Denny's work on pauses as having great methodological and substantive significance. We regard the technology she used in measuring pauses as a major development in pause research. Based on widely available technology for digitizing speech, and using the DTEDIT program on the PDP-11 computer, it was possible to measure each pause individually with an accuracy of $\pm$ 5 ms. Because the digitized speech could be played back through speakers, the location of each pause in the stream of speech could be determined, between-word pauses could be distinguished from within-word pauses, and other interaction phenomena could be verified, such as whether a pause between participants separated speaking turns or occurred between the speaker's speech and auditor's back channel. Considered together, these elements permitted a unique accuracy and specificity in her analyses.

Not mentioned in Denny's chapter was one of the more astonishing results to emerge from her improved measurement technique: Smooth exchanges of the turn (i.e., with no overlap in speech) can occur in 5 ms. At this length, absolutely no pause can be heard; nevertheless, the oscilloscope confirms that there is no speech overlap. Other such exchanges occurred in the 5- to 65-ms range. Although most investigators of conversation have commented on the remarkable facility and coordination that participants have in exchanging the turn, no other measurements have been so precise as Denny's. It seems reasonable to expect that, as investigation continues, this facility will be observed in many other aspects of interaction.

The accuracy and interactional specificity in Denny's study contrast sharply with the currently standard technology in which pause lengths are measured automatically by computers using a 300-ms sampling interval (Jaffe & Feldstein, 1970; Natale, Entin, & Jaffe, 1979). This technique requires the inference that a 600-ms pause has occurred if a pause is detected in a speaker's speech on two successive samplings (cf. Jaffe & Feldstein, 1970, Figure II-2). Denny's data (reported more fully in her 1982 dissertation) clearly document that this inference is not always justified. There can be successive, brief pauses within that interval.

Furthermore, it is clear that, even if the 300-ms interval contained only one pause, its length cannot be accurately assessed using Jaffe and Feldstein's sampling technique. Such a pause, recorded as 600 ms in that approach, could have ranged from 301 to 899 ms (i.e., through essentially all of the preceding and subsequent intervals). Given Denny's results, this level of measurement accuracy no longer seems acceptable.

Even more significant is Denny's documentation of sharply different distributions of interparticipant pause lengths for turn exchanges, as opposed to verbal auditor back channels. The probability of a turn exchange increases as a function of pause length, whereas the probability of an auditor back channel decreases slightly. These two forms of auditor response thus have sharply contrasting temporal parameters. This result suggests that the lumping of both sorts of pauses in current computerized studies has the potential of introducing considerable noise in the data, distorting results for both turn exchanges and auditor back channels. In view of Denny's results, there seems to be little justification for continuing the widespread practice of aggregating pause-length data on turn exchanges and auditor back channels.

This argument need not be confined to the turn-exchange/back-channel distinction. Denny's study, part of which is described in Chapter 8, showed distinct pause-length distributions, depending on the interactional precedents and concomitants of the pause. For example, her Figure 8.1 shows that the pause-length distribution for GCGZ-AGZ (the co-occurring combination of grammatical completion, speaker gaze, and auditor gazing away) is sharply different from the distribution for any one of these actions occurring alone. It thus seems questionable even to aggregate pause-length data for different types of turn exchange.

The apparent advantage of approaches such as Jaffe and Feldstein's (1970) AVTA is that pauses are measured automatically by the computer, so that the data need not be "touched by human hands." This greatly speeds the data collection process. In this regard, Denny's approach sharply contrasts. She measured by hand (i.e., by indicating on the apparatus) and categorized each and every pause in the digitalized speech. However, there seems to be no technical reason why this process cannot be more completely automatized. We believe that the increased accuracy of pause measurement, together with the ability to identify each pause within the speech stream—and thus the interactional context of that pause—can only improve the quality of research on interactional pause length.

More broadly, Denny's research calls into question the very notion of research that focuses exclusively or primarily on pause length, as opposed to incorporating pause length within a more inclusive consideration of interactional elements. It would seem that the appropriate evaluation of pause length would require information on its interactional context. For pauses to be understood, each must first be categorized in terms of the pattern of other actions present at its initiation. Then, within each such category, relationships between pause length and type of termination can be examined.

The evaluation of a variable in terms of its interactional context is a general principle of interaction research that we advocated in D&F. "Nonverbal communication" research has for too long tended to focus exclusively on some single element, such as gaze direction or pause length. The complexity of interaction, increasingly documented in integrative studies, militates against piecemeal analysis. Denny's results on pause length would seem to lend further validation to this point. Obviously, it is not now possible, given our limited knowledge and techniques, to identify and include all potentially relevant variables in a single study. Nonetheless, research will benefit as the behavioral scope and coverage of studies are increased.

Linguistics and statistics

Another interesting aspect of Denny's method is the integration of a linguistic sensibility with a hardheaded approach to statistical data analysis. It is quickly apparent to the reader of Denny's chapter that she approaches her topic from a distinctly linguistic or anthropological linguistic point of view. Her rhetorical style and some of her terms may be somewhat unfamiliar to some psychologists, but not her emphasis on thoroughgoing data analysis; and conversely, for some linguists and ethnomethodologists.

There has been a tendency in interaction research for linguistically oriented researchers to avoid statistical tests of their hypotheses. And more generally, statistical analysis has not been prominent in the linguistic literature. Similarly, many psychologists working on interaction have not emphasized the linguistic aspect of their materials. However, extensive statistical analysis is routine in their studies. This divergence of research styles is current but certainly not necessary or constructive. There can be little doubt that language is an integral part of many interactions, and that comprehensive treatment of these interactions must take language into account. At the same time, appropriate statistical treatment of interaction data can usually facilitate and strengthen the investigator's work.

Historical precedent notwithstanding, there seems to be no compelling reason why linguistic consideration and statistical analysis should be mutually exclusive in interaction research. (It never was in psycho-linguistics.) Denny's work is a case in point, where both formal models and case-by-case analysis (analysis of residuals) were used in describing the data. Occupants of both camps may be both reassured and challenged. We have already considered this general issue in our discussion of ethno-methodology in Chapter 4.

Points of difference

There are two points on which Denny's interpretation of the data differs from ours. These should be pointed out to avoid possible confusion for readers, as well as to highlight legitimate issues in interaction research.

Given her heavy emphasis on predictive models, it seems natural that Denny should view her results in those terms. Thus, she views the GCGZ-AGZ behavioral combination as predictive of turn exchange. She finds for GCGZ-AGZ that, as pause length (PL) increases, the probability of turn exchange reaches an asymptote near 1.0.

In D&F and in Duncan, Brunner, and Fiske (1979) we characterized this phenomenon in a somewhat different way. We viewed the GC as an element of the turn signal, the GZ as a strategy signal that increases the probability of the auditor's taking the turn, and the AGZ as a speaker-state signal indicating that the auditor is shifting to the speaker state (i.e., taking the turn) at that point. From this point of view, the GCGZ-AGZ combination constitutes an instance of turn exchange, rather than predicts it. In this case, AGZ is the critical element. GCGZ merely provides a point at which the auditor may appropriately take the turn. AGZ, if it occurs, indicates that the auditor chooses to exercise the available turn-exchange option, thereby actuating the exchange. Thus, it is not surprising that there is a strong relationship between GCGZ-AGZ and turn exchange.

On the other hand, it seems consonant with our point of view for Denny to say that GCGZ-AGZ-PL, taken as a whole, indexes a turn exchange. In the same sense, GC indexes the opportunity for turn exchange, co-occurring GZ indexes a heightened speaker readiness for turn exchange, and co-occurring AGZ indexes the auditor's shift to the speaker state. It was this sort of indexical relationship that was the point of the discussions of "transition readiness" in D&F (e.g., pp. 196–198)—discussions that would have benefited had Silverstein's (1976) excellent paper been available.

Finally, by conceptualizing each combination of behavioral elements marking turn exchange as a distinct index, Denny's discussion of strategy differs from, but does not conflict with, Duncan et al. (1979). Rather than documenting strategy signals, she discusses the indexical signals in terms of their pragmatic markedness. A component of strategy, she would argue, is found in the use of pragmatically marked and unmarked indexes. A resulting hypothesis would be that conversations differing in their patterning of pragmatically marked and unmarked indexes accomplish different social ends.

Speech event

The rather complex relationship of what Denny calls "speech event" to the other phenomena suggests another, virtually inevitable line along which interaction research can be developed. Denny uses a simple, three-part category system: Question, Answer, and Comment. "Question" is defined in virtually the simplest possible way: verb inversion or rising pitch contour. The other two categories might be characterized as "that which follows a Question" (Answer), and "that which does not follow a Question" (Comment).

In spite of the simple categories—or because of them—Denny shows distinct patterns of statistical interaction between speech event and the other variables, both in negotiating the process of turn exchange and in the auditor's producing a back channel. The speech-event effects are widespread in our data, having shown up in some of our earliest analyses (now discarded because of changed techniques). They are, we believe, further testimony to the desirability and fruitfulness of more integrated analyses of interaction, as opposed to those focusing more narrowly on one or two "nonverbal" actions or on linguistic elements alone.

Conclusion

In considering her results, Denny emphasizes two major points: (a) the deeply pragmatic—as opposed to purely referential—aspect of utterances, and (b) the role of both linguistic and nonlinguistic ("nonverbal") elements in achieving pragmatic functions in interaction. Language serves not only to convey referential information, but also to manage—in conjunction with other actions—the coordination of action by interacting participants. Her detailed analyses suggest specific elements of a system of indexical rules relating to both structure and strategy, operating within the conversations we observed.

11.8. Patterns of persistence and change in action sequences

Mokros's study reported in Chapter 9 is a pure example of exploratory research. First, he significantly expands the D&F action-sequence variable by inventing the run-sequence variable. As we stated in Chapter 1, the run-sequence variable is the most information-packed that we have encountered in interaction research. Having devised the variable, Mokros proceeds to use it in exploratory analyses, leading to results unlike any that we have obtained so far. These results are reported in Studies 1 and 3. Finally, he proposes that the results reflect, in part, the operation of cognitive processing constraints in the participants, a kind of regularity altogether different from any that we have proposed to date. In Study 2,

Mokros uses a more familiar sort of data—state transitions (he terms them "events")—but he analyzes these data in an unusual and apparently productive way via log-linear analysis.

Taken as a whole, Mokros's work strays the furthest from our initial notion of strategy. In fact, it turned out not to be about strategy at all. In this sense, the development of the research reported in Chapter 9 was the most unexpected product of this project and one of the most interesting.

Variables

We view the run-sequence variable as a valuable addition to the armamentarium of interaction investigators. Mokros makes the reasonable point that it is useful to know not only where the onset and offset of an action occured in the stream of interaction, but also how long it lasted. Whereas the durations of actions such as gaze have been the topic of many studies, the data have been treated in a summary fashion. Analysis has not focused on distributions of the durations. As Mokros demonstrates, these distributions are analyzable using log-linear methods. We expect to make continued heavy use of run-sequence variables, applying them to issues extending well beyond those that Mokros examines.

It may be noted that many investigators will be interested in measuring durations using some temporal index, such as seconds. This approach is obviously entirely compatible with the run-sequence notion. In contrast, Mokros chose the unit of analysis, an interactionally defined measure, extensively used in our studies of structure and strategy. These units, although not at all of constant temporal length, do tend to last about a second or a little longer (cf. Table 5.2).

Benefits typically carry costs, and run-sequence variables are no exception. In a sense, they are a kind of luxury that should be indulged when it can be afforded. The cost may be measured in terms of data partitions. It is the nature of run-sequence variables to impose a number of partitions (one for each length), in addition to those partitions that are part of the investigator's design. For example, in Table 9.7 Mokros uses seven run lengths. Thus, there are seven partitions of the data prior to any other cross-classifications that may be used.

Mokros could use run sequences because his major analyses pooled across all participants in the conversations we analyzed. In contrast, Kanki (discussed in the next section) analyzed individual participants and conversations. In this case, run-sequence variables were out of the question; the data simply could not support the partitioning by run length, participant, and the signal and response cross-classification she needed. The partitioning cost of run-sequence variables is clearly a factor for investigators considering their use. Nevertheless, their unusual richness of information permit analyses of considerable power. They provide yet another useful tool for the investigator.

Cognitive constraints

Mokros's exploratory work led him to hypothesize cognitive-processing constraints as the source of the regularities he discovered. He then proceeded to further analyses designed to rule out, insofar as possible, reasonable interactional interpretations of his basic regularities. As indicated in the studies he cites, some investigators have begun to address cognitive issues using data from interaction, mainly speaker gaze. The kinds of questions involved are related to those addressed in psycholinguistics and in research on skilled performance. An early antecedent would be Goldman-Eisler's (e.g., 1968) studies of speech encoding based on pause phenomena. We regard interactional phenomena as a potentially rich resource for investigating cognitive phenomena.

In Chapter 9, Mokros presents three studies. In Study 1, he examines cycles of speaker gazing toward and away from the auditor; in Study 2, changes in speaker signal display; and in Study 3, participant smiling and partner response.

Study 2 is concerned exclusively with sequences of speaker signal display with no intervening auditor response, and thus the auditor is excluded by definition. Mokros finds constraints on changes in signal display that have no known interactional cause or effect. (He has analyses, not included in Chapter 9, indicating that auditor response is influenced almost exclusively by the latest speaker signal display, and not by sequences of displays having various properties. That is, he was able to identify no sequence of two signal displays that had an effect on auditor response beyond that of the the most recent display.)

Studies 1 and 3 deeply involve the auditor's response. Study 1 highlights a number of properties of speaker gaze duration. Of particular interest to Mokros is the regular cycling of gaze toward and away from the auditor during the midst of turns when auditor turn taking is not a direct factor. Study 3 shows strong regularities in the durations of smile initiations contingent on a smiling response—or lack thereof—by the partner. Further, some of these regularities are closely matched by the timing of smile responses when they occur.

In each study, the task of the analyses is to peel away as many of the strictly interactional effects as possible, leaving exposed those regularities that might plausibly be regarded as properties of the speaker. When these properties show strong regularities across speakers (contrasting with the distinct individual differences evident in many phases of the data), Mokros raises the possibility that the regularities stem from processing constraints within each participant.

Clearly, this is intricate and tricky business. At this stage, Mokros's exploratory analyses are primarily suggestive. First, it can always be claimed that the regularities are due to yet undiscovered interactional properties. Recall that convention-based regularities are similarly constant across the participants we studied. However, this objection is uninteresting in the abstract. It would become interesting if specific conventions were hypothesized that encompass Mokros's regularities, and these hypotheses were supported by appropriate evidence.

Second, Mokros's analyses are based on relatively natural interactions. More detailed examination of the regularities he reports would almost certainly require some sort of properly controlled experimental manipulation. As we pointed out in Chapter 1, some types of control in interaction research seem unproblematic, but attempts at control through the use of confederates seem doomed to failure.

To the extent that there are processing constraints, it is clear that, although they operate at a more fundamental level than do structure and strategy, they must also operate in interaction with convention, and it is chiefly (but not exclusively) in relation to convention that they will be manifest. For example, Mokros would not have been able to observe the regularities in internal speaker-ended gazes if the convention used by our participants stipulated (as it apparently does in some societies) that the speaker minimize gaze toward the auditor.

Further, conventions may well capitalize on processing constraints as a vehicle for transmitting information. As Mokros points out, turn exchanges are related to speaker gazes slightly longer than is typical in the gaze/no-gaze cycle. Thus, a slight extension of speaker gaze at the auditor during turns, relative to the typical gaze/no-gaze cycle, is associated with the auditor's acting to take the speaking turn.

At the same time, Mokros acknowledges the operation in his data of common participation: the partner's effect on the participant's action. For example, as has already been noted, a speaker's turn-internal gaze cannot be three units long if the auditor always takes the turn after two units of gaze. However, assuming that the speaker is given sufficient latitude by the auditor, it is possible to examine regularities in the speaker's action.

It seems reasonable, therefore, to expect a complex relation among processing constraints, convention, and strategy involving the respective actions of the two participants. Investigators must be at pains to differentiate these sources of regularity insofar as possible. This research problem should challenge the most ingenious investigators. However difficult it might be, it would appear to be an essential element of interaction research.

Conclusion

Mokros does not prove the operation of processing constraints in his data. But his results do involve regularities that do not seem to stem from interaction phenomena of which we are aware. In the three studies, he considers three types of regularities, expanding our notion of the range of actions that may be subject to processing constraints. At the same time, he also points out interesting new interactional regularities. If the phenomena Mokros examines indeed involve processing constraints, then there should be more awaiting discovery. It is clearly not necessary to remain exclusively concerned with, for example, speaker gaze. To us this is a fascinating possibility. Finally, in his use of variables and analytic techniques, he suggests some novel ways to examine the phenomenon. In addition to their own usefulness, these approaches may inspire further development by other investigators.

11.9. Participant differences and interactive strategy

Kanki's study of participant differences in interaction represents the kind of research that we had in mind when we began this project—the kind of research that led us to use the term "strategy" in the first place. Certainly, we thought we were well positioned with respect to strategy research. Structural studies had led to hypothesized conventions that formed the basis of strategy research. In D&F, we had considered to some extent what strategy research might look like. (This will be briefly outlined below.)

Obviously, we could not have predicted the course that the project took. Various other types of "strategy research" (described in Chapters 8 and 9) emerged as the project evolved, some of which were not so aptly termed strategy. And Kanki's individual-differences study took a shape very different from what we had anticipated. As it stands, her study bears little resemblance to individual-differences studies encountered in either standard psychological research or in the "nonverbal communication" literature. In order for Kanki's study to be completed, it was necessary both to change our notion of how to approach individual-differences research on interaction, and to formulate methods that embodied, at least to some extent, our new conceptions.

The study represents an effort to incorporate in individual-differences research two related but distinguishable notions: the interactional context of an individual's strategy, and common participation.

Interactional context of strategy

One element of our current strategy research was anticipated in D&F: the idea that an individual's strategy could not be viewed in isolation from its interactional context. (It will be apparent that we intend "interactional context" here in a sense quite different from the notion of situation discussed in Chapter 2.) In considering what strategy research might look like, we observed in D&F:

> The first task of the investigator of interaction strategy would seem to be the identification of those action-sequence variables most effective in the description of a strategy. Each effective variable relates to one element of a participant's interaction strategy, for example, tendency for an auditor to interrupt following some action by the speaker. But it can be shown that an element of strategy cannot be fully described in terms of a single action-sequence variable. Rather, that strategy element for a participant would be described in terms of an action-sequence variable, given some pattern of action by the partner.
>
> The frequently used example of the gesticulation signal may serve as an illustration of this point. Imagine a conversation in which a partner as speaker gesticulates across a large proportion of boundaries at which the turn signal is also active. In this situation it may become something of a strategy issue for the participant as auditor whether to continue respecting the gesticulation signal, or to begin "breaking in" by claiming the turn at such points in order to get a word in edgewise. Let us say that the participant chooses to break in frequently. In contrast, imagine a partner as speaker using the gesticulation signal over a very moderate proportion of unit boundaries at which the turn signal is also active, but once again the participant as auditor breaks in at a large number of these points.
>
> In both interactions we are looking at the same action-sequence variable: turn claims when both turn and gesticulation signal are active; and in both interactions there is a similar, high rate of such

turn claims. Nevertheless, it seems reasonable to interpret the participant's frequent turn claims in these two situations as reflecting two distinguishable strategies: the first as a more straighforward effort to maintain a certain balance in the conversation, given a somewhat difficult situation; the second as a more "grabby," aggressive strategy. In this manner, a difference in a participant's strategy in two interactions may be observed, even when that participant's rate of response is essentially the same in the interactions. (pp. 334–335)

These paragraphs express the common-sense reasoning behind our feeling a need for a more complex analysis of individual differences in interaction, one that does not focus exclusively on the individual participant. It is clear that a participant's action is constrained by a number of factors, only some of which are presently known. We had anticipated that situation constrains choice of convention, and that convention constrains choice of action. Finally, everyday interpretation of a participant's course of action takes into account, among other things, the interactional context of that action—that is, the partner's action. Each participant is at least partly understood in the light of what the other is doing. This much seemed both reasonable and clear enough. It was much less clear how this sort of concern might actually be incorporated in data analysis. Kanki's study addresses this issue.

Interactional context of individual action

What was altogether unanticipated in the individual-differences research was the notion of common participation. As psychologists, we were not expecting to encounter something like common participation in the context of individual-differences research. It seems reasonable to say that the general notion of individual differences in psychology does not immediately suggest that common participation is an important element. This phenomenon was the source of considerable difficulty until we began to incorporate it in our data analyses.

Our lack of anticipation was caused simply by our failure to generalize sufficiently from the structural research reported in D&F. Common participation was built into the definition of convention-based action. Conventions were said to require the cooperative action of both participants. Each participant makes a distinct contribution to carrying out the convention, where the convention is defined as involving a sequence of actions involving both participants. For example, the exchange of a speaking turn in a two-person conversation was said to require a coordinated sequence of three actions involving both participants: (a) The speaker displays the turn signal in the absence of the gesticulation signal, (b) the auditor acts to take the turn, displaying the speaker-state signal, and (c) the original speaker relinquishes the turn, becoming silent. None of this seems to involve extensive common participation as we have defined it. (But other conventions almost certainly will.)

Although common participation was essentially taken for granted in the structure research, we did not give it exclusive consideration in terms of individual differences. The need for accommodating common participation in the strategy research became apparent, however, early on. It became critically important to appreciate the extent to which the actions of individual participants could be affected by the partner. From one perspective, one might view Kanki's study as an attempt to implement on the level of data analysis and interpretation the notions concerning both the definition of variables that we discussed in Chapter 1 under "pseudo-unilaterality," and the common-participation theme considered earlier in this chapter.

With respect to variables in interaction research, we emphasized that a variable should not be considered the product solely of a single individual's action. To treat it as such would be the error of pseudounilaterality. Rather, the values that a variable takes should be considered a joint product of the actions of both participants, even when that variable appears to be centered entirely on one. In Kanki's study, both main variables involved the action of both participants: a signal display by the speaker, and a response by the auditor. One variable focuses on the nature of the signal, and the other, on the nature of the response. Given this property of variables and the broader common-participation perspective on interaction process, it obviously will not do to view these concerns as operating only on the level of variable definition, however. These issues pervade all aspects of research on individual differences in interaction.

What was altogether unclear was how this understanding might be implemented in data analysis. Kanki's study may be viewed as an initial and partial solution to this issue. We see the problem as a thorny, complex one that almost certainly admits of several sorts of solutions. The solution posed in Kanki's chapter should hardly exhaust the analytic approaches to dealing with the common-participation theme in individual-differences research; and it is reasonable to expect that our own approach will continue to develop over time.

Nevertheless, Kanki's solution has some properties that we view as highly desirable. The notions of common participation and interactional context of action seem to be well realized in the analysis. A conversation is treated as a product constructed mutually by the two participants. Each participant's contribution to this product is then evaluated, *relative to the other participant's contribution.*

Kanki did not ask specifically how one participant acted, but rather how each participant acted in relation to the other's action. Thus, the results do not focus on, say, a participant's level of back-channel responses to speaker displays of grammatical completion and gaze. Rather, the level of this type of response to this type of signal is related to the partner's level, among other things.

Kanki's analysis is based on the conversation, not the participant. The participant's action is placed in the context of the conversation as a whole. In this way, Kanki's study has moved a long way from studies relating, for example, a participant's gaze rate to affiliation.

Kanki has, we believe, achieved an effective interactional contextualization of individual conduct in interaction. In so doing, Kanki's approach involves a basic paradigm shift in individual-differences research on interaction. We expect, however, that there may be a number of ways of contextualizing a participant's action. It remains for further research to continue clarifying and elaborating this paradigm.

It seems imperative for studies of individual differences to view action in both a more differentiated and a more inclusive manner. There seems little justification now for treating participants' actions as if they were occurring in some sort of interactional vacuum. The whole issue of contextualizing action suggests once again the complexity of interaction and challenges investigators to devise appropriate methods for dealing with it.

Kanki's relational approach to studying participant differences is, in our view, necessary in interaction research. But it is highly unfamiliar to us as psychologists—a difficult mode in which to conceptualize things. We are trained to interpret groups of test items or to label personality traits, but describing individuals in terms of relative actions in interactions is strictly new territory.

To illustrate, many of the conversations Kanki studied involved a general matching of auditor responses. We should be careful in characterizing what this means and does not mean. For example, it does not mean that there was extensive and detailed similarity between these conversations. Recall that the analysis is within conversations. There are numerous ways in which two participants might match each other, and many of these were realized in the data. To oversimplify, matching might be achieved in one conversation by participants' having similarly high rates of back channels, and in another conversation by their having similarly low rates, and the like. A major ongoing task will be further development of modes of characterizing results from this sort of individual-differences study.

Constructing interactions

The notion of treating an interaction as a product constructed by the participants suggests a line of research that has not, to our knowledge, been attempted. This research would focus on the manner in which participants go about constructing this product on a moment-to-moment basis. This phenomenon would seem to be one of the two or three ultimate issues in interaction research, requiring the integration of extensive knowledge of both structure and strategy.

Several phenomena suggest the potentially great complexity and fascination of this construction process, as well as its unpredictability. In everyday life, when one has two friends who have not met, it is often difficult to predict accurately how they will get along. In the same vein, parents of school-age children often find that their children have experiences with teachers very different from those of other children who are friends of their own children or who are considered to be similar in many ways to their own. Again, one of the writers had the experience at one time of conducting structured interviews with applicants for therapy at a counseling center. His reactions—both positive and negative—to these clients had very little to do with the subsequent reactions of the therapist, or to the relative success of the therapy.

Kanki's results clearly illustrate this phenomenon. Although the matching of participants' actions was a major interaction outcome in her data, there were many types of matches. Matching required that the two participants were similar in their general profile of action. The profiles themselves varied considerably among the matching interactions. Further, within this rather small group of participants there were no clear patterns of consistency for participants between the first and second conversations. A participant who matched the partner in one interaction might not in the second, and so on.

In short, it was hard to find evidence that one participant or one type of participant was effectively determining in some unilateral sense the shape of the interaction. Instead, the evidence strongly suggested that the interaction was constructed through the joint contributions of both participants, and that the nature of a participant's contribution to the second conversation was essentially impossible to determine on the basis of conduct in the first. This is not to say, of course, that there is no consistency or patterning in the construction of these conversations, only that the phenomenon is evidently a complex and therefore interesting one.

11.10. Conclusion

As we commented in D&F regarding our structural research, this monograph reports a voyage of discovery. It is clear that we did not return with a comprehensive mapping of the terrain. Our purpose was to explore the area of strategy research, considering methods and hoping to discover phenomena. Our notion of strategy began as a rather limited phenomenon related to personal style and influence in interaction. In the course of the project, strategy research came to mean for us any sort of interaction research based on the notion of structure. This expanded definition was forced upon us as the research branched in several different directions.

In the sense that the respective studies took several highly distinct paths, the project was more productive than we would have anticipated. There was a series of genuine surprises along the way, both methodological (such as the pseudounilaterality problem) and substantive (such as strategy signals). These developments and others have been considered in detail.

Nevertheless, as is perhaps to be expected in research, we have more of a sense now of being at the beginning of things than we did when we started. We view none of these studies as some sort of definitive statement—indeed, quite the reverse. Each is an initial scouting of an area or a possible area of interaction research. (And there are undoubtedly more interaction research areas to be discovered.) Further, each chapter presents sample data from a larger, more complex study. We hope we have included in each chapter sufficient material on method and results to illustrate a possible area of research, and to suggest an approach to pursuing it.

We are left with a heightened appreciation of the complexity of interaction and of the limits of current research findings. It would appear that a virtually unlimited number of conventions remain to be described; strategy has been only tentatively explored; and there has been minimal study of situation.

What we have presented, then, is a kind of invitation—or rather, set of invitations—to investigators, each invitation having to do with broadening the scope of interaction research or shifting the paradigm in an existing area. We hope that we have suggested, if nothing else, the great, unexploited potential of interaction research for pursuing central issues in psychology in particular and social science in general. We submit our work to the scrutiny of fellow investigators in the hope that, by stimulating further discussion and investigation, it will contribute to the development of research on face-to-face interaction.

References

Allison, P. D., & Liker, J. K. (1982). Analyzing sequential categorical data on dyadic interaction: A comment on Gottman. *Psychological Bulletin, 91*, 393-403.

Argyle, M., & Cook, M. (1976). *Gaze and mutual gaze.* Cambridge: Cambridge University Press.

Barker, R. G. (1963). *The stream of behavior.* New York: Appleton-Century-Crofts.

Basso, K. (1970). 'To give up on words': Silence in Western Apache culture. *Southwest Journal of Anthropology, 26*, 213-231.

Bates, E., & Begnini, L. (1975). Rules of address in Italy: A sociological survey. *Language in Society, 4*, 272-288.

Bauman, R., & Sherzer, J. (Eds.). (1973). *Explorations in the ethnography of speaking.* Cambridge: Cambridge University Press.

Beattie, G. (1978a). Floor apportionment and gaze in conversational dyads. *British Journal of Social and Clinical Psychology, 17*, 7-15.

Beattie, G. (1978b). Sequential temporal patterns of speech and gaze in dialogue. *Semiotica, 23*, 29-51.

Beattie, G. (1979). Planning units in spontaneous speech: Some evidence from hesitation in speech and speaker gaze direction in conversation. *Linguistics, 17*, 61-78.

Beattie, G. (1980). The role of language production processes in the organization of behavior in face-to-face interaction. In B. Butterworth (Ed.), *Language production* (pp. 69-107). New York: Academic Press.

Beattie, G. (1981). A further investigation of the cognitive interference hypothesis of gaze patterns during conversation. *British Journal of Social Psychology, 20*, 243-248.

328

Berlin, B., & Kay, P. (1969). *Basic color terms: Their universality and evolution.* Berkeley: University of California Press.

Bernstein, B. (1962). Social class, linguistic codes, and grammatical elements. *Language and Speech, 5,* 221-240.

Bernstein, N. (1967). *The coordination and regulation of movements.* Oxford: Pergamon Press.

Bishop, Y. M. M., Fienberg, S. E., & Holland, P. W. (1975). *Discrete multivariate analysis.* Cambridge, MA: MIT Press.

Bock, R. D. (1975). *Multivariate statistical methods in behavioral research.* New York: McGraw-Hill.

Bock, R. D. (in press). *Multivariate analysis of qualitative data.* Chicago: National Educational Resources.

Bock, R. D., & Yates, G. (1973). *MULTIQUAL: Log-linear analysis of nominal or ordinal qualitative data by the method of maximum likelihood.* Chicago: National Educational Resources.

Brown, R., & Ford, M. (1961). Address in American English. *Journal of Abnormal and Social Psychology, 62,* 375-385.

Brown, R., & Gilman, A. (1960). The pronouns of power and solidarity. In T. A. Sebeok (Ed.), *Style in language* (pp. 253-276). Cambridge, MA: MIT Press.

Brunner, L. J. (1979). Smiles can be back channels. *Journal of Personality and Social Psychology, 37,* 728-734.

Butterworth, B., & Goldman-Eisler, F. (1979). Recent studies on cognitive rhythm. In A. W. Siegman, & S. Feldstein (Eds.), *Of speech and time: Temporal speech patterns in interpersonal contexts* (pp. 211-224). Hillsdale, N.J.: Lawrence Erlbaum Associates.

Cappella, J., & Streibel, M. (1979). Computer analysis of talk-silence sequences: The FIASSCO system. *Behavior Research Methods and Instrumentation, 11,* 384-392.

Castellan, N. J., Jr. (1979). The analysis of behavioral sequences. In R. B. Cairns (Ed.), *The analysis of social interactions: Methods, issues, and illustrations* (pp. 81-116). Hillsdale, N.J.: Lawrence Erlbaum Associates.

Chase, L. J. (1978). Elementary information processes. In W. K. Estes (Ed.), *Handbook of learning and cognitive processes* (Vol. 5): *Human information processing* (pp. 19-90). Hillsdale, NJ: Lawrence Erlbaum Associates.

Collett, P., & Lamb, R. (1982). Describing sequences of social interaction. In M. von Cranach & R. Harre (Eds.), *The analysis of action* (pp. 161-186). Cambridge: Cambridge University Press.

Cook, M. (1979). Gaze and mutual gaze in social encounters. In S. Weitz (Ed.), *Nonverbal communication: Readings with commentary* (2nd ed., pp. 77-86). New York: Oxford University Press.

Cronbach, L. J. (1957). The two disciplines of scientific psychology. *American Psychologist, 12,* 671-684.

Denny, R. (1982a). To talk or be silent: Functional specialization in a system regulating the sequence of talk in conversation. Doctoral dissertation, University of Chicago.

Denny, R. (1982b). Closing up openings: The realization of adjacency pairs in casual conversation. In R. Schneider, K. Tuite, & R. Chametsky (Eds.), *Nondeclaratives* (pp. 43-54). Chicago: Chicago Linguistic Society.

Dittmann, A. T. (1972). The body movement-speech rhythm relationship as a cue to speech encoding. In A. W. Siegman & B. Pope (Eds.), *Studies in dyadic communication* (pp. 135-151). New York: Pergamon Press.

Dixon, R. (1972). *The Dyirbal language of North Queensland.* Cambridge: Cambridge University Press.

Duncan, S. D., Jr. (1969). Nonverbal communication. *Psychological Bulletin, 72,* 118-137.

Duncan, S. D., Jr. (1972). Some signals and rules for taking speaking turns in conversations. *Journal of Personality and Social Psychology, 23,* 283-292.

Duncan, S. D., Jr. (1983). Speaking turns: Studies of structure and individual differences. In J. M. Wiemann, & R. P. Harrison (Eds.), *Nonverbal interaction* (pp. 149-178). Beverly Hills, CA: Sage.

Duncan, S. D., Jr., & Fiske, D. W. (1977). *Face-to-face interaction: Research, methods, and theory.* Hillsdale, NJ: Lawrence Erlbaum Associates.

Duncan, S. D., Jr., & Rosenthal, R. (1968). Vocal emphasis in experimenters' instruction reading as unintended determinant of subjects' responses. *Language and Speech, 11,* 20-26.

Duncan, S. D., Jr., Rosenberg, M. J., & Finkelstein, J. (1969). The paralanguage of experimenter bias. *Sociometry, 32,* 207-219.

Duncan, S. D., Jr., Brunner, L. J., & Fiske, D. W. (1979). Strategy signals in face-to-face interaction. *Journal of Personality and Social Psychology, 37,* 301-313.

Duncan, S. D., Jr., Kanki, B. G., Mokros, H. B., & Fiske, D. W. (1984). Pseudounilaterality, simple-rate variables, and other ills to which interaction research is heir. *Journal of Personality and Social Psychology, 46,* 1335-1348.

Eads, D. (1982). You gotta know how to talk . . . : Information seeking in southeast Queensland Aboriginal society. *Australian Journal of Linguistics, 2,* 61-82.

Ehrlichman, H. (1981). From gaze aversion to eye-movement suppression: An investigation of the cognitive interference explanation of gaze patterns during conversation. *British Journal of Social Psychology, 20,* 233-241.

Ehrlichman, H., & Barrett, J. (1983). Random saccadic eye movements during verbal-linguistic and visual-imaginal tasks. *Acta Psychologica, 53,* 9-26.

Ekman, P., & Friesen, W. V. (1969). The repertoire of nonverbal behavior: Categories, origins, usage, and coding. *Semiotica, 1,* 49-98.

Ekman, P., Friesen, W. V., & Ellsworth, P. (1972). *Emotion in the human face.* Oxford: Pergamon Press.

Ervin-Tripp, S. (1972). On sociolinguistic rules: Alternation and co-occurrence. In J. J. Gumperz, & D. Hymes (Eds.), *Directions in sociolinguistics* (pp. 213-258). New York: Holt, Rinehart and Winston.

Exline, R. V. (1971). Visual interaction: The glances of power and preference. In J. K. Cole (Ed.), *Nebraska symposium on motivation* (Vol. 19) (pp. 163-206). Lincoln: University of Nebraska Press. [Republished in S. Weitz (Ed.), *Nonverbal communication* (pp. 65-92). New York: Oxford University Press.]

Fiske, D. W. (1977). Personologies, abstractions, and interactions. In D. Magnusson, & N. S. Endler (Eds.), *Personality at the crossroad: Current issues in interactional psychology* (pp. 273-286). Hillsdale, NJ: Lawrence Erlbaum Associates.

Fiske, D. W. (1978). *Strategies for personality research: The observation versus interpretation of behavior.* San Francisco: Jossey-Bass.

Franck, D. (1979). Speech act and conversational move. *Journal of Pragmatics, 3,* 461-466.

Friedrich, P. (1966). Structural implications of Russian pronominal usage. In W. Bright (Ed.), *Sociolinguistics* (pp. 214-259). The Hague: Mouton.

Geertz, C. (1968). Linguistic etiquette. In J. Fishman, (Ed.), *Readings in the sociology of language* (pp. 282-295). The Hague: Mouton.

Gerstman, L., Feldstein, S., & Jaffe, J. (1967). Syntactical versus temporal cues for speaker switching in natural dialogue. *Journal of the Acoustical Society of America, 42,* 1183.

Goffman, E. (1967). *Interaction ritual.* Garden City, NY: Anchor.

Goffman, E. (1971). *Relations in public.* New York: Basic Books.

Goffman, E. (1974). *Frame analysis.* New York: Harper and Row.

Goffman, E. (1981). *Forms of talk.* Philadelphia: University of Pennsylvania Press.

Goldman-Eisler, F. (1968). *Psycholinguistics: Experiments in spontaneous speech.* New York: Academic Press.

Good, C. (1979). Language as social activity: Negotiating conversation. *Journal of Pragmatics, 3,* 151.

Goodman, L. A. (1968). The analysis of cross-classified data: Independence, quasi-independence, and interactions in contingency tables with or without missing entries. *Journal of the American Statistical Association, 63,* 1091-1131.

Goodman, L. A. (1969). How to ransack social mobility tables and other kinds of cross classification tables. *American Journal of Sociology, 75,* 1-40.

Goodman, L. A. (1970). The multivariate analysis of qualitative data: Interactions among multiple classifications. *Journal of the American Statistical Association, 65,* 226-256.

Goodman, L. A. (1971). The analysis of multidimensional contingency tables: Stepwise procedures and direct estimation methods for building models for multiple classifications. *Technometrics, 13,* 33-61.

Goodman, L.A. (1972a) A general model for the analysis of surveys. *American Journal of Sociology, 77,* 1035-1086.

Goodman, L. A. (1972b). A modified multiple regression approach to the analysis of dichotomous variables. *American Sociological Review, 37,* 28-46.

Goodman, L. A. (1978). *Analyzing qualitative/categorical data: Log-linear models and latent structure analysis.* Cambridge, MA: Abt.

Goodwin, C. (1981). *Conversational organization: Interaction between speakers and hearers.* New York: Academic Press.

Gottman, J. M., & Bakeman, R. (1979). The sequential analysis of observational data. In M. E. Lamb, S. Suomi, J. Stephenson, & R. Gordon (Eds.), *Social interaction analysis: Methodological issues* (pp. 185-206). Madison: University of Wisconsin Press.

Greene, P. H. (1972). Problems of organization of motor systems. *Progress in Theoretical Biology, 2,* 303-338.

Haberman, S. J. (1973). The analysis of residuals in cross-classified tables. *Biometrics, 29,* 205-211.

Halliday, M., & Hasan, R. (1976). *Cohesion in English.* London: Longman Group.

Hanushek, E., & Jackson, J. (1977). *Statistical methods for social scientists.* New York: Academic Press.

Harper, R. G., Wiens, A. N., & Matarazzo, J. D. (1978). *Nonverbal communication: The state of the art.* New York: Wiley.

Havranek, B. (1955). The functional differentiation of the standard language. In P. Garvin (Ed.), *A Prague School reader on aesthetics, literary structure and style* (pp. 3-16). Washington, D.C.: Washington Linguistics Club.

Jaffe, J., & Feldstein, S. (1970). *Rhythms of dialogue.* New York: Academic Press.

Just, M. A., & Carpenter, P. A. (1976). Eye fixations and cognitive processes. *Cognitive Psychology, 8,* 441-480.

Kaye, K. (1982). *The mental and social life of babies: How parents create persons.* Chicago: University of Chicago Press.

Keller, E. (1979). Gambits: Conversational strategy signals. *Journal of Pragmatics, 3,* 219-238.

Kendon, A. (1967). Some functions of gaze-direction in social interaction. *Acta Psychologica, 26,* 22-63.

Kendon, A. (1974). The behavior of communication [Review of *Body language and the social order: Communication as behavioral control,* and *How behavior means*]. *Contemporary Psychology, 19,* 526-527.

Kendon, A. (1977). *Studies in the behavior of social interaction.* Bloomington, IN: Indiana University Press.

Kendon, A. (1980). The sign language of the women of Yuendumu: A preliminary report on the structure of Walpiri sign language. *Sign Language Studies, 27,* 101-112.

Kendon, A. (1982). The organization of behavior in face-to-face interaction: Observations on the development of a methodology. In K. R. Scherer & P. Ekman (Eds.), *Handbook of methods in nonverbal behavior research* (pp. 441-505). Cambridge: Cambridge University Press.

Kendon, A., Harris, R. M., & Key, M. R. (Eds.). (1975). *The organization of behavior in face-to-face interaction.* The Hague: Mouton.

Kinsbourne, M. (1972). Eye and head turning indicates lateralization. *Science, 176,* 539-541.

Knoke, D., & Burke, P. J. (1980). *Log-linear models.* Beverly Hills, CA: Sage.

Labov, W. (1966). *Sociolinguistic patterns.* Philadelphia: University of Pennsylvania Press.

Levinson, S. (1983). *Pragmatics.* Cambridge: Cambridge University Press.

Lewis, D. K. *Convention.* (1969). Cambridge, MA: Harvard University Press.

Mackey, W. C. (1976). Parameters of the smile as a social signal. *Journal of Genetic Psychology, 129,* 125-130.

Maclay, H., & Osgood, C. (1959). Hesitation phenomena in spontaneous English speech. *Word, 15,* 19-44.

McDowell, J. (1983). The semiotic constitution of Kamsa ritual language. *Language in Society, 12,* 23-46.

McNeill, D. (1979). *The conceptual basis of language.* Hillsdale, NJ: Lawrence Erlbaum Associates.

McQuown, N. A. (1959). *Natural history method – A frontier method.* In A. R. Mahrer & L. Pearson (Eds.), *Creative developments in psychotherapy* (Vol. 2, pp. 431-438). New York: Appleton-Century-Crofts.

McQuown, N. A. (Ed.). (1971). The natural history of an interview. Microfilm Collection of Manuscripts on Cultural Anthropology, Fifteenth Series. Chicago: The University of Chicago Joseph Regenstein Library Department of Photoduplication.

Mehrabian, A., & Ksionzky, S. (1972). Some determiners of social interaction. *Sociometry, 35,* 588-609.

Mokros, H. B. (1983). *Production regularities: A consideration for the description of social interactions.* Paper presented at the annual meeting of the American Psychological Association, Anaheim, CA, September, 1983.

Mukarovsky, J. (1977). Dialogue and monologue. In J. Burbank & P. Steiner (Trans.). *The word and verbal art* (pp. 81-112). New Haven: Yale University. (Original work published 1940).

Natale, M., Entin, E., & Jaffe, J. (1979). Vocal interruptions in dyadic communication as a function of speech and social anxiety. *Journal of Personality and Social Psychology, 37*, 865-878.

Newson, J. (1978). Dialogue and development. In A. Lock (Ed.), *Action, gesture and symbol: The emergence of language* (pp. 31-42). New York: Academic Press.

Philips, S. (1976). Some sources of cultural variability in the regulation of talk. *Language in Society, 5*, 81-95.

Posner, M. I. (1978). *Chronometric explorations of mind.* Hillsdale, NJ: Lawrence Erlbaum Associates.

Posner, M. I., & McLeod, P. (1982). Information processing models: In search of elementary operations. *Annual Review of Psychology, 33*, 477-514.

Rosch, E. (1977). Human categorization. In N. Warren (Ed.), *Advances in cross-cultural psychology.* London: Academic Press.

Rosenfeld, H. M. (1966). Approval-seeking and approval-inducing functions of verbal and nonverbal responses in dyads. *Journal of Personality and Social Psychology, 4*, 597-605.

Rosenfeld, H. M. (1967). Nonverbal reciprocation of approval: An experimental analysis. *Journal of Experimental Social Psychology, 3*, 102-111.

Rosenfeld, H. M. (1972). The experimental analysis of interpersonal influence processes. *Journal of Communication, 22*, 424-442.

Rosenthal, N. E., Sack, D. A., Gillin, C., Lewy, A. J., Goodwin, F. K., Davenport, Y., Mueller, P. S., Newsome, D. A., & Wehr. T. A. (1984). Seasonal affective disorder. *Archives of General Psychiatry, 41*, 72-80.

Rosenthal, R. (1966). *Experimenter effects in behavioral research.* New York: Appleton-Century-Crofts.

Rosenthal, R., & Rosnow, R. (1969). *Artifact in behavioral research.* New York: Academic Press.

Russo, J., & Rosen, L. (1975). An eye fixation analysis of multialternative choice. *Memory and Cognition, 3*, 267-276.

Rutter, D., Stephenson, G., Ayling, K., & White, P. (1978). The timing of looks in dyadic conversation. *British Journal of Social and Clinical Psychology, 17*, 17-21.

Sacks, H., Schegloff, E. A., & Jefferson, G. (1974). A simplest systematics for the organization of turn-taking for conversation. *Language, 50*, 696-735.

Sankoff, G. (1980). *The social life of language.* Philadelphia: University of Pennsylvania Press.

Sanson, B. (1980). *The camp at Wallaby Cross.* Canberra: Australian Institute for Aboriginal Studies.

SAS Institute. (1980). *SAS supplemental library user's guide.* Cary, NC.

Schaffer, H. R. (1979). Early interactive development. In M. H. Bornstein & W. Kessen (Eds.), *Psychological development from infancy: Image to intention* (pp. 279-305). Hillsdale, NJ: Lawrence Erlbaum Associates.

Scheflen, A. E. (1961). *A psychotherapy of schizophrenia: A study of direct analysis.* Springfield, IL: Thomas.

Scheflen, A. E. (1963). Communication and regulation in psychotherapy. *Psychiatry, 26*, 126-136.

Scheflen, A. E. (1965). Quasi-courtship behavior in psychotherapy. *Psychiatry, 28*, 245-257.

Scheflen, A. E. (1966). Natural history method in psychotherapy: Communicational research. In L. A. Gottschalk, & A. H. Auerbach (Eds.), *Methods of research in psychotherapy* (pp. 263–289). New York: Appleton-Century-Crofts.

Scheflen, A. E. (1967). On the structuring of human communication. *American Behavioral Scientist, 10*, 8-12.

Scheflen, A. E. (1968). Human communication: Behavioral programs and their integration in interaction. *Behavioral Science, 13*, 44-55.

Scheflen, A. E. (1972). *Body language and the social order.* Englewood Cliffs, NJ: Prentice-Hall.

Scheflen, A. E. (1973a). *Communicational structure: Analysis of a psychotherapy transaction.* Bloomington: University of Indiana Press.

Scheflen, A. E. (1973b). *How behavior means.* New York: Gordon & Breach.

Scheflen, A. E. (1975). *Human territories: How we behave in space-time.* Englewood Cliffs, NJ: Prentice-Hall.

Schegloff, E. A. (1982). Discourse as an interactional achievement: Some uses of 'uh huh' and other things that come between sentences. In D. Tannen (Ed.), *Analyzing discourse: Text and talk* (pp. 71-93). Washington, D. C: Georgetown University Press.

Schegloff, E. A., & Sacks, H. (1973). Opening up closings. *Semiotica, 8*, 289-327.

Scherer, K. R., & Ekman, P. (Eds.). (1982). *Handbook of methods in nonverbal behavior research.* New York: Cambridge University Press.

Shannon, C. E., & Weaver, W. (1949). *The mathematical theory of communication.* Urbana: University of Illinois Press.

Siegman, A. W., & Feldstein, S. (1978). *Nonverbal behavior and communication.* Hillsdale, NJ: Lawrence Erlbaum Associates.

Silverstein, M. (1976). Shifters, linguistic categories, and cultural description. In K. A. Basso & H. A. Selby (Eds.), *Meaning in anthropology* (pp. 11-55). Albuquerque: University of New Mexico Press.

Simon, H. A. (1979) Information processing models of cognition. *Annual Review of Psychology, 30*, 363-396.

Stern, D. N. (1974). Mother and infant at play: The dyadic interaction involving facial, vocal, and gaze behaviors. In M. Lewis & L. Rosenblum (Eds.), *The effect of the infant on its caregiver* (pp. 187-213). New York: Wiley.

Trager, G. L., & Smith, H. L., Jr. (1957). *An outline of English structure.* Washington, D. C.: American Council of Learned Societies.

Turvey, M. T. (1977). Preliminaries to a theory of action with reference to vision. In R. Shaw & J. Bransford (Eds.), *Perceiving, acting, and knowing.* Hillsdale, NJ: Lawrence Erlbaum Associates.

van Hoof, J. A. R. A. M. (1972). A comparative approach to the phylogeny of laughter and smiling. In R. A. Hinde (Ed.), *Non-verbal communication* (pp. 209-238). Cambridge: Cambridge University Press.

von Wright, G. H. (1963). *Norms and action.* New York: Humanities Press.

Wampold, B. E., & Margolin, G. (1982). Nonparametric strategies to test the independence of behavioral states in sequential data. *Psychological Bulletin, 92*, 755-765.

Whorf, B. L. (1956). *Language, thought, and reality.* J. Carroll (Ed.). Cambridge, MA: MIT Press.

Yngve, V. H. (1970). On getting a word in edgewise. *Papers from the sixth regional meeting, Chicago Linguistic Society*, 567-577.

Author index

Subject index

action sequence, *see* sequence variables;
   turn system, interaction unit; turn
   system, rules; response preferences,
   and control of interactive options
adjacency pair, 165, 170
antecedent probability, *see* probabilities
auditor back channel, *see* back channel;
   pragmatic marking, back channels;
   turn system, auditor back channel
auditor state, *see* turn system, participant
   states postulated

back channel, 96–7, 188, 227; *see also*
   pragmatic marking, back channels,
   auditor; turn system, auditor back
   channel
behavioral samples, averaging over, 234–5

change in actions, 176, 183, 204–14; *see
   also* sequence variables; speaker signal
   sequences
   and cognitive processes, 213
   constraints on, 213–14
   patterns of
      across events, 210–12
      by individuals, 212
      and turn taking, 213
coding, *see also* transcription system
   of smiles, 215–17

of speaker gaze states and runs, 194–5
of speaker signal sequences, 206
coefficient of multiple determination (R^2),
   196–7
common participation, 297, 299–302, 304,
   319, 322–5
confederates, *see* experimental control
consequent probability, *see* probabilities
consequentiality of alternatives, 304
constraints on action, 176, 179, 182, 226,
   230
   on change, 213–14
   on smiles, 218, 224, 225–6
   sources of, 179–82
      environmental, 179–80
      information processing, 176, 181–2
      interactional, 180–1
   on speaker gaze, 203–4
   on speaker signal sequences, 204
context, *see* interactive context; situation
context analysis, 73–5
   and structural unit, 74–5
   and transcription, 77–82
control, *see* experimental control
convention, 177, 180; *see also* interaction
   strategy; situation
   and coordination problems, 34, 298
   generalizing with respect to, 62–4, 100–
   1, 303